PRAISE FOR
HEIRS OF AN HONORED NAME

"This is a story of declension: the intergenerational devolution of a great American family line. In vivid and graceful prose, Douglas Egerton recounts the political and moral decay of the Adamses. In his time, John Quincy Adams became a leading, even heroic figure in the fight against slavery, a fight that eventually achieved victory through civil war. But in later years, his descendants turned their back on the principles that animated that struggle. In doing so, they paralleled and illuminated the retreat of the northern business and political elite as a whole from the goals of the nation's second democratic revolution."

—BRUCE LEVINE, author of *The Fall of the House of Dixie: The Civil War and the Social Revolution that Transformed the South*

"The Adams family contributed a stunning procession of presidents, diplomats, historians, and intellectuals who played crucial roles in the birth and maturation of the Republic and its salvation during the Civil War. In this wonderfully engaging book, one of the most eminent historians of this period tells a compelling story of how this seemingly indispensable family became superfluous to the nation it had so dutifully served."

—DON H. DOYLE, author of *The Cause of All Nations: An International History of the American Civil War*

"In this riveting saga of the personal tribulations of America's first family's later generations, Douglas Egerton beautifully charts the declension of the American Republic from its revolutionary and antislavery ideals. He adeptly mirrors the betrayal of emancipation and hopes for an interracial democracy after the Civil War in the Adams family's retreat from the duties of patriotism to narrow elitism. This is a collective historical biography of a superior order."

—MANISHA SINHA, author of *The Slave's Cause: A History of Abolition*

"If good biography tells us what we need to know about its subjects and the society they inhabit, then in this splendid life story of the Adams family, Douglas Egerton takes us on a troubling journey through the many ways this patrician family, and the country, abandoned their lofty principles and commitment to equality for a crass denial of rights."

—RICHARD BLACKETT, author of *The Captive's Quest for Freedom* and *Making Freedom*

HEIRS
of an
HONORED
NAME

HEIRS
of an
HONORED
NAME

*The Decline of the Adams Family
and the Rise of Modern America*

Douglas R. Egerton

BASIC BOOKS
NEW YORK

Basic Books
Hachette Book Group
1290 Avenue of the Americas, New York, NY 10104
www.basicbooks.com

Printed in the United States of America
First Edition: October 2019

Published by Basic Books, an imprint of Perseus Books, LLC, a subsidiary of Hachette Book Group, Inc. The Basic Books name and logo is a trademark of the Hachette Book Group.

The Hachette Speakers Bureau provides a wide range of authors for speaking events. To find out more, go to www.hachettespeakersbureau.com or call (866) 376-6591. The publisher is not responsible for websites (or their content) that are not owned by the publisher.

Library of Congress Cataloging-in-Publication Data
Names: Egerton, Douglas R., author.
Title: Heirs of an honored name : the decline of the Adams family and the rise of modern America / Douglas Egerton.
Other titles: Decline of the Adams family and the rise of modern America
Description: First edition. | New York : Basic Books, [2019] | Includes bibliographical references and index.
Identifiers: LCCN 2019011712 (print) | LCCN 2019981423 (ebook) | ISBN 9780465093885 (hardcover) | ISBN 9781541699700 (ebook)
Subjects: LCSH: Adams family. | Adams, John Quincy, 1767–1848. | Adams, Charles Francis, 1807–1886. | United States—Politics and government—1783–1865. | Statesmen—United States—Biography. | Statesmen's families—United States—Biography. | Braintree (Mass.)—Biography.
Classification: LCC E322.1.A39 E36 2019 (print) | LCC E322.1.A39 (ebook) | DDC 973.5/50922 [B]—dc23
LC record available at https://lccn.loc.gov/2019011712
LC ebook record available at https://lccn.loc.gov/2019981423
ISBNs: 978-0-465-09388-5 (hardcover), 978-1-5416-9970-0 (ebook)

LSC-C

10 9 8 7 6 5 4 3 2 1

For *MY* honored family,
Hannah
Kearney
Leigh
Marc

CONTENTS

Contents

I met a traveller from an antique land
Who said: "Two vast and trunkless legs of stone
Stand in the desert . . . near them, on the sand,
Half sunk, a shattered visage lies, whose frown,
And wrinkled lip, and sneer of cold command,
Tell that its sculptor well those passions read
Which yet survive, stamped on these lifeless things,
The hand that mocked them and the heart that fed;

And on the pedestal these words appear:
'My name is Ozymandias, king of kings:
Look on my works, ye Mighty, and despair!'
Nothing beside remains. Round the decay
Of that colossal wreck, boundless and bare
The lone and level sands stretch far away."

—Percy Shelley, "Ozymandias," 1816

ADAMS FAMILY TREE

(Third, Fourth, and Fifth Generations)

JOHN QUINCY ADAMS married LOUISA CATHERINE JOHNSON
(February 12, 1775–May 15, 1852) on July 26, 1797, and was the
father of four children and the grandfather of nine grandchildren.

1. **George Washington Adams** (April 12, 1801–April 30, 1829).
2. **John Adams II** (July 4, 1803–October 23, 1834) married Mary Catherine
   Hellen (1806–1870) on February 25, 1828.

    1. **Mary Louisa Adams** (February 23, 1829–July 16, 1859) married
       William Clarkson Johnson (August 16, 1823–January 28, 1893) on
       June 30, 1853.

    2. **Georgeanna Francis Adams** (September 10, 1830–October 2, 1839).

3. **Charles Francis Adams Sr.** (August 18, 1807–November 21, 1886)
   married **Abigail Brown Brooks** (April 25, 1808–June 6, 1889) on
   September 3, 1829.

    1. **Louisa Catherine Adams** (August 13, 1831–July 13, 1870) married
       Charles Kuhn (November 2, 1821–October 18, 1899) on April 13,
       1854.

        1. **Mary Elizabeth Kuhn** (October 1857).

    2. **John Quincy Adams II** (September 22, 1833–August 14, 1894)
       married **Frances "Fanny" Cadwallader Crowninshield** (October 15,
       1839–May 16, 1911) on April 29, 1861.

        1. **John Quincy Adams III** (February 23, 1862–April 12, 1876).
        2. **George Caspar Adams** (April 24, 1863–July 13, 1900).
        3. **Charles Francis Adams III** (August 2, 1866–June 10, 1954).
           married Francis Lovering.
        4. **Fanny Crowninshield Adams** (August 8, 1873–April 11, 1876).

5. **Arthur Adams** (May 20, 1877–May 19, 1943) married **Margery Lee** on October 5, 1921.
6. **Abigail Adams** (September 16, 1879–February 15, 1974) married **Robert Homans** on June 10, 1907.

3. **Charles Francis Adams Jr.** (May 27, 1835–May 20, 1915) married **Mary "Minnie" Hone Ogden** (February 23, 1843–March 23, 1935) on November 8, 1865.

   1. **Mary Ogden Adams** (July 27, 1867–July 21, 1933) married **Grafton St. Leon Abbott** on September 30, 1890.
   2. **Louisa Catherine Adams** (December 28, 1871–October 13, 1958) married **Thomas Nelson Perkins** (1879–1937) on June 6, 1900.
   3. **Elizabeth "Elsie" Ogden Adams** (December 3, 1873–October 19, 1945).
   4. **Henry Adams** (July 17, 1875–April 26, 1951).
   5. **John Adams** (July 17, 1875–August 30, 1964) married **Marian Morse** (1878–1959).

4. **Henry Brooks Adams** (February 16, 1838–March 27, 1918) married **Marian "Clover" Hooper** (September 14, 1843–December 6, 1885) on June 27, 1872.

5. **Arthur Adams** (July 23, 1841–February 9, 1846).

6. **Mary Gardiner Adams** (February 19, 1846–August 19, 1928). married **Henry Parker Quincy** (October 27, 1838– March 11, 1899) on June 20, 1877.

   1. **Emme M. Quincy** (1881).
   2. **William Brazics Quincy** (February 3, 1884–December 24, 1958).
   3. **Dorothy Adams Quincy** (December 4, 1885–April 6, 1939).
   4. **Edwin P. Quincy** (1888).
   5. **Eleanor Adams Quincy** (March 11, 1888–1939).

7. **Peter Chardon Brooks Adams** (June 24, 1848–February 13, 1927). married **Evelyn "Daisy" Davis** (1853–1926) on September 7, 1889.

4. **Louisa Catherine Adams** (August 12, 1811–September 15, 1812).

PROLOGUE:
"THE LAST OF THE EARTH"
February 1848

H ENRY BREWER STANTON WAS THE FIRST TO NOTICE. THE United States House of Representatives had just wrapped up debate on a resolution to thank American officers and soldiers for their "splendid victories" in Mexico, and John Quincy Adams, who had long denounced the conflict as a "most unrighteous war," had cast one of the few nays, voicing his disgust in an "emphatic manner and an unusually loud tone." Stanton, a reporter for the antislavery *Boston Emancipator and Republican* and the husband of feminist Elizabeth Cady Stanton, was sitting twenty feet from Adams when he observed the eighty-year-old congressman suddenly make an "effort to rise," reaching out "with his right hand as if to take his pen from the inkstand." Adams grew flushed, then paled and clutched the desk with a "convulsive effort" before sinking to the left side of his chair. Congressman David Fisher, an Ohio Whig, caught Adams as he fell, while Congressmen George Fries and Henry Nes, both of whom were physicians, rushed to his aid. "Mr. Adams is dying," somebody shouted.[1]

Both the House and Senate promptly adjourned, as did the Supreme Court, housed downstairs, but no one left the building. Many crowded in to see whether Adams yet lived. "Stand back! Give him air! Remove him!" Fries bellowed. Adams's colleagues bore him first to a settee near the door and then into the Rotunda. But the throng followed, so Speaker Robert Winthrop suggested they carry him to the sofa in his private chamber. "Cupping, mustard poultices and friction have been resorted to," Stanton reported. "It is probably an apoplectic stroke." In a few "broken, disjointed and incoherent words," Adams mumbled something about his wife, and those in the chamber believed they heard him whisper, "My son, my son." Most of what he said next was hard to comprehend; some understood him to say, "This is the end of the earth. I am composed." Others thought him to murmur, "This is the last of the earth. I am content."[2]

Around two o'clock that afternoon—Monday, February 21—Louisa Johnson Adams received a message at their F Street home, summoning her to the Capitol. Her husband had appeared in good health that morning and had even walked part of the way to the House, so she little knew what to expect. Her companion, Mary Elizabeth Cutts, accompanied her, and when they arrived at the building, someone assured her that her "poor husband had had a faint turn from which he had recovered." Even when Louisa saw the throng crowded outside the Speaker's chamber, she was "altogether unsuspicious of the awful shock" that awaited her. Louisa bent over her husband and spoke his name, but Adams gave no sign of recognition. At length, the attending doctors prevailed on the two women to withdraw.[3]

At some point, Adams regained consciousness enough to ask for Henry Clay, his long-ago secretary of state. Although not then a member of the Senate, Clay was in Washington, and he reached the Capitol that evening. By the time Clay arrived, Adams was again unconscious; Clay, one journalist recorded, "grasped the hand of the dying patriot, held it, and wept." An artist, Arthur Stansbury, elbowed his way into the room and drew a detailed "crayon sketch" of Adams as he lay on the sofa.[4]

The next morning, some four hundred miles to the north, Charles Francis Adams Sr., John Quincy's and Louisa's only surviving child,

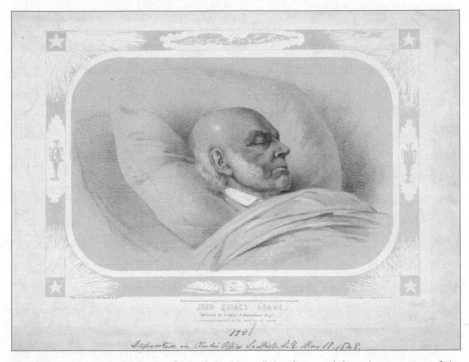

The first man ever to die in the Capitol Building, John Quincy Adams became one of the leading congressional voices against the so-called "slave power" and was much admired by the antislavery community. His private life was far sadder. By his death in February 1848, he and his wife, Louisa, had buried three of their four children. *Courtesy Library of Congress.*

stopped by his Boston office at the *Daily Whig* and spied a telegraph sent by his friend, Congressman John Gorham Palfrey, dated the previous afternoon. "Here was a shock," Charles Francis scribbled into his diary. His father "was taken in another fit of paralysis and it was not thought he could survive the day." Adams dashed home to inform his family and then caught the next train south. "The day was gloomy enough," Adams mused, and the novel he brought with him, Charlotte Brontë's *Jane Eyre*, did little to improve his mood. John Quincy had suffered a small stroke two years before but had quickly regained his health. "He has been the great landmark of my life," Charles Francis wrote. Although he was now forty-one and had been "accustoming myself to go alone," the son yet regarded his father as his "stay and companion." The train initially made good time, but his transfer to a boat heading for the capital made for a "vexatious delay" of four hours. At length, Adams booked a stateroom and tried to sleep.[5]

"Hon. John Quincy Adams is not yet dead," one Massachusetts newspaper reported on Tuesday, although the editor held out little hope for his recovery: "The pallor of death is upon his face, and he has ceased to struggle with nature." Louisa returned and sat beside her husband of fifty-one years for several hours. She returned the next day, Wednesday, February 23, as well, but when it became clear that Adams was near death, Speaker Winthrop encouraged her to withdraw. "I was forced to leave him," Louisa fumed to her sister. "My senses almost gave way and it seemed as if I had become callus to suffering while my heart seemed breaking." Adams died that evening without uttering another sound, the speaker announcing his death to the assembled chamber on Thursday. Old John Adams had perished, fittingly, on the Fourth of July, but his son, one journalist marveled, "died in the Capitol itself, and almost upon the birthday of Washington." It was a "fit end for a career so glorious."[6]

Charles Francis had reached Philadelphia on Wednesday evening and took a room at the Jones Hotel. He awoke on Thursday morning with "the dull, heavy sense of existing pain which comes with calamity." Seeing a man reading a newspaper with black borders, Adams purchased a copy at the depot but tucked it under his arm until the train was under way. "I threw open the paper I had bought and the first thing I saw was the announcement that at a quarter past seven last night my father had ceased to breathe," he confided to his diary. "I have no longer a Father. The glory of the family is departed and I, a solitary and unworthy scion, remain overwhelmed with a sense of my responsibilities." Charles Francis at last arrived in Washington on February 24. He found his mother calm and preparing for her husband's funeral. In the meantime, the body rested in the Capitol.[7]

By the time that Charles Francis reached the building, undertakers had placed his father in a lead-lined, partially windowed coffin; a glass plate above the face permitted mourners to view the deceased (a popular feature in an age that feared premature burial). A steady stream of the curious flowed through the room, but Speaker Winthrop—a conservative Whig recently condemned by young Adams and other antislavery activists—emptied the chamber so that Charles Francis might be alone. John Quincy's face, he thought, "was little changed from life," apart from "some marks of the instruments used to recover animation, which by the way were ridiculous." For four decades, Charles Francis had looked to his father "for support and aid and encouragement." Now he "must walk alone and others must lean on" him. Two brothers and a sister had died young, leaving Charles Francis "alone in the generation." But one deceased brother left behind two children, and Charles Francis had five of his own, with a sixth due in four months. That realization "brought me to a sense of my duty," Adams wrote that evening in a sentiment his father would have admired. "A tear or two was all," and then Charles Francis returned to the Committee Room to talk politics.[8]

The capital descended into mourning. A hastily assembled committee of Congressman Abraham Lincoln and Senator Jefferson Davis, together with their future vice presidents, Hannibal Hamlin and Alexander Stephens, gathered to make arrangements for the first state funeral since President William Henry Harrison's death in 1841. President James K. Polk put aside his long-standing disdain for the antislavery congressman and ordered the executive mansion and all the departments draped with black cloth. Most private residences in Washington followed suit. Shops closed their doors and shuttered their windows. Within the House of Representatives, doorkeeper Robert Horner shrouded the statues in the chamber, with the exception of the white marble figure representing History. A New York congressman introduced a resolution that Adams's desk and chair "remain unoccupied for thirty days." Secretary of War William Marcy instructed his senior officers to wear black crepe and fire a salute of twenty-nine guns, as did Secretary of the Navy John Y. Mason, a proslavery Virginian who had scant use for Adams in life.[9]

The funeral was held the following Saturday, February 26. Pennsylvania Avenue was "dressed in mourning throughout," newspapers reported, and "flags everywhere floated at half mast." A long black pennant waved from atop the Capitol dome. The service itself was held in the House chamber. Louisa could not bring herself to attend, so Charles Francis and his sister-in-law, Mary Hellen Adams—the widow of his brother John—represented the family and sat facing the coffin, now covered with black velvet fringed with silver. Seated behind the family was Washington's elite, from Polk and his vice president, George Dallas, to his cabinet and members of the Supreme Court. To one side, Sarah Childress Polk sat beside eighty-year-old Dolley Madison, while longtime rivals John C. Calhoun of South Carolina—whom Adams had long despised—and Thomas Hart Benton of Missouri entered arm in arm, prompting one journalist to describe them as a "curious juxtaposition." After a eulogy by House Chaplain Ralph Gurley, pallbearers loaded the casket aboard a carriage decorated with a gilt eagle and pulled by six white horses. Capitol bells rang out as the procession shuffled toward the Congressional Cemetery on the banks of the Anacostia River, from where Adams's remains would be shipped north to the family plot in Quincy, Massachusetts.[10]

Editors filled their columns with tributes to John Quincy, who had received his first public position in 1796, when President George Washington had nominated the twenty-six-year-old youth to serve as minister to the Netherlands. President Polk chose to ignore the congressman's denunciation of his invasion of Mexico and praised Adams for his political service of "more than half a century." Numerous publishers remarked that Adams had "fallen on the very area of his highest intellectual efforts—beneath the roof of the capitol." He "fought a good fight, and kept the faith towards his God and his country," observed another. Even in a day of extreme partisanship and growing sectionalism, newspapers remembered him as a "pure patriot," a "man of high-toned morals, and of the strictest integrity," a statesman "above all reproach," a politician who "never pandered in any way," and a world traveler who lived "more of a varied and romantic" life than any of his colleagues. The Massachusetts legislature passed a series of resolutions in honor of his memory and invited former Governor Edward Everett—brother-in-law to Charles Francis—to provide yet another eulogy. In Albany, New York, former Governor William Henry Seward delivered a similar address to his state's assembly, prompting a grieving Louisa to publicly thank both legislatures for honoring her "dear deceased husband."[11]

The antislavery press was particularly generous to the man who had fought for many of their causes even while stubbornly refusing to embrace the term "abolitionist." Henry Stanton, who had earlier charged the congressman with inconsistency in voting against the congressional declaration of war with Mexico while agreeing to fund it, now characterized Adams as a "brave old man" who had fallen "in a last struggle for peace and liberty." New England editors applauded him for opposing an "extension of slave states by the acquisition of territory" taken from Mexico and for fighting to overturn the so-called Gag Rule, the 1836 prohibition on accepting antislavery petitions. "The venerable Adams lived to see the scales broken and the subject of slavery opened for debate in the House," one Massachusetts publisher recalled. Another contrasted the late congressman with Senator Daniel Webster, who labored to conciliate the South while Adams defended "the *Liberties of Mankind*." In Rochester, New York, abolitionist Frederick Douglass penned a series of tributes for his *North Star*, arguing that "the last ten years [were] the heroic years" of Adams's life. Despite his never once attending an abolitionist meeting, Douglass observed, Adams had demonstrated a "sincere desire for the eradication of [the national] curse, Slavery," and championed the right of all Americans, black and white, male and female, to submit petitions to Congress. Antislavery activists, Douglass insisted, should remember Adams "not only as a friend of his country, but of us, the oppressed portion of his countrymen." In a final essay that April, Douglass challenged his readers to adopt Adams as their "example," to dedicate themselves "to action," and to "do quickly, what we have to do for ourselves, our fellow-men, and for our God."[12]

Douglass was far from the lone mourner in the black community. In Buffalo, congregants at the Vine Street Methodist Church agreed that Adams's life and career should "serve as a way-mark to every principle of moral excellence and intellectual ability." Black activists at a second meeting, noting the praise heaped upon Adams by white editors and politicians, maintained that "this feeling of respect and veneration, is not felt entirely by white persons, but is shared by the oppressed and despised colored people." His "mighty exposures of the slave power" earned

Adams the enmity of southern whites, but they led black Americans "to honor his memory, now that he is dead." The *North Star* reprinted resolution after resolution, each extolling Adams's "bold and manly efforts to rescue the oppressed," which "endeared him to us as a friend to humanity and to God."[13]

The fact that the aged Senator Calhoun, known as the "cast iron man" for his rigid defense of slaveholders' rights, had not only attended Adams's funeral but had even stepped in as a pallbearer to replace an ailing Daniel Webster, did little to appease the New Englander's southern foes. A handful of Virginia Whigs introduced resolutions honoring Adams into the House of Delegates, but the Democratic majority in the state Senate voted to table them the following day. Although the influential *Richmond Times* denounced the Senate's action as a "discreditable fact," the resolutions were never passed.[14]

As Charles Francis prepared to return north with his father's remains, a lengthy note of sympathy arrived from Henry Clay, who had known John Quincy since their days as peace negotiators in Ghent during the War of 1812. "No surviving friend of your father sympathizes and condoles with you all, with more sincerity and cordiality than I do," Clay insisted. Predictable hosannas to the former president's career as "patriotic, bright, and glorious" followed. But then Clay signed off with a comment that surely gave Charles Francis—the son and grandson of presidents—a moment of pause. Since the 1770s, the name Adams had "shone out, with the brightest beams, at home and abroad," Clay observed. "May its lustre, in their descendants, continue undiminished." Whether Clay meant it as such, *that* was a daunting challenge.[15]

It was also a challenge the son would have to face alone. Each time an American founder died, the nation debated what that loss meant for the present and what that statesman's legacy held for future generations. One newspaper editor pondered the math. The Constitution had been in effect since 1789, and in that "period of 59 years, we have had eleven Presidents." Eight of that number had "sunk into the tomb; and only one of them (Mr. Adams) leaves a son behind." Of the three living presidents, both Martin Van Buren and John Tyler (who sired fifteen children by two wives) had living sons. But Charles Francis was unique among the group in that he could claim two of the eleven presidents as his lineage. Later generations would come to regard the Adams family as America's *first* political dynasty, but for those trying to take the measure of a man who had literally died within the Capitol's walls, Charles Francis represented the hopes of what was then American's *only* political dynasty.[16]

A decade later, on the eve of his own election to Congress, Charles Francis reflected on the almost crippling burden that this inheritance imposed on his family. "The heir of an honored name, and of men who have distinguished themselves in the most difficult of all careers, has a trying position anywhere, but most of all in America," he wrote. "Every act of his is contrasted, not with those of common men, but with those of persons whom all have united to produce very extraordinary specimens of the race." Should he or his sons fail to obtain the status achieved by earlier generations, his countrymen might regard that as a tragic "moral about the degeneracy of families." But "if by some miracle he should happen to reach a still higher point" than his illustrious ancestors, residents of "all free countries," Charles Francis worried, could rightly grow concerned about one family's claim to govern on the grounds of "inherited abilities, or greatness." As a boy and then a young man, Adams had watched as his grandfather and father were not merely criticized but also bested by men they regarded as of lesser abilities, and throughout the remainder of his life, he would ever be ambivalent about taking up Clay's challenge.[17]

FOR A FAMILY THAT RANKED INDEPENDENCE AND INFLEXIBILITY AS among the most cherished qualities in a person, it stood to reason that the Adamses were often singular in their achievements. It surprised almost nobody, for example, that in 1830, two years after he was soundly beaten by Andrew Jackson in his bid to be returned to the White House, John Quincy became the first former president to seek congressional office. Adams won the seat handily, defeating two opponents by a two-to-one margin. "My election as president of the United States was not half so gratifying to my innermost soul," he replied when told the news. Louisa was less pleased. Having accompanied her husband to London, Paris, St. Petersburg, and Washington, she had hoped for a peaceful retirement in New England. For his part, Charles Francis was embarrassed by what he regarded as his father's acceptance of an inferior position. "To neither of us can it prove beneficial to always be struggling before the public without rest or intermission," he groaned.[18]

Yet as Frederick Douglass later remarked, Congressman Adams's eighteen years in the House provided some of the finest moments of his career. Liberated from having to please a national constituency, the former president became the champion of both free speech and free labor. Although John Quincy had never defended slavery, neither had his ambitions permitted him to openly condemn it. Now he represented the voters of Massachusetts's eleventh district, who were increasingly bitter about what they saw as southern domination of the federal government: the Slave Power, as they dubbed it. As a Whig and a man of the law, Adams conceded that the Constitution protected unfree labor, but that did not mean that free states were obligated to assist in slavery's expansion westward. Even those protections, he theorized, had limits. As a congressman, Adams began to argue that under certain circumstances, such as the emergency of war, the federal government enjoyed the authority to emancipate southern slaves in the name of national security. The year 1831 witnessed a bloody slave revolt in Southampton County, Virginia. Local militiamen succeeded in putting down the uprising, but had Virginia requested the assistance of the US Army and federal funds to suppress the rebellion, who then, Adams reasoned, could claim that Congress possessed "no authority to interfere with the institution of slavery?"[19]

Initially, Adams was more concerned about northern rights than he was with demands for black freedom. In 1831, shortly after William Lloyd Garrison began publishing the *Liberator*, abolitionists proceeded to pepper Congress with petitions praying for the abolition or restriction of slavery. Adams routinely presented these entreaties, even though he often regarded their requests as unrealistic or unconstitutional, as he saw the right to petition elected leaders as basic to American freedoms and enshrined in the First Amendment. In response, southern politicians demanded that the petitions be tabled without discussion. Undeterred by their complaints and threats, Adams continued to present the petitions. In early January 1836, the congressman submitted an antislavery petition signed by 153 residents of Millbury, Massachusetts, and two weeks later he was back with a document bearing the signatures of 363 inhabitants of Weymouth calling for the end of buying and selling of slaves in Washington, a request Adams privately conceded was "utterly impracticable."[20]

On one occasion, Adams rose to introduce a petition demanding the right of northern citizens to travel within the South without "danger to their lives." As was by now common, southern politicians bellowed for the petition to be tabled. Adams paused, then continued: "In another part of the Capitol it had been threatened that if a Northern abolitionist should go to North Carolina and utter a principle of the Declaration of Independence . . ." (cries of "Order! Order!" rode over his words, but Adams patiently waited for silence). "That if they could catch him they would hang him," Adams finished, but not without infuriating his proslavery colleagues. As Henry Wise of Virginia threatened, were it not for the fact that Adams was an "old man, protected by the imbecility of age, he would not have enjoyed, as long as he has, the mercy of my mere words."[21]

In the wake of such melees, the House formed a special committee chaired by South Carolina's Henry Pinckney to investigate the right of petition and report back to the entire body. In what came to be known as the Gag Resolution, on May 18, 1836, Pinckney recommended that "all petitions, memorials, resolutions, propositions or papers relating in any way or to any extent whatever on the subject of slavery or the abolition of slavery shall, without being printed or referred, be laid upon the table and that no further action whatever shall be had thereon." When it came time to vote and his name was called, Adams calmly observed, "I hold the resolutions to be a direct violation of the Constitution of the United States and of the rights of my constituents." Adams lost that argument by a tally of 117 to 68, but not before Massachusetts had submitted 362 petitions—the most of any state—and Adams had brought forward a record

693—roughly half of them from states other than his own—an effort that secured him the honorific title of "dean of the Conscience Whigs."[22]

Just days later, Adams found another opportunity to elevate his standing within the antislavery community. By the spring of 1836, news of the victory by Texas secessionists over Mexican forces at the Battle of San Jacinto reached Washington, and close behind followed a series of memorials and petitions calling for the recognition of Texan independence. A few urged annexation. Mexico had abolished slavery in 1824, and in a fiery pamphlet, abolitionist Benjamin Lundy charged that Texans sought independence in hopes of reversing that ban. On May 25, Adams rose to fire the first congressional volley. His lengthy speech grew longer still as Adams paused to allow endless interruptions and catcalls to die down. "A war for the restoration of slavery where it has been abolished, if successful in Texas, must extend all over Mexico," Adams warned. He thought it curious that his republic, which spoke of "freedom, independence, and democracy," should support a rebellious new country "waging a war" designed to "forge new manacles and fetters." Turning to his southern colleagues, Adams cautioned that in any great conflict between slavery and emancipation, Congress might be forced to "interfere with the institution of slavery" in the southern states.[23]

Although the congressman never grew egalitarian enough to enjoy the friendship of black Americans, he was color-blind when it came to the question of political rights. When William Costin, a Washington-based activist widely believed to be the son of John Parke Custis—and so the mixed-race grandson of Martha Washington—died in May 1842, Adams attended his funeral and pronounced him "as much respected as any man in the district." Why, Adams asked one journalist covering the memorial service, "should such a man as that be excluded from the elective franchise, when you admit the vilest individuals of the white race to exercise it?" Not surprisingly, such testimonials to racial equality earned Adams the enmity of white supremacists. One Virginian wrote to assure Adams that his neighbors were pooling their money to pay a "large premium" for his murder. A Georgian was furious about the congressman's willingness to establish diplomatic relations with Haiti, which he feared would result in a "Big Black, Thick lipped, Cracked Heeled, Wooly headed, Skunk smelling, damned Negro" arriving as an envoy from the black republic. Should Adams persist, the Georgian warned, he would "be shot down in the street, or your damned guts will be cut out in the dark." Several others mailed missives containing a bullet or a drawing of a knife, together with a threat: "You will be *lynched* if it is to be done by *drawing* you from your *seat* in the *house* by force."[24]

It was never in an Adams to back down, and certainly not in one who had recently turned seventy. For his growing band of antislavery admirers, the congressman's greatest triumph was reached in January 1841 when he accepted the position of senior counsel to the fifty-three Africans captured aboard the *Amistad* after it was seized off the coast of Long Island by the US Navy. Abducted from Sierra Leone by Portuguese slave hunters and sold into Spanish Cuba, the Africans' captivity violated treaties signed by both European nations. After the captives were put aboard the *Amistad* for reshipment around the island, the Africans seized control of the vessel, killing the captain and the cook before sailing north. Spanish authorities claimed that the rebels were enslaved Cubans, not Africans, and demanded their return. When the trial regarding their legal status moved to the Supreme Court, abolitionists begged Adams to supply the final argument. In the process, Adams at last came to see human bondage as a crime against humanity rather than as a free speech or constitutional issue. Adams visited the prisoners in New Haven, after which several of the Africans began to correspond with him. Eleven-year-old Kale, surely with the help of his American teacher, wished to advise his "dear friend" on what he should tell the "Great Court." The Mende people, he explained, simply wanted to go home. "All we want is make us free [and] not send us to Havanna." Kale signed off with a simple "your friend."[25]

In a seven-hour argument that spanned two days, Adams devoted less time to the legal and diplomatic aspects of the case than to its violation of American ideals. The Spanish, Adams charged, expected the president to "turn himself into a jailer" and hold Africans illegally captured until they might be returned to "the slave-traders of the barracoons." What of their violation of American principles, Adams wondered? Had the

Fourth of July "become a day of ignominy and reproach?" Ever aware of the burden levied upon his surname, Adams pointed dramatically to the copy of the Declaration of Independence—a statement drafted in part by his father—hanging on the courtroom wall. "The moment you come to the Declaration of Independence, that every man has a right to life and liberty, as an unalienable right, this case is decided," Adams insisted, his voice overcome by emotion. "I ask nothing more on behalf of these unfortunate men, than this declaration." Adams won his case, and the Africans were released. "These poor negroes have had some good fortune after all," Charles Francis applauded. Now on the eve of his seventy-fourth birthday, the congressman, as would become a family trait, promptly published his oration in pamphlet form. "Some of us may have at times done thee injustice," admitted Quaker abolitionist John Greenleaf Whittier, "but, I believe we now appreciate thy motives."[26]

ALTHOUGH INITIALLY EMBARRASSED BY HIS FATHER'S CONGRESSIOnal run, and even more mortified by John Quincy's failed 1833 bid for the governor's chair on the conspiratorial Anti-Masonic ticket, Charles Francis later came to agree with Douglass in regarding "the period between 1835 and 1845 [as] the most brilliant portion of my father's career." Some family members might disagree, Charles Francis conceded, having wished the former president to quietly retire in Quincy, as had his father before him. But the son took "satisfaction" in knowing that his father's postpresidential years, and especially his unexpected emergence as an antislavery champion, provided his father with some contentment in his final years and "met with his [own] entire and uniform approbation." Special envoy to the United Kingdom, minister to Russia, Prussia, and the Netherlands, US senator, eighth secretary of state, sixth president, and, finally, eighteen years of service in the House, Charles Francis reflected, constituted greatness enough for any man.[27]

Yet honesty forced Charles Francis to also admit that there was a darker side to this saga, one that had bedeviled earlier generations of

Adamses and imposed enormous responsibilities on both him and his children. "The history of my family is not a pleasant one to remember," he once fretted. "It is one of great triumphs in the world but of deep groans within, one of extraordinary brilliancy and deep corroding mortification." His father and grandfather, rather like his own young children, had been favored with more than their share of intelligence, resolve, and determination. But they were also prickly, fussy, usually in a huff about something, and crippled with self-doubt. Adams men harbored overly competitive natures—particularly toward one another—while concealing deep sadness, often to the point of considering or committing suicide. John Adams, the founder of the dynasty, had been habitually depressed, irascible, tactless, vain, and able to discover a slight in almost everything. Charles Francis could recall his grandmother Abigail scolding her husband for his "intolerable" habit of silently staring at guests. "Tis impossible for a Stranger to be tranquil in your presence," she once sighed. John had replied that his solitary nature and tendency toward brusqueness were typical of all New Englanders of Calvinist background, and while that was true in part, his inability to connect with his fellow creatures became an oft-repeated family curse. "I am never happy in their Company," John once admitted of his colleagues. "This has made me a recluse."[28]

Although John Adams had been painfully aware of his personal idiosyncrasies—Abigail had reminded him of his faults often enough—and even made numerous efforts to improve himself, each subsequent generation not only failed to overcome these "corroding mortification[s]"; they also passed them along, together with their admirable traits, to their offspring. Like his father, who was rarely comfortable in the company of women, John Quincy once admitted that he was "cold" around ladies, even after decades of marriage. Tellingly, he blamed this flaw on his mother, who had cautioned him to sit silently in polite company, fearing he would say something rude or improper that could embarrass the family. Because each generation of Adams parents poured a steady barrage of advice into their children, either verbally or in correspondence, their progeny grew up aware of the perfectionist standards demanded of them, but equally mindful of their failures to reach those goals. John Quincy filled his diary with self-reproach for failing to live up to his father's expectations, just as Charles Francis later confessed to his diary of his own failure to accomplish as much as his father had by his age. "God of Heavens!" John Quincy agonized at the age of twenty-one, "take me from this world before I curse the day of my birth."[29]

The family cycle of public success and private torment never ceased, stretching into the first decades of the twentieth century. If John Adams saw his fondest hopes fulfilled in the elevation of John Quincy to the presidency, his grandchildren and great-grandchildren witnessed (and frequently orchestrated) their family's decline and fall. Although the elder Charles Francis achieved a level of fame and accomplishment enough to satisfy almost any Victorian, his dream of becoming the third President Adams eluded him, and he died a sour, discontented patrician. And in the years after John Quincy's death, his grandchildren continued to exhibit both the best and the worst of the family's traits. Although talented and highly educated, they all grew to dislike themselves, detest one another, and loathe their lineage. Charles Francis Jr. condemned his father in print, remembering that while his grandfather John Quincy was a "solitary man," he was also a kind "as well as a great one." But "not so with my father," the younger Charles Francis revealed to the world. "He was built on more rigid and narrower lines [and] was even less companionable." To his siblings, Charles Francis Jr.'s private appraisals of their father's character were harsher still.[30]

As grave as these private doubts were for the Adamses, they also had consequences for the wider public and for their nation. All four generations of the Adams family exhibited a distrust of democracy and a distaste for the public they felt compelled to serve. John Quincy befriended many of the *Amistad* captives, but his grandson Charles Francis Jr. never wished to understand the black cavalrymen who served under his command during the Civil War. Wartime service tended to erode the genteel racism of most white officers, but Charles Francis Jr. never ceased to employ racist epithets when discussing African Americans. Like his brothers Henry and John Quincy II, the former Union colonel condemned Reconstruction-era reforms and came to embrace the Lost

Cause ideology of former Confederates—even to the point of recommending a statue of Robert E. Lee be erected in Washington—before easing into the life of a robber baron as president of the Union Pacific Railroad. Henry, too, rejected a career in reform and retreated into the mists of a distant and imaginary Christian past, one, unlike Gilded Age America, as he put it, uninhabited by "the Jew, the Czar, the socialist, and above all the total, irremediable, radical rottenness of our whole social, industrial, financial, and political system."[31]

Although Charles Francis Sr.'s failure to capture the White House—largely because he refused to fight for the nomination in 1872 and 1876—lessened some of the pressure on his children that his grandfather's and father's political successes had placed upon him, the fourth generation of the family remained spectacularly dysfunctional (even by the standards of influential political dynasties). Charles Francis Jr. enlisted in the Massachusetts cavalry largely to spite his "cold" diplomat father and took pride in his own chronic discourtesy. "Nothing tells like being contemptuous," he once counseled Henry. His sister Louisa Catherine Adams was regarded by all her siblings as the most gifted of their generation. But Adams women, even the firstborn, were not destined for political office; instead, Louisa entered into an unhappy marriage, returned home at the end of her disastrous honeymoon, and spent much of her short life wandering about Europe. Charles Francis Jr. and his brother Brooks cared little for Henry's wife, Marian "Clover" Hooper, or even for Henry's prizewinning *The Education of Henry Adams*, which Charles Francis dismissed as "simply silly." Henry, in turn, thought Brooks's draft biography of John Quincy unworthy of publication, calling it a "psychological nightmare to his degenerate and decadent grandson." After Brooks reluctantly deferred to Henry's opinion and set the project aside, Charles Francis Jr. published a dry biography of their father, a volume much disliked by Henry and one that focused exclusively on the public man, while also producing an autobiography in response to Henry's celebrated tome.[32]

In tragic ways the family's disturbing internal dynamic reflected the troubled mood of the nation. Great political dynasties shape their country even as they themselves are shaped by it. Diplomats, politicians, historians, soldiers, professors, and authors, the Adamses served their country with distinction. From laboring to end the Massachusetts ban on interracial marriage to fighting to keep slavery out of the territories, and from leading black cavalrymen into Richmond to helping invent the modern avocation of history, the reform-minded Adams family helped to create modern America. Yet as socially conservative Brahmins, they also often resisted the rise of an egalitarian nation and clung to early American notions about the better sorts' natural right to govern, just as, ironically, they resisted much of the postbellum progress in civil rights achieved through their own efforts.

The war years and their aftermath molded the Adamses, and rarely for the better. By the late 1860s the Adamses collectively had scant regard for the modern republic that was emerging after Appomattox. They were not alone, of course, and the family's retreat from greatness during these decades mirrored the decay of the Republican Party's ideals as the party deteriorated from a progressive, free-soil movement that spoke to the aspirations of the northern middle class—and even, in the case of striving young Whigs like Abraham Lincoln, to the upwardly mobile working class—into a party of wealthy barons and railroad magnates. But then neither were they just another American family, and had they sought to slow their party's descent or battle for the causes embraced by their grandfather, the course of their nation might have been far different. Instead, in their final days the Adams brothers, as Brooks conceded, regarded themselves as "displaced intellectuals of patrician descent who sought desperately to fathom the meaning of the changes that displaced them." The "greatest tragedy of all for us, and for all optimists who believe in the advent of perfection through the influence of democracy," Brooks admitted toward the end of his life, "is the condition in which we have been left since the close of the war." Once the first family of the republic, the fourth generation, Brooks mused, were "appendages only." They neither recognized the country their family had nurtured over the long decades of the nineteenth century nor wished to serve it. As the last surviving member of his generation, Brooks alluded to both his nation and his ancestry and even wondered whether "I must refer to myself as part of this family tree." That seventy-year decline and fall is the subject of this book.[33]

1

"NOT EXPECTING TO MAKE
A VERY GREAT FIGURE IN THE WORLD"
Generations

FOR A MAN WHOSE POLITICAL STAR WOULD ONE DAY RISE SO high, his was hardly an auspicious start in the world. Although Louisa Catherine Adams had previously given birth to two healthy boys, she also had a history of miscarriages. When she went into labor at 2:00 A.M. on August 18, 1807, the pains were so severe that her nurse grew alarmed, burst into tears, and was sent out of the room. Instead, for the first time in four births, Louisa's husband John Quincy assisted and, like many a young father, claimed to have "witnessed sufferings that he had no idea of." After six hours of labor, Louisa gave birth to "another *apparently dead Child*." Within thirty minutes, however, she rejoiced to hear that "the Child had recovered the play of his lungs." The couple had already named their first son George, after the late president, and the second one John, after the child's grandfather. This boy was christened Charles Francis, after the newborn's deceased, alcoholic uncle and after Francis Dana, a minor diplomat who had served as American minister to St. Petersburg when John Quincy was thirteen. But then third sons seemed rarely destined for greatness.[1]

Born in London, Louisa was one of seven daughters of an English-woman and a well-connected Maryland merchant, whose brother served as governor of Maryland before his elevation to the Supreme Court. Louisa had met John Quincy in 1795, during his tenure as minister to the Netherlands, and they wed two years later at a parish church on London's Tower Hill. For the next several years, the couple lived in Prussia, where John Quincy negotiated a maritime treaty and where George Adams was born on April 12, 1801. (Concerned for Louisa's health, King Frederick William III ordered the street on which the Adamses lived sealed at both ends to cut down on horse-drawn carriage noise.) After his father lost the presidency to Thomas Jefferson in the bitterly fought contest of 1800, John Quincy resigned his position, assuming, perhaps incorrectly, that Jefferson intended to name a Republican to the post. On July 17 the three Adamses boarded the *America* and sailed for Boston, a city that Louisa had never visited, to meet in-laws she had not yet encountered.[2]

Only thirty-four years old, John Quincy was unsure about his future. He began to practice law, an occupation that bored him. However, in April 1802 his neighbors elected him to the state assembly. That November, he sought a seat in the national Congress but lost to his Republican opponent by fifty-nine votes. His fortunes improved early in 1803 when the Federalist-controlled legislature selected him for the US Senate, and that July, Louisa gave birth to his second son. But after Senator Adams broke with his party to endorse the Louisiana Purchase in 1803 and President Jefferson's Embargo Act in 1807, the Federalists made it clear that he would not be chosen for a second term. Adams chose, yet again, to resign his office and return to Boston. As he had in 1801, Adams believed his political career to be at its end, although he took some solace in the praise of the pro-Jeffersonian *Richmond Enquirer*, which applauded his reply to his Federalist critics as "one of the ablest and most eloquent political papers." John Quincy moved his growing family into a large, airy house on Boylston and Tremont Streets, and it was there, only two weeks after they arrived from Washington, that Charles Francis was born.[3]

John Quincy did not wander long in the political wasteland. In July 1809, President James Madison appointed Adams to serve as the nation's first minister to Russia. (Still furious over John Quincy's defection to the Republicans, both senators from Massachusetts voted against his confirmation.) It was imperative that he leave before the fall: once the harbor of St. Petersburg froze, the city was virtually unreachable until late spring. Abigail Adams, the boys' grandmother and unquestioned matriarch of the Adams clan, decreed—much to Louisa's dismay—that George and John, the two eldest sons, should remain in Massachusetts to pursue their education. Louisa, John Quincy, and one-year-old Charles Francis boarded the *Horace* on August 10. "Eight full and eventful years" were to lapse, Charles Francis later observed, before he would, as a boy of ten, return to American shores.[4]

Charles Francis later derided his education in St. Petersburg as "of a very desultory character," but in important ways it prepared the future diplomat for a career in foreign courts. The official language of Russian society was French, which both John Quincy and Louisa spoke fluently thanks to respective childhoods partly spent in Paris and Nantes. For three hours each morning, John Quincy instructed his son in French and German, and so fluent did he quickly become that on one occasion Tsar Alexander I and Empress Elizabeth chatted with the boy for nearly an hour before pronouncing him a "charming child." Believing that five-year-old Charles Francis possessed a "thirst for learning beyond his years," John Quincy expanded the morning work schedule to six hours and added mathematics. Lacking a background in New England Calvinism and having not been raised by the demanding John and Abigail, Louisa came to fear that her husband was pushing their son too hard. John Quincy remained convinced that his third son was a prodigy, a view that the praise from the royal family only served to reinforce. For his part, young Charles Francis found subtle ways to assert his independence. When he realized that he could annoy his father by incorrectly "reading or pronouncing words when he knows perfectly well the right," Charles Francis continued to do so, prompting John Quincy to fret that the boy had a "singular aversion to being taught."[5]

While mornings in Russia were devoted to study, the evenings were given over to an elegance and festivity rarely found in dour Quincy. Charles Francis understood enough German—the native language of the empress—to enjoy the German theater, and one "hobgoblin story," John Quincy remarked, left his son "much diverted." Charles Francis routinely donned exotic costumes for fancy-dress bells, once appearing as Bacchus, although he preferred American Indian dress, Louisa sighed, to satisfy his "taste for Savages." John Quincy also took his son to see the circus acts in St. Isaac's Square and on occasion tried the role of tender companion, playing games with Charles Francis or holding his hand for long walks along the Neva River. What Charles Francis could not then appreciate was that his father gave him what was denied to his brothers: time alone with his parents. But for an Adams, that was ever the mixed blessing. By the time he turned seventeen, Charles Francis would admit that he little enjoyed the company of his father. "He is the only man I ever saw, whose feelings I could not penetrate," he confided to his diary. "I can study his countenance for ever and very seldom find any guide by which to move."[6]

If he found his father cold and unfathomable, Charles Francis quickly learned to discern his mother's moods. In turn, Louisa thought her son fascinating and, bored as she was in frigid St. Petersburg, came to regard him as both a child and a companion. They spent afternoons together, taking a turn under the blossoms in her garden during the brief summer months or devising fantastical stories for one another. Charles Francis was especially sensitive to his mother's needs after the birth of his sister, Louisa Catherine Adams, in August 1811. The baby was never well and lived but thirteen months. It had been another troubled delivery, and Louisa knew this would be her last. She and Charles Francis sometimes visited the grave at the city's Lutheran Cemetery, and Louisa took comfort in her son's "little tender assiduities; attentions gentle and affectionate beyond [his] years." The two enjoyed cards, and Charles Francis assured his father that "Mama is a great amateur of cards." Louisa also took an interest in her son's education, but the tender companionship that Charles Francis found in his mother was precisely what he found lacking in his severe father.[7]

THE OUTBREAK OF WAR BETWEEN RUSSIA AND NAPOLEONIC FRANCE in June 1812 surprised few court insiders, just as the nearly simultaneous congressional declaration of war against Britain was equally anticipated. But events took an unexpected turn when Tsar Alexander, who desperately needed British aid, offered to act the role of mediator between Washington and London. Madison promptly named a bipartisan commission to join Adams in St. Petersburg, but when the British rejected the tsar's offer and instead suggested direct negotiations in the Belgian port of Ghent, John Quincy prepared to leave wife and child in Russia while he journeyed west. The enforced absence from his family brought a surprisingly affectionate quality to his correspondence. The letters they exchanged, Charles Francis later told his sons, revealed "the kindlier, more domestic, and less austere features" of John Quincy's character. However, Louisa so dreaded the coming winter and feared the French invasion that she considered taking Charles Francis and sailing for home: "I am so sick and weary of it I would willingly run all the risks attached to the Voyage in the present state of things than undergo it much longer."[8]

After signing a draft peace treaty on Christmas Day of 1814, Adams quit Ghent for Paris, writing to Louisa that she and Charles Francis should join him there. With the Neva frozen, Louisa prepared for a brutal cross-country trip of 40 days and 1,600 miles. Louisa, who had just turned forty, left St. Petersburg on February 12 in a large carriage known as a *berline,* its runners designed to be replaced with spring heels when the snows turned to frozen earth. Traveling with the two were a Russian nurse and one soldier to serve as both guard and driver. "We were jolted over hills, through swamps and holes, and into valleys, into which no Carriage had surely ever passed before," she wrote, "and my whole heart was filled with unspeakable terrors for the safety of my Child." Although Louisa carried Russian, French, and Prussian passports, as they neared the Marne River, the carriage was surrounded by a crowd of French camp followers who screamed that she and Charles Francis were Russians: "Take them out and kill them." Louisa stepped out of the carriage and in her perfect French explained that she was the wife of an American diplomat before shouting back, "Viva Napoleon!" The mob parted, and Louisa waved her handkerchief as they drove away. The Adamses were reunited on March 23, the same day that Napoleon Bonaparte marched into the city and began his final reign of one hundred days. Charles Francis was not yet eight years old.[9]

The boy was fascinated by the chaos of wartime France and thrilled, as part of "the surging crowd," to look up and see Bonaparte waving from the balcony at the Tuileries. "I well remember the scenes of Paris during the hundred days," he later wrote, "reviews by Napoleon, the excitement of the city, the theaters, the exhibitions." In early May, word arrived that Madison had appointed John Quincy as minister to Great Britain, a post once held by his father. The three departed for London, arriving just ahead of the news from Waterloo. With the war at last finally over, John Quincy and Louisa decided that the time had arrived for George and John, whom they had not seen in six years, to join them in England.[10]

The entire family was finally reunited later that month when the two eldest sons, one fourteen and the other nearly twelve, arrived at their hotel in Cavendish Square. A directive from their grandmother warned John Quincy to be gentle with the sensitive, talented George, although as Abigail feared that her husband had been too lenient with his namesake John, she cautioned that the "wild" boy had a "little too much confidence in himself." As for Charles Francis, he scarcely knew his brothers and had almost come to regard himself as an only child. Having had little contact with other children his own age in St. Petersburg or Paris, Charles Francis now had to learn to share his parents' attention with two older and far less urbane brothers. Even communicating was a trial. John Quincy regarded George's Greek and Latin as unacceptable, while Charles Francis was more fluent in French and Russian than in English.[11]

John Quincy enrolled the three boys in a large boarding school in Ealing, a few hours' coach drive from London, run by Dr. George Nicholas. At this home to roughly 250 boys, the gregarious George and John were instantly popular, although George struggled with his Latin classes, which were taught exclusively in that language. Charles Francis took considerable pride in the fact that while his brothers "made several friends, I had none." As the War of 1812 was but recently over, both Dr. Nicholas and the well-to-do students picked on Charles Francis and routinely sang "Rule, Britannia" on the playground. The headmaster reported him a "dull boy," and in turn, Charles Francis retorted that he "learned nothing, but the necessity of fighting English boys in defense of the honor of a country of which I knew practically nothing." The one virtue of the school, he later reflected, was that it taught him the importance of "standing up to the support of my own opinions." The experience also taught him much about "the English character," which was to be of "very appreciable value" fifty years later, as he would admit to his own sons.[12]

In the late spring of 1817, word reached London that the new president, James Monroe, intended to appoint John Quincy his secretary of state. Accordingly, on June 10 the five Adamses sailed for home aboard the *Washington* after final visits from British abolitionist William Wilberforce and philosopher-reformer Jeremy Bentham. Charles Francis was ten. America "did not look to me as I expected," he later remarked. "The people were all strange, the habits very different from what I had been used to." The experience, ironically, turned the boy "shy and cold," two defects that he so disliked in his father. After first leaving the boys in the care of their grandparents, both strangers to Charles Francis, John Quincy and Louisa hastened to Washington. Abigail Adams was then seventy-three but remained a formidable presence in the old house in Quincy. George was then sixteen and "quite grown up," in his youngest brother's estimation. Yet the smallest admonition from Abigail reduced both George and John to tears. At the time, Charles Francis little understood their terror or their feelings of "admiration and affection" for their grandmother. But by the day she died thirteen months hence, he realized that "he himself fully shared in it."[13]

Having been rarely separated from his parents even while at Ealing, Charles Francis took the parting hard. When his grandparents entrusted him to Benjamin Anthorp Gould's Boston Latin School, the traditional preparatory institute for Harvard College, Charles Francis tried to remain with John and Abigail in Quincy by feigning chronic dysentery. Only when John Adams raised the prospect of "medicine and emetics" did the symptoms disappear. Unlike Dr. Nicholas, Gould took to the boy, and Charles Francis thought himself "somewhat of a favorite" of the headmaster. John Quincy was less confident. When the boys visited their parents in Washington over the Christmas holiday, their father confided to Abigail that he was resigned to the dismal prospect of his sons being "like other men," the goal of perfection and "ideal excellence" being beyond their meager capabilities. Curiously, George agreed, thinking that "the comparative idleness" of his recent travels "unfitted the mind for that severe application necessary for the attainment of profound and useful knowledge." Even so, the secretary of state still planned to send all his sons to his old college and that of his father, with George destined to enter the class of 1821.[14]

When John II also left for Harvard, in September 1819, the Adamses decided to send for Charles Francis, now twelve, and enroll him in a Catholic school run by a Reverend Ironside. The boy enjoyed being once more in his parents' company, as well as again having them to himself. Discipline at the school was evidently casual, as Charles Francis approvingly told his grandfather that "talking playing and whistling" were common in the hallways, a confession that earned a rebuke from Quincy. Such amusements, the eighty-four-year-old patriarch warned, were "not fit to be indulged or tolerated in the scene of education for Youth."[15]

Charles Francis's extensive training in Latin in both Boston and Washington convinced his father that the boy was ready for Harvard at the age of fourteen. When his brothers returned north in February 1821 after the Christmas holidays in Washington, Charles Francis traveled with them. Much to John Quincy's dismay, Charles bungled his Latin examination and had to sit for it again. Since the examiner was Edward Channing, a professor whose appointment John Quincy had publicly opposed just the year before, the secretary warned Harvard president John Kirkland that his son had been "unfairly treated." Charles Francis took the exam again, this time with his father observing, and he passed with but one small mistake. Yet even in an era when boys attended college in their late teens, a fourteen-year-old, Charles Francis later conceded, was "very imperfectly fitted for admission." Although he rightly believed that he had "read more extensively" than any other boy of his age, his mind "was without discipline," and his "memory for things in which I took no interest, utterly useless." By the end of his first year, Charles Francis was ranked near the bottom of his class, and he was as friendless as at Ealing. He was mortified that he "was in no condition to enter the list as a competitor for college honors." Having rushed his youngest son into college, John Quincy now regretted his boys' collective "blast of mediocrity." Whether the three spent the next winter vacation in Washington or in Cambridge, he concluded, "would depend on their standing as Scholars."[16]

The secretary grew further alarmed when he paid a visit to Cambridge and inquired about his other sons' rankings. George's records revealed a mediocre standing of thirtieth in his class while John, ranked forty-fifth, was, like Charles Francis, close to the bottom of his cohort. "You boast of your studying hard, and pray for whose benefit do you study?" John Quincy demanded of John. "Are you so much a baby that you must be taxed to spell your letters by sugar plums?" Toward George, the disappointed father was equally harsh. Given George's "propensity to skulk from real study," John Quincy thundered, he should perhaps write his senior dissertation on the maxim "Mind your [own] business." George at least received his diploma. Just months before his graduation, however, John was one of forty students expelled for violation of Harvard's code of conduct, probably for drunkenness. John Quincy posted two letters to Kirkland begging him to reconsider, but to no avail.[17]

Charles Francis responded to his father's admonitions by proposing that he quit college altogether. Still three months away from his fifteenth birthday, the teenage Adams, as he sorrowfully confided to his diary, had grown "addicted [to] depraved habits," particularly "billiards, drinking parties and riding." Charles Francis had also grown infatuated with his cousin Mary Hellen, the orphaned daughter of his mother's eldest sister, who had moved in with John Quincy and Louisa in 1817. Although the same age as Charles Francis, Mary enjoyed flirting with all three cousins, prompting Louisa to reprimand her niece for "behaving shamefully." Worried about his younger brother, George rode out to Cambridge to discover whether a leave of absence "would in any way prejudice" Charles Francis's standing at Harvard. Their father was not so understanding.

In a lengthy letter, John Quincy assured his son that while he did not "absolutely reject" the idea of his abandoning his studies, he could only "consent to it upon condition that he should determine upon some other course of life to which he could immediately resort." Charles Francis's personal flaws and immorality, John Quincy chided, were an altogether different matter: "If I must give up all expectation of success or distinction for you in this life," at least "preserve me from the harrowing thought of your perdition in the next." Deciding that eternal damnation was too high a price to pay, Charles Francis remained at Harvard and graduated in 1825.[18]

Charles Francis reached Washington in late May of that year, arriving two months after his father's inaugural. The early months in his parents' White House were pleasant ones. Charles Francis spent the mornings reading law and the afternoons listening to debates in Congress, but only "when they were worth hearing." He also found time to enjoy fiction and verse, which earned him yet another long-distance reprimand from his aged grandfather. "Mathematicks and Law are the true rocks on which a man of business may surely found his reputation," the eighty-nine-year-old patriarch snapped. "It is not novels or poetry." Charles Francis posted a polite dissent to Massachusetts and continued to relish his "Segars," wine, champagne, and billiards. Secretary of State Henry Clay was a frequent visitor, and Charles Francis enjoyed meeting "all the leading men of the country" while "analyz[ing] their qualities." At length, Charles Francis decided that his grandfather was right and "went back to classical studies, and began a new formation for my mind in a more rigorous method of application."[19]

While Charles Francis studied, his mother gazed ahead toward her husband's reelection campaign. Using her mother-in-law as a model, Louisa regarded herself as John Quincy's political partner and advisor, a role Adams accepted, in part because the political culture of the era required men to maintain the pose of indifference to one's career. As a relative newcomer to Washington, Louisa was free to forge new alliances, and her invitations to dine were carefully calculated for political effect. Sophisticated and European educated, the First Lady was the perfect hostess for a rustic city desperate to rival the great European capitals. Postwar America retained many of the early republic's deferential attitudes, at least along the Eastern seaboard, and from her selections of music to her choice of food, Louisa sought to present the Adams family in the earlier traditions of Martha Washington and Abigail Adams. As her aged father-in-law assured her, "Your experience in Berlin, St. Petersburg and St. James's, your sense, wit, and perfect fluency and purity in the French language will hold you constantly besieged" by Washington's political wives.[20]

Among those residing in Louisa's White House was Mary Hellen, who first transferred her affections from Charles Francis to George before eventually settling upon John, who in 1826 informed his stunned parents that he hoped to marry her after an engagement of several years. Any promises Mary had made to George, John sneered, were an "utter absurdity." Mary's cruel indecision only added to George's crippling self-doubt while also convincing young Charles Francis of the dangers of romantic entanglements. Mary, Charles Francis fumed, was "one of the most capricious women that were ever formed in a capricious race." Rather than risk further pain, Charles Francis instead took a "Mistress," evidently a working-class woman whose name he declined to list in his diary.[21]

Charles Francis's low opinion of women changed abruptly in the winter of 1826 when he met eighteen-year-old Abigail Brown Brooks. Abby, as she preferred to be called, was the daughter of Ann and Peter Chardon Brooks, a banker and maritime insurance executive who was reputedly the wealthiest man in Boston. Abby had traveled to Washington to visit her sister, Charlotte Everett, the wife of Congressman Edward Everett, and experience the city's social season. Charles Francis fell in love almost immediately, and by early February he admitted to his journal that he was miserable when not in her presence. He loved her, he thought, as a "woman ought to be loved—sincerely, fervently, and yet with purity and respect," terms he did not ascribe to his mistress, whom, to his discredit, he continued to visit. Being an Adams, of course, meant that he felt it necessary to tabulate Abby's defects as well. Her temper was "too high," and because her education was "faulty," she frequently expressed her opinions with "unmeaning and loud nonsense." Nor was she beautiful. But

AT LEFT:
Born in April 1808 in Medford, Massachusetts, Abigail Brooks Adams was thirty-nine when she sat for painter William Edward West in 1847. By that the time, Abigail had given birth to six children. Her youngest, Brooks, had been born two years before, and her son Arthur had died during the previous year. *Courtesy National Park Service.*

AT RIGHT:
Charles Francis Adams Sr. was twenty when he sat for the Washington-based portraitist Charles Bird King in 1827. Adams had graduated from Harvard two years before and was studying law in the office of Congressman Daniel Webster. Months before, Adams had met and promptly fallen in love with Abigail Brown Brooks, prompting him to break off his relationship with his mistress. *Courtesy National Park Service.*

her face was "expressive," and most of all, Abby possessed a "frankness, a simplicity about her manner" that he much approved of. And as he felt himself stagnating under his father's roof, Adams hoped that an engagement might serve to bolster his flagging ambitions.[22]

On the night of February 10, at a dance hosted by the French envoy, Abby chanced to take Charles Francis's arm for a stroll about the residence, and he seized the opportunity to propose. Although fluent in several languages, the flustered suitor so botched the effort that Abby took him only to mean that he wished to see more of her in the future. Trying again, Adams finally got the words out but later pronounced the moment "painful." Abby replied that she had to consult her family, leaving Charles

Francis to seek out Charlotte Everett and explain his hopes. Charlotte promised to arrange a meeting with her father—who had known John Quincy at least since 1809—while Adams rushed back to the White House to inform his startled parents. Although both believed the couple too young, John Quincy judged the match a wise one. John Adams had died the year before, and much to Louisa's dismay, John Quincy had recently gone into debt in order to satisfy his father's will. As Charles Francis assured them, the Brooks money was "such as to prevent any uneasiness as to our condition in life." Perhaps also John Quincy guessed where his son spent many of his evenings. Because Charles Francis was still six months away from his twentieth birthday, his parents gave their consent, provided that the marriage was postponed until he turned twenty-one.[23]

Peter Chardon Brooks was less enthusiastic. When Charles Francis asked for his permission, Abby's father replied that it was "not a thing to be spoken of," although he eased the sting by adding "at least at present." Charles Francis was the son and grandson of presidents, but he had yet to be certified to practice law. When Brooks heard that John Quincy approved of the relationship, his opposition melted a bit, and Abby assured her mother that she returned Charles Francis's love. Brooks also wished the marriage delayed for several years. Both families agreed that for a time, Abby would return to the family's estate in Medford. Charles Francis was to move back to Massachusetts, board with his brother George, and complete the final year of his legal studies by clerking in the office of Congressman Daniel Webster. Before leaving Washington in late April, he paid one final visit to his paramour. "In the evening I went through one of those disagreeable scenes which occur sometimes in life," he confided to his diary. "No man of sense will ever keep a Mistress," he lectured himself. "For if she is valuable, the separation when it comes is terrible, and if she is not, she is more plague than profit." Adams was surely correct in thinking that the misuse of working-class women by well-to-do young men was a habit practiced by "each succeeding generation," but his remark that he had "been preparing for a close of my licentious intrigues" ever "since my engagement" suggests that Charles Francis continued to see his mistress even after professing his love to Abby.[24]

As he pursued his legal studies in Boston—where he almost never laid eyes upon Webster, who was elevated to the Senate that June—Charles Francis continued to discuss his career plans with his future father-in-law, even as he subtly hinted that the wedding ceremony need not be delayed for two years. Brooks, he complained, had agreed to "the earliest possible time of it taking place" after Charles Francis "commenced the work in the practice of a Profession." But precisely when that exact moment arrived depended "upon a diversity of circumstances entirely beyond present calculations." Charles Francis candidly confessed to Brooks that his father's "fortune is totally handsome but of a nature not very serviceable to himself." Part of his dilemma was that his father at present financially supported all three of his sons. Yet while George had recently been elected to the state legislature and was reading law, "His disposition [seemed] to be such as to make it impossible [that] he will ever seriously pursue it." If by this admission Charles Francis hoped to convince Brooks that he required Abby's promised dowry of $20,000 sooner rather than later, it surely instead renewed doubts that Adams men made for suitable husbands.[25]

This confessional mode continued for more than a year, as Charles Francis penned a series of extraordinary letters to both his father and to Peter Brooks, missives that displayed the brutal honesty common to his family. John Quincy had been forced to pay his father's estate $12,000 in exchange for the house in Quincy, but at the time his presidential salary was only $25,000 annually. As the election of 1828 approached, Charles Francis counseled his father that he should "enter into some arrangement for the future in case you must leave Washington." At the same time, the young law student warned John Quincy that he did "not expect to make a very great figure in the world," hinting that in future years his parents should not plan on receiving any financial assistance from a third President Adams. "I cannot get over my dislike to the idea of a political existence," he added. It "shackles the independence of mind and feeling." To Brooks, Charles Francis again pushed for an early date. "My reasons for it are few and simple," Adams wrote in October 1828: "*Delay will do me no good.*" His allowance of $1,000 per year might actually decrease after the

Named for the first president, and the eldest son of his generation, George Adams was expected to achieve great things in life. But upon graduating from Harvard in 1821, the depressive George drank too much and served only one year in the state legislature. Entrusted with his father's investments, George failed at that as well because of his "indolence and self-delusion." After fathering a child with the chambermaid of a Boston doctor, George died of an apparent suicide at the age of twenty-eight. *Courtesy National Park Service.*

election, while his "profession will hardly do me any service for some years at least." The only way to attract wealthy clients, he lectured, was himself to be wealthy, "and that fitness is hardly created by the employment of time as I have done."[26]

Brooks refused to reconsider the agreed-upon timetable, and when Charles Francis pestered his father about an increase in his allowance, John Quincy shot back that he was but a "beggar, living on charity." Instead of complaining about money, the elder Adams instructed, his son should practice "self control" and rise each day at five. Three hours of study before breakfast, he thought, was "worth more than all the mines in Mexico, in *Virtue*." Charles Francis was little happier with Brooks, whom he condemned in his diary for his "miserly timid policy." But Charles Francis was eventually admitted to the bar in January 1829, at the age of twenty-two, and nine months later, on September 5, 1829, he and Abby were married at her father's estate in Medford. (John Quincy chose the date to coincide with the anniversary of his father's signing of the 1783 Treaty of Paris, which ended the Revolutionary War.) The bride's father, one newspaper remarked, was "the richest man in New England." Evidently impressed by Charles Francis's abilities, if not his patience, Brooks suggested that his son-in-law invest Abby's properties and yearly income on her behalf, a privilege he had not granted to Edward Everett or to his other son-in-law, Unitarian minister Nathaniel Frothingham.[27]

As Charles Francis's fortunes rose, his brother George's continued to decline. Even before his failed romance with Mary Hellen, the sensitive George appeared lost. Elected to the state assembly in 1826, George served only a single term before returning to his law practice on Court Street, although he never attracted many clients. Charles Francis worried that George drank too much and thought his brother's behavior "very strange." Burdened with the pressure of being his parents' firstborn and so destined for greatness, George instead sank into debt. Without telling Louisa, John Quincy paid off his son's creditors in the summer of 1827, a liability of nearly $1,000 that he could ill-afford. Foolishly, John Quincy also placed George in charge of managing the family's real estate ventures, praying that responsibility might force the twenty-six-year-old to act sensibly. Should George apply himself to the task, John Quincy lectured, "you will have no time to indulge moments of despondency." Whatever George's flaws, dissembling was not among them. His own "indolence and self-delusion," George confessed, led him to mismanage his father's accounts. As for Charles Francis, hoping to impress his future father-in-law on the matter of his family's solvency, he grew increasingly miserable about his brother's failings. "George has changed for the worse," he fretted, and "is in danger of a relapse."[28]

George was as hard on himself as was his father. In a typical diary entry, George berated himself for staying up too late, drinking too heavily, and indulging in an "inclination to sleep" away the afternoon rather than "go down to the office." As John Quincy encouraged all his sons to do, George crafted a precise schedule of daily activities but repeatedly failed to carry it through. "Of this I am ashamed," he admitted. Having wasted the day, George was victimized by "unpleasant and restless nights" as he wrestled with his guilt. The result, invariably, was a "wretched night" in which he "slept at most three hours" and so began each day's cycle of failure all over again. At times, George wondered whether the six years he spent without his parents while John Quincy served in Europe had somehow damaged him. "Could my youth have been passed with them its present results would have been probably very different," he mused. Even upon John Quincy's return, his position in Washington left "little time" for George's "instruction," so he grew up "altogether ignorant of ill and unsuspicious of the future man" he was to be. That Louisa shared his regrets did little to ease George's sorrow.[29]

Never the dedicated diarist, George abandoned his daily exercise in self-recrimination in late August 1825 before posting one final entry on New Year's Eve. However, he promised himself that the next morning he would draft a brief autobiographical statement, with a special emphasis on the past year, which would be "at once both historical and reflective." By scribbling down "the worst results of the preceding years of life," a period "far from commendable and far from happy," he might divine a "more satisfactory path of life." Referring, perhaps, to his increasing abuse of alcohol, George wished to overcome "those vices the germ of which has been planted by irresolution and [have] recently alarmed me by its gradual expansion." An appeal to the "Almighty Being," George hoped, might help him "to escape from the domination and corrupt passions." Evidently, he had no faith that such reform would come to pass. The last sentence he would ever write in his diary said only that "I close the year in melancholy feeling; its course cannot meet approval from a strict and serializing conscience."[30]

Louisa begged George to abandon Quincy and come live in Washington, but it was more than terror of his father that kept him in Massachusetts. In 1828 George became a father when Eliza Dolph, a chambermaid in the household of Dr. Thomas Welsh—where George sometimes boarded—gave birth to a daughter. The child was unwell, and George persuaded a second doctor, David Storer, to care for the child and find a new position for Dolph. Storer, in turn, prevailed upon Miles Farmer, one of his patients, to take Eliza in. Mrs. Farmer agreed but, concerned about appearances, stipulated that Adams could visit only twice a week, that he could never remain after ten o'clock, and that she or her husband must be present during his calls. Adams paid Eliza's rent but promptly ignored Mrs. Farmer's conditions, arriving drunk on several occasions and, Farmer complained, "annoying the family until a late hour in the evening." Upon being thrown out of the house, a sober George returned the next morning, "exhibiting the deepest penitence" and pleading "that the unfortunate girl might not be turned out [of] doors for his sins."[31]

As he prepared to journey to Quincy, John Quincy wrote to George on April 20, 1829, instructing him to meet them in Washington and assist with their baggage. Charles Francis cautioned his father that despite promises to mend his ways, George's law office was a hub of "loose-living and debauchery." Terrified by the prospect of facing his father, George finally took the stage to Providence. There he boarded the steamer *Benjamin Franklin* for Manhattan, where he was to transfer to another stage for Washington. Just before dawn on Thursday, April 30, George approached Captain Elihu Bunker and demanded to be put ashore. "There is a combination among the passengers against me," Adams explained. "I heard them talking and laughing at me." After Bunker refused George's request, George approached John Stevens, another passenger, and told him that the ship's rhythmic engines were telling him to "let it be, let it be." Stevens continued his morning stroll about the deck, but when he returned about ten minutes later, he found only George's hat and cloak lying near the stern.[32]

Two days later, Charles Francis left his Boston office to attend court. When he returned, his father-in-law was awaiting him. Brooks carried several newspaper accounts of George's disappearance. (The body would not wash ashore for another six weeks. Among his recovered possessions was his watch, frozen in time at 3:40.) Charles Francis nearly crumpled but then rallied, thinking of his parents. "My father almost lived in him and the loss will to him indeed be dreadful," Adams assured Brooks. Charles Francis was not wrong, as Louisa wrote that the grim news drove her husband "almost to madness."[33]

John Quincy's anguish was made worse by the arrival of a letter from Dr. Storer, informing him of the situation regarding Eliza and her daughter. At about the same time, Miles Farmer wrote to Charles Francis, informing him that while Eliza had regained her health, the child had died. George had left debts, Farmer added, but instead of simply asking for payment from the Adams family, he attempted blackmail. "I am still disposed to keep silent," he threatened. "If not [reimbursed], all the particulars will be made public," which "will not only make some people's hearts but their ears also tingle." After Charles Francis declined any correspondence "of the subject," Farmer called at his office and demanded a "settlement of the board of Eliza Dolph, and also for an adjustment of the whole affair." Coolly self-controlled, Charles Francis cautioned Farmer that "he did not believe a word" of the story before ordering him to leave his office. The story of George's secret family reached the public two years later, when Farmer sued Storer for libel, but no Adams compensated Farmer for George's debts, and Eliza vanished from history.[34]

On occasion, the romantic George had tried his hand at poetry but, doubting his abilities, had confined his lines to the privacy of his journal. Shortly before his final journey, however, he penned a short piece titled "The Spark at Sea," which he sent to several friends. One of them passed it along to the editor of the Wilmington *Register*, who published it as a fitting, if tragic, epitaph:

> *There is a little spark at sea*
> *Which glows 'mid darkness brilliantly,*
> *But when the Moon looks clear and bright.*
> *Emits a pale and feeble light;*
> *And when the tempest shakes the wave,*
> *It glimmers o'er the seaman's grave.*[35]

NOR DID JOHN ADAMS II LIVE UP TO HIS FATHER'S EXPECTATIONS. His wedding to Mary Hellen, although bitterly opposed by his parents, finally took place on February 25, 1828, in Washington's Episcopal Church. John Quincy was so upset about the ceremony—which the jilted suitors George and Charles Francis declined to attend—that he lost track of the time and had to be reminded to walk the few blocks from the White House to the church. Five weeks after the nuptials, Mary became pregnant. To assist the young couple, John Quincy invited them to reside in the White House while John worked as his father's secretary. Louisa opposed the arrangement but was somewhat mollified that December when Mary gave birth to a girl, whom her parents named Mary Louisa Johnson Adams. The birth was a rugged one. Mary declared herself an invalid, so Louisa took charge of her first granddaughter.[36]

By the time of John's marriage, his father was in the heat of his presidential reelection bid, and his sons discovered that they could not escape the capital's bitter partisanship. The wife of Russell Jarvis, a pro-Jacksonian reporter for the Washington *Daily Telegraph*, along with several female visitors to Washington, attended a party at the White House, and John, resenting Jarvis's politics, allegedly declared their presence an "impropriety." Jarvis wrote to John, demanding an explanation or apology, to which Adams replied that he thought their attendance "highly improper, considering the *political relation*, which [Jarvis] bore to his father." A month later, when John was delivering the president's messages to Congress, Jarvis assaulted him in the Capitol Rotunda, pulling his nose and slapping him soundly, both actions understood to be an invitation to duel. John refused to be provoked, and a congressional inquiry ruled that "whatever may have been the causes of provocation," Jarvis's attack "was done in contempt to the dignity of the House." But Jarvis was never arrested, and pro-Jackson papers made much of the affair, charging John with cowardice.[37]

To remove John from harm's way, John Quincy placed his son in charge of the family's Columbia Mills on Rock Creek, which he had purchased in 1824 from one of Louisa's cousins. The president prayed that the responsibility would turn around the failing venture and give his son a purpose in life. Louisa had no confidence in either the mill—which routinely flooded during heavy rains—or her son, whom she regarded as weak and under the thumb of his unwell but domineering wife. In the fall of 1829, after John Quincy and Louisa had returned north, John urged his father

The second son of John Quincy and Louisa Johnson Adams, John Adams II led a troubled life. Expelled from Harvard during his senior year for drunkenness and taking part in a student protest, Adams married his cousin Mary Hellen over the objections of his parents. John sank into alcoholism and bankruptcy. After his death at the age of thirty-one, his father became the legal guardian of his two daughters, but both had died by 1859. *Courtesy National Park Service.*

to invest thousands more in the mill. The elder Adams declined, gently advising his son that his "calculations may be a little over-sanguine." John persevered, but the pressure and his increasingly excessive drinking took a toll on his body, damaging his health and weakening his eyesight. The mill finally closed its doors in early 1834, by which time John Quincy was back in Washington as a congressman. "You have met with severe disappointments," John Quincy counseled, "but let them not overcome your resolution." Louisa begged the couple, whose family now included a second daughter, Georgiana Frances (named for her doomed uncle), to relocate to Quincy, but certain that some new opportunity would present itself, John chose to remain in Washington.[38]

That October, Charles Francis received word from Caroline Frey, Louisa's older sister and a resident of Washington, that John and Mary were both dangerously ill. Charles Francis rode out from Boston immediately to inform his father. "Then came the most trying part of it," he admitted in his diary, "the disclosure to my Mother." John Quincy promptly departed for Washington, traveling part of the way aboard the *Benjamin Franklin*, the steamer from which George had vanished. When Adams arrived at his son's Lafayette Place home on October 22, John was already unconscious while Mary, who sat nearby sobbing, was "emaciated." John Quincy kissed his son's brow before promising Mary that he "would be father to her and her children." John Quincy dozed fitfully downstairs before waking at half past four, when he went upstairs to find Nathaniel Frey, Caroline's husband, closing the eyes of the thirty-one-year-old John. A doctor arrived but declined to diagnose the cause of death; almost certainly, it was the alcoholism that had carried off two uncles and contributed to George's death. When Charles broke the news to his mother, "She lay in a state of almost stupor for some time," he remembered, "followed by a violent and indefinite emotion."[39]

John's finances, the family discovered, were far worse than anticipated. John Quincy had signed John's initial loans on the mills, which totaled $9,000. John had borrowed another $3,000 from several family friends and also owed an additional $3,000 to his servants, druggist, tailor, and butcher. As had been the case with George's suicide five years earlier, Charles Francis worried only that the death and the debts would crush his father's soul. To the privacy of his diary, Charles Francis concluded that by dying young, his elder brothers "were saved much misery which would have been otherwise inevitable, and their friends the harrowing anxieties of witnessing a remediless evil." Such a pronouncement, Adams admitted, could with "possible justice" be regarded as cold and unfeeling. But he insisted also that a "calm judgment could come to no other conclusion." Charles Francis, who had turned twenty-seven the previous August, was now the last of his generation.[40]

That realization prompted Charles Francis to understand the time had come for him to shoulder the responsibilities of masculinity as defined by the Victorian era.[41] With a growing family of his own—two children, and a third on the way—together with an impoverished sister-in-law and two young nieces, as well as aging parents, he had to accept this mantle. No longer a lonely mother's sole companion in St. Petersburg, the adult Charles Francis was suddenly expected to doggedly pursue a career and prosper in the legal world rather than merely dabble in what he had previously regarded as little more than an intellectual hobby. He was also expected to manage his entire family's finances and investments, and raise his sons to understand what it meant to be an Adams. The day had not yet arrived for the decline of the nation's most eminent family. Having once warned his father that he did not intend to distinguish himself in society, this son and grandson of presidents was forced to confront the possibility that, as with those who came before him, his future lay in politics and diplomacy. The earlier generations had wrestled with the issues that dominated their era: a revolutionary conflict with Britain and then a second war with the colonial power. As Charles Francis watched his father battle the rising clout of the "Slave Power" in Congress, a course of action and a first step began to grow clear.

2

"SINGULARLY LACKING IN WHAT IS KNOWN AS TACT"

The Assemblyman

T HE TRAGIC REALITY THAT THE THIRD SON HAD BECOME THE last of his generation and the man on whom any further Adams dynasty depended forced Charles Francis, not yet thirty years of age, to reconsider his future. Had his brothers lived, and had they become the sort of political men John Quincy had desired them to be, Charles Francis might have been content to manage his wife's investments, to litigate the occasional case—especially where property was concerned—to educate his sons, and to engage in his latest hobby, the collection of ancient coins. But now, greatness beckoned. It seemed as if each time Adams opened his morning newspaper, he discovered himself proposed for this or that position, and from Washington his aged father made his expectations for his remaining son all too clear. The result would be one of the most productive and liberal-minded periods of his life, as he pursued a variety of reforms—most of them dealing with race—in the state assembly. In doing so, he became for a time the last honorable Adams, the heights from which both he and his family would slowly decline over the next decades.

By the time of his brother John's death in 1834, Charles Francis and Abby had begun their own family. Even before George's death, which came a short five months before their wedding, the young couple grasped the importance of producing the fourth generation of Adamses. Perhaps her husband reminded her of this burden, or possibly Abby herself understood, as shortly after her marriage she became and remained unwell, much to the puzzlement of her doctors. Abby's condition was evidently psychosomatic, as it worsened after the birth of Mary Louisa Adams, John and Mary's first child, in December 1828. Abby slowly rallied, but after the birth of John's second daughter, Georgiana, Charles Francis sank into despair, fearing that the family name would die with him. Should that be the case, he supposed, better it was "that it should cease than degenerate to become a proverb." Ironically, the gloomy realization that Charles Francis would be the last Adams eased the pressure on the young couple. On August 13, 1831, Abby gave birth to a healthy child. To Charles Francis's chagrin, it was a girl. Had the firstborn been a boy, New England traditions designated that the child be named after a grandfather (although John Quincy had already defied that custom). Parents often named daughters after one of their siblings, usually so that those siblings might care for their namesakes should the parents die young. Yet even in a time of high infant mortality, which prompted new parents to defer naming their infant for a few weeks, Charles Francis and Abby waited until her christening on Sunday, October 23, to announce her as Louisa Catherine Adams, named for the sister buried in Russia. Grandmother Louisa was more horrified than flattered, admitting that the news brought a "pang in my heart." And when she finally saw the infant, Louisa was troubled. "She has superb eyes," she wrote, "but they indicate high temper and want sweetness."[1]

Although a daughter did not liberate Abby from the responsibility of producing an Adams male, it did free her of her fears that she could not bear children. Six more would follow, mostly at two- or three-year intervals. In September 1833 Abby gave birth to a boy, named John Quincy II after his overjoyed grandfather, and two years later, on the centennial of John Adams's birth, Abby presented her husband with a second son, christened Charles Francis Jr. after his father. Henry Brooks entered the world in February 1838, followed by Arthur in July 1841. A second girl, Mary Gardner, was born in February 1845, and although Abby had just turned forty, her last child, Peter Chardon Brooks, named for Abby's father, was born in June 1848.

Charles Francis's young family lived in a modest home that Abby's father had given her as a wedding gift. The house was on Boston's Hancock Street, near the state capitol, but with seven children, Charles Francis judged it too small. He had noticed a larger house near the top of Beacon Hill at 57 Mount Vernon Street quite near his Court Street law office. Built in 1804 and several times remodeled, the home was less "showy," Charles Francis rationalized, than the mansions inhabited by Abby's sisters. Even so, it was beyond his financial reach, and so in 1842 Charles Francis accepted $14,000 from his father-in-law for the purchase. Charles Francis Jr., who was seven when the family relocated, never cared for the house. The boy thought it gloomy, later remarking that it "threw a shadow across my whole early life." It contained just one sunny, "really desirable room," the younger Charles remembered, but "my father fixed on it for his library regardless of other considerations."[2]

Adams believed that his sons, future leaders all, should read widely and educate themselves so that they might later educate the public about morality and proper policies. The "study of ethics is of the highest value to a man in active life," Charles Francis assured his sons. To that end, Grandfather John Quincy encouraged them to borrow any book they wished from his vast library, and Charles Francis devoted a few hours each day to read to his children until they were old enough to do so themselves. The senior Adams preferred to read his sons "political literature" and essays by educational reformer Horace Mann, while the boys, Henry remembered, "took possession of Dickens and Thackeray for themselves." Henry embraced the bookish life. "Henry *is* Henry," Abby commented to her husband, and "when in the house [is] mostly curled up in your big chair with a book." However, Charles Francis Jr. desired to balance his education with exercise, but his father discouraged physical fitness, believing it deleterious to the brain. "My father saw no good whatever in athletics," he complained, "and he had a prejudice against the gymnasium." Tragically, having as a boy thought his own father cold and unfeeling, as an adult Charles Francis Sr. found himself unable to break the family's destructive cycle of parental taciturnity.[3]

Spiritual training, Charles Francis believed, was his most significant task as a father, and each Sunday morning he required his children to recite aloud from the Bible for an hour, after which they committed verses or a religious poem to memory. His diary entries for Sunday were the lengthiest of the week, commenting on his children's varying abilities to remember passages. Church services followed. As had his father and grandfather, Charles Francis insisted his children attend two services. "Lord! Twice a day, rain or shine, summer and winter," Charles Francis Jr. complained. "I was glad when Monday came." Although other boys lamented the end of the weekend and the resumption of school, he rejoiced in the fact that it "was six days before another Sunday." Abby shared her son's disdain for the family's Sunday traditions, but unlike her mother-in-law, she meekly did as her husband wished when it came to issues of child rearing. Finally, in 1843 Abby, who had previously declined to take part herself, agreed to accompany her family in "their sedate walk," as her son drolly put it, to the Reverend Nathaniel Frothingham's "dreary old Congregational barn in Chauncy Street." If Charles Francis Jr. was depressed by the "sombre idleness" of the day, having Abby join them in church moved her husband "to tears." A renewed faith, he hoped, would do Abby good and might provide "firmness to her determinations."[4]

For her part, Louisa Catherine demonstrated far too much firmness to please her parents. Sister Lou or Loo, as her younger brothers called her, possessed a "haughty dominating spirit," her father sighed, which he prayed she might learn to tame. Had she been a boy, Adams would not have been so concerned, as that vice had propelled a good many Harvard men into political life. But Louisa's curse was to be the eldest and brightest of her generation, and to be a girl. Her brother Henry, seven years her junior, later judged her to be "one of the most sparkling creatures I met in a long and varied experience of bright women." Like Charles Francis Jr., her second brother, Louisa enjoyed the vigorous life and bragged to her dismayed parents that she was a far more daring sleigh rider than any boy. Abby sought to develop Louisa's feminine side, at one point urging her to organize a "little dance upon the occasion" of Henry's birthday. When that too failed, her parents enrolled her in novelist Catherine Sedgwick's school for girls in distant Lenox, Massachusetts. There, her father hoped, she might "learn a lesson of moral discipline she does not obtain at home." Sedgwick found her a difficult case. Louisa was unimpressed with her instructors and regarded her classmates—perhaps rightly—as intellectually inferior. After reading widely in her grandfather's library, the gifted thirteen-year-old grew bored by the second-rate education provided girls, which was intended solely to train young women to be suitable companions to their husbands and capable mothers of their politically minded sons. "It is very fine for people that are amiable and good to be loved and praised," she wrote to her parents by way of defense, "for they don't have to try, while those that try are disliked and blamed although I am sure if they all tried as hard as I do to do right, they deserve the praise the good ones get." Louisa and Sedgwick endured two years of this contest of wills before she was allowed to return home.[5]

Louisa's two nearest siblings were a study in contrasts. An Adams to the core, Charles Francis Jr. was seldom happy for long; given to mood swings, he was moody and withdrawn one day, companionable and intimate the next. He took especial pride in not being particularly popular, as if he regarded social acceptance to be almost a character flaw. Normally competitive, Charles Francis Jr. readily admitted that his elder brother, John Quincy, was well-liked: "He had a charming, ingratiating presence and manner. He was essentially 'a good fellow,' as the term went, and a charming companion." Henry agreed that his oldest brother grew up to become "one of the best talkers in Boston society, and perhaps the most popular man in the State." Charles Francis Jr., by comparison, "was singularly lacking in what is known as tact," as he confessed. He had "almost a faculty for doing or saying the wrong thing at any given time." The boys' parents were no more enamored of Charles Francis Jr.'s rudeness than they were with what they perceived to be John Quincy's glibness, and so in 1848, both were shipped off to the Boston Latin School, their father's old academy. The boys fared no better than had Louisa. "I loathed it, and John loathed it worse than I," Charles Francis Jr. grumbled. "Not one single cheerful or satisfactory memory is with me associated therewith."[6]

As the fourth child and third son, Henry was intimidated by what he described as his "large and overpowering set" of siblings. Perhaps because of their brilliance, Henry feared himself to be "very nearly the average of most boys in physical and mental stature." (None of the Adams boys towered above their fellows, and as an adult Henry stood but four inches above five feet.) Henry was less impressed by his mother, however, believing her too easily bent to his father's will and too indulgent toward his older siblings. "Certainly no one was strong enough to control" his sister Louisa and his two elder brothers, Henry mused, "least of all their mother." But he took to his worldly grandmother Louisa, who outlived her husband by four years and died in 1852, when Henry was fourteen. Henry felt a special kinship with his grandmother and thought himself to be more like her than any other member of his family. As he grew older, Henry came to share his father's estimation of Abby's faulty education and modest reading habits; by comparison to the well-traveled Louisa, Abby struck her son as hopelessly provincial. What Henry failed to observe, evidently, was that while earlier generations of Adamses desired wives who doubled as political helpmates, his own father sought nothing more than a domestic partner, a wife who understood her domestic role and submitted to her husband's will.[7]

Unlike his brother Charles Francis Jr., Henry was drawn to his father. Where Charles Francis thought him cold and distant, Henry judged that their father "possessed the only perfectly balanced mind that ever existed in the name" of Adams. He was "singular for [his] mental poise—absence of self-assertion or self-consciousness," Henry marveled. His character "neither challenged nor avoided notice, nor admitted question of superiority, of jealousy, or personal motives," even when "under great pressure." Much later in life, Henry admitted that he and his siblings "continued to discuss this subject with a good deal of difference in their points of view." True it was, Henry once conceded, that Charles Francis Sr.'s "mind was not bold like his grandfather's or restless like his father's." But "it worked with singular perfection, admirable self-restraint, and instinctive mastery of form." However, it was suggestive that Henry's admiration did not necessarily contradict Charles Francis Jr.'s deprecation; perhaps because of their own needs, they simply chose to emphasize different facets of their father's personality. Henry instinctively grasped that his family was not as demonstrative as that of his neighbors; he responded to intellect and neither expected nor desired affection. Nor would he ever.[8]

Charles Francis Sr.'s children witnessed a previously unknown side to their father in early February 1846, when Arthur developed a case of "the croup," a respiratory condition caused by a viral infection or an allergic reaction, and died six days later at the age of five. Charles Francis was particularly distraught: just days before, he had severely chastised his son for some minor failing. Late that evening, Adams poured his sorrows into his diary: "My poor, beautiful boy, Arthur, expired at a quarter past six o'clock this day, having carried on a most terrible contest with this arch disease." Charles Francis had buried two brothers and an infant sister, but the death of his child left him undone. "Stunned by this blow, and exhausted by watching and attendance night and day," Adams could do little more than drop his "swimming head and yielding limbs upon my bed." As her husband collapsed, Abby, understanding that her children—and especially Mary, who was ten days shy of her first birthday—needed her, found an untapped source of strength. Louisa Adams had long regarded her daughter-in-law as weak, but now she praised her as "ready and active." Charles Francis Sr. also noted the transformation, although his approbation, as always, contained a veiled barb. Arthur's death, he assured his wife, had the "remarkable effect [of] exalting and refining your character."[9]

DESPITE FAMILY CONCERNS, "THE GREAT POLITICAL ISSUE OF HIS generation," that of African slavery, began to intrude upon Charles Francis's well-ordered existence, even before the death of his father. Initially, Adams sought to avoid political affairs or claimed he was content to leave national issues to his brother-in-law Edward Everett, a moderate Whig to whom he had never truly warmed. As late as 1835, when publisher William Lloyd Garrison was attacked by an anti-abolitionist mob in Boston, Adams dismissed "slavery and abolition [as] a subject which it might be wiser not to touch." Even as his father began to devote his final years to battling "the slave power," Charles Francis recorded only his "regret though not my surprise." As a man who prized cool, rational thought, Adams derided abolitionists as angry "out of all proportion to the apparent menace" and as scheming politicians in search of political advancement. In the Massachusetts statehouse, Charles Francis warned his father, abolitionists were "going without knowing it into the most ultra doctrine." So extreme were they, Adams assured the congressman, "your antislavery is nuts and gingerbread [compared] to this."[10]

If at no point in his long life did he devote much thought to the plight of enslaved Americans, like his father Adams regarded the so-called Gag Rule as an assault on the First Amendment. When Andrew Jackson relinquished the presidency in March 1837, Charles Francis rejoiced that the "incubus upon the freedom of thought and speech in the Nation" was gone. But for him the turning point came that November when a proslavery mob in Alton, Illinois, murdered publisher and minister Elijah Lovejoy. When Boston abolitionists attempted to book Faneuil Hall for a public protest against the violence, the mayor and aldermen voted to deny the application. Given his upbringing and education, Charles Francis was more incensed about the killing of a white activist than he was about slavery itself, and as a member of New England's natural aristocracy, crowd action struck him as especially horrific. Adams regarded the mayor's decision, rather like the Gag Rule, as he stated in a letter published by the *Boston Morning Post*, a violation "of our free republican institutions." Acceding to southern demands, he fumed, revealed that the "craven spirit has got about as far in Boston as it can well go." Twelve-year-old Charles Francis Jr. concluded that while his father "was a cold man outwardly, once fairly in motion he was apt to be impetuous." Peter Chardon Brooks, Charles Francis's father-in-law, and his two brothers-in-law did not approve of his editorial, and the four endured a "warm argument" over the issue one evening. "They will always be of the conservative order," he scribbled into his diary, "and I cannot often be." Whether Charles Francis realized it or not, his letter was a step into the political arena.[11]

That step was far from easy. Part of Charles Francis desperately wished to break the cycle of Adams family public service. "I wish I could be an entire abolitionist; but it is impossible," he confessed to his diary. "My mind will not come down to the point." Adams also admitted "some repugnance" to public speaking, believing he was "not naturally endowed with" the abilities of a Daniel Webster. (He rightly suspected, however, that Webster's fame as an orator had less to do with intellectual "study" than with his booming voice, and Adams was to become a much-valued antislavery speaker because he emphasized facts above showmanship.) But as the son and grandson of presidents, Charles Francis was to discover— as would his sons—that whenever a position fell vacant, Massachusetts residents instinctively thought of an Adams. In October 1839, leaders of the state's Whig Party arrived at his door to offer him a nomination to the Massachusetts legislature. Because the Whigs dominated the state, nomination was tantamount to election. Stunned by the honor, Adams declined "without a moment's hesitation." Although he approved of Whig principles, he acknowledged in a lengthy reply, he preferred "the position of an *unpledged* citizen who may say exactly what he thinks upon public affairs." Having found his voice in his editorial on the Faneuil Hall dispute, Charles Francis had then published a number of essays on national economic issues in the Boston *Columbian Centinel* and the *Advocate*. A seat in the legislature would burden him with a "multitude of harassing local questions" and deny him the opportunity to address questions of "the general or particular good."[12]

The Whigs carried his district that year, but their margin of victory was small enough to encourage them to try Adams again in 1840. In an act that served to further sour their already-frosty personal relationship, Adams's brother-in-law Everett, then the state's governor, begged John Quincy to demand that his son stand for office. The aged congressman had "expressed so much regret at my decision" not to run in 1839, Charles

Francis admitted, "that I would gladly have recalled it, had there been an opportunity." Over the next months he pondered his options, carefully tabulating the positives and negatives. "I have still children to whom I owe something," he reasoned. But his country "was now in danger from evil and vicious counsels," and he owed it to the nation "to extend my sphere of activity and usefulness, and to benefit my fellows" at the cost of his own happiness. On October 28, 1840, he contacted the party's leadership, assuring them that "the opinions of my friends" prompted him to "accept it upon this occasion."[13]

Adams's seat was never in doubt, but even so, he thought the "result of the Election beyond" anything he had anticipated. He won the highest number of ballots bestowed upon any Boston assemblyman. The Whigs captured eleven of his state's congressional districts and control of the national House of Representatives for the first time in their brief history. Bedeviled by the ongoing depression of 1837, President Martin Van Buren retained only 60 electoral votes to Whig candidate William Henry Harrison's 234. "So much for the Northern man with Southern principles," Adams gloated. "May this year's experience be a lesson to all future politicians who sacrifice the interests that ought to be most dear to them for the sake of truckling to Slaveholders." Yet as a reminder that he was no typical state assemblyman, the far-away Indiana *Richmond Palladium* proudly reported that "Charles Francis Adams, son of the ex-President, is elected to the Massachusetts legislature."[14]

A congratulatory letter of sorts promptly arrived from Washington. "You have so reluctantly consented to engage in public life, that I fear you will feel too much annoyed by its troubles and perplexities," lectured John Quincy. Yet the old congressman believed his son knew his duty. "Your father and grandfather have fought their way through the world against hosts of adversaries," he added, but they never grew "discouraged nor soured." The letter only dampened Charles Francis's spirits. His father's words, he mused, proved "very prejudicial to my comfort," as he was quite certain that "political life would not suit me at all." The assemblyman-elect admitted that "the confidence of my fellow citizens" pleased him. But not enough: "It is the commencement of another kind of life in which I must be tried perhaps beyond my strength to bear."[15]

Two months later, on January 6, 1841, thirty-three-year-old Charles Francis strode into the General Court—the name a holdover from the earliest days of the Massachusetts Bay Colony—and took the seat assigned to him by lottery. As he had feared, his days were consumed by parochial affairs, making it "dull work to spend the day hearing such stupid stuff." Of greater moment was the assembly's decision regarding Daniel Webster's replacement in the Senate, as Webster had been tapped by Harrison as his secretary of state. Following considerable debate, the assembly chose former congressman Rufus Choate. "After much patient reflection," Adams wrote, he voted for Choate, yet he "felt that his election was a slight upon" his own father. National concerns intruded a second time in April, when word arrived of the unexpected death of Harrison and the elevation of Virginia planter John Tyler to the presidency. Mainstream Whigs thought Tyler's advancement a national calamity, and given the new president's proslavery ideology, Adams suspected, it was "hardly probable that it would not be."[16]

By the end of his first single-year term, Adams was inclined to retire. For an Adams, even one still so young, the General Court, he fretted, was a "place of no great distinction." But because of Harrison's death, the Whigs were in disarray. Entangled in negotiations with Britain over a border dispute, Webster opted to remain loyal to Tyler, whose states' rights orientation placed him at odds with his party's nationalistic, loose construction approach to the Constitution. Adams agreed to run again in 1841 and won, although the results, he worried, revealed a "prodigious falling off" from the previous year's Whig majority. Yet the rise of "His Accidency," as New England Whigs dubbed Tyler, provided Charles Francis with a clue on how to rationalize a political office that he professed to detest. Rather than bury himself in the minutia of local constituent service, Charles Francis decided to mirror his father's course and confront the slave power in his home state.[17]

The first issue to arise was that of fugitive slaves. Decades before, in 1793, Congress had passed the Fugitive Slave Act, based upon Article

IV, Section 2, of the Constitution, which stipulated that persons "held to service or labor in one state" who escaped into another were not freed but might be "delivered up" to their owners. In response, in 1826 the state of Pennsylvania made it a felony for anyone "to take or carry away, by force and violence," any black resident of the state. Six years later, a slave catcher named Edward Prigg seized Margaret Morgan, a Maryland runaway, on behalf of her deceased owner's heirs. When Prigg was arrested, he appealed to the US Supreme Court. Finally, in 1842, in the case of *Prigg v. Pennsylvania*, Justice Joseph Story, writing for the majority, struck down the state law as a violation of both federal law and the Constitution. But while the Court gutted the Pennsylvania act, Story, a native of Massachusetts, also held that because the Fugitive Slave Act was a federal law, states were under no obligation to help enforce it.[18]

The ruling became a Massachusetts concern later that year, when George and Rebecca Latimer, fugitives from Virginia, were arrested by Boston police after being recognized by a former employee of their owner. Technically, under the 1793 law, runaways had committed no crime, and because the *Prigg* decision did not compel local authorities to act, black activists posted signs denouncing the city constabularies as "Human Kidnappers." Abolitionists Frederick Douglass and Charles Remond addressed fund-raising meetings in hopes of purchasing the couple from James Gray, their Norfolk owner. At length, Boston's antislavery community was able to raise enough money to liberate the Latimers. But the movement against slave catchers continued as abolitionists began two petition drives on the issue, one for the state assembly and a second for Congress. When finally delivered to the General Court, the former bore 62,791 signatures and weighed 150 pounds.[19]

Because Charles Francis chaired the committee tasked with drafting memorials and remonstrances, the petitioners asked him to present their appeals to Congress. "This is perhaps the most memorable event of my life," he thought. "I feel some degree of pride in the fact that I was selected for such a purpose." Charles Francis's report, which led to the state's first personal-liberty law, conceded the validity of the *Prigg* decision. "Nullification was never any part of my policy," he assured one supporter. But whereas Story had ruled that state authorities were not *required* to assist in corralling fugitives, Adams recommended that Massachusetts law *forbid* state and local officials from "aiding in or abetting the arrest or detention of any person who may be claimed as a fugitive from slavery." Even city "jails or other public property of the State" were to be denied to federal marshals or professional slave catchers. Unlike more militant abolitionists, Charles Francis believed that the Constitution protected slavery from federal interference; the proper middle ground, he argued, was to remove Massachusetts from any connection to what Adams's report dubbed a "despicable" institution. After the legislature approved the report, Adams at last felt he had found his role in politics. "Public life is to me nothing excepting insofar as it contains something honest to contend for," he assured his journal.[20]

If Massachusetts reformers could not erase contemptible sections of the Constitution, they could address their own shameful past. In 1786, just as slavery was dying in the Bay State, the assembly restored colonial prohibitions against marriages between whites and blacks (and Native Americans). The issue remained divisive. Early on, abolitionist William Lloyd Garrison condemned the ban, yet after being warned off by his antislavery allies, he briefly backtracked, announcing that he had "never advocated nor recommended" interracial marriage. In 1840 and again in 1841, Whig assemblyman George Bradburn introduced legislation for the law's repeal, but on both occasions a coalition of conservative Democrats and Whigs defeated it in one or the other chamber. The bill's critics, Charles Francis groused, were "better as exponents of popular prejudices and old habits than in advancing any ultimate principles." When Bradburn retired, Adams took up the challenge. During his second term, he successfully guided the bill through the Senate, only to watch it fail in the House. Adams persevered, and the bill finally passed in February 1843 by a vote of 143 to 126. "Thus is passed under my care one of the most difficult bills that ever had to run the gauntlet of Legislative Assemblies," Charles Francis sighed. "I think it is the last remnant of Slavery in our Statute book."[21]

To Adams's chagrin, no other state followed Massachusetts' lead. Not only did the other original thirteen colonies maintain their old legislation, but in the two decades leading up to the Civil War, seven more states, including California and Ohio, passed laws banning interracial marriage. And even in victory, Adams remained a conflicted reformer, one more dedicated to principle than actual people. "I am glad to have aided in removing" the 1786 ban, he wrote in the privacy of his diary, "although nothing can be more disagreeable to me than the consideration of the subject which it involves."[22]

That done, and at age thirty-five, Adams nursed his habitual pro-testations to quit public life, insisting that he saw "no issue for honest men in the United states, but retirement." His emergence as a leader of New England's antislavery Whigs made that unlikely, however, and in a demonstration of his growing clout, in November 1843 his party elevated him into the state Senate. With forty members, the Senate was one-tenth the size of the House, providing Charles Francis with greater state and regional prominence. Devoting almost all of his energies to battling the slave South, Adams presented petitions on behalf of Boston abolition-ist Wendell Phillips and sided with black activist Charles Remond in his fight against segregated train cars. As did his father, Charles Fran-cis regarded the right of petition a basic Constitutional entitlement, even when he dissented from a petitioner's sentiments. Yet while he privately noted Remond's race in a way he did not with Phillips, neither did he feel it necessary to elaborate on that fact in his diary, instead praising Remond's speech to the General Court on the Latimers's freedom as a "very strong appeal." He also supported the rights of his state's black mar-iners by denouncing South Carolina's 1822 Negro Seamen's Act (which required that black mariners be incarcerated while in that state's ports) and, at the request of the legislature, forwarded to his congressman father a resolution demanding that the Constitution be amended to remove the three-fifths clause (which counted five southern slaves as three citizens, thus giving the South an advantage in congressional apportionment), a symbolic effort that failed 156 to 13 in the House and earned Charles Francis an editorial rebuke from the powerful *Richmond Enquirer*.[23]

In recognition of his rising fame, the mayor and aldermen of Boston invited Adams to deliver the annual Fourth of July oration there in 1843.

The day had long been one of celebration in Boston, but in recent years it had grown into a major event, with the New England Guards escorting the procession of speaker and city elders through the streets to Faneuil Hall. Far from a small honor, the invitation brought Charles Francis to the attention of the New York press. The offer also revealed how dramatically public opinion in the city had shifted against the South in the six years since the 1837 murder of antislavery minister Elijah Lovejoy. Although asked to speak on the topic of liberty, Adams abandoned traditional odes to the Revolutionary generation in favor of "the encroachment of the Slave power." For the young politician, the day was made especially dramatic by a bust of John Adams on one side of his podium while on the other, John Quincy sat beneath his own portrait. No newspaper reported the full contents of the speech, but one Manhattan journalist recorded that Adams "acquitted himself in a manner which must have given complete satisfaction to his most ardent friends." However, more-conservative Whigs were displeased with the oration, and quite possibly the invitation was made in hopes of luring Adams back into a more moderate stance. Had he done so, his son Henry later remarked, he "might then have taken his inherited rights of political leadership in succession" to Webster and Everett. But he "could not make terms with the slave-power, and the slave-power overshadowed all the great Boston interests."[24]

Much to the dismay of business-minded Whigs, whose industrial ventures tethered them to southern cotton planters, in September 1844 Charles Francis next shared a Boston stage with Liberty Party activist Cassius Clay, the antislavery cousin of perennial Whig presidential candidate Henry Clay. Sponsored by the Young Men's Whig Club, the rally at the city's Tremont Temple exposed the growing divide between the younger, antislavery wing of the party—whose members styled themselves Conscience Whigs—and the older, establishment Cotton Whigs, who conducted textile business with southern planters. Although Adams, as president of the club, humorously introduced Clay as a statesman who "had merits of his own, *other* than that of coincidence in name with our distinguished candidate for president," the speeches that followed, according to one horrified Vermont reporter, were filled with "insulting denunciations of Henry Clay," whose shifting positions on annexing the slaveholding Republic of Texas had alienated antislavery New Englanders.[25]

Adams initially judged Henry Clay's May 1844 nomination to be a "very good one in itself," although he also felt "uncertain as to Mr. Clay on the point of Texas" and increasingly thought that the "Whigs as a party are but a single step above their opponents." In truth, Adams had good cause to worry about the candidate's stance on Texas. Having initially opposed annexation, Clay published a letter in mid-August announcing that he "should be glad" to welcome Texas into the republic provided it could be obtained "without dishonor, without war, with the common consent of the Union, and upon just and fair terms." In Massachusetts and New York, younger Whigs abandoned the party in droves and cast their ballots for James G. Birney and the Liberty Party. Adams took solace in the fact that his father was "reelected by [a] nearly two thousand majority," while he himself trounced his Democratic opponent and captured more votes than any other Whig candidate for the state Senate. But Birney earned 15,812 of his 470,062 third-party votes in the Empire State, and that allowed James K. Polk, the Democratic candidate, to win New York's thirty-six electoral votes after edging out Clay by a mere 5,106 ballots. When Adams, "dull headed" from a celebratory dinner, awoke to hear of Polk's victory, he considered it a "disappointment" that all but erased his own good electoral news.[26]

Outgoing President John Tyler, who favored annexation, regarded Polk's election as a national referendum on the issue and urged Congress to admit Texas under a simple (and unprecedented) joint resolution. After the House of Representatives voted to do so in late January 1845, with John Quincy in the minority, Charles Francis leapt into action. "There must be a new spirit in the people of the free States," he wrote. To that end, he called upon the state Senate to allow him to chair a joint legislative committee to prepare a "report and resolutions on the subject of Texas." On January 29 he joined abolitionists Garrison, Abby Kelley, Maria Weston Chapman, and 350 other delegates in a "Great Abolition Anti-Texas Convention" in Faneuil Hall. Although the meeting was billed as open to all who opposed annexation "without distinction of party," his presence marked yet another step away from Whig orthodoxy.[27]

On February 20, Charles Francis rose in the Senate to present five resolutions and his accompanying report. Privately, he regarded the final result as "somewhat tame," but after five years in the General Court he had developed a keen sense of what might win the support of both chambers. The resolutions held that because Texas had been an independent republic for nearly a decade, there was no precedent for its acquisition and that its admission by joint resolution by Congress was equally without precedent. The fourth formed the state's core complaint: Massachusetts could "never consent" to the admission of Texas or any other territory except upon "the perfect basis of freemen," and never "while slavery or slave representation form any part" of it. The legislature approved the resolutions and requested that Governor George Briggs submit them to the president, the state's two senators, and, knowing that John Quincy Adams could be counted on to support them in the House, its congressional delegation.[28]

As Charles Francis expected, Congress refused to debate the resolutions, although John Quincy's determination to be heard on the matter further enhanced his reputation among abolitionists and earned him the title of "our Wilberforce," after the British antislavery activist. However, the younger Adams was satisfied that his entire state had formally gone on the record in opposing annexation. He wished to place the South on notice that New England's antislavery sentiment was no longer the concern only of the apolitical supporters of William Lloyd Garrison, who refused to vote on moral grounds. Take notice it did. When one Manhattan paper quoted Adams as saying that he "rejoiced heartily" in combating "this high-handed Texas scheme," journalists in both North Carolina and Washington denounced his remarks as "fanaticism [that] almost amounts to insanity."[29]

After five years in the General Court, Charles Francis was prepared to retire, although not from political activism. He had long believed a "political position is now among the most laborious and difficult of professions," and with the Texas resolutions, the Latimer law, and the legalization of interracial marriage successfully concluded, Adams considered these accomplishments a "fair termination of my labors." These achievements were done, he assured his diary, not in search of "vain glory" but through "hard and incessant labour, in opposition to popular opinion and [with] the overshadowing influence of my father." His plan, however, was not to step aside but rather to continue to shape public opinion through the press. In a move that made news even in Virginia, in 1846 Adams, together with John Gorham Palfrey, the secretary of state, and investor Stephen Phillips, purchased the nearly defunct *Boston Daily Whig*. Because the family's responsibilities to the public would not go unattended, John Quincy announced that "did not at that time disapprove" of Charles Francis's decision to decline renomination in the fall.[30]

At two cents per copy, the *Daily Whig* never turned a profit, and Charles Francis, who required no salary because of his wife's properties, kept the newspaper afloat with his own purse. However, the hope of the editors was that the paper would serve as the voice of the Conscience Whigs while silencing the old guard and winning over Liberty Party voters. Adams was weary of "Whig apathy" and the willingness of the party's national leadership "to surrender further opposition to Texas and slavery," although Polk's victory in 1844, he was convinced, also demonstrated the dangers of third-party candidates. The need for a staunchly antislavery Whig journal in New England, Adams believed, only became greater in March 1845 when Polk was sworn in as president. "Polk's inaugural address [was] a singular compound of cant and hypocrisy," Adams fumed. The new "administration [planned] to make this great people subservient to an oligarchy of slaveholders."[31]

The staid business wing of the party tolerated Charles Francis and the *Daily Whig* until the outbreak of war with Mexico in May 1846. Although most northern Whigs in the House believed that Polk had unconstitutionally provoked the Mexicans into the conflict, in the end only fourteen members of Congress, including John Quincy Adams, cast their votes against the war. Charles Francis and Charles Sumner, a law professor at Harvard who contributed numerous editorials to the *Daily Whig*, were furious with what they regarded as the cowardice of the party's elder statesmen; Senator Daniel Webster was traveling in New

England at the time and refused to go on the record concerning the war resolutions. "When will her pusillanimous advisors understand that the issue must sooner or later be met in America?" Adams editorialized in the *Daily Whig.* "Slavery must be abolished, or there will be no freedom left." So identified was he as the leader of the Conscience Whigs that Garrison and Phillips stopped at his office and urged him to sponsor an antiwar rally. Disagreeing with Garrison's advocacy of disunion, Adams declined. But when the party met at Faneuil Hall that September in their state convention, the Conscience wing was determined to be heard. "The Whigs," Sumner shouted during his turn at the podium, "ought to be the party of Freedom." Adams agreed. In a "very warm and emphatic speech," as one journalist characterized it, Adams took issue with those who argued "the Whig Party could not touch the slave question in a manner to suit abolitionists without killing itself." To the contrary, Adams observed, the reason why its candidates often lost votes to third-party Liberty contenders "was because there was a shade of suspicion of their sincerity on the subject of slavery."[32]

Largely because the state convention demonstrated that most of the delegates remained loyal to the old party, both Adams and Charles Sumner resolved to cast their lot elsewhere. Charles Francis was now convinced "that little or nothing can be done with the Old Whig Party," and his newspaper was openly contemptuous of Webster and Massachusetts Congressman Robert Winthrop, who had reluctantly voted for war. Sumner considered challenging Winthrop by running as a Liberty candidate. Adams dissuaded him from doing so but then editorialized that "there are two divisions of the party, one based on public principle and the other upon manufacturing and commercial interests." Although still professing a disdain for political office, Adams also began to quietly approach Liberty partisans, assuring one abolitionist that "all rigid party associations tend rather to weaken" the crusade against slavery. To Ohio Congressman Joshua Giddings, an ally of his father and a fellow Conscience Whig on the verge of leaving the party, Charles Francis confessed himself "very tired of the equivocation of the Whigs" and "fully prepared for any movement which may be made from any quarter." Understanding the influence that Adams and his newspaper could bring to their cause, abolitionists responded enthusiastically to his overtures. An agent of the Massachusetts Anti-Slavery Society urged Adams to attend an upcoming meeting in Westminster, and Frederick Douglass sent him a lengthy missive in reply to a notice in the *Daily Whig*.[33]

Party elders believed they had the upper hand, and shortly after the convention, Adams discovered that despite the "formidable demonstrations" he and Sumner had made at Faneuil, their "risk" had not paid off. Adams and Sumner "are no longer Whigs and have no further right to claim affinity to the Whig Party," charged the influential *Boston Atlas*. "We publicly denounce them as deserters from its ranks, and traitors to the true political faith." Remembering President John Adams's firing of reactionary members of his cabinet and John Quincy's youthful embrace of the Republicans, the *Pittsfield Sun* added that "Adams has an hereditary right to abandon his party and his friends, [as] it has been rather too prevailing a trait in [his] family." The southern press, which despised both father and son, took heart in the fact that "in Massachusetts the Whigs are positively and openly at war." Although Charles Francis had not coveted that result, hoping instead to end, as one Richmond paper sarcastically phrased it, "the truckling spirit shown to the South [by] the old Whigs," he accepted his fate with equanimity and continued to promote antislavery in the *Daily Whig*. "I trust in God and go right forward," he promised himself.[34]

By the time the telegram alerting him about his father's stroke arrived at his office in late February 1848, the tide had begun to turn. The inability of Congress to resolve the destiny of the southwestern territories seized from Mexico during the war, together with Senator Webster's willingness to compromise with his southern colleagues, rendered Massachusetts increasingly inhospitable to conciliatory politicians. Newspapers in New York and Boston advanced the names of State Senator Henry Wilson and antislavery attorneys Solomon Lincoln and William Jackson for the special election to fill John Quincy's seat. All had either abandoned the Whigs for the Liberty Party or had all but done so. "None other than a decidedly anti-slavery Whig can probably be chosen," one editor admitted. Charles Francis's Beacon Hill address placed him outside of his father's Quincy district. Otherwise, the editor added, "Charles Francis Adams would, most likely, be the man" for the seat. In the end, the party nominated Horace Mann, an educational reformer and former member of the state legislature.[35]

The death of his father immediately altered Charles Francis's life, and not merely because he was now without the parent—their complicated, troubled relationship notwithstanding—to whom he had routinely turned for advice and looked to as his role model. Because of two large purchases of land around Quincy, together with rising land values in the decade after the Depression of 1837, John Quincy left behind property valued "at not less than half a million of dollars." Charles Francis and his family were already sufficiently wealthy thanks to Abby's dowry and investments, but because Charles Francis was the only surviving child, his father's estate made him one of the wealthiest men in Massachusetts. Political life was not as yet an avenue to private wealth, so his inheritance liberated the forty-year-old Adams to pursue any course he might desire.[36]

There was also an inheritance of another kind, one demanding enough to determine Charles Francis's future course for him. By the time that John Quincy's body was returned north and interred in the family crypt at the United First Parish Church, large numbers of northern Democrats had concluded, as had their youthful Whig brethren, that the established two-party system was not responsive to the sectional crisis wrought by the war with Mexico. As a political vehicle, a militant abolitionist faction like the Liberty Party stood little chance of rising to the challenge. But a party dedicated only to keeping slavery out of the newly acquired territories had the potential to quickly emerge as a potent force in American life. And if so, who better to help guide it than an Adams?

3

"TO UNITE THE ANTI-SLAVERY FEELING OF THE UNION"

The Free-Soiler

THE DEATH OF HIS FATHER SEVERED ANY REMAINING TIES THAT bound Charles Francis to the Whig Party. The brief movement to elevate Adams into the vacant congressional seat held by John Quincy foundered, as he confided to his diary, on "the objection of nonresidence." But for Charles Francis, both personal and political considerations also blocked his path to Washington. The Conscience Whigs had lost the state contest with their conservative elders, and as yet, no replacement party presented itself. "Although no one feels more strongly than I do the kindness" paid by his late father's constituents, he added, Adams professed to have a "profound aversion to finding myself in any way connected with office seeking." It was one thing for the aged former president to serve as a lonely voice against the slave power, but Charles Francis was ambivalent about beginning his national career where his father had finished his. The "trials of that House I am not very eager to endure," he insisted, and with Abby again pregnant, he faced "private responsibilities which ought first to demand my time." National concerns, he promised himself, might wait.[1]

Within two months of his father's death, Adams discovered that providence had other plans in store. For more than three decades, politicians had sought to avoid any sectional issues that divided the North from the South in favor of vigorous debates over economic policies. Virtually since John Quincy's election to Congress in 1830, his Whigs had pursued a pro-business agenda, while the rival Democrats backed low-tariff policies on behalf of the farmer and urban laborer. With few abolitionist voices in Congress, many mainstream Democrats and Whigs wished to avoid discussing slavery, which they were often able to do, provided that the question focused on unfree labor where it already existed as opposed to where it might expand. The conflict with Mexico changed all of that. Even before the February 1848 Treaty of Guadalupe Hidalgo brought 529,000 square miles of new land into the Union, it was clear to all that Polk's war was dissolving old political affiliations. In hopes of surviving an anticipated antiwar backlash at the polls, in August 1846 Congressman David Wilmot, a Pennsylvania Democrat, had tried to amend a war-appropriations bill to require that slavery be banned from any territory annexed from Mexico. By a vote of 85 to 79, the northern-dominated House approved the Wilmot Proviso, with John Quincy siding with the majority. However, thanks to Senator John Davis, a Massachusetts Cotton Whig, the Senate defeated the bipartisan northern coalition, so the war ended with no resolution of the fate of the territories.[2]

The future of the Southwest, Americans hoped, would be settled by the upcoming presidential contest. As was traditional, the Democrats held their national convention first, meeting in Baltimore in May 1848. On the fourth ballot, the convention nominated a sectionally balanced ticket of Senator Lewis Cass of Michigan and General and Congressman William Butler of Kentucky. In an era when party platforms were both brief and widely read, the Democrats opted for silence, choosing to take no formal position on the territories. But Cass had been public in his criticism of the Wilmot Proviso, initially denouncing it as "mischievous & foolish" before finally arguing that it was unconstitutional, claiming that Congress lacked any legal authority over the West beyond the creation of territorial governments. Because settlers enjoyed the right of self-government, only they might regulate slavery when it came to framing local laws. In time, Cass's theory came to be known as "popular sovereignty." Empty platform or not, with the candidate came his positions.[3]

The Whigs met in Philadelphia on June 7. As always, perennial candidate Henry Clay of Kentucky angled for the nomination, but his loss four years before, together with his refusal to explicitly embrace the Wilmot Proviso, worried delegates who remembered his earlier equivocation over Texas. Conscience Whigs then looked to Daniel Webster, back in the Senate following his stint in the State Department. Webster had famously condemned the Mexican War as "universally odious" and was friendlier to the free-soil movement—which sought the prohibition of slavery in western territories—but his attempt to ignore the proviso by advocating that the United States simply return the Mexican cession of 1848 was regarded as untenable even with northern voters. At length, the nomination went to Zachary Taylor, an apolitical but effective general and a bitter critic of Polk. Because he was also a Louisiana slaveholder, most of Taylor's 171 votes came, unsurprisingly, from southern delegates. An attempt by Charles Allen, a Massachusetts Conscience advocate, to adopt the Wilmot Proviso was ruled out of order. The Whigs, believing that any statement regarding slavery would weaken their chances against Cass, declined to issue any platform at all.[4]

As was customary, the convention's chairman called upon the delegates to unify and make the nomination unanimous, but Allen and a disgusted Massachusetts delegation refused to do so. The question remained of how New England Whigs would respond. One Vermont editor, recalling how disenchanted Liberty voters had inadvertently assisted in Polk's victory, speculated that even Charles Francis would come to accept Taylor's nomination: "Adams will think 'Birneyism' is decidedly worse than 'Taylorism,' and so choosing the least of two evils, he will bite his lips, eat his [earlier antislavery] words, and vote for Taylor under protest."[5]

The editor could not have been more wrong. On the eve of the Philadelphia convention, which Adams declined to attend, he correctly predicted that Taylor's victory would be "decided by the Slave States." His own policy toward free soil, Adams observed, was "almost identical with the view taken by my father in the House at the time when the Wilmot proviso was first moved." Adams supposed that whether Cass or Taylor captured the White House, the new president would deploy the military to secure the frontier, so any future application for statehood "will come with a Slaveholding form of government." It was imperative, Adams counseled, for free-soil advocates in both parties "to unite the anti Slavery feeling of the Union." To plan strategy, Adams invited his *Daily Whig* colleagues to convene in his Boston office on May 27. Stephen Phillips, Charles Sumner, and Henry Wilson, himself a delegate to the national convention, agreed to meet, as did state senator Ebenezer Hoar. "Our course is plain," Adams wrote to Congressman John Gorham Palfrey, his friend and Conscience ally in Washington. "The issue must be made at some time or other, and there is no fairer time than this."[6]

As far as the Whig antislavery faction was concerned, they had not left the party; the party had abandoned them. "Whiggism has virtually committed suicide," Adams charged in a brutal editorial, and "has *thrown itself* into the arms of slavery." Taylor, who confessed in an interview to never having voted, "was not a Whig" but rather a general who fought "in order to keep his two hundred slaves longer under his unrighteous power." Their collective goal, Adams argued, must be to awaken northern sensibilities, perhaps with a new party, so that "the Christian citizens" could find the courage to "contest the black piratical flag of African Slavery." The group finally decided to issue the call for a regional "Anti-Cass, Anti-Taylor" convention to meet a month later in Worcester, in the central part of Massachusetts. The call for delegates was published by the *Whig* and the Boston *Courier*, and it bore the names of Adams, Sumner, Wilson, and Charles Allen. To choose either Cass or Taylor, the advertisement asserted, was "treacherous to the cause of Freedom, and the utter prostration of the interests of Free Labor and the Rights of Freemen."[7]

The effort to unite free-soil advocates on both sides of the aisle had been quietly discussed in congressional hallways and legislative chambers since Wilmot first advanced his amendment. Antebellum reformers had embraced a wide variety of causes, from temperance to women's rights, and were enthusiastic conventioneers, so they knew whom to contact outside their districts. Since the summer of 1846, Conscience Whigs had been corresponding with Barnburner Democrats—antislavery politicians accused of being willing to torch their political barn to eliminate conservative candidates—such as Preston King, a New York congressman, and Salmon Chase, a radical attorney and leader of the Liberty Party in Ohio. Adams himself had penned dozens of missives to reformers and journalists outside of New England, assuring one New York Democrat that the time had come for "the forgetting of past differences." If the "Barnburners of New York are true and can present the best men for this crisis," he argued, "in God's name, let them lead." At the same time, several Liberty Party newspapers, including the Massachusetts-based *Emancipator*, dropped their objections to cooperation with Free-Soilers.[8]

Although there was no formal delegation selection process, the June 28 meeting was a tremendous success, with as many as five thousand attendees. Conventioneers booked a special train of fourteen cars from Boston, "fuller than full," as one sympathetic journalist bragged. So many arrived that the convention was forced to set up in a clearing amid a large oak grove adjacent to an insane asylum (which provided the meeting's conservative critics, one journalist laughed, with several "scurvy jests"). Wishing to counter the charge—true although it was—that this was predominantly a young man's summit, the planners prevailed upon the aged Samuel Hoar, a former congressman and Ebenezer's father, to serve as chairman. However, journalists correctly identified Adams, Sumner, Wilson, and Allen as "the leading spirits" of the group. Congressman Joshua Giddings led a small delegation from Ohio, and there "were not a few members of the [far more militant] American Anti-Slavery Society among the spectators," Ohio's *Anti-Slavery Bugle* reported.[9]

Following Giddings's opening remarks, Charles Francis took the podium. Journalists from outside of his home state invariably referred to him as the "son of John Quincy Adams." But even those unfamiliar with the former state senator were impressed. Adams "made a most severe and caustic speech in which his 'cotton Whig' friends had to suffer some," reported one New Hampshire newspaper. As the Massachusetts state legislator tasked with "preparing resolutions against the extension of slavery," Adams formally announced his opposition to "the nomination of a military chieftain, who had not given the least evidence of agreeing with the great body of the Whigs in a single principle." The old party existed only to capture offices for its political class, while the Worcester delegates, he insisted, were "not engaged in politics as a trade." As for himself, he concluded, "he could have nothing more to do with a party whose course had exhibited such monstrous falsehood." Sumner followed, but the audience remained with what a Massachusetts journalist judged Adams's "thorough-going bolting speech." The reporter had heard Adams address the General Court in the past "but never knew him to speak so well as on this evening. He appeared to be in a very happy state of mind."[10]

Long critical of third parties, Charles Francis believed that the free-soil movement might soon replace the Whigs and blossom into the nation's second party. But he was not so naive to think that it could secure the White House that November. Understanding the necessity of advancing the name of an important politician, some delegates hoped that Webster, who had initially threatened to "stand quite aloof" from Taylor's nomination, might accept a leadership role. Adams considered this a dreadful notion, and not merely because of his father's longtime distrust of the conservative Webster. "My idea always has been to put the West in the lead if possible," he counseled journalist Henry Stanton. Wisely, the predominantly New England–based convention decided against making any nominations at that time and instead issued a call for northern Free-Soilers of both parties to convene in Buffalo, New York, on August 9 for a "Free State Convention" to nominate an antislavery ticket. To better coordinate with other states, the Massachusetts delegation appointed a fifteen-member Central Committee, to be chaired by Adams and Henry Wilson. One loyal Whig editor had already condemned the Worcester delegates as men who had "been acting against the Whig party for the past three years," so the group issued a final resolution observing that they were advancing "no new principles" but rather adhering to "the memorable" Ordinance of 1787, which banned slavery from the Old Northwest and "has for more than half a century been the fundamental law of human liberty."[11]

There was much to do and little time. Personal issues intruded, but in a most welcome fashion, when on the eve of the Worcester meeting Abby gave birth to their final child, Peter Chardon Brooks. "Mother and child doing well," Adams scribbled into his diary. "Blessed be to God, for my anxieties on this score have been manifold and painful." Yet within hours, Charles Francis was huddled with Sumner. The weeks before Buffalo were critical, he believed: it was easier for disaffected voters and activists to unite on behalf of an idea than it would be after the convention elected nominees and the ticket was no longer an "abstraction." With Webster grudgingly coming to accept Taylor's nomination, leading Free-Soilers began to advance favorite sons. Owen Lovejoy, the editor of the *Emancipator* and brother of the martyred abolitionist, suggested Senator John P. Hale of New Hampshire. The Liberty Party, which advocated the immediate end to slavery, had nominated Hale and former Ohio Whig Leicester King several weeks before at a small convention in Buffalo. But a majority of Liberty activists favored fusion with the more gradualist Free-Soilers, so the party formally dissolved and, with it, its nominations. Even so, Hale remained a front-runner for the August candidacy.[12]

More pragmatic activists thought that Hale, a former Democrat who had been in the Senate less than two years, lacked enough clout to carry many states in the Electoral College. Adams was stunned to read that three Massachusetts newspapers endorsed former President Martin Van Buren of New York. "The confusion of the political world seems rather to increase than to diminish," Adams remarked to Palfrey in early July. "Van Buren is not my candidate." Sumner disagreed, telling Adams that he was growing "reconciled to him as our candidate, [as his] name gives our movement a national character." At length, Adams saw the wisdom in that argument and began to rationalize the choice in his diary. "He *did* oppose the annexation of Texas," Adams conceded. Perhaps he also saw something of his father's political progression in that of the New Yorker: "In his early life, [and] in middle life," Van Buren was "swayed to the wrong by his ambition." But "he seems toward the close of his career to be again falling into the right channel." Most Liberty voters thought Van Buren an "old sinner," little better than Cass or Taylor. But Salmon Chase and Henry Stanton sided with Sumner and labored to convince their allies of the logic in selecting a former president.[13]

Adopting his customary pose of indifference, Adams informed Stanton in late July that he had "no desire to be present" in Buffalo. Despite spearheading the movement, he professed to hope that Massachusetts might select other delegates "who have zeal enough to sustain the cause." But there was never any doubt that he and Sumner would attend. Remembering the occasional strolls he took with his father in and about St. Petersburg, Adams decided to take thirteen-year-old Charles Francis Jr. with him, with a promised side trip to Niagara Falls. The journey was uneventful apart from a chance encounter with a traveling slaveholder who found himself in the car with a number of "pretty violent abolitionists" and was "unlucky as to declare his opinions." Sumner and the two Adamses arrived in Buffalo around two o'clock in the afternoon of August 8 and checked into the American Hotel. Adams was immediately pressed into service as a member of a four-person Whig Committee, whose job it was to confer with their Democratic counterpart and finalize arrangements. So it fell to Sumner to escort Charles Francis Jr. to the falls. "I felt for him an admiration closely verging on affection," Charles Francis Jr. remarked in later years. "He was very kind and considerate to us children, taking a deep interest in us." Then, in a phrase that he never applied to his own father, the boy added that Sumner was "very companionable."[14]

With as many as 20,000 delegates expected, the committee turned the Second Universalist Church it had originally intended as their meeting hall into an office and ordered an enormous tarp—once used to cover evangelist Charles Grandison Finney when he spoke at Oberlin College—erected over Courtyard Square. One of the planners urged Adams to accept the role of convention chairman. He insisted that his voice lacked the power to reach such an assemblage, but the other seven, recognizing the expected protest of reticence, approved the motion with a "perfect breeze of enthusiasm." All evening, trains and boats continued to unload hundreds of delegates. "The city swarms with strangers," Frederick Douglass reported in his *North Star.* "Every hotel, every boardinghouse, steamboats, main street, the by-ways, private families are all full, crowded and jammed." Although the conference had not officially begun, Chase closed the day's events with an impromptu speech on the "great power of the Proviso principle upon the Constitution."[15]

At noon on Wednesday, August 9, delegates began to present their credentials. They represented all fifteen northern states, with a handful of brave souls from Maryland, Delaware, and Virginia. The majority were Barnburner Democrats or Conscience Whigs, but a scattering of Liberty men and abolitionists attended, including Douglass, physician and journalist Martin R. Delany, and former Kentucky slave Henry Bibb. Giddings once again led the Ohio delegation, and young Walt Whitman, the editor of the *Brooklyn Eagle*, sent back reports to his readers. New York's Preston King introduced Adams, who took his seat upon the low stage to the "most vociferous and repeated cheers from the multitude." Benjamin F. Butler, a New York Barnburner, rose to introduce three resolutions. The first, reflecting Adams's position on the Fugitive Slave Act, called upon the federal government to "relieve itself of all responsibility for the extension or continuance of slavery." The second advanced the long-standing Whig position that Washington could not "establish or regulate slavery within the States," while the third held "that the only safe means of preventing the extension of slavery" into the territories was its prohibition "by an act of Congress." The audience was called upon to approve them, and, Adams observed, "There arose such a shout, and waving of hats, handkerchiefs, and all conceivable things." Somebody then called upon Douglass to speak, but the celebrated orator begged off, insisting that "his diseased throat [was] preventing him from responding."[16]

Following what one reporter lamented was an "eloquent, but very long prayer," it was Adams's turn. Despite his previous evening's reluctance, Adams had been given the prime slot, and he did not intend to waste it. The afternoon had turned steamy, but "the Park filled to its utmost capacity," and the crowd spilled down Main Street. Adams's oration began with the traditional "apologies for [his] own unfitness" but quickly eased into a rousing combination of logic, history, and, uncharacteristically, humor. Leading members of both parties had denounced the Wilmot Proviso as an idea only, an "abstraction" under the theory that slavery could not survive in the arid Southwest. "It is an abstraction to be sure, and so was [the idea of] the Magna Carta an abstraction," Adams shouted. "And so was the Declaration of Independence an abstraction." The audience rose as one, and Adams paused while shouts of "Yes, yes. That's it. There you have 'em" filled the tent. "It is these abstractions that raise a people and carry them on to glory forever," Adams continued. As was typical of Free-Soilers, he emphasized the threats that the slave power posed to American "freedom and truth." His brief assertion that the Founders "never contemplated that we as a people should allow the creating of a system of injustice in any country which we may ever populate" was as close as he came to denouncing the crimes against black Americans. Even so, Delany enthusiastically reported on the speech at length for the *North Star*, signing off with "Yours for liberty for all mankind."[17]

The speech made Charles Francis's career. "Mr. Adams took his seat amidst the most enthusiastic and long continued applause," one journalist observed. That night, he even allowed himself a rare bit of self-congratulation in his diary. "My address met with great favor," Adams wrote, "was applauded at various points and at the close, I felt greatly relieved when I got through with it." The speech was covered in both abolitionist and Whig newspapers, and even in a handful of disapproving southern journals. Before August 9, Charles Francis had been a crusader on the state level, primarily famous for his illustrious surname. By the next morning, he was the intellectual leader of the free-soil movement.[18]

That did not mean that the conclave intended to slow its political momentum by nominating a forty-year-old former state senator. After his speech, balloting began for the presidential nomination, with the Committee on Conferences—consisting of nine delegates from every represented state—rather than the entire gathering, casting what was announced to be an "informal" tally. Supreme Court Justice John McLean, who had received some support at the recent Whig convention, was much discussed, but he had written days before to withdraw his name from consideration. "It soon became apparent that the struggle had narrowed down" to sixty-five-year-old Van Buren and Hale, Adams observed. Because he had already heard "rumors" that his own name might be advanced for the vice presidency, Charles Francis "determined to throw away" his vote for another candidate, not wishing "any thing like an appearance of a bargain." The balloting gave Van Buren 244 votes to Hale's 181. Forty-one other delegates scattered their votes, with thirteen men from the Midwest voting for Adams. Although that gave Van Buren only a twenty-two-vote majority over all others, Joshua Leavitt of Massachusetts moved that the vote be considered unanimous. Somebody raised the question of whether Van Buren would accept, but Butler replied by reading a letter from the New Yorker, which "satisfied all scruples on this point."[19]

That evening, a delegate from Ohio approached Adams to say that his state intended to nominate him for the vice presidency. Given the rumors earlier that day, the honor came as no surprise. Briefly dropping his habitual posture of reluctance, Adams thanked him for his "friendly support." But Adams was aware that Hale, like Van Buren, was a former Democrat; for balance, the second spot on the ticket had to go to a former Whig. As it was unusual in that era for candidates to appear at conventions, even to accept their nomination, Adams fled the church where the second day's business was being conducted. "But shout upon shout" could be heard from across the square, Adams noted, alerting him to his nomination by "unanimous voice and enthusiastic acclamation." "Marvelous are thy ways, O Lord!" the normally dour Adams rejoiced. In the privacy of his diary, he assured himself that he cared "little for the worldly honor." Having his peers deem him "worthy to stand before the people for the second office in their gift" was reward enough. It had been only six months since the death of John Quincy, but now, he mused, the position "places me somewhat near the level of my father." As friends crowded around in congratulations, Adams "escaped to the Hotel to marvel at the change that had suddenly come over me."[20]

The two-page Free Soil Party platform of fifteen points was designed to appeal to northern men of both major parties. As Whig statements had for years, the platform called for federally funded internal improvements and a tariff high enough to defray those expenses. For Democrats, the document promised free homesteads in the West. Mostly, of course, it addressed slavery. As had the convention's resolutions, the platform supported long-standing demands by both Chase and Adams that the government divorce itself from slavery where it had the constitutional power to do so: in Washington, on military installations, and in the territories. "Congress has no more power to make a slave than to make a king," it declared. Yet while upholding "the rights of Free Labor against the aggressions of the Slave Power," the platform abandoned earlier Liberty Party pronouncements on the political rights of free blacks. Four years earlier, the Liberty platform had called upon white voters to reject "any inequality of rights and privileges" based on race. However, the abolitionist Liberty Party had campaigned to promote a cause. The antislavery Free-Soilers, by comparison, campaigned to win, if perhaps only in 1852 after first establishing itself as the new second party. As such, the party's slogan—"Free Soil, Free Speech, Free Labor, and Free Men"—spoke more to the desires of white settlers than it did to the plight of enslaved Americans.[21]

That Friday, August 11, Adams prepared to board the steamer *Emerald* for Niagara Falls to rejoin Sumner and his son. The two had enjoyed touring the area, and as Sumner preferred to speak only after memorizing a carefully prepared script, he was content to stay away from Buffalo, lest he be asked to address the gathering. As he departed, Adams found himself "in the midst of a crowd of persons warmly congratulating" him, and the entire Pennsylvania delegation wished to shake his hand. So long delayed was he that he missed the morning steamer, and when he finally arrived at the Clifton House, he discovered that the pair had already passed over to the American side of the falls. The last ferry had sailed, so Adams dined with four Manhattan Barnburners before retiring to reflect on the events in his journal. "This was the closing act of the most memorable two days of my life," he thought. Adams was sure that the convention was the beginning of the end for slavery, as he could not "imagine that any event of the age will lead to consequences more important."[22]

Even in a day when candidates neither campaigned nor met the running mate selected for them by their party's convention, the pairing of Charles Francis Sr. with the architect of the Democratic Party and his father's longtime political adversary raised eyebrows across New England. Activists loyal to the Whigs had little trouble digging up Charles Francis's old published criticisms of Martin Van Buren. *Courtesy Library of Congress.*

Tradition required that candidates deliver formal statements accepting the nomination, usually from their front steps after a group deputized by the convention formally notified them of their good fortune. Adams was at the old estate in Quincy, tending to his father's affairs, when the time came to reply. His widely reprinted letter of August 22 was far more somber in tone than was his Buffalo address and advanced a cautionary note that would come to be a staple in free-soil speeches of the next decade. The nation had reached a turning point, Adams warned, and had "either to turn back" to its founding ideals or voluntarily "abandon the principles with which their fathers started." Slavery and freedom were so incompatible that either unfree labor would eventually extend "over the whole breadth of the North American continent" or Americans would embrace "the maintenance of the fundamental doctrines of the Declaration of Independence." Adams prayed that the latter might prevail, but he urged northern voters to achieve that victory without "any feelings of acrimony or ill will toward" southern planters. "The slaveholding section of the Union merits our sympathy," Adams ventured in the sort of conciliatory remark not shared by former slaves Douglass and Bibb. The *North Star*, however, eagerly endorsed Adams's concluding promise to confront the slave power's "aggressive policy with the firmest resistance."[23]

If pragmatic Free-Soilers believed that a former president atop their ticket could help with the Electoral College, the choice of Van Buren immediately proved to be problematic. New England Whigs who might have been tempted to vote for yet another Adams denounced Van Buren's nomination as a "farce." One editor judged his "subservency to the South too notorious and of too recent a date to be forgotten, or overlooked." Another remarked that while Van Buren had opposed the annexation of Texas, he eventually endorsed the pro-expansion ticket of Polk and George Dallas "while their flag was flying for Texas." A third editorial characterized Van Buren as the former leader of a "profligate and wicked" party before hitting a personal note regarding Adams: "'Old Man Eloquent' is scarcely hushed in the grave, before his 'son and heir' actually links his fortune to that of his father's most bitter enemy!"[24]

Charles Francis was hardly alone in facing charges of inconsistency. One editor observed that the same Joshua Leavitt who had published an essay on the *Amistad* case alleging that Van Buren desired to "deliver up the negroes" had attended the Buffalo conference and was now a "chief priest in the Van Buren Sanhedrin." It was all too easy for hostile journalists to dredge up quotations from John Quincy: his lengthy argument before the Supreme Court was public record. Van Buren's "order" to arrest the Africans "was on its face sweeping, unconstitutional," the elder Adams had insisted. But far more embarrassing were Charles Francis's own words, now seized upon by almost every loyal Whig newspaper. "Van Buren must be judged by his preceding course, taken as a whole," Charles

Francis had editorialized four years earlier. "From that let no man delude himself with the belief that he is fixed to any thing but his own interest." Could Adams identify a "solitary item of principle" that Van Buren had changed in the intervening period to justify this union of "strange bedfellows?" a home-state editor wondered.[25]

Then there was the invasion of Mexico, a decision universally condemned by the free-soil movement and an act that had led to the current crisis regarding western territories. Pro-Taylor journalists quoted Van Buren as praying that the war effort "be triumphantly sustained," while in the following paragraph they cited Charles Francis's essay that criticized the conflict as "unconstitutional in its origin, unjust in character, and detestable in its objects." The Whig Party was itself inconstant on the question, however, because it had formally censured Polk's movement of troops into the disputed zone above the Rio Grande River claimed by both Mexico and the United States before nominating one of the war's heroes. Even so, it was hard to disguise the enmity that the Adams family had long held for Van Buren. Having already banished Charles Francis from the Whig Party, the influential *Boston Atlas* praised the late John Quincy as "the last Adams" and belittled Charles Francis as an ungrateful son "who lives upon the reputation as well as the wealth of his ancestors, intense *egoism* being the characteristic of his appearance, and selfishness that of his action." To engage in such a "strange and most unnatural alliance," a Vermont newspaper suggested, "dishonored the memory of his father." Even a Whig journal in Ohio, a region that had advanced Charles Francis's name in Buffalo, wondered "on what question of public policy have they ever agreed," laughing: "What a beautiful pair!"[26]

For weeks, Adams declined to respond publicly to these charges. Instead, he poured his anguish over this "coarsest and grossest abuse" into his diary. "It has been the fate of three generations of our race to stand as the guardians of Liberty," he groused, and "so long as I live there shall be another Adams who will denounce every bargain that shall trade away the honor of this country." But when a Democratic New Hampshire paper ventured the absurd theory that were he still alive, John Quincy "would support Gen. Cass in preference for either Taylor or Van Buren," Charles

Francis was forced to reply. In a lengthy explanation published in friendly newspapers, including Douglass's *North Star*, Adams conceded that as a former Whig, there were a good many economic issues on which he and the former Democratic president disagreed. But while the Free Soil platform contained provisions designed to appeal to voters from both parties, its sole reason for existing was to stand against the spread of slavery into the Southwest. As early as 1844, Adams insisted, it became clear "that there was a point beyond which [Van Buren] would not go, and that point had been reached" with the annexation of Texas. The only issue that truly mattered in 1848 was the fate of the Mexican Cession. Van Buren, Adams concluded in a devastating indictment of his old party, had "done more to concentrate and rally the friends of Liberty of all parties in the Free States" than had any politicians loyal to the Whigs, who "by way of proving their zeal against the extension of slavery, advocate the claims to the Presidency of the only slaveholder in the field."[27]

Rationalize his course of action though he might, a part of Adams knew the Whig charges had merit; they would not have stung so much otherwise. He could claim that the nomination placed him on par with his father's accomplishments, but as the Whig press insisted, it was also a betrayal of his father. Each Adams generation wished to best the previous one, as well as other males of their own age, and his decision to serve on the same ticket with his father's longtime antagonist was meant not only to match his father's enormous accomplishments but, in a curious fashion, to vanquish his father's towering ghost.

At a time when Americans thought it unseemly for candidates to campaign on their own behalf or give more than a single speech in their hometown, regional ratifying conventions were one method of spreading the candidates' message and selecting presidential electors. However, what each meeting emphasized tended to vary by region. An October convention in Springfield, Massachusetts, never once mentioned Van Buren while claiming that nobody was "as sound on the constitutional question of slavery as Charles Francis Adams." A meeting in Milford, New Hampshire, approved a brief resolution endorsing Van Buren and Adams as "the only candidates who are unequivocally pledged to Free

Soil Principles," but only after a lengthy tribute to Hale, "the Wilberforce of America." Yet when activists met in the Utica, New York, courthouse, they proclaimed themselves the "Democratic Free Soil Convention" and praised Van Buren's "consummate abilities as a statesman, as well as the integrity and purity of his character." A September rally at Philadelphia's Chinese Museum was more balanced, thanks to Pennsylvania's status as a swing state. Resolutions passed by the large gathering lauded Van Buren as a "self-denying champion of the principles of Free Soil" and applauded Adams as a "scholar and a philanthropist, the whole tenor of whose past life is a guarantee of his energy and fidelity in the cause of Truth and Freedom."[28]

Free Soil meetings in Boston opted simply to call themselves the "State Liberty Convention." One group met in the Melodeon before marching through the streets to the Tremont Temple, where it named electors and nominated candidates for state office who "support the Buffalo platform." Much to the chagrin of loyal Whigs, a late August Free Soil meeting at Faneuil Hall was so well attended that hundreds were turned away for want of room. Skirting the tradition against campaigning, Adams spoke at the Faneuil meeting, and his address revealed the depth of his pain over the personal attacks by what he characterized as "Taylor newspapers." The Buffalo convention was "the dearest day of my life," he confessed. But those who were not there "get nothing like the spirit of that meeting" from the Whig press, especially the Boston *Atlas*. Bostonians who wished to "get the truth of this movement," Adams shouted, should "not go to the lying Atlas," a remark that drew "great cheers and laughter." The free-soil crusade, he concluded in an eloquent if somewhat disingenuous flourish, was "not a contest with a geographically defined section of the country." Rather, it was a "struggle to sustain principles of inestimable value in every land, of general application wherever society is established."[29]

The slurs hurled against Adams suggested just how much the emerging Free Soil Party worried the Whigs, who fretted that their nomination of a Louisiana planter would hurt them far more than Van Buren's prestige might damage Cass and the Democrats. "Those who are conscientiously opposed to slavery never can vote for a man who holds in bondage 280 negroes," lectured one Ohio editor. In Michigan a young men's "Taylor Club" formally dissolved after concluding that both major parties were willing to allow slavery into the lands acquired from Mexico, pledging to support the Free Soil ticket. After debating whether Taylor would sign or veto a bill containing the Wilmot Proviso, several delegates at a Pittsfield, Massachusetts, "Whig meeting" announced their decision "to leave the Taylor ranks." The *Providence Transcript* withdrew its endorsement of Taylor and announced for Free Soil. And in Adams, Massachusetts, a hamlet in the far western part of the state, more than one hundred Whigs quit the party and endorsed Charles Francis's party. "The truth is that the Whig party is rotten," Adams wrote Joshua Giddings. Its elder statesmen cared only for issues of an earlier day, such as a "high tariff and Bank discounts." The only option was to "take the bold, open, straightforward course [and] stick to the principle" of liberty that mattered to younger voters.[30]

When not heaping abuse on Adams, conservative Whigs pretended they were pleased that he was no longer in good standing with the party. In an editorial that surely persuaded no reader, one editor pronounced it a "real blessing" that "calculating, self-seeking men like Sumner, Adams, [and] Palfrey" had been banished from their ranks. Former senator Rufus Choate kept up the refrain that John Quincy was "the last Adams" and defended his party's lack of a formal platform with the argument that Whig principles "were the same now as they have always been, the same principles on which we elected the elder Adams" to Congress. Wiser voices played on the likelihood that the new party could not secure the 146 electoral votes necessary to win. Whig editors made much of Ohio elector Joseph Roop's defection to Taylor after the antislavery activist concluded that Van Buren and Adams could not carry his state. "To vote for them," Roop reasoned, was "equivalent to not voting at all." Other New England editors argued that the likeliest outcome was that none of the candidates could secure an electoral majority, so throwing the decision to the House, where "Lewis Cass, the slavery candidate," might emerge as the winner. "A party which commands so much money and which has so much financial interest at stake in an Election is not going to abandon everything without a struggle," Adams observed of the Whigs. But so sure was he that his former party was a spent force, Adams refused to lose "confidence in the result," believing that the Whig Party was "destined to a heavy defeat from which it will not recover."[31]

The Democrats, who were equally unprepared for a serious third-party challenge, also faced defections, especially in Van Buren's Empire State. "In my judgment the decision will turn upon New York" and its thirty-six electoral votes—the most of any state—Adams speculated. But even to the west in Illinois, the *Alton Monitor* dropped its support for Cass "and hoisted the Free Soil banner," while to the south in Maryland, former governor Francis Thomas, a Democrat but a staunch antislavery man, published an editorial explaining his support for Van Buren and Adams. In 1844 Polk had lost Maryland but carried New York and Illinois, and Democrats understood that their path to victory narrowed with each potential defection.[32]

Hoping their constituents' historical dislike of any Adams was stronger than their fondness for Van Buren, most Democratic newspapers focused their fire on Charles Francis. "Any man who can vote for *Charles F. Adams* should never pretend to be a Democrat," one editor scoffed. "A more bitter federalist or a more arrogant and haughty aristocrat cannot be found even in Boston." Another alleged that Adams did not expect to win as much as he plotted "to annihilate the Democratic party by carrying it over to federalism through that portion of the party 'now and always' hostile to the Union, the abolitionists." Born in 1807, the same year that his father broke with the Federalists, Charles Francis had no connection to the party of his grandfather, but he was an Adams, and that was enough for the Washington *Daily Union* to remind its readers that he had "been educated in the school of Massachusetts whiggery" and hailed from a state that was arrayed "against the War of 1812." The New York *Evening Post* urged credulous readers who wished to support Van Buren to "throw overboard the federal-abolition wing of the combination, Charles F. Adams, and rally at once upon Van Buren *and* [Cass's running mate] *Butler*," a physical impossibility in a day when voters obtained card-like "tickets" from party functionaries that bore the names of all of the candidates affiliated with that party.[33]

FREE SOIL
ELECTORAL TICKET.

For President of the United States,
MARTIN VAN BUREN,
OF NEW YORK.
For Vice-President of the United States,
CHARLES FRANCIS ADAMS,
OF MASSACHUSETTS.

Electors for the State at Large.

DAVID GAMBLE, of Frederick County,
JOHN REYNOLDS, of Cecil County,

For the Congressional Districts,

DARIUS THOMAS,
ELISHA B. CUNNINGHAM,
EDMUND H. LEWIS,
JOHN HAMPDEN WILLIAMS,
ELLIS P. HOWARD,
SAMUEL S. STEVENS.

Voters in 1848 did not yet use paper ballots or vote behind curtains. They had to obtain a ticket, which included all state party candidates and electors, from a party functionary and then publicly deposit the ticket into a bowl or box marked by party affiliation. Only 129 Maryland voters, or 0.18 percent of the state's voters, obtained a Free Soil ticket. *Courtesy National Park Service.*

On November 7, American voters flocked to the polls on the same day for the first time. The Free Soil ticket failed to carry a single state, but as many Democrats had feared, it cost Cass the election. Van Buren captured 10.1 percent of the national vote and 26.4 percent of New York's, outpolling Cass by more than six thousand in his home state and handing the reliably Democratic state to Taylor. In Vermont and Massachusetts, thanks to the Adams name, the party won 29.6 and 28.3 percent of the vote, respectively. A small band of dedicated Liberty men had prevailed upon New York's Gerrit Smith to run in place of Hale, insisting that he "was the candidate of the *Abolitionists*, while Adams represented the *Anti-slavery* party." However accurate that sentiment, the majority of Liberty voters stood with Free Soil, and Smith won only 2,733 ballots, or 0.056 percent of the national vote. Adams also took heart in the news that a deal between Democrats and Free-Soilers in Ohio had elevated Chase into the Senate. The Massachusetts returns were a most "gratifying result," Adams mused. "At least it shows that my nomination has received the sanction of a full third of the intelligent voters of this commonwealth." Left unsaid was his certainty that those who voted otherwise were bigoted or ignorant, a view that ignored the fact that many antislavery Whigs—Congressman Abraham Lincoln of Illinois, newly elected Senator William Henry Seward of New York, and Adams's own brother-in-law, Edward Everett—had reluctantly endorsed Taylor.[34]

Two nights later, Adams delivered a concession speech at Faneuil Hall. "The Hall was crowded in the galleries and full though not crowded on the floor," Adams wrote upon returning home. "I was received with prodigious cheering and made my speech apparently to the acceptance of the audience." The campaign left Adams with a national reputation. No longer merely the son and grandson of illustrious ancestors, Charles Francis, who had turned forty-one just days after the Buffalo convention, was now recognized as one of the nation's leading antislavery voices. Even so, electoral defeat was never kind. One Massachusetts wag chuckled that now that he had ample free time, Adams "has recently been lecturing on 'Paradise Lost!'"[35]

The election behind him, Charles Francis temporarily retreated into private and family affairs. For several years, he had planned to edit and publish his grandfather's papers, a task that he believed fell to him as the only surviving grandson, but also one that would keep the Adams name before the public. During the campaign, Adams had reduced both his hours and his financial contribution to the *Boston Daily Whig*—renamed the *Boston Republican*—and tried to hand the editorship to Sumner, who declined the responsibility. But despite all claims to the contrary, Adams paid close attention to events in Washington and the yet-unsolved fate of the Mexican Cession. Although Taylor, who had begun to diversify his financial holdings and invest heavily in bank stock, hardly proved to be the militant expansionist that Free-Soilers had feared, Adams continued to regard him as "so much of a cipher" and thought his cabinet rightly deserving of "so little respect." Nor did he place much hope in either party's elder statesmen. In his view, Cass and Clay, both back in the Senate, hoped "to play the part of peacemaker by a grand compromise." But

Adams scoffed that they "scarcely know at which end to begin," while Webster, "according to his practice, keeps out of the way whilst things are in doubt."[36]

With angry planters demanding the right to carry their human property into the territories and again "rattling the sabre"—as their dubious northern critics had long dubbed their threats of disunion—in late January of 1850 seventy-two-year-old Clay prepared a comprehensive, five-part compromise package designed to stitch the nation back together. California, whose population had boomed since the discovery of gold, was to enter the Union as a free state, while the remainder of the Mexican Cession would be decided according to Cass's popular sovereignty. The disputed border between Texas and the vast New Mexico territory was to be redrawn, and in exchange for Texas's reduction in size, the federal government would assume the old 1836 Texas war debt. To appease Upper South slaveholders, Clay, on the urging of Virginia senator (and Charles Francis's future diplomatic antagonist) James Murry Mason, sought to replace the weak, state-centered Fugitive Slave Act of 1793 with a far more draconian law. Finally, a fifth section of the so-called Omnibus bill would ban the interstate slave trade, but not human bondage itself, in Washington. Adams was disgusted. In caving to the "tyrannical disposition of our slaveholding brethren," he wrote Liberty Party leader John Hale, Clay had "thrown off all his disguises and thus completely justified the distrust of him entertained by the Liberty men in 1844." In early February, Adams met with Congressman John Gorham Palfrey, Sumner, author Richard Henry Dana, and other Free Soil "members of the Legislature and the County Committee" to plan strategy. After "much good speaking," the group opted to host a regional convention to defeat Clay's bill.[37]

In his convention speech later that month, Adams anticipated a fear that was to become a staple among antislavery politicians in the next decade: if the North gave way on the Wilmot Proviso now and allowed slavery into the territories, what was to stop southern expansions from then demanding a "new measure of Cuban annexation, another Mexican War," or even a "crusade on the West Indies, now free, and so on to the 'crack of doom?'" Charles Francis counted himself among those who doubted that planters were serious in their threats of disunion, assuring his son John Quincy that he judged the crisis not "so desperate as the Taylor men do." Northern cowards, he now charged, reconciled "themselves to the abomination of Mr. Clay's bill" by pretending that planters were innocent victims of a labor system that had been "entailed upon them" by their fathers. As always, the *Boston Atlas* aimed for the personal rather than defend the merits of Clay's compromise package. "The son of the last Adams took the stand and threw off his usual quantity of bile," it reported. "This is a philanthropic gentleman who rolls in wealth, but who has never been known to do an act of liberality." This time, Adams took little notice of the criticism, remarking to Palfrey that the "politicians of the old school" utterly failed to recognize the "moral effect of the Free Soil movement" and engaged in nothing "but intrigue for personal ends."[38]

Curiously, Webster initially agreed with Adams that Clay's fears were overblown. "All this agitation will, I think, subside, without serious result," he assured one correspondent in mid-January. But Webster was as concerned about organized antislavery as he was by southern rhetoric, fearing both were a danger to the nation, a strained equivalency that Adams regarded as immoral. But prodded into action by the dying Senator John C. Calhoun's March 4 speech, which claimed a constitutional right for southerners to carry their slaves into all western territories, including the Pacific Northwest, Webster replied in the Senate to Calhoun three days later. Insisting that "the law of nature, of physical geography" would limit slavery to its current boundaries, Webster deprecated the Wilmot Proviso as a "taunt or a reproach" against the South, and he criticized abolitionists as dogmatists who had precipitated the looming crisis by characterizing slavery as immoral and unchristian.[39]

No Adams had ever expressed any confidence in Webster. In response to the senator, Charles Francis remarked, "My soul entertains such a loathing, that the idea of Judas Iscariot, who at least hung himself by way of conscience, is a relief to it." Charles Francis was particularly disgusted by Webster's view that patriotism required Americans to remain silent on antislavery. "I deny that Slavery and the Union are one and the same thing," he lectured a correspondent. "I deny that the

Constitution was made to protect, to defend and to disseminate one of the most gigantic evils that ever distressed humanity." Living under his father's roof and spending so many dinners with weekly visitor Sumner, twelve-year-old Henry absorbed their disdain for Webster and all career politicians who "depended on others for machine work and money." The "Free Soil conclave in Mount Vernon Street," as the boy labeled their household, "had nothing to do with [party] machinery," which he thought a "noble position." A disgruntled correspondent leaked to the press one of Charles Francis's private letters, in which he complained that Webster's "loose private and wavering public career" had done more to "shake the principles" of his region "than that of any man known to history." But Adams refused to retract or apologize for stating what he assumed all antislavery activists knew to be true.[40]

Furious with what he regarded as President Taylor's willingness to grant California admission as a free state, Georgia governor George Towns issued a call for a bipartisan, all-southern convention to meet in Nashville in early June. Legislatures from nine southern states agreed, selecting 176 delegates; in preparation, South Carolina's governor proposed that his state appropriate $50,000 for arms and ammunition. Southern nationalists were deprived of their best mind, however, when Senator Calhoun died of tuberculosis on March 31. The delegates ultimately voted to extend the Missouri Compromise line to the Pacific, securing the broad New Mexico Territory and south California for slaveholders. Charles Francis wasted no tears over the demise of his father's old enemy. "The death of Mr. Calhoun goes far to break the power of the Slaveholding interests in its scheme of disunion," he believed. Although he was grudgingly willing to admit that Calhoun "was a man of talent considerably beyond the common level," Adams regarded the militant defender of slavery as the chief "supporter of old and intolerable abuses." As for the Nashville Convention's demands, Adams was willing to test southern resolve. "The secession of seven states from the Union," he counseled Palfrey, "could scarcely be a fatal [blow] to the twenty three or four others." Adams was confident that a breakaway confederacy could not long survive and that the Lower South would at length "return to the Union with a broken spirit and diminished influence." Charles Francis, of course, could hardly know that many of his coming years would be devoted to seeing what he dubbed the "experiment of secession" ending in failure.[41]

The unexpected death of President Taylor from acute gastroenteritis on July 9, 1850, dramatically upended the political landscape. Vice President Millard Fillmore of New York promptly asked Taylor's entire cabinet to resign, including Secretary of State John Clayton, who as senator had been the only southerner to vote in favor of the Wilmot Proviso. Much to Adams's dismay, Fillmore tapped Webster as Clayton's replacement, a sign that he favored Clay's compromise; worse yet, from the Free Soil perspective, the Massachusetts assembly then selected Robert Winthrop, a Whig loyalist whom Charles Francis had spent much of the early decade publicly criticizing, to fill Webster's seat in the Senate. Having deplored the late president as a "cipher" only months before, Adams now praised Taylor as a leader who "had made up his mind to carry through a policy looking to the maintenance of freedom in the territories." With a new White House hoping for sectional armistice, Senator Stephen Douglas, an Illinois Democrat, proceeded to chop apart Clay's failed omnibus bill—which had served only to unite its various opponents—into five separate bills. "The course of political affairs ever since the death of General Taylor has run in a channel uniformly bad," Adams concluded.[42]

Douglas was able to forge a majority vote for each bill by obtaining fragile bisectional majorities for regionally favored portions of the compromise, together with a handful of border-state moderates who desired national peace. Adams was not much mollified by the fact that of the 261 procedural and final votes to approve popular sovereignty in the Utah and New Mexico Territories and to pass the Fugitive Slave bill, only 37 of those votes were cast by northern Whigs. "Thus the triumph of boasting and braggard threats is complete," he fumed. "It seems as if no effort could rouse the sluggishness of the people of the Free States."[43]

Having devoted numerous hours to limiting his state's involvement with the 1793 Fugitive Slave Act, Adams was particularly incensed by the invasive new fugitive slave law. On October 15, at the invitation of black activists William C. Nell and Lewis Hayden, Adams presided over a meeting in Faneuil Hall called "to repudiate the Fugitive Bill." With the threat to black residents now replacing the territories as the most pressing issue facing northern reformers, the gathering witnessed an increasing fusion of remaining Liberty Party and Free Soil activists. Richard Henry Dana spoke briefly, as did abolitionists Charles Remond and Wendell Phillips, a member of Boston's Vigilance Committee, an organization founded to assist runaway slaves. Standing once again between the bust of his grandfather and the portrait of his father, Adams delivered an un-usually angry oration, an indication of just how much the events of the summer had shaken his faith in the republic. Webster was "the Benedict Arnold of the age," he charged, echoing Phillips's earlier remarks that Webster was a "traitor to the constitution and an apostate to humanity." As for the new fugitive slave law, Adams shouted, "No imperial edict of Rome's worst days, was ever marked with a more burning stamp of human passion than this bill." Webster had promised that Clay's com-promise had forever "settled the slavery question," Adams mocked, but only as the British forces "on Bunker Hill settled the payment of a tax on tea." Before closing, the meeting resolved to submit an appeal to Congress entreating repeal of the law, and approved a resolution submitted by Rev-erend Nathaniel Colver that they would "not allow a fugitive to be taken from Massachusetts."[44]

Just as Adams was concluding, the cry of "Douglass, Douglass" went up, and Charles Francis for the first time found himself sharing the stage with the abolitionist who had so fondly eulogized his father. Taking the podium, Frederick Douglass warned the audience that he spoke for those Americans who had liberated themselves—as he once had—but now feared "that the man-hunters of the South would be here in Boston." Al-though Douglass was to be proven prescient, his brief speech infuriated conservatives. The *Washington Union* reported that the meeting "consisted of four thousand negroes, over whom Charles Francis Adams presided!" Farther south, the coverage was even more hostile. "Fred Douglass and Charles Francis Adams [entered] arm and arm," Tennessee's *Athens Post* mocked, marching before "The Benedict Arnold Society, The Aaron Burr Association."[45]

No journalist reported how Charles Francis voted on Reverend Colver's motion. It appealed to a "higher law" that superseded human enactments and demanded that, "constitution or no constitution, law or no law," Bostonians assist fugitives. Over the years, Adams took enormous pride in crafting his state's first personal-liberty law, but he also took satisfaction in the fact that his Latimer law's "constitutionality has never been questioned so as to weaken its force." He thought there to be "assailable points" in the new federal law, but thanks to the Supreme Court's 1842 *Prigg* decision, which upheld the Fugitive Slave Act of 1793, Adams did not believe that the right of southern masters to reclaim their slaves worthy of legal challenge. However, Adams did contribute $100 to a legal fund organized by black abolitionist Francis Jackson. And if Adams remained a man of the law, his diary revealed a respect for those black abolitionists who professed more-radical views. He invariably described the African Americans he shared the stage with as "colored persons" while neglecting to mention the race of his white allies. Yet even as one abolitionist writer paid Douglass the curious tribute of dubbing him the "Fugitive Othello" (evidently forgetting that Shakespeare's protagonist murdered his white wife), Charles Francis simply referred to him as "Mr. Frederick Douglass" in the privacy of his journal. No racist epithet ever tainted his diary or correspondence. Unhappily, Charles Francis's sons were not to inherit that trait.[46]

Adams cared little about the enmity of slaveholders or even of Whig loyalists. But the glares he began to receive from his neighbors pained him. That November, when Adams again spoke at a Boston meeting, he found the audience "cold, disappointed, and restive." When he criticized Webster, this time with greater prudence, some "fifty or sixty friends" of the secretary began to hiss. Adams persevered and finished his oration, but "it was a disagreeable process," he sighed, and he returned home "full of painful and discontented thoughts." As much as his state might crave sectional harmony, public opinion against the Fugitive Slave Act remained strong, and Adams believed that the "domination of Daniel Webster has been demolished." Even so, Adams noticed that at parties, "for the first time people avoided recognizing" him, ostracisms he stoically bore "with great resignation." A chance encounter with outgoing Senator Winthrop proved "most embarrassing" to both, he reported. "I care not to revive old grudges," Adams scribbled into his diary, just before noting precisely how long it had been since Winthrop and his allies had "reveled in a most merciless triumph" over the Conscience Whigs.[47]

In mid-February 1851, Robert Rantoul, an antislavery lawyer who had taken Winthrop's seat in the Senate only weeks before, introduced into that legislative body the resolutions crafted at the end of the Faneuil meeting. Supported by a petition of several thousand signatures—Adams's name appeared at the top—the resolutions charged that the Fugitive Slave Act "caused great anxiety amongst our fellow-citizens of color" and violated the "moral sense" of the state's Christians. Drafted by Adams, the three-paragraph statement denounced the law "as contradictory to the Declaration of Independence [and] inconsistent with the purposes of the Constitution." That carefully crafted clause did not flatly state that the entire law was unconstitutional, but as it denied an accused runaway a jury trial, Adams thought himself justified in charging that it deprived "men of their liberty without due process." Led by Illinois Democrat Jesse Bright, who announced that he planned to introduce legislation "to increase the efficiency" of the 1850 law, the Senate voted to table the resolutions "without any consideration." Undaunted, Adams would submit similar resolutions and petitions the next spring.[48]

At the same time, Adams helped to organize a "general convention in opposition" to the Fugitive Slave Act, which was held in Boston's Tremont Temple in April. Palfrey spoke first. Having left Congress the previous year and taken over the editorship of the *Boston Republican*—rechristened yet again as the *Commonwealth*—Palfrey was now at liberty to promise that he intended to violate the law. "He would shelter the fugitive and bide the result," he promised. At his turn, Adams again counseled "firm, persevering and resolute opposition in legitimate modes" to the law. Although he could not countenance "violence," he promised "agitation and opposition as long as that statute shall remain a dishonor to American legislation." While far from the most radical voice at the April meeting, the Adams name, together with his training as an attorney, placed

Charles Francis in the forefront of Boston resistance. "There is not a week passes that does not bring me propositions either to redeem [purchase] slaves, or to assist fugitives here or elsewhere, or to promote anti-slavery enterprises, or to aid the establishment of a free colored man," Adams complained. "I do what I think reasonable, but the demand so far exceeds all ability to meet it."[49]

The resolutions submitted to Congress in February did not overstate the fears of black Bostonians, who had since begun to flee to Canada. To an extent, the Fugitive Slave Act was in response to protections like the Latimer law; if state officials were denied the authority to arrest fugitives, white southerners who normally professed to believe in small government demanded federal officials to fill the void. When Jerry Henry was arrested in Syracuse, New York, in October 1851 after escaping from Missouri eight years before, Liberty Party activists at a nearby convention broke him out of jail and smuggled him into Canada. Even Adams, despite his devotion to the rule of law and abhorrence for mobs, believed their actions to be just. "It is a bad sign for a country when a number of virtuous and respectable citizens feel justified in rejoicing that a law has been success-fully resisted," he confided to Syracuse minister Samuel May. Three years later, when Boston authorities seized Virginia runaway Anthony Burns, President Franklin Pierce would effectively declare martial law and order a company of US Marines to protect his deportation south. "Massachusetts has bent to the dust before the idol who its own servants have clothed with the power to humiliate her," an increasingly radicalized Adams groused.[50]

ALMOST EVERY SUNDAY, AFTER THEY DEVOTED MOST OF THE DAY TO divine services, the Adamses returned home to dine with Charles Sumner. At six feet, four inches, the handsome bachelor towered over Charles Francis, and the four Adams boys idolized him. Henry, thirteen years old in 1851, absolutely "worshipped" Sumner. "The relation of Mr. Sumner in the household was far closer than any relation of blood," Henry remembered. Uncles Everett and Frothingham never "approached such intimacy." Although long active in antislavery politics, Sumner had never held elective office, and he regarded Charles Francis, four years his elder and a former legislator, as the senior partner in their relationship. All of this began to change in early 1851 when a coalition of antislavery Democrats and Free-Soilers wrestled control of the state assembly from the Whigs. Senator Rantoul was a reliably antislavery voice in Washington, but he was in ill health (and would soon die at the age of forty-seven). Advisors to newly elected Governor George Boutwell, an antislavery Democrat, began to advance Adams's name, either as senator or chief counselor to the governor. Adams regarded the Senate position as his due, thanks to his name, his service in the General Court, and his nomination by a third party. But perhaps remembering his uneasy 1848 alliance with Van Buren, he distrusted any cooperation with the Democrats and regarded the idea of serving under Boutwell and his "confounded coalition" as utterly "monstrous."[51]

Privately, Charles Francis dreamed of the Senate, telling his diary of his anxiety "to stand upon something like a level with my family." But the honor must come to him; he would not lift a finger to achieve it. "Should the Anti Slavery Whigs choose to support me in conjunction with our [Free Soil] friends," Adams admitted, "I would consent to stand for the purpose of breaking this unholy combination" of Democrats and Free-Soilers. But since any man who still called himself a Whig regarded Adams as a turncoat, "there is little or no real probability" of that. When Sumner asked if Adams might allow to have his "name connected with the place of Senator," Charles Francis demurred, believing his chances slim. Instead, Adams replied that Sumner would "make an efficient and true Senator in the cause." After Sumner persisted in urging Adams to run, Charles Francis contacted George White, a state Free Soil leader. Dutifully he announced, and perhaps even half-believed, that he "could not think of serving in the Senate this year, if elected," and so declined having his "name used as a candidate."[52]

"Sumner does not see the thing as I do," Adams complained about his friend's willingness to accept the support of Democrats, a peculiar position for a man who had recently joined a ticket headed by Van Buren. Over yet another Sunday dinner, Sumner insisted that "the possession of a Senator's place" by an antislavery man was more important than which "traitors or opponents" placed him there. Sumner also protested that he could not bring himself "to desire the post, or even be willing to take it," although in his case, he was honestly willing to step aside in favor of his older colleague. But with Adams continuing to refuse it, Sumner was content to lobby for it. By mid-January 1851, newspapers in Boston and Washington reported that "the first fruits of the coalition between free-soilers and the democracy" would be the election of Charles Sumner rather than the "expected elevation" of Charles Francis. Adams published a letter in the *Boston Atlas* recommending Sumner, after which he complained to Palfrey that Sumner "wanted the place" and maneuvered the legislature in his own behalf. Adams's criticism somehow got back to Sumner, who promptly wrote to say that he "cannot contemplate without emotion that there should be any political separation between us."[53]

The spat healed enough that within weeks Sumner and Adams resumed their weekly dinners. Adams was correct, at least, in thinking the coalition a troubled one, as the state's Democrats preferred anyone besides Sumner for the position, believing him, as the *Boston Post* editorialized, too willing to denounce "the democratic party as the tool of the South." Sumner was with the Adamses on April 24 when the General Court, on the twenty-sixth ballot, gave Sumner 193 votes, the precise number required for election. Henry had slipped away and run the two blocks to the statehouse, where to his joy he heard the good news. Henry raced for their Beacon Street home, pretending to be downcast and disappointed before announcing the news. Sixteen-year-old Charles Francis Jr. jumped to his feet, saying, "Mr. Sumner, I want to shake hands with you first." As neighbors began to pour into the house, Adams was likely too preoccupied to ponder—as he surely had in previous weeks—how the same Senate seat vacated by his father four decades before might one day have elevated a third Adams into the presidency.[54]

"SUMNER'S LARGER AND MORE IMPOSING PRESENCE, COMBINED WITH the magnetism, eloquence, and zeal," Charles Francis Jr. wrote years later, raised the once-junior partner "into greater prominence." The elder Charles Francis retreated to his ongoing project of editing his grandfather's papers while attending the occasional Free Soil meeting. Adams spoke at state conventions in Worcester and Cleveland and sent a lengthy missive to be read at a meeting in Ravenna, Ohio. But his refusal to indicate any interest in the Senate, his son Charles correctly observed, meant that despite his prominent role in the 1848 Free Soil campaign, within his home state, at least, control of "the antislavery movement was passing from Adams."[55]

His travels and speeches maintained Adams's political visibility outside of Massachusetts, and as 1852 dawned, editors from Manhattan to Vermont, and from Pennsylvania to the nation's capital, began to speculate that when the Free Soil Party met that summer in Pittsburgh in their second national convention, Adams would this time sit atop the ticket. "John P. Hale, Charles Francis Adams, and John A. Dix are spoken of as candidates for President," the Washington *Southern Press* reported. "As the grandson of John Adams," the *New York Herald* added, there was a "fitness in choosing him that does not always characterize such things." By this time, Americans had come to regard the Adams family as the republic's first and finest dynasty. "The talent of the family has descended to its present representative to a very fair extent," the *Herald* believed. Having just bungled the opportunity to serve in the Senate, Adams again proposed to let events unfold without his assistance, and he neither encouraged nor discouraged the rumors.[56]

Before the summer's political season could begin in earnest, Adams's personal concerns intruded when his sister-in-law Mary sent word that his mother, now seventy-seven, was quickly failing. Louisa had been in poor health for years, and because she was too weak to travel, Charles Francis and Abby separately journeyed to Washington several times each year to visit her. As he had four years before, Adams boarded a southbound train, hoping to arrive in time to say his good-byes. His train pulled into Washington just after six on the morning of May 16, but when he reached his parents' F Street residence, he found a black ribbon tied to the bell. Two days later, Louisa's funeral was held at the church at the Congressional Cemetery until her body could be reinterred in Quincy. Both houses of Congress adjourned, and the president of the Senate and the Speaker of the House served as pallbearers. President Fillmore also attended, as did his cabinet, but the brokenhearted Charles Francis scarcely noticed their presence. He was her only surviving child, and his thoughts returned to his childhood days in Russia. "I never questioned her kindness or her love," he reflected on the night of her funeral, "and her going leaves a blank which nothing can replace."[57]

As he had after losing his father, Charles Francis turned philosophical, reflecting on his parents and his own responsibilities to his five surviving children. As a boy, he had thought his father cold and remote, but now, reading through his father's diary, Charles Francis judged himself "inferior" as a parent. As he pored over John Quincy's journals, he saw for the first time "the evidence of the care and labor bestowed by him upon myself during my infancy." Fearing that he would never "be able to repay it" to his own children, Adams resolved to at least care for them financially, consulting with his banker about a proper sum "to be paid to his daughter Louisa" upon her coming of age and checking with his attorney about provisions for his niece in John Quincy's will. He also sent his sister-in-law Mary a check for five thousand dollars. Characteristically, Adams said nothing about being a less rigid father or trying to understand his son Charles Francis's obvious antipathy toward him.[58]

There was little time to mourn or deal with family affairs. In early June, after nearly deadlocking, the Democrats selected former New Hampshire Senator Franklin Pierce as their presidential candidate on the forty-ninth ballot. Two weeks later, the Whigs tapped General Winfield Scott. The two parties issued similar platforms in which both pledged to uphold the Compromise of 1850, Fugitive Slave Act and all. "I do not well comprehend how any man, Whig or democrat, can assent to the platform[s] without at the same time disavowing every particle of practical hostility to slavery," Adams complained to Sumner. "Both are intensely anti-republican." But even though Pierce's running mate was Alabama senator and slaveholder William King, Adams guessed correctly that most Barn-burners were content with the Democratic ticket. Without a name of Van Buren's caliber, he believed, the Whigs would lose and "the democratic party will once more come into power despite of all its internal divisions." Adams suspected the Whigs were "very likely to owe their future destruction" to their indecision on slavery, but 1852 was not to be the year that a party dedicated to free soil would emerge as the major alternative to the Democrats. As Charles Francis had no desire to lead a doomed crusade, Pierce's popularity meant that he determined not to be the Free Soil nominee. "My present intention is to go to the National Convention and vote for Messrs. Hale and [Cassius] Clay," Adams wrote in his diary on June 23, "and to take little or no part in the state election."[59]

The Free Soil convention opened in Pittsburgh on August 11. "We had not a multitude as at Buffalo," Adams admitted, and that was an understatement. Although the delegates "seemed sincerely in the cause," only 2,000 conventioneers turned out, compared to 20,000 four years before. A handful of delegates visited Adams in his room at the Monongahela House, all of them urging him to accept the top position, but Charles Francis advocated for John Hale "as strongly as [he] could," and the delegates finally grasped that his refusal was not a pose. However, Adams did agree to chair the convention. The assembly made quick work of nominating Hale and Indiana congressman George Julian, although one delegate stubbornly cast his ballot for Adams. Their platform, a Manhattan paper reported, was "deadly hostile to any more slave States—dead against [the annexation of] Cuba, dead against the introduction of slavery into the territories—dead set against the Fugitive Slave law." Adams himself was pleased, informing Sumner that the convention "has done me good by convincing me that the movement has more steam than ever." Journalists farther South were predictably hostile. "These anti-slavery folks 'spit upon' Gen. Scott and Gen. Pierce with equal bitterness," the Washington *Southern Press* editorialized, while the *Richmond Enquirer* thought it unsurprising that the Adams family planned "schemes of revenge, swearing its sons to eternal hostility" to the slave states.[60]

Although Adams believed his labors completed for the fall, New England's Free-Soilers understood that while they would again not capture the White House, they might pick up a number of seats in Congress. Adams first caught wind of their plans to advance his name for the Third District in late September, when his Charles Francis Jr. showed him a loyal Whig newspaper "containing a bitter and malignant attack upon" him, evidence that his old party took a possible Adams candidacy seriously. Having missed his opportunity to secure a seat in the Senate, Adams supposed that the nomination "would be agreeable" provided it was "spontaneous." It was not his own fame that mattered, he promised himself, but rather that he "could do something to modify the politics of this State." On October 21, Adams was formally notified of the honor, and four days later he published his reply. His acceptance began with the requisite protest that the party "generously over-estimates" his ability and reminded it that he never *solicited* a nomination." But he promised to pursue "the sacred cause in which we are engaged" in the few short weeks before the election.[61]

"General Scott will scarcely reach the Presidency this time," Adams predicted in mid-September, and his guess proved no exaggeration. As was his habit by now, Henry raced to the statehouse to get the election-night news, which he hurried back to his father and Sumner. "A total and overwhelming defeat of the Whig party," Charles Francis recorded. Scott carried only four states, one of them Massachusetts, but even there Scott's tally barely bested that of Hale's Liberty Party. "The democratic party now comes into power upon ultra pro-slavery ground," Adams wrote, "and the Whigs are eliminated." As much as he mourned Pierce's triumph, he took pleasure in the fact, as he assured Sumner, that the election was the Whigs' "last gasp," while the Free Soil Party, which had captured 22 percent of the vote in Massachusetts but only 6.6 percent of the northern vote, was "no longer the third party of the nation."[62]

Unhappily for Charles Francis's career, the Whigs were not as thoroughly smashed as he anticipated. Adams took it as an omen that Whig Party founder Daniel Webster died at the age of seventy on the eve of the election; no more charitable to him in death than in life, Adams privately denounced him as a "corrupt politician and a bad man." But despite the support of the moribund Liberty Party, which praised Adams as a man of "high-souled integrity" worthy of "the third generation" of a great family, Adams lost his race to Whig stalwart John Wiley Edmands by 674 votes. Massachusetts Free-Soilers were "much chagrined" by the outcome, one disappointed journalist remarked, evidently having thought they did not need to "exert" themselves to hold the seat. Worse yet for Adams, Webster's position in the State Department passed to his brother-in-law Everett, as recompense for his loyalty to the party.[63]

EDMANDS WAS EQUALLY AWARE THAT HIS PARTY WAS COLLAPSING, and when in 1854 he declined to run again, Adams's old supporters made a modest effort in his behalf. But by then, family issues were paramount, always an important consideration for a father raising the next generation of statesmen. John Quincy II, his eldest son, had started at Harvard the previous year. "During the last year he has done very well and has certainly made much progress," a proud Adams boasted that September. More concerning, however, was the education of Charles Francis Jr., whose career at his father's old academy, the Boston Latin School, was increasingly troubled. In mid-May 1851, Charles wrote to say that he had "fallen behind [his] class" and was "extremely dejected." Charles was then nearing the end of his third year, and for his final term he begged to transfer to Andover. When his austere father declined to reply, Charles wrote a second and then a third time, "waiting with much anxiety the answer to my last, in respect to my schooling."[64]

At length, Adams agreed to allow Charles Francis Jr. to withdraw and prepare for college with a private tutor. Never happy in his brother John Quincy's shadow, Charles Francis Jr. then begged to be sent to Yale, but any college besides Harvard—the college of three previous generations—was unthinkable for an Adams. The stern father packed

Charles Francis and Henry off to Cambridge. Charles Francis was nineteen, Henry but sixteen. Choosing to ignore his own unhappy experience when enrolled in Harvard just before turning fifteen, Adams judged this a "critical period" for Henry and prayed "that he may go through with honor." Despite his complaints, Charles Francis Jr. did well, winning the college's Bowdoin Prize in 1855. Rather to his surprise, the intellectual Henry also enjoyed the experience. The undersized boy promptly became close pals with another heir to a famous name when he befriended William Henry Fitzhugh Lee, the grandson of Virginia governor "Light Horse Harry" Lee and the son of Robert E. Lee. The tall, affable Virginian, known as "Roony," was "the most popular and prominent young man in his class," Henry later remembered. But he was also "ignorant [and] childlike." When Lee finally decided to drop out, Henry wrote his letter of resignation, and another to Winfield Scott, requesting a commission on the expedition the general was preparing to lead against Mormons in Utah Territory. Henry remained at Harvard, with plans to graduate in May 1858.[65]

As ever, Louisa Catherine, or Sister Lou, was an altogether different story. For the oldest of the fourth generation, there was of course no Harvard in her future. Some young women, such as Elizabeth Cady of New York, attended the Troy Female Academy, which was intended to provide women with the same educational opportunities as their brothers. But nobody in the family considered that possibility. Instead, to the consternation of her parents, she used her brilliance and spirit to attract and then abandon suitors. For several years, Louisa had on occasion mentioned a Charles Kuhn, a Manhattan attorney and businessman ten years her elder who hailed from a prominent Philadelphia family. Even so, it came as a shock to Charles Francis when in December 1853 Kuhn appeared in Boston to ask for Louisa's hand in marriage. Louisa agreed, and so the Adamses saw no objection, although they urged their twenty-two-year-old daughter to delay the wedding for at least a year. But Charles Francis had also once pushed for a brief engagement, and so the couple was married in a small ceremony in the old house in Quincy

Known to the family as Peacefield or simply the Old House, the estate in Quincy was acquired by John and Abigail Adams in 1787 after its original Loyalist owners abandoned Massachusetts during the Revolution. The house was expanded over the years, and most of the fourth generation preferred it to Charles Francis Sr.'s house on Beacon Hill. "How we did hate Boston!" Charles Francis Jr. remembered. "How we loved Quincy!" *Courtesy National Park Service.*

on April 13, 1854. Adams promised them $1,800 each year, together with $5,000 to furnish their home.[66]

The relationship between Louisa and Charles was troubled from the start. Following a disastrous honeymoon due to causes no family member ever put to paper, Lou spent more time in Boston than in New York City with her husband, and when in Manhattan, she complained of "cramps" and demanded that Abby come for lengthy visits. "A letter from my wife [was] not very encouraging," Charles Francis remarked that June, "as it respects Louisa's condition." Charles Francis had come to fear "that the disease is deeper seated than the physicians yet understand." Three months later, when the couple journeyed to Boston for Charles Francis's

The brilliant eldest child of Charles Francis and Abby Adams, Louisa Catherine Adams Kuhn was denied the Harvard education and public fame that her brothers regarded as their birthright. An unhappy marriage to a Manhattan-based attorney whom the family believed to be her intellectual inferior led to a restless existence in Europe. "Poor girl," her brother Henry observed, "she always was and always will be the most impulsive and unhappy of beings." *Courtesy Massachusetts Historical Society.*

and Abby's anniversary, Adams fretted that Louisa "did not look so well as I had hoped."[67]

By Christmas, Louisa was back in Manhattan, celebrating the holiday with the Kuhns. "You mustn't worry about my health any more," she assured her father on one occasion, telling Abby on another that she continued "very well, not the least nervous, and perfectly regular." Abby journeyed down to New York in March 1855 to see for herself, and she was not assured. "Poor child if her health was really good things would look very different," she reported to Charles Francis Sr. Abby's sons had Harvard and career prospects, but the brilliant Louisa had only Kuhn. "She is restless," Abby worried, with "nothing to take up [her] free time." Should Louisa never "have children," Abby feared "the effect, for she already settles to nothing." Clearly, the twenty-four-year-old Louisa resented her parents' suffocating concerns. "I think I am more capable of doing what I believe to be right even at cost to myself," she promised her father, before adding, in a nasty aside worthy of her brother Charles Francis Jr., that she found the Kuhns a "charming family, more like a home in the ways of talking than any I know."[68]

Louisa's mysterious illness, which her family diagnosed as "nervous prostration," was quite common to upper-class women of her era. The Adams boys were dependent on their father only until they graduated college. But the brilliant Louisa was completely dependent on her husband, an affluent but unambitious attorney who clearly lacked her intellectual gifts. Feminists Charlotte Perkins Gilman and Olive Schreiner, who wrote about Louisa's condition—often dubbed "neurasthenia" by male doctors—noted that working-class women did not suffer from this syndrome. Charles Francis Sr. expected his sons to make their mark in politics and the law, but Louisa was doomed to a pointless existence in which she performed reproductive duties in exchange for financial support. Schreiner described such relationships as "female parasitism." Had her father, perhaps, been more interested in his wife being the sort of political partner that his grandmother Abigail or his mother, Louisa, had been, the younger Louisa might at least have had ambitions to marry the sort of politician or reformer who desired a professional helpmate. But with no model to emulate, Louisa settled, unhappily, into the role of a genteel lady of leisure, an ornamental wife.[69]

THE PASSAGE OF SENATOR STEPHEN DOUGLAS'S KANSAS-NEBRASKA Act in May 1854, which overturned the thirty-four-year-old Missouri Compromise and allowed for the possibility of slavery in the Upper Midwest under the guise of popular sovereignty, drew Adams back into the public eye. "The events in Washington and in Kansas show in a clear light how much of the savage still inheres in the social and political character of Slaveholders," he remarked. Following hard on slaveholders' victories with popular sovereignty in the southwestern territories and the Fugitive Slave Act, what was at issue, Adams believed, was "no less than the control of the general government." As was the case with many Free-Soilers, Kansas also served to radicalize Adams. Within the year, Charles Francis contributed to a endowment designed to keep Douglass's *North Star* afloat. Adams assured Julia Griffiths, Douglass's business manager, that although he did not always "concur in the views which [Douglass] entertains," he "never had occasion to regret the manner in which he thinks fit to express them."[70]

For most of the next year, Adams's schedule was a blur of speaking engagements. His lecture "What Makes Slavery a Question of National Concern" was delivered in Syracuse and other New York canal towns, in Manhattan, and in a number of "Anti-Nebraska" meetings in Massachusetts. Despite his professed admiration for Douglass, Adams's standard speech continued to emphasize the crimes of the "Slave Power" against white Americans, from the assaults on free speech and the right of petition to its corruptive power on national culture. "There is no path to distinction in the South (where commerce, literature, and art don't exist), save that of politics," he insisted, "and that leads but one way," toward proslavery expansion. After listening to the lecture, one hostile journalist characterized Adams as an "ultra freesoil abolition politician," even while admitting that "the audience was large." The tour left Adams weary but gratified. "This is the first year since 1848 that I have been able to act with the most perfect reliance on the soundness of my position," he told an admirer in November 1855.[71]

Adams also correctly surmised that a law as despised as the Kansas-Nebraska Act would revive the free-soil movement, just as he believed that he was the man to help guide its course. As disgusted Democrats quit their party, and as the Whigs continued to collapse, antislavery activists staged "fusion conventions" across the North. Adams, state senator Ebenezer Hoar, and Sumner labored to forge a new party with the support, as the abolitionist *National Era* reported, of "Anti-Slavery Whigs, the Free-Soilers, or Independent Democrats, and the Anti-Slavery Know Nothings." Formally known as the American Party, the Know-Nothings built their platform upon hatred of Catholics and immigrants, a nativist strain that Adams, despite his devout Protestantism, denounced as "in conflict with the first dictates of humanity." The fusionists were soon calling themselves Republicans. Having been banished from his old party seven years before, Charles Francis was far quicker than the two men he would one day serve—Seward and Lincoln—to embrace the new coalition. "I have been industrious in the labor of constructing the party here," he informed antislavery editor Gamaliel Bailey, "and with a greater share of success than I expected."[72]

Southern whites returned fire. After Sumner delivered a furious speech denouncing the two authors of the Kansas law, Stephen Douglas and Andrew Butler of South Carolina, Congressman Preston Brooks, Butler's nephew, assaulted the Massachusetts senator with his gold-headed cane on May 22, 1856, while Sumner was sitting at his desk. Adams was horrified, although he also surmised that the brutal attack was likely to advance "the general issue [of free soil] that is inevitable." Adams worried about his friend's head trauma, of course, and rightly so: Sumner would not return to the Senate until 1859. But as Adams was also mourning the ten-year anniversary of the death of his "beautiful boy," Arthur, he felt strangely fragile and thanked God he had not witnessed the assault: "My nerves have become so shaken that such a scene would be too much for them."[73]

In June, Adams journeyed to Philadelphia for the first national Republican nominating convention. The opening session convened on June 17 in the city's Music Fund Hall, formerly a Presbyterian Church, on Locust Street. Adams desired the nomination to fall to either Seward of New York or Supreme Court Justice John McLean, a Free-Soiler from Ohio, but the senator's handlers held him back until 1860, suspecting the new party yet lacked the political infrastructure necessary for victory. On the eleventh ballot, the conclave of 565 men chose the handsome and politically connected explorer John C. Frémont. Although born in Savannah, Frémont had briefly represented California in the Senate, which meant that an eastern man had to take the second spot. Hoping to play a minor role at the convention, Adams worried that he might be asked to run, but rather to his consternation, delegates sounded him out on Sumner's availability. Adams fretted that his "lukewarm" response might be taken as "jealousy," while if he endorsed the idea, the delegates might suspect his enthusiasm "sprang from a wish to [take] the Senator's place" in Washington. In the end, the convention selected William Dayton of New Jersey and merely asked Adams to address the delegates. In a fiery speech that drew prolonged cheers, Adams warned his audience "that the great battle is coming on." Had the North stood its ground in the previous decade, he added, "we should not have come to gutta-percha canes in the Senate."[74]

Far more gratifying for Charles Francis was that in July the town fathers of Quincy invited him, together with twenty-three-year-old John Quincy II, to jointly deliver the Fourth of July oration. Remembering his own triumph in 1843 while conveniently forgetting the pressure he felt performing before his father, Adams was elated. Although John Quincy was just three years out of Harvard and still studying law, the widely publicized event reminded him that his state and nation, as one editor promised, expected great things of "the fourth generation." Ohio's *Anti-Slavery Bugle* was "pleased" to announce the affair, noting—surely unnecessarily—that John Quincy was "the grandson of the President whose honored name he bears." Even in far-away Honolulu, the fact that this "direct descendant of two Presidents" was to carry on the family tradition made news. The Adams family, which had heretofore recorded every public utterance of its members, kept no record of the speech. Yet it was sound enough, evidently, for Boston to invite John Quincy to repeat the performance in 1857.[75]

That fall, Charles Francis kept a fairly low profile, speaking only at the Republican state convention in Worcester and at a Frémont rally in Philadelphia. The Democrats had nominated Pennsylvania native James Buchanan, and Republicans were nervous enough about losing the state to import Adams as their keynote speaker before an open-air rally of perhaps forty thousand in Independence Square. "The spectacle was a very imposing one," Adams thought. Gas jets on either side of the stage lit the night sky. Buchanan, he advised the audience, was "not the man for the crisis," as he was yet another northern politician under the control "of the same men who ground [dominated] President Pierce." But feeling the return of his "old enemy the head ache," Adams cut his speech short. At least he "was listened to with patience and approbation [and] hit my argument," he reflected, all without "straining my voice."[76]

Privately, what Adams desired was another chance at a seat in the House. But William Damrell, an antislavery Know-Nothing, had replaced the retiring Edmands in March 1855, and in the intervening months he had switched to Republicanism. Local party leaders thought it unwise to deny him nomination, much to Adams's dismay. To his political friends, Adams swore he had never "directly or indirectly sought a nomination" and that when unknowingly put forward by his supporters, he "guided [his] acceptances or otherwise" by his judgment of the "precise circumstances in each particular case." Adams retreated to his study to finalize publication of the tenth volume of *Life and Works of John Adams* and to promise his diary that he was content to stump for his party. "My personal interest in this kind of life is so much diminished that I now keep in it at all only from a sense of duty to my name," he wrote. "My nerves no longer bear it well."[77]

As Election Day approached, Adams was confident that the Republicans would at least sweep New England. "I have never entertained a doubt of their complete success from the day of the assault upon Sumner," he confided to one New Yorker. Charles Francis Jr., who at age twenty-two was reading law in Dana's office, proudly cast his first vote, saying that he "was from childhood a part of the anti-slavery agitation." Frémont carried only eleven states to Buchanan's nineteen—with one going to former President Fillmore and the Know-Nothings—and the Republicans emerged in their first national contest as the republic's second party. The Democrats captured only five free states. As Adams predicted, Buchanan won in just four congressional districts in New England, none of them in Massachusetts. "We have gone through the great struggle and failed," Adams groused. But as he had every confidence that the incoming administration would be a disaster, he was "on the whole content to stand still and wait" for the next election cycle, when "the people shall have made up their minds more clearly."[78]

It was not to be a long wait. Although Adams consoled himself with the sentiment that a "kind providence" had saved him from being "called to represent in the next Congress," thus allowing him to be "better and more usefully occupied in my private station," fate had other plans for Charles Francis and his family. Just days after the election, Adams correctly surmised that despite Frémont's defeat, "The elements of a new combination are now assembled which will, if this administration continues its [proslavery] policy, ultimately control the government." If so, "We may yet save the country." And, as it was to turn out, newly elected Congressmen Damrell was unwell and on the verge of suffering a debilitating paralytic stroke.[79]

4

"THE GHOST OF THIS MURDERED REPUBLIC"

The Congressman

THE RUMORS BEGAN AS 1858 DAWNED. SIX MONTHS AFTER Charles Sumner's brutal beating, the Massachusetts General Court reelected him to the Senate, believing that his empty chair stood as a powerful statement against the slave power. Sumner had returned to Washington once in 1857 but could not withstand a single day of business and fled to Europe. Upon his return, his doctors judged him little improved, and on May 22, 1858, the second anniversary of the attack, he again sailed for the Continent. Sumner called on Adams before his departure, and Charles Francis agreed that his condition remained "much the same," guessing that "he will never be a well man again." Other party leaders, including Maine Senator William Pitt Fessenden and Boston abolitionist Samuel Gridley Howe, concurred and quietly began to suggest that the time had arrived to fill the seat. Newspapers caught wind of the rumors and began to report that should Sumner resign, Adams "was to take his place." Charles Francis was mortified. Having refused to campaign for the position seven years before, he flatly refused to shove his old ally aside, particularly since he guessed that Sumner's offers of resignation were not sincere. "I do hope this matter may be set at rest at once," he groused.[1]

Other developments were more welcome. In mid-March, journalists reported that Charles Francis was "spoken of as a candidate for Congress in the district in Massachusetts now represented by Mr. Damrell, whom ill health obliges to decline being a candidate for re-election." As ever, the possibility that a son of the nation's first political dynasty might one day sit in the White House captured the imaginations of editors from Cleveland to Alexandria, Virginia.[2]

Now fifty-one, Charles Francis scribbled his habitual doubts about such an eventuality into his journal, although gossip about William Damrell's health was commonplace in both Boston and Washington. Nor were there any Republicans in the Bay State more active than Adams. During the previous year, he had attended a small, private dinner for former candidate John C. Frémont (and was surprised to discover the explorer "modest yet firm and courteous") and had shared the stage with Joshua Giddings at the June 1857 "Black Republican State Convention" in Worcester. A number of abolitionists turned out for the meeting, including William Lloyd Garrison and Unitarian minister Thomas Wentworth Higginson. Adams's address, which one journalist described as a "flat key-note," reminded them that most Republicans were not always kindred spirits. "I do not mean to charge upon slaveholders, as a class, that they are irredeemably wicked, any more than I should upon bankers, or brokers, or hotel keepers, or liquor-sellers, or horse drivers," Adams argued, adding that in "this imperfect world we must mix with and tolerate common sinners." Although the 1856 Republican platform had not demanded the immediate end to slavery where it yet existed, many of those in attendance regarded southern whites who owned black Americans to be far more sinful than hotel keepers. Despite this, Garrison dutifully included Adams's speech in the convention's published proceedings, which his office sold for fifteen cents.[3]

The speech did Adams little harm with party regulars, however. It had been ten years since his father's death, he reflected, and that decade had "on the whole been not ill employed." As always, Charles Francis assured himself that he could not accept a congressional nomination if it required "any effort of my own to secure it." But should the voters of his district "think well enough of me to call me into their service," Adams believed, he "recognized the obligation as a citizen to obey" and to "acquit myself as well as my ability would go." To one supporter, Adams trotted out his habitual pose of indifference, remarking that "at no time in my life have I ever solicited office." Yet the times were perilous, he admitted, and as an Adams he recognized "the right of the public to require the services of any citizen." Should his political friends advance his name, Adams promised, he would not waver: "To *me*, the notion comes with tenfold force when my name is presented in connection with a situation in which to fail would be indelible disgrace to me."[4]

Republican delegates congregated in Dedham's Temperance Hall on October 7, 1858, to choose their nominee for the Third District. Out of 128 votes cast, Adams won 82; his closest competitor captured only 24. Newspapers across the North hailed the choice, with Gamaliel Bailey's *National Era* praising the nomination as "eminently fit to be made." An Ohio journal remarked on Adams's "long and distinguished service in the legislature," adding that he "has some of the inflexibility of his father and may be warranted to stand proof against the popular sovereignty theories" prevalent in Washington. A triumphant Adams wrote to Sumner that his supporters had "been indefatigable in making an opinion in my favor" and that the selection was made "by a very decided vote." Yet, as ever, Charles Francis could not help but warn Sumner that should he succeed in carrying his heavily Republican district, "no one will be more surprised than your humble servant."[5]

On October 12, Adams formally acknowledged his selection, informing the committee that he accepted the nomination "in the spirit in which it was made." His widely reprinted public letter followed, which was then expanded into a lengthy oration. Speaking in Boston, Adams pointedly observed that he was "not inclined to solicit office," and he cautioned his audience not to vote for him "only because I am the son of my father and the grandson of my grandfather." He did not wish "even to mention" himself but rather to explain what was at stake in the coming election and the presidential contest of 1860. "The Democratic party are exceedingly concerned when there is anything said about human rights," he shouted. "Last summer they felt under the necessity of seceding from the customary assemblies for the general celebration of the Fourth of July," Adams continued, provoking laughter and applause, "because it was a time when there was a great deal too much said about liberty." As had been the case a decade before in Buffalo, when Adams took to the podium, his normally staid facade fell away, and the passionate orator emerged.[6]

As one Ohio journalist observed, Adams's nomination in a district that had not elected a Democrat since 1835 was "equivalent to an election." Even the *Boston Ledger*, a Democratic newspaper, was so hostile to the party's candidate, Arthur Austin, that it instead endorsed Adams as a "man of character, independence, and truth, and not a trading politician." However, the pessimistic Adams fretted that Moses Cobb, the third-party Know-Nothing candidate, might attract old-line Whigs who yet despised Adams as a turncoat. "My confidence in my own success has never been brilliant," he confessed, "and I have habitually schooled myself to low expectations." But while Adams had refused to lobby for his party's backing, once he had it he threw himself into the race with enthusiasm. "There is [so] much intrigue going on in secret to defeat me," Adams believed, that he had little choice. October 26 found him in Dedham, speaking at a Republican rally in the Agricultural Society Hall. Maine Governor (and future Vice President) Hannibal Hamlin warmed up the audience, and then state assemblyman John A. Andrew introduced Adams. "I found myself cheered almost at every period," Adams remarked later. "I have seldom heard a more responsive auditory."[7]

Following the campaign from Paris, Sumner never harbored any doubts about its outcome. "I do not understand how any person, who is not indifferent on the question of slavery, can hesitate to support you for Congress," he predicted, and rightly so. The Republicans swept the state, from congressional seats to the governor's chair, and from the statehouse to the Senate. Adams earned 6,524 votes to Austin's 3,893 and Cobb's 1,464. As the returns trickled in on the evening of November 2, Adams thought it "the crowning of all the wishes I ever had in political life." As he was no longer young, he supposed, the victory "will not turn my head." The day was proof, he assured Sumner, of a "triumph exclusively of the anti slavery sentiment." Although still undecided about returning to the Senate, Sumner was delighted by the news. "Returning justice lifts aloft her scales," he exclaimed. "The election has taken place & yr husband has at last the first installment on what is due to his ability, integrity & loyalty to our cause," he lectured Abby, correctly guessing that she was not as enthusiastic about her new life as was Charles Francis.[8]

Elsewhere in the northern states, the Republicans performed nearly as well, thanks to the fratricidal war within the Democratic ranks over President James Buchanan's maladroit attempts to force the proslavery Lecompton Constitution on the settlers in Kansas in violation of Stephen Douglas's popular-sovereignty theories. Adams was just one of twenty-one Republicans elected to the House, but among the freshmen congressmen, only Adams, thanks to his illustrious surname and his labors in the General Court, was to arrive in Washington with name recognition and a national reputation. Contrary to tradition in the Senate, seniority meant little in the lower chamber, so if he desired, he might exercise considerable influence when the next session of Congress began in December 1859.[9]

Democrats, including those in New England, were dismayed by the Republican wave. The statewide election, one Pittsfield paper lamented, "confirms and endorses the wildest and most extraordinary sectional doctrines." Of the "whole agitating crowd" of Republicans Ebenezer Hoar, Henry Wilson, and Maine's Hannibal Hamlin, the worst and "father of these measures is Charles Francis Adams." A Nashville paper agreed: "The extreme men have triumphed while in the act of arraigning in the extreme manner, the slaveholders of the south." For Adams, who had crafted his state's "personal liberty bill" to be "selected out and sent to Congress," the editor fumed, demonstrated that Republicans intended to "hold up these slaveholders for public odium as an oligarchy, an aristocracy, as having hands red with the blood of their fellow men." The editor, of course, assumed that all "intelligent and patriotic" Americans shared his fears and disdain, but in truth, Adams could not have put it better.[10]

JUST DAYS BEFORE HIS ELECTION, CHARLES FRANCIS AND ABBY HAD bid farewell to Louisa and Charles Kuhn, who left on an extended tour of Europe. One year earlier, in October 1857, Louisa had gone into labor with a baby girl they intended to name Mary Elizabeth—the first child of the fifth generation of Adamses—but the "child suffocated" in the process, and "the disappointment to her is grievous," her devastated father recorded. Doctors treated Louisa with mercury and pronounced her cured. In early 1858, Lou, as her husband also called her, informed her mother that they planned to sail for Europe in early June. "What does that mean?" Charles Francis wondered. Frantic over his always-volatile daughter's state of mind, Adams briefly decided to sail with them, and to also take Henry, who was to graduate from Harvard that May. But then the campaign season intervened. At length, Charles Francis and Abby persuaded the Kuhns to remain in the country until the late summer. The pair arrived in Paris in early September 1858. They were welcomed by Charles Sumner, who was preparing to leave for southeastern France for further treatments.[11]

Having captured Harvard's Bowdoin Prize for senior composition before being elected Class Orator that May, Henry believed that he also deserved a year or two on the Continent. While in Cambridge, Henry had fallen in love with Caroline Bigelow, the daughter of the state's chief justice, but after three years of courtship, it became clear to Henry that Caroline merely enjoyed the chase. "It cost me the hardest heart-aches ever I had before I could sit quiet under the conviction that she is—what she is," he confessed to his brother Charles Francis Jr. Lacking direction, the young graduate determined to pursue legal studies at the University of Berlin, not that he "knew what the Civil Law was," Henry later admitted, "or [had] any reason for his studying it." Charles Francis Sr. was willing to finance the venture, largely because he hoped Henry might keep an eye on Louisa. "But the best resolutions of young men often melt like wax before the attractive warmth of sensual enjoyments," his dubious father sighed. "And industry will degenerate when out of the reach of observation into selfish indolence." Henry sailed on the *Persia* on September 29, five weeks before Adams's election to Congress.[12]

Taken for his Harvard graduation in 1858, this photograph depicts Henry, then age twenty, as he prepared to embark on a grand tour of Europe and study law at the University of Berlin. Charles Francis Sr. was willing to finance the venture, largely because he hoped Henry might keep an eye on his troubled sister Louisa. "But the best resolutions of young men often melt like wax before the attractive warmth of sensual enjoyments," his father worried. *Courtesy National Park Service.*

John Quincy II, the eldest son, had graduated from Harvard five years before, in 1853, and had passed the bar and settled into the practice of law in Boston. As a matter of course, Charles Francis Jr. soon joined him. His two-year apprenticeship to Richard Henry Dana ended around the time of his father's election. Although the twenty-three-year-old judged himself "no more fit to be admitted [to the bar] than a child," rather to his amazement he passed the exam, probably, he guessed, because of the help of Justice Bigelow, Caroline's father. "I never took to the law," Charles Francis Jr. later acknowledged, "and I am sure the law never came my way." But as lacking in direction as Henry, Charles consented to practice with his brother John Quincy at 23 Court Street, a building owned by their father. Most of his labors were devoted to managing his father's properties and dealing with Adams family clients, a job that made him little more, he complained, than a "real estate agent." The congressman-elect, as usual, appeared not to notice his son's unhappiness. "The success of my son Henry, the advance in his profession of my son John, the steady promise of Charles," he wrote, a week after his own victory, "have all contributed to surround the memories of this season with delight."[13]

Henry survived a brutal crossing, which, he reported, "for mere physical misery passed endurance." Both Sumner and Louisa were in Paris to greet him, which raised "his spirits" considerably. The Kuhns tarried only long enough to see Henry before setting off for Dresden. On the last evening before their departure, Louisa "had a bad night," Henry reported to Charles Francis Jr., without specifying the cause of her distress. Despite his own wanderings, Sumner seconded Adams's fears that Henry might waste his time abroad. "He must not lose his early habits of industry," he warned. "Wherever he is—although for a day—he must work." Indeed, none of Henry's dreams worked as planned. His German-language skills were so inferior that he had to devote three months to its study before he could turn to the law. "The German students were strange animals," in his estimation, and "their professors were beyond pay." His teachers "mumbled" out their lectures, and Henry quickly discovered that he could learn more from his books "in a day" than he could from his professors "in a month." The students he befriended "enjoyed the beer and music, but they refused to be responsible for their education."[14]

Henry also disliked the "gloom" of a Berlin winter, gray even by Massachusetts standards. Curiously, given his later views, he also found the anti-Semitism of his fellows troubling, reflecting that "the Germans are still a semi-barbarous people." His lengthy absence prompted him to think about the family he had left behind. "One doesn't appreciate home properly, at home," he assured Charles Jr. Henry had always thought his mother weak while admiring his father, a sentiment his brother Charles Francis failed to share. Just before he departed for Europe, Henry and his mother shared "two or three long talks," he told Charles Francis Jr., which left him "feeling more like a damned selfish, low-minded fool" than ever before in his life. Henry resolved not only "to show more respect and affection" toward her but also to persuade his brother Charles Francis to do so as well. The penitent Henry even resolved that upon his return, he would be kinder to his brother Peter Chardon Brooks—by now, referred to simply as Brooks—then ten years of age and notorious for pestering his older brothers with endless questions. "We ought to try our hardest to tolerate the child," he advised Charles. But Henry was less sure about how to treat thirteen-year-old Mary. He suspected she would grow into a "great, strapping girl," a curious prediction for a family not known for height. "Her manners too will never be good, I'm afraid," he supposed. "She has too many brothers."[15]

If Abby was pleased by Henry's resolution to be kinder to his youngest brother, she shared his opinion that Brooks was a most unusual child. "Papa reads aloud for an hour or two evenings, & poor Brooks screams, & laughs, & rants, & twists, & jumps, & worries about so, that we have been obliged to set him on a footstool, in the middle of the room," Abby reported to Henry. They at last found him a school that catered to his special needs, but he could not "study close, or read, or spell tolerably." Abby doubted that he would ever attend college, "for he has no taste for books at all." Charles Francis Sr. disagreed. While he admitted that Brooks was "peculiar [and] developed too slowly," he otherwise pronounced him "sensible [and] above common boys in intellect." Abby conceded that Brooks was "good, dutiful, & honest as the day." Perhaps, she assured Henry, he was as bright as other children, "but not so clever as you three."[16]

Henry also began to reconsider his childhood adoration of Sumner. In mid-January 1859, he informed his brother Charles Francis that he had come to share their father's view that the senator would never be the man that he had been, writing: "Sumner can't return and won't resign." Audaciously, Henry dropped Sumner a note, "hinting that I wished and hoped that he would give up all idea of returning until he was really recovered and resign his seat." Young Adams was rather surprised when Sumner refused to accept medical advice from a student not yet twenty-one, declined to respond, and prepared to sail for America in November 1859. Otherwise, Henry was embarrassed by the state of American politics under President Buchanan and felt "disgraced when a German asks about them." Believing, as did family friend and New York senator William Henry Seward, that an "irrepressible conflict" was looming, Henry hoped to stay in Europe until the day that he heard the senator was "quietly elected President."[17]

When on holiday, Henry visited his sister and her husband, on one occasion traveling to Florence, on another to Switzerland. "Loo loves to have everyone about her gay, brilliant, and amusing, and dislikes stupid people, as she calls them." Their father was displeased. "All this experience may do him good," Adams grumbled, "but I cannot help doubting it." For her part, Abby continued to worry about her daughter's health and contentment, but if she expected Henry to put her mind at ease, an Adams was ever blunt. "Your complaints and fears about her may be perfectly just," he responded. Henry blamed much of her unhappiness on Charles Kuhn. The wealthy attorney was "willful and has always had his own way," Henry thought (in a curious criticism from an Adams), "and perhaps doesn't regard people's wishes so much as he might." Privately, Henry cautioned his brother Charles that the couple would probably never return to America. However brilliant she might be, Louisa was a woman and so not destined for greatness. "If she can't lead a useful life, at least lead a happy one," he hoped. "Loo's object in life is now so far as I see, pretty much reduced to that of being happy." Should she return home, he warned Charles Jr., "she would make you angry; you would make her more unhappy than ever." A life in Europe could not "make matters much worse," Henry supposed. "At least I hope not."[18]

Abby disagreed and wrote to inform Louisa that she and Charles Francis Sr. believed she had been gone too long and was spending too much money. An indignant Louisa replied that Abby, of all people, should know "that one's husband is *the* person and if he is satisfied, no one has a right not to be." Although the Adamses helped to finance her travels, most of the money spent came from the Kuhn family, and Louisa was annoyed "at the way in which everyone seems to think Mr. Kuhn is not capable of judging his own movement & plans." Regarding her father, Louisa added, "he ought to be ashamed to beg us not to become Europeanized Americans," especially after spending his youth in Britain and Russia. "I am and always shall be as thoroughly American as I ever was in my life," she promised, before adding a final twist: "I thought Papa had a better opinion of me, than to fancy that a few years passed away from home would destroy my character."[19]

Although he knew she did not wish to hear it, Henry also urged his mother to allow Louisa to "remain in Europe all of her life if she wanted to." She was "not meant for America." Not usually the most empathetic of people, Henry understood his older sister better than anyone in the family. The problem, Henry counseled, was that Louisa was far too brilliant to settle into the role of a Manhattan businessman's wife. Although inferior, her education made Louisa aware enough of this to "destroy her happiness, and till now the only happiness that I know of for her is this life in Italy." For her part, Louisa was aware that her parents blamed her husband for her misery, and that realization made her unhappier yet. "Poor girl, she always was and always will be the most impulsive and unhappy of beings," Henry sighed. "Where on earth did she get her disposition from? The rest of us are cold-blooded enough." Henry wished that "Loo" could accept her proper role as a wife and woman, but he admitted to his mother that "she has no object" to her life "and would have no more if she came home now than if she never came home at all."[20]

IN THAT ERA, CONGRESS MET ONLY FROM LATE WINTER THROUGH early March, unless called into special session by the president. The thirty-sixth Congress did not assemble until December 5, 1859, thirteen months after Adams's election. In the interim, Adams purchased a large farm in Boston, the Melodeon estate, at an auction price of $76,000. To enhance his role as a gentleman farmer, he also bought two "full blooded Ayrshire bulls" imported from Britain. The acquisition made Adams the largest taxpayer in the county; his annual burden of $1,440 was nearly three times that of the second-highest ratepayer, Josiah Quincy. His constituents could not claim that Adams failed to shoulder his share of the state's finances.[21]

Several months later, on July 2, Abby's brother-in-law Edward Everett wrote with the sad news that her sister Charlotte had died at the age of fifty-nine "after a lingering and painful illness." Abby's other sister, Ann Frothingham, was traveling abroad. Abby was bereft but tried to focus on the impending move to Washington, although she made it clear to her husband that she was "becoming a little exercised, as the prospect grew nearer," and that she could not help but "feel as if [his] election to Congress had not been so much desired as she thought last year." Mary and Brooks were to accompany their parents in late November, with Charles Francis Jr. to follow soon after and John Quincy directed to remain behind and manage the family's properties.[22]

Two days before Congress began its deliberations, Virginia authorities hanged abolitionist John Brown for his failed October raid at Harpers Ferry. "It will infuse a great portion of bitterness into all the intercourse between parties," the new congressman fretted. Unlike Abby, who regarded Brown as a "holy saint and martyr," Adams had little sympathy for the fiery abolitionist, in part because he regarded the raid a "desperately treasonable enterprise." He also feared that southern Democrats intended to play upon "the panic which it has excited" across the South to recapture the White House during the next year's elections and "uphold for one more term the domination of the oligarchy." His task over the coming months, Adams believed, was to repeatedly place "the cause of freedom in an advantageous light before the people and the world."[23]

The Adamses rented a spacious residence at the corner of K Street and Pennsylvania Avenue once owned by the British ambassador and designed more for entertaining than for a family of five. But creating a place for Republicans to gather was paramount. Many congressmen spent the four-month political season in Washington without their families, and most of those who brought their wives were southern Democrats. "The Republican party at that time was at a great disadvantage socially," twenty-four-year-old Charles Francis Jr. observed upon his arrival. Republicans often rented rooms in "wretched hotels or still less-inviting boarding-houses," and so the Adams abode was intended to be a "Republican social centre." The Adamses had shipped crates of dishes, books, and furniture south, but Charles Francis Jr., who had never visited Washington, was unimpressed by the capital, or at least by its racial composition. "A dirtier city materially—'Nigger'—it would not have been easy to imagine," young Adams remarked, easily adopting a racial slur never once used by his father, and one he would repeatedly toss into speeches and correspondence in later years.[24]

Charles Francis Sr. and Abby threw themselves into the Republican fray, hosting so many dinners and parties that Adams, according to one admiring journalist, quickly earned himself the reputation as a "gentleman who dispenses liberal hospitalities." Among the frequent guests was Senator William Henry Seward, whose temperance-inclined wife Frances despised Washington and its manners and morals. The younger Adamses found the New Yorker fascinating. "A slouching, slender figure; a head like a wise macaw; a beaked nose; shaggy eyebrows; unorderly hair and clothes; hoarse voice; off-hand manner; free talk, and perpetual cigar," Henry reported after returning home in time for the upcoming presidential contest. "From the first sight," Henry admitted, he "loved the Governor." Seward attempted to return the favor, but his dinners were all-male affairs, and Adams found them dull. "The usual assemblage of persons in whom I take very little interest," Charles Francis Sr. complained after one dinner at Seward's, where he found "not a single person whose conversation seems to me worth courting."[25]

Initially, the elder Adams assumed that the 1860 presidential nomination was Seward's for the asking. However, many of the senator's supporters were dismayed by Seward's three-hour speech of January 29, which was designed to position him for the fall in what were already being dubbed "swing states." Gone was his inflammatory terminology of earlier years. In place of an "irrepressible conflict," Seward now implored his southern colleagues to "distinguish between [the] legitimate and constitutional resistance to the extension of slavery" practiced by Republicans and the "unconstitutional aggression against slavery" waged by militant abolitionist John Brown. Reading the speech in Boston, William Lloyd Garrison insisted that "thousands" of New England Republicans were "mortified, disappointed, and privately indignant" at Seward's "cautious, calculating, retreating policy." Adams found himself torn between his personal fondness for Seward, who regarded himself as a disciple of John Quincy Adams, and his political connections to Sumner, who was furious about the speech. "The movement against Mr. Seward is earnest and active," Adams admitted. When New Hampshire senator John P. Hale came to dine, he hinted to Abby that "somebody had to interfere" and tell

Seward to step aside for the good of the party. Hale thought that Charles Francis "was the proper man to do it." But while Adams agreed that "Seward may not be the strongest man to run," the senator would "never forgive" him if he broached the subject. In any case, it remained unclear to Adams what other candidate "might carry the day" in November.[26]

Unlike Seward, Adams honestly feared that "the federal government [was] slowly but steadily losing its character of a free republic" and that southern influence in Washington tended toward "the renunciation of the principles which animated the revolutionary struggle." All new congressmen were expected to deliver a maiden speech, but Adams chose to wait until June 2; by that date, the presidential season would be well under way. Word quickly spread that Adams intended to speak, and the chamber filled. "There were no loiterers in the cloak rooms, no writers at the tables, none reading newspapers; all were earnest, anxious listeners," one Ohio journalist reported. Because he was the son of John Quincy, "even pages" expected fireworks. The congressman "bears a very strong resemblance to his late father," a second journalist remarked. "Quite bald, light complexioned, quiet and unobtrusive in manners, accessible and easy," Adams "dressed with great simplicity and plainness."[27]

Ostensibly a reply to an unnamed colleague from Mississippi, Adams's lengthy oration was a classic free-soil disquisition, in that Adams challenged the prerogatives of southern politicians and questioned their concerns without ever once expressing sympathy for enslaved Americans. "Ninety members stand upon this floor" because of seats bestowed upon the South by the three-fifths compromise, Adams alleged, and in addition they controlled nearly half of the Senate, more than half of the cabinet, and five of nine Supreme Court slots. Over the decades, however, the "old revolutionary dogma that slavery was an evil" had given way to the "modern dictum that slavery was a benefit to the African, and a positive blessing to the master." The South, Adams concluded, had abandoned "the fundamental principles of the Declaration," leaving it to the Republicans to "maintain the cause of freedom and free institutions. *There can be no compromise whatever on this issue.*"[28]

Charles Francis Adams's reelection to Congress in 1860 coincided with Lincoln's victory and the secession of South Carolina. As a moderate Republican, the congressman found himself caught between his desire to forge a compromise that might save the Union—created in part by his grandfather—without abandoning his long-held free-soil principles. *Courtesy of Library of Congress.*

As he delivered his speech, Adams stood not by his desk but near what had come to be known as "the imaginary Mason and Dixon's line" between clusters of Republican and Democratic desks. His position was no accident. By that date, the Democrats were in disarray. As did Seward, Adams had assumed that Illinois Senator Stephen A. Douglas would gain his party's nomination when the Democrats gathered in Charleston on April 23. Republicans loathed Douglas for overturning the ban on slavery in the upper Midwest with his Kansas-Nebraska bill, a view shared by Charles Francis Jr., who enjoyed comparing Sumner's "air of large refinement" with Douglas, a "squab, vulgar little man, with an immense frowsy head." But the gamble of popular sovereignty was not guarantee enough for southern Democrats, who demanded federal protection for slavery in the territories. Douglas's delegates numbered a majority, but not the two-thirds required for nomination. After ten angry, fruitless days, the Democrats adjourned, with plans to meet again on June 18 in Baltimore. Most Republicans rejoiced at the implosion of the once-dominant Democrats, with only Adams thinking that the Charleston debacle "has elated our friends more than I think is altogether justifiable." All would be different, he admitted, should the squabbling sections fail again in Baltimore and end up making "separate nominations."[29]

The Republican national convention had met in Chicago on May 15. Adams did not attend, but as Charles Francis Jr. later observed, he "was an earnest, though quiet, advocate" of Seward. In truth, he was more than that. Earlier in the month, Adams assured journalist Edward Pierce that were it within his power, he "should select Mr. Seward, as the representative of the ideas of the party [and] as the most efficient laborer in the cause" of free soil. The choice posed a problem within the family, however, as Sumner, who held the safest of Senate seats, was bitterly critical of Seward's sudden moderation. "The two men would have disliked each other by instinct had they lived in different planets," Henry commented. "Each was created only for exasperating the other." As a longtime friend of Sumner, Adams hoped to somehow mediate between the radical senator and his new ally on Capitol Hill.[30]

Concerned that Seward would not run well in Pennsylvania, Indiana, and Illinois—all states captured by Buchanan in 1856—the convention instead nominated Abraham Lincoln, a former one-term congressman, on the third ballot. Having believed that the "present drift is clearly toward Mr. Seward," Adams was stunned by the news. Publicly, Adams assured his constituents that "the republican nomination seems to be generally acceptable" and would most likely prove victorious in November. Privately, the Massachusetts congressman had his doubts. The relatively obscure Lincoln, he suspected, was far from "timid," quite sound "on the slave question," and both "honest and tolerably capable." But Lincoln had "no experience and no business habits." Regarding the former concern, Adams was correct enough, although Buchanan's lengthy résumé had not protected his administration from failure. And as Adams was to discover in coming years, Lincoln was the most industrious of politicians.[31]

The Adams family knew a good deal about crushed hopes and lost elections. Adams immediately wrote to Seward. "No statesman of the first class is likely to be called to the Presidency," he counseled. "Yet your services are more necessary to the cause than they ever were," he added, trusting that Seward would "indulge no notions of retirement." In fact, after thirty years in public life, Seward had informed his overjoyed wife, Frances, that he was considering just that. On May 30 he returned to Washington from his home in Auburn. That evening, as he dined with the Adamses, Seward promised that, while he intended to "withdraw himself from public life," he would do so only after campaigning for Lincoln that fall. Adams assured his friend of his "great satisfaction at the last idea" but lobbied against his retiring to Auburn. Seward should quit the Senate only if called to serve in Lincoln's cabinet, he argued, as the "new President should not be left to a cabinet, which from his want of experience will necessarily be the guide of his system." Seward remained noncommittal.[32]

Complicating matters both for Adams and for the nation, remnants of the Whig and the so-called "Know-Nothing" Parties met in Baltimore in mid-May to create the Constitutional Union Party, an organization dedicated solely to compromise and sectional reconciliation. The short-lived party selected as their presidential nominee John Bell, a former Tennessee senator who both owned and leased slaves for his iron foundries, and for vice president Adams's brother-in-law Edward Everett. But even before the death of Abby's sister, the two men had not been close, and Everett had sided with the Whigs against the Free Soil ticket in 1848. Adams fretted that "the so-called Constitutional Union party" might damage his Republicans in the lower North. "The tardiness with which the people of the Free States come up to a sense of their duty on this inevitable slave question may yet postpone our success." Better news arrived in June, when the Democrats met again but failed to advance a unified ticket. Instead, as Adams remarked, "the great democratic organization has finally burst into pieces," resulting in the separate presidential nominations of Douglas and Vice President John C. Breckinridge, an ardent proslavery Kentuckian. The dissolution of the last remaining bisectional party elevated Republican prospects. Even so, Adams wondered if northern voters understood "what the crisis requires of them." Thinking of many of his colleagues in the House, Adams "almost tremble[d] at the answer to the question."[33]

In mid-August, Seward arrived in Boston, having spoken around Massachusetts. Adams and his son Charles Francis met him at the station and drove him to the old family estate in Quincy. Seward's purpose was to propose that Charles Francis Sr. accompany him on a western political tour, an idea, Adams sourly noted, "for which [he] had not the smallest fancy." But Seward turned Adams's previous arguments against him, insisting that they both had the "duty" to help elect Lincoln. Hearing that Charles Francis Jr. was bored with his legal duties, Seward suggested that he too join the expedition, adding that his daughter Fanny and her friend Ellen Perry intended to accompany him. Privately, Adams worried that Seward was less interested in the campaign than in having the opportunity to persuade him to assist in "the construction of the incoming administration" by accepting a cabinet post. But Charles Francis Jr. "eagerly caught at the idea" and prevailed on his father "to fall into it." Ten days later, Adams wrote to Seward to say that they would both join the excursion and that if business called him back to Massachusetts, Charles Francis Jr. planned to continue on without him.[34]

The group rendezvoused in Albany on September 1. When they reached Syracuse, the party was joined by General James Nye, a local politician, and his seventeen-year-old daughter Mary. Charles Francis Jr. thought the elder Nye "excellent company" but was especially taken with Mary, whom he described as a "pretty, bright girl, with whom I became very intimate." The young Harvard graduate was also impressed by Seward's prodigious "consumption of liquors and cigars" during their journey. Charles Francis Jr. took up cigars as well, and the two smoked so heavily that they were routinely asked to relocate to the baggage car. "When it came to drinking, Seward was, for a man of sixty, a free liver," Charles Francis Jr. remarked. "At times his brandy-and-water would excite him, and set his tongue going," while in other moments he "was very fond of champagne; and when loaded, his tongue wagged." Despite that, at each stop Seward impressed his young friend by delivering "really remarkable speeches in rapid succession."[35]

It was approaching midnight when the train reached Kalamazoo, Michigan, and even the ever-cautious Charles Francis Sr. was enthralled by a crowd of 1,000 strong, together with "100 Wide-awakes," young Republican men who paraded about in black capes and fatigue caps while bearing torches. The next day's weather was a "cold, drizzling rain," but as many as 15,000 people from the city and surrounding counties braved the weather to hear Seward, Adams, and Nye speak. Seward thought the turnout spectacular, shouting that he "found everywhere a spirit and enthusiasm unsurpassed, a zeal that needed no stimulation." Charles Francis Jr. also gaped at the throng, but unlike the energetic campaigner, he quickly grew weary of the journey's hardships. "The eating-houses were wretched," he complained, "and the hotels overgrown taverns."[36]

The senior Adams left the tour for a speaking engagement in Philadelphia before they reached Springfield, Illinois. Lincoln had considered traveling to Chicago to meet the group, but his advisors persuaded him to let the former front-runner come to him. "It was the first time I ever saw Lincoln," Charles Francis Jr. later wrote. Lincoln boarded the car with Lyman Trumbull, an Illinois senator and a critic of Seward's. "'Old Abe' was a revelation," Charles Francis Jr. marveled. "There he was, tall, shambling, plain and good-natured." Trumbull conducted the introductions as they stood in the aisle, almost as if a "couple of ordinary businessmen" had encountered each other on a packed train, Charles Francis thought. When Seward introduced the members of his party, Lincoln gazed down at Charles Francis, saying only, "A son of Charles Francis Adams? I am glad to see you, Sir." As Lincoln left the car, Adams thought he "saw a look of interest" cross his face. Like his father, however, Charles Francis Jr. was generally unimpressed by the candidate. Lincoln had a "mild, dreamy, meditative eye which one would scarcely expect to see in a successful chief magistrate."[37]

Just days later, Charles Francis Jr. met yet another presidential aspirant when their train arrived in Toledo, Ohio. In the middle of the night, Adams was awakened with shouts of "Where's Seward?" Peering out of his sleeping berth, Charles Francis recognized Senator Douglas, who had spoken there earlier in the evening. "Come, Governor, they want to see you," Douglas insisted. "Come out and speak to the boys." Seward was polite but begged off as being "sleepy." Douglas "had a bottle of whiskey" in hand and was "more than half drunk," and as he watched Douglas leave the car, the senator threw back his head "to take a drink." Charles was not much surprised when Douglas died of cirrhosis of the liver eleven months later at the age of forty-eight.[38]

The Adamses were all back in Massachusetts when on October 17, Henry sailed into Boston aboard the *Arabia*. "I was cheered to see him come home safe," Charles Francis Sr. reflected, noting that his third son, now twenty-two, was already balding and had picked up a "few grey hairs." All of Charles Francis Sr.'s children were home to greet Henry, excepting Louisa, who planned to return shortly after the new year. Henry witnessed one procession of Wide Awakes "stretching in ranks of torches along the hill-side," as they marched to the Adams home, where the congressman received them with a short speech. Adams doubted that Henry's two years of study abroad had prepared him to practice law at home and suggested instead that his son act as his private secretary when Congress resumed in December. "Profoundly ignorant, anxious and curious," Henry admitted, he "packed his modest trunks again" in preparation for Washington.[39]

Election Day fell on Tuesday, November 6. With four candidates in the contest, Lincoln gathered 1,865,908 ballots, or just 39.8 percent of the total popular vote. In the electoral count, however, Lincoln carried every northern state except New Jersey, which he split with Douglas. His tally reached 180 electoral votes, far more than the 152 required to win, and 57 more than his four rivals' combined count of 123. Republicans captured 62.8 percent of the vote in Massachusetts and carried every county in the state. Democrats did not even bother to put forth a candidate in the state's Third District, and Adams easily bested Constitutional Union candidate Leverett Saltonstall 10,521 to 7,508. "There is now scarcely a shadow of doubt that the great revolution has actually taken place," Adams exulted. The "country has once [and] for all thrown off the domination of slaveholders." Adams was also thrilled to discover that his own victory was "by a majority greater even than the plurality I had two years ago." Days later, however, he chided himself for boasting: "Lord, suffer not thy servant to be puffed up with vain glory." Even so, Adams was pleased enough to believe that "the outside world" now regarded him as more than simply "the son of my father." His position in Congress was "not unworthy of

[his] ancestry," he mused, and his political fortune was ample for all "reasonable desires."[40]

Five days later, Adams wrote to Seward, imploring him to remain in Washington and work with the incoming administration. *"Of course* Mr. Lincoln will offer you the chief place in his Cabinet," Adams counseled. "I trust no considerations will deter you from accepting it." Concerned that the inexperienced president-elect was not the man for the impending crisis, Adams believed that Seward was "the only person who can give the country confidence that the administration will be capable." After Lincoln tendered the position of secretary of state to Seward on December 8, Adams again "prayed him to meet the responsibility." When Seward at last agreed to serve, Adams was "greatly relieved" by the news, "first, because he is in the government; second, because I am not."[41]

Adams's fear that he might be offered a position in Lincoln's cabinet was not an idle one. Even before the election was decided, former congressman John Gorham Palfrey had written to Lincoln to suggest that his state deserved a seat in the cabinet. "We have in New England a man singularly qualified for a position," he observed. "I refer to Mr. Charles Francis Adams." His education, Palfrey added, "was conducted under singular advantages, in the houses of his father & grandfather." Newspapers in Lincoln's Midwest reported that other Massachusetts Republicans "recommended Charles Francis Adams for a seat in Mr. Lincoln's Cabinet." However, Adams was not merely content with his rising power and influence in Congress; he also feared that even with Seward onboard, Lincoln's administration would be a rocky one. Scarcely a day passed, Adams noted, without somebody expressing "his wish that I should be in the cabinet," and just ten days after his reelection, Adams caught rumors that his name was being discussed "as a proper person for the Treasury." Horrified, he contacted Palfrey, asking him to desist and promising that if "the New England member" hailed from Connecticut, he would "be relieved by" the news. If the president-elect called upon him to serve, Adams knew, he would be honor-bound to accept, so he indulged himself in his semiannual desire to retire and live on his newly acquired farm. "This kind of life scarcely suits me," he scribbled into his diary on November 15. "I am beginning to feel the effects of it."[42]

THREE DAYS AFTER WORD OF LINCOLN'S ELECTION REACHED SOUTH Carolina, James Chesnut became the first southerner to quit his seat in the Senate. The following morning, South Carolina's other senator, James Henry Hammond, withdrew as well, as did a number of federal judges and US attorneys. Adams regarded the state's impending departure as nothing less than an assault on American democracy. "Secession is boldly declared at once," he observed, the "only cause assigned for it being the election of Abraham Lincoln by a strictly constitutional vote." Adams was less sure as to whether Carolina planters truly intended to secede, suggesting that their rhetoric was designed to force the president-elect to abandon his free-soil positions and "declare himself in opposition to the principles of the party that has elected him." Doubting the ability of a handful of states to survive as an independent nation, Adams was almost willing "to wish them to go on in their experiment." With southern Democrats temporarily absent from Washington, Republicans could control both chambers, "establish their authority in the federal government, and the whole game is played."[43]

President James Buchanan sent his annual address to Congress on December 3. Seward guessed that Buchanan might attempt to placate the South by attacking "the Free States and most especially Massachusetts," and hoping to defuse the mounting crisis, he encouraged Adams to prevail upon his state congressional delegation not "to speak on the spur of the moment." Buchanan's message was even worse than Seward had feared. The "immediate peril," Buchanan charged, arose from "the incessant and violent agitation of the slavery question throughout the North for the last quarter of the century," which "produced its malignant influence on the slaves, and inspired them with vague notions of freedom." Listening as a clerk droned out the message, Adams judged it "in all respects like the author. Timid and vacillating in the face of Slaveholding rebellion, bold and insulting towards his countrymen who he does not fear." Buchanan should "be impeached," Adams concluded. Always kinder toward his father than was his older brother, Henry was impressed by Adams's resolution. "Our father is firmer than Mt. Ararat," he assured Charles. "I never saw a more precious old flint."[44]

Delegates from across South Carolina convened in Charleston on December 20. Their first order of business was to rename Institute Hall—the same building that had played host to the Democratic convention the previous spring—as Secession Hall. The vote to repeal the act of May 23, 1788, that had ratified the Constitution was a unanimous 169 to 0. Adams now understood that this was no bluff, and he supposed that a "few of the Cotton States will follow." He yet hoped that the brief moment of southern independence would prove a failure, "after which they might come [back] in and very likely would be cured of their madness forever." Either way, he resolutely opposed Buchanan's proposal that Republicans turn their backs on the voters who had cast their ballots for Free Soil candidates. "Must we consent to insert pledges in the Constitution that *we* will uphold, perpetuate and extend slavery in one half of the Union?" he asked Dana. Noting the South's abandonment of its professed love of states' rights, southern whites had no "grievance to complain of," he instructed one constituent, "excepting the refusal" to "establish slavery under the direction of the Federal Government" in the territories "stolen from our Mexican neighbors."[45]

Having agreed to serve as his father's secretary—and having once again abandoned all thoughts of the law—Henry accepted his brother Charles Francis's advice to also practice political journalism. "We can't help it," Henry told his mother. "This taste for politics is a perfect mania in us." The Adams name won him the title of Washington correspondent for the *Boston Daily Advertiser*, and with his pen, he decided, he might play a small role in helping to shape public opinion at home. As his editorials were to be anonymous, Henry could defend any position his father might choose to take. Initially, at least, Henry embraced Sumner's view that all the North had to do was to hold firm, and the South, "like petulant, passionate children, prone to violence," would quickly yield. "No

compromise that a republican could offer would stand a chance of acceptance with them," he posted on December 27. But after Henry realized
that Seward was advocating compromise and that his father, while far
less optimistic than the New Yorker, thought accommodation might be
possible, he too began to defend moderation. "Sumner always acts with
his eye on his personal figure before posterity," the disillusioned Henry
cautioned his brother Charles Francis, while "our father [keeps] his eye on
the national future."[46]

As did many northerners, Charles Francis Sr. and Henry believed that
the nation's fate resided not with the president-elect but with Seward,
often dubbed "Mr. Republican." The difficulty, Adams supposed, was not
to give in to Lower South demands while providing "the Union party
of the [Upper] South an opportunity to contest the elections next summer with the secessionists." Adams believed that the only member of the
incoming administration able to retain the confidence of the North "in
such a process would be Mr. Seward." With president-elect Lincoln yet
in Springfield and Seward in Washington, the senator, Henry told his
brother Charles Francis, was the "virtual ruler of this country." Lincoln
would require a seasoned hand at the helm, and "Seward will be Premier."
Charles Francis Sr. would remain in the House, gaining "national fame
and power inferior to no one unless it be Seward," Henry added. Then it
would be Adams's turn "to be Premier, in '64." Charles Francis Jr., still in
Massachusetts, agreed that his father and Seward were the "chief concil-
iators" but thought that "the secession movement had by its force, volume
and intensity taken [Seward] by surprise." Either because of hindsight or
simply because he was far less infatuated with his father than was Henry,
Charles Jr. later judged the two as "wholly wrong in basing any hopes on
this misconception of the real attitude and feelings of the South."[47]

In hopes of slowing the secession movement, House Speaker William Pennington, a New Jersey Republican, created a committee tasked
with forging yet another sectional compromise. The numerically equitable
group of sixteen Republicans, fourteen Democrats, and three Constitutional Unionists was chaired by Ohio Republican Thomas Corwin and
was quickly labeled the Committee of Thirty-Three. Adams agreed to

serve, but while one journalist praised the committee members as "all very excellent men," Adams worried that some "were selected mainly on account of their conservatism, to use the popular phrase for pliability." The committee met for the first time on December 11 and promptly got off to a rocky start when Albert Rust, an Arkansas Democrat, introduced a resolution claiming that "the existing discontents among the Southern people, and the growing hostility among them to the Federal Government, are not without cause." Adams was predictably unimpressed. Southern members could point to "little beyond alarms and apprehensions" of what might happen once Lincoln was inaugurated, he fumed. Rust's resolution "was curious from its utter want of any real ground for the revolution they are initiating."[48]

At about the same time, the Senate followed suit with the creation of a Select Committee of Thirteen. The roster boasted many of the leading men in the Senate, including a good number of southerners—Mississippi's Jefferson Davis, Georgia's Robert Toombs, and Virginia's James M. Mason—who had no interest in compromise and were merely marking time until their states withdrew from the Union. But Seward and Douglas also served on the committee, as did John J. Crittenden, a seventy-three-year-old Kentucky Whig turned Constitutional Unionist esteemed as the *"Pater Senatus,"* the oldest member of the Senate. On December 22, Adams found himself at a dinner with the Kentucky senator. As the party was breaking up, Adams heard Crittenden loudly announce that the fate of the nation "was in his hands." Turning, Adams realized Crittenden was speaking of him. Crittenden touched Adams's arm, saying, "This is the man." Evidently, the Kentuckian believed that Adams was not merely a leading member of the House but a man destined for a spot in Lincoln's cabinet. Adams noted in his diary that he "laughed as if enjoying the joke." Although he had heard rumors to that effect, he had "not the smallest reason to believe that it is more than one of the thousand passing noises that float through this metropolis."[49]

That did not mean, however, that Adams was opposed to Crittenden's hopes of compromise, particularly if proposed solutions did not violate the Republican platform and served to dampen secessionist plans in the

Upper South. "I do not believe it becomes a victorious party to be surly and vindictive," Adams remarked. He announced himself willing to at least "listen to the complaints of the defeated" party and section. If their demands were "unreasonable things, they should be firmly refused." But neither could Adams countenance those antislavery voices who desired the South to go in peace. If "the dissolution of the Union *is in any way promoted by us*," Adams warned John A. Andrew, recently elected governor of Massachusetts, that would amount to a "great political blunder, if not a crime."[50]

Although it was painful to contemplate, given his youthful labors in the state assembly, Adams was even willing to consider repealing or modifying northern personal-liberty laws, a position also endorsed by Seward and the president-elect. Lower South secessionists cared little about the issue, as runaways from Alabama or Mississippi stood little chance of reaching Canada or Massachusetts. But petty slaveholders in Virginia and Maryland could be bankrupted by the loss of even four young bondmen. Should House Republicans urge repeal of state laws that provided jury trials or writs of habeas corpus for accused fugitives, Adams told one constituent, that might provide anti-secession moderates "some help in the April elections in Virginia." Minor changes, although repugnant to the abolitionist community, would not violate his Latimer law but would grant Upper South members of the committee a "graceful opportunity for reciprocation" on other issues. Privately, Adams doubted that even New York's tough personal-liberty laws "had any effect at all" in assisting runaways, as the Fugitive Slave Act was unenforceable in much of the state. If southern demands on this issue were merely a "pretext," the wise response was to call their bluff. Henry agreed, warning his more critical brother Charles Francis that "if Virginia goes out," he did "not see how [war] is to be avoided."[51]

Rather harder to justify was Adams's willingness to compromise on the vast New Mexico Territory. Although the 1860 Republican platform was technically silent on New Mexico, it had denied "the authority of Congress, of a territorial legislature, or of any individuals, to give legal existence to Slavery in any Territory." But in the Senate, Crittenden proposed an amendment to extend the Missouri Compromise line to the Pacific, thereby permanently protecting "slavery of the African race" in the Southwest, and Adams believed that some concession was necessary, if only to avoid Crittenden's openly proslavery suggestion. Congressman Henry Winter Davis, a Maryland Republican, suggested the House committee simply bypass the territorial stage and immediately grant statehood to New Mexico (which stretched from Texas to California). Because New Mexico's residents could then write a state constitution with or without slavery, Davis's proposal amounted to an acceptance of Douglas's popular sovereignty. In exchange for this concession, Adams insisted, the South should agree that "all the rest of the [Mexican Cession] territory north of the compromise parallel was to make a second state," which presumably would opt against slavery.[52]

Adams reached this position after the committee spoke with a federal judge who had lived in New Mexico for nine years. The testimony confirmed Adams's suspicions that the dry Southwest was inhospitable to "any system of African slavery," which "flourishes only in rich agricultural regions." Although this widely shared view ignored the fact that some southerners coveted the region for its mining potential, or that rivers and canals could in time irrigate cotton estates, Adams at least had data on his side. Because the Compromise of 1850 allowed for both the New Mexico and Utah Territories to be settled under the guise of popular sovereignty, slaveholders had already had ten years to emigrate into the region. Yet the recent census revealed that there were but twelve slaves in the territory, and those, Adams observed, were "mostly females, domestics brought by the Government" officials and army officers. "I doubt if there be a single male field hand in the whole region," he assured a correspondent. Southern whites, of course, were reluctant to carry their expensive human property into territories that might liberate them upon statehood, which was why they insisted on the extension of the Missouri line. For Adams, to agree to such an amendment was no compromise but a capitulation of Republican policy.[53]

As a man of the law, Adams also reminded puzzled constituents that Congress had already allowed for the possibility of slavery in the Southwest as part of the 1850 compromise and that following the 1857 *Dred Scott* decision, which prohibited Congress from banning slavery in the territories, Roger B. Taney's Supreme Court would surely rule against federal attempts to flatly prohibit slavery in New Mexico. The moderate Washington *National Republican* endorsed Adams's "statesmanlike" position of allowing New Mexico's residents to decide, noting that the late Zachary Taylor had been "in favor of similar action more than ten years since." The newspaper also agreed that because the words "New Mexico" had not appeared in the Republican platform, Adams's solution did "not conflict with" the party's free-soil roots, before confounding its own argument by noting that his position was supported by voters who had cast ballots for Douglas, Bell, and Everett, none of them, of course, Republicans.[54]

The angry mood of what Henry Adams was to call "the secession winter" was not sympathetic to voices of moderation. Any hopes of sectional reconciliation were troubled by the resignation of committee members as their states voted for secession, as well as by southern demands that the Missouri line not only be extended westward but that slavery also be protected by the federal government in any Mexican territory that might be acquired in future years. As Adams complained to former New York senator John A. Dix, he and Ohio Republican Corwin were prepared to settle the Utah and New Mexico question, but his compromise was rebuffed by southern men who demanded that lands "hereafter wrested from the hands of Mexico [become] a slaveholding empire." A furious Crittenden warned Adams that he was "the greatest block in the way of conciliation" and that without congressional guarantees, New Mexico would essentially enter the Union as a "Free State." That prospect, of course, was precisely what Adams hoped for. Despite Crittenden's endless pleas for bisectional compromise, Adams understood that what the Kentuckian had in mind was nothing but a package of northern concessions. "Our good father in considering the ultimatum of the south," Henry assured Charles Francis Jr., would rather "see the Union dissolved" than see the

Constitution "turned into an instrument discountenancing freedom and protecting slavery."[55]

For many Republicans, however, Adams's willingness to negotiate amounted to a repudiation of their November victory. "The *worst* thing I have seen is Adams's *dodge* to admit New Mexico into the Union, really as a Slave State," an irate New Hampshire editor wrote to Lincoln. "The scheme is a scheme of treason to Republicanism, and will ruin those Republicans who indorse it." One home-state supporter, Judge Jacob Collamer, wrote to warn Adams that he never could "be reelected in Massachusetts on such a measure." As ever, Adams was confident that his course was correct and was prepared to suffer the consequences. "My letters and the newspapers from home shew a continued stream of indignation against me for what I have done, in regard to the New Mexico proposition," he confided to his journal. "Such are the hazards of politics, in critical times." When journalist Edward Pierce penned a polite dissent, Adams replied that he knew "the difference between surrendering unimportant points and sacrificing principles." Should events prove him wrong, Adams added, "nobody will suffer besides myself." In saying this, Adams again unconsciously identified himself as a white free-soiler rather than as a militant abolitionist, for African Americans who might be sold into New Mexico would obviously "suffer" far more than the wealthy congressman. However, Adams was right enough in reminding Pierce that if Massachusetts voters disagreed, they "will have the coast clear in the third District for a new man."[56]

When the resolution on New Mexico came to a vote on December 29, the remaining southern members of the Committee of Thirty-Three made one final attempt to insert the words "hereafter acquired." After Corwin advanced a motion to strike the phrase, the resolution passed by a vote of 13 to 11, with a majority of Republicans siding with Adams and southerners voting 5 to 2 against. Without a guarantee of a "Compromise line and protections for slavery south of it," Adams crowed to one constituent, "slave-holders would not accept" the compromise. "They consider themselves as having gained nothing by our action." The best evidence that New Mexico "will not remain a slave state," a vindicated Adams told another, was that Missouri and Texas congressmen "voted *against* my proposition." Committee Chairman Corwin, who wished to avoid the appearance of Republican intransigence, praised Adams as "the Archbishop of antislavery," while Henry, still posting anonymous columns in the *Boston Daily Advertiser*, gloated that "the seceders" had at last asserted "their real grievance. Republicans will not guarantee slavery in a Territory they haven't got."[57]

For abolitionists, the possibility, however slight, that New Mexico might become a slave state proved that Republicans were untrustworthy allies. Speaking in Boston, Wendell Phillips, who had united with Adams over protecting fugitive slaves, "denounced the compromise spirit manifested by Mr. Seward and Charles Francis Adams with much severity of language." The growing partnership between Adams and Seward also served to further alienate Sumner. All of Adams's efforts in the Committee of Thirty-Three were based on the hope that small compromises could bolster the influence of those Upper South unionists who had supported Bell months before, while Sumner regarded the immediate admission of New Mexico as "*a fatal dismal mistake*" and an "abandonment of principle." Even Charles Francis Jr., who could rarely be counted on to approve of anything his father did, thought it absurd that Sumner regarded Seward and Adams as "compromisers," a term he believed better suited to "Crittenden and his supporters of his East-and-West line project." As did his father and brother, however, Charles Francis Jr. recognized that no concessions could win back Lower South "extremists." They "were intent on a separate, slave-holding nationality, and nothing short of that."[58]

Henry believed his father's position back home was precarious enough to craft a disingenuous essay for the *Boston Daily Advertiser* in which he passed the blame for the New Mexico issue to other Republicans on the Committee of Thirty-Three. Charles Francis Sr. surely did not see the anonymous piece in advance, as Henry depicted his father as a somewhat passive follower, rather than a decisive leader who embraced Henry Winter Davis's proposal and then persuaded other Republicans to join in support. In any event, the editorial was probably unnecessary. Business-minded Republicans in Massachusetts flooded Congress with petitions totaling 35,000 signatures, begging for concessions to save the country. Some even took Adams to task for not being still more conciliatory.[59]

The disagreement over New Mexico took a nasty personal turn on January 13, 1861, when Sumner and Preston King, New York's other Republican senator, dined at the Adams home. The party remained polite, Henry reported, until late in the evening, when "mamma & Loo and Mary" retired." After King "got his cigar and decanter of wine," the conversation turned to the territorial question, with King criticizing Seward and his host, and Sumner supporting King's positions. As the three sparred, a fascinated Henry "sucked [his] cigar and kept still." Finally, after an inebriated King struck a nerve and Sumner insisted that "the South must be made to bend," Charles Francis Sr. lost his temper. "Sumner, you don't know what you're talking about," he snapped. "Yours is the very kind of stiff-necked obstinacy that will break you down if you persevere." Henry judged his father the winner of the debate, laughing that Sumner, a man he had once idolized, could "no more argue than a cat." A somewhat contrite Sumner returned the next day and "expressed himself much pained at what [Adams] had said." Adams replied that he also regretted saying anything "offensive to him" and offered "all suitable apology." But the damage had been done. "Hereafter there will be no intimacy," Adams told Palfrey.[60]

Promoting his father's views in the northern press, Henry agreed that the Republicans needed to "set themselves right before the country, and to show that they did not wish to force a quarrel upon the South." To that end, Adams and the other Republicans on the committee reluctantly agreed to support what he sourly dubbed the southern "ultimatum, the protection to Slavery nailed on to the constitution." Kentucky's Francis Bristow crafted a simple paragraph that acknowledged slavery as the lawful system in fifteen states and recognized "no authority, legally or otherwise, outside of a State where it so exists, to interfere with slaves or slavery in such States, in disregard of the rights of their owners." Joshua Giddings, who had retired from Congress the previous year, begged Adams to disagree. But as the president-elect signaled that he could endorse any compromise proposal that did not violate the party's platform, committee members felt secure in voting for Bristow's proposed constitutional amendment. Adams even offered to write "the doctrine of the Chicago platform into an Amendment" to prove to worried Upper South members that the incoming administration had no plans "to interfere with slavery in the states" where it already existed. Corwin reported to Lincoln that although "Southern men are theoretically crazy," the amendment and the repeal of personal-liberty laws might spare the nation a "long & bloody civil war."[61]

Corwin scheduled a final meeting of the committee for January 14. The day ended in chaos. Twenty-nine of the original thirty-three were in attendance, but after an acrimonious debate the committee failed to agree on a concise package to recommend to the entire House. Adams submitted a resolution asserting the duty of states to acquiesce in Lincoln's election. After seven southern members refused to vote on the measure, Adams introduced a second resolution stating that because members of the committee refused to acknowledge the validity of Lincoln's victory, "there could be no further discussions." Corwin then advanced Bristow's language on what would have become the Thirteenth Amendment to the Constitution, protecting slavery in the southern states. Adams waited to vote until he "saw how the majority of slaveholders voted," and when most voted no, he too "gave a negative." Their votes against constitutional protections, Adams surmised, "show that they will be pacified by nothing short of the indefinite expansion of slave institutions in the south through the joint agency of money and arms." The committee finally voted to report on whatever measures the chairman might "think proper to submit," and Corwin sent Bristow's amendment to the floor. Adams suspected that the "results [were] pushed forward without any guarantee of support in any quarter," and he drafted a minority report explaining that the amendment "would be powerless to afford a remedy" to the secession crisis. "Now I fear I must make a speech," Adams sighed.[62]

As hope for compromise vanished, Henry observed, talk of "certain civil war" became commonplace, and permanent residents of the capital prepared to ship their wives and children farther north. "The ghost of this murdered republic rises everywhere," Henry wrote, "and meets everyone." It appeared to the third and fourth generations of the Adams family that they were witnessing the death of what the first two generations had created. As for Charles Francis Sr., despite the promises he scribbled into his diary to care only about doing his "duty faithfully" and seeking no "other object in life than that of being useful," the congressman knew that he had to justify himself to the voters of his district. "You don't know how strong the feeling is against him," journalist Edward Pierce cautioned Sumner. "I have not heard of the first constituent who defends him."[63]

On January 31, Adams rose in the House to speak. Moving from his desk to the center of the chamber, Adams gazed up at the "densely packed and breathlessly silent" galleries. A number of senators had crowded into the hall, but Sumner, he observed, "was noticeable for his absence." Adams began by describing the "sublime spectacle" of Americans flocking to the polls for the nineteenth time in their history: "No complaint of unfairness or fraud was heard." Yet even before the electors could gather, South Carolina, without a "single cause, suddenly broke out into violent remonstrance, and dashed into immediate efforts to annul all of their obligations to the Constitution." As he admitted on many occasions, Adams lacked a powerful voice, and southern congressmen moved toward him as they sought to catch each word, some of them perched atop the desks of Republicans.[64]

Adams then chided members of his own party, "rigid friends" who refused "to listen to complaints." These grievances, he suggested, concerned personal-liberty laws, a growing northern population that might one day pass amendments infringing "on the right of the slave States to manage their domestic affairs," and a "denial of equal rights in the Territories." The Fugitive Slave Act of 1850, Adams conceded, was "inoperative in a very large section of the free States" that regarded the return of runaways as "cruel." But was this cause for disunion, he wondered? At present, federal law was on the side of the South, but if southern states abandoned the Union, he warned, "you will never get anything like such security again." As for the territories, Adams reminded, slaveholders had enjoyed the right to carry slaves into the Southwest for ten years, and thanks to Roger

Taney, they could now bring them into *any* territory: "Why do they not use that right? The law of political economy regulates this matter much better than any specific statute." Yet southern members of the Committee of Thirty-Three demanded a constitutional "pledge that we will protect slavery in the States of Sonora, or Coahuila, or Chihuahua, or New Leon, *when we get them.*"[65]

Turning at last to the possibility of future antislavery amendments, Adams gently mocked southern fears. "The chivalrous State of South Carolina frightened!" Here was a complaint, Adams scolded, based upon an "apprehension of what may be done hereafter." Even should Congress at some future day propose an amendment banning slavery, with every free state in agreement, achieving the necessary ratification by three-fourths of all states would require the admission of twenty-seven new free states into the Union, bringing the total number of states to sixty. Since the Corwin committee offered an amendment to protect slavery, did the South not "have a security, so long as this Government shall endure, that no sister State shall dictate any change against their will?" Should war come, Adams concluded, it was no fault of the North, but rather a result of "the willful passions of infatuated men, who demand it of us to destroy the great principles for which our fathers struggled. Rather than this, let the Heavens fall. My duty is performed."[66]

His speech, Adams recorded that evening, lasted eighty minutes, "in silence so that you could have heard a pin drop." At several points, the galleries burst into applause. Louisa, who had arrived home several weeks before, and sixteen-year-old Mary "called him out from the middle of a swarm of people," Henry assured Charles, "and hugged and kissed him in the passage." Others crowded in to shake his hand, with some pronouncing the speech "the finest delivered this session" and one telling Adams he "had equaled the best of my race." It was just as well that he was "old" (he was fifty-three); otherwise, his "head might be turned" by the praise. Henry suspected that the speech would win over his father's Third District constituents and indeed most readers "except the abolitionists and disunionists." The Washington *National Republican* agreed, reporting that it reflected "the eloquence of his grandfather" and was "worthy of the statesmen's blood that courses in its author's veins." Even Alabama's Howell Cobb, within weeks of serving as the president of the Provisional Congress of the Confederate States, thanked Adams for his civility and lack of rancor.[67]

There was little time or reason to celebrate, however. By refusing to permanently set aside all lands south of Utah Territory as slave soil, Adams believed, "the slave-power" had failed in its efforts "to retain its hold on the Government by fraud or force." But until March 4, the presidency remained in the hands of the indecisive James Buchanan, whom Adams believed "guilty of treason [and] at least" worthy of impeachment. "At one moment he authorizes measures to sustain the Law," Adams complained to Palfrey. "At another he recalls them." Yet neither did he believe the president-elect was the man for the troubled hour. Adams thought it "folly" that Lincoln did not publicly endorse all of Seward's positions and so jeopardized "the only hope of the country's salvation." In the Senate, Seward had endorsed the immediate admission of New Mexico as a slave state, and both men understood they had damaged their careers no matter what course the Upper South followed. Dining with the Adamses shortly after Charles Francis Sr.'s speech, a glum Seward announced that "if there's no [further] secession now, you and I are ruined."[68]

On the morning of February 23, Lincoln reached Washington and checked into Willard's Hotel. Seward promptly raced over to call on the president-elect, and the following day Adams and Henry walked over for their first meeting with the incoming president. "Mr. Lincoln is a tall, ill-formed man, with little grace of manner or polish of appearance," Adams thought, "but with a plain, good-natured, frank expression which rather attracts one to him." The two chatted mostly of Lincoln's trip from Philadelphia and the threats to his party as they passed through Maryland. Henry was more taken with John Hay, one of Lincoln's two private secretaries. "Friends are born, not made," Henry later wrote of Hay, and from "the first slight meeting in February and March, 1861, he recognized Hay as a friend, and never lost sight of him." The Indiana-born Hay was then twenty-three, Henry's age. Educated at Brown University, Hay was also about Henry's height, and Henry's drooping mustache matched his new friend's. Sumner soon arrived to greet Lincoln, so the Adamses took their leave.[69]

On March 4 the entire Adams family ventured to the capitol to witness the inauguration. The congressman elbowed his way into the Senate chamber while the rest of the family secured seats above in the gallery. At noon, Lincoln and Buchanan walked in together, and once again, the Illinois attorney failed to impress the Brahmins. Charles Francis Jr. judged the aged outgoing president "the more presentable man of the two" and groused that Lincoln's simple suit "did not indicate that knowledge of the proprieties of the place which was desirable." His father agreed: "Mr. Lincoln looked awkward and out of place." The procession then moved out to the Eastern Portico, where Lincoln, standing on what Charles Jr. complained was a "miserable scaffold," began to speak to the assembled crowd.[70]

Rather to his surprise, the senior Adams approved of the new president's address. "As a whole it was well timed, and raised my opinion of the man," he admitted. "It was fortunate in pleasing both wings of the party, and bringing all to stand upon a common ground." Lincoln insisted that "he intended no war, but that his duty was by his oath to see the laws were faithfully executed." Adams was especially pleased to hear Lincoln endorse the Corwin amendment. "Of all people I had the greatest occasion to be gratified," he thought, "as the amendment which was the main point in the policy which goes by my name has thus been fully justified in the face of the country by the head of the nation as well as of the republican party." As ever at such moments, Adams guessed that his fame could never rise to greater heights, and he thought he "should be fortunate if I closed my political career now." "I have gained all that I can for myself, and I shall never have such another opportunity," Adams supposed, "to benefit my country."[71]

That evening, the Adamses attended the inaugural ball at City Hall, where their brief flash of praise for Lincoln abruptly ended. Henry denounced the affair as "melancholy," and his father was unimpressed by the first couple. "They are evidently wanting in all the arts to grace their position," Adams remarked. "He is simple, awkward and hearty. She is more artificial and pretentious." Mary Adams wished to be introduced to the First Lady, and upon presenting his young daughter, Adams was irritated to discover that the president had forgotten who he was. "Were it anybody but a Western man I should have construed it as an intentional slight," he fumed. "But we cannot measure such a free and easy people by the standard of courtly civilization." Henry also believed Lincoln's thoughts to be elsewhere, his "mind absent in part." In time, the family would come to change their views of the president's abilities, but only very slowly. "Had young Adams been told that his life was to hang on the correctness of his estimate of the new president," Henry conceded in later years, "he would have lost."[72]

With the thirty-sixth Congress concluded, the Adamses began to prepare for their return to Boston. Henry and Charles Francis Jr. found time to dine at Arlington plantation with "Rooney" Lee, Henry's failed Harvard classmate. Charles Francis found Rooney's sister Eleanor Agnes Lee to be "extremely attractive," but he wondered whether he might soon be "arrayed against" the young Virginians who made up the rest of the party. Neither Adams, despite being the sons of a pioneering free-soil politician, bothered to comment on the domestic slaves who served their food and cleared the dishes.[73]

Congressman Adams watched in dismay as Lincoln ignored Secretary Seward's recommendations of appeasement, believing that if left alone, southern tempers might cool and wise voices of unionism could seize control of events. Having regarded Buchanan's response to secession to be one "of feebleness," Adams now feared that "the course of the new president [was] drifting the country into war." Lincoln was reluctant to abandon the besieged Fort Sumter in Charleston Harbor, which was rapidly running out of supplies. "For my part I see nothing but incompetency in the head," Adams fretted. "The man is not equal to the hour." Upon reaching Boston, Adams again threatened his diary with retirement. "As brilliant as has been my brief career in public life," he told himself, he longed to put Washington behind him and, "for whatever was left of my days," prepare his father's papers for publication. Just as predictably, his son Charles thought his father quite "wrong in his inclination." So desirous was Adams for compromise, Charles Jr. wrote, "he failed to see that the time for action had at last come, and the issue must be met." The two disagreed about Fort Sumter, with Charles Jr. later claiming that his father's "horror of civil war was such that I find myself at a loss to fix the point on which he would have made a stand." Although it would be men of young Charles's age who would have to fight, he recognized that by late March, the choices were war or a "peaceable separation," and that he opposed.[74]

Nobody in the Adams household was surprised to read that at 4:30 in the morning of April 12, South Carolina shore batteries opened fire on the fort. Adams still believed that his policy, and Seward's, of conciliation had been the proper one. He thought the event a "perfect verification of Governor Seward's prediction that the President, instead of withdrawing Major [Robert] Anderson at once, and appearing thereby to act magnanimously, would hesitate and delay and thus end by doing the thing from necessity." Two days later, Adams continued to blame the outbreak of war on Lincoln, but he had come to hope that the results might justify the carnage. "Perhaps this is not in the end to be regretted so much, as the Slave States have always been troublesome and dictatorial partners." Yet the president, Adams thought, lacked anything like a "systematic plan adequate to the emergency." However, he professed to take considerable solace in the fact that he was not needed in Washington until the following December. "On the whole I feel so little confidence that it is a fortunate thing," he insisted, perhaps in hope of convincing himself that he was not offered a position with the administration where "confidence would be most needed."[75]

5

"PROFOUNDLY ANXIOUS FOR THE SAFETY OF THE COUNTRY"

The Minister

THE TELEGRAM ARRIVED JUST BEFORE BREAKFAST ON TUESDAY, March 19, 1861. Richard Henry Dana, the writer, activist, and attorney who had mentored Charles Francis Jr., stopped by to visit the Adamses, only just returned from Washington. Despite their recent estrangement over the New Mexico question, Charles Sumner continued to regard the congressman as a "political & personal friend," and his telegram announced that President Abraham Lincoln had submitted the name of Charles Francis Adams to the Senate as the new minister to Great Britain. The news "fell on our breakfast-table like a veritable bombshell, scattering confusion and dismay," Charles Francis Jr. scribbled into his diary. Abby, who just the previous fall had fretted about spending the winter in Washington, burst into tears, "absolutely refusing to be comforted," Charles Francis observed, while his father "looked dismayed."[1]

And with good reason. Thanks to the voracious British appetite for southern cotton, as well as the English aristocracy's long-standing affection for southern landlords, Parliament could be expected to lean toward

Confederate independence. Adams was also surely aware of the irony of the grandson of John Adams—who in Holland and France had argued in behalf of foreign recognition of American rebels—demanding the British government now do no such thing regarding southern renegades. Additionally, a posting abroad meant dividing his family, perhaps for years. Remembering his own childhood in Russia and the years he was unable to see his brothers as painful, part of him undoubtedly agreed with his son Henry's judgment that John Quincy had been "abominably selfish" and even "demonic" in separating Louisa from most of her children.[2]

The following day's newspapers confirmed the telegram. But official word from either Lincoln or Secretary of State William Henry Seward had yet to reach Adams, prompting him to await making a decision. While Abby remained disconsolate, her children were less distressed. Only sixteen, Mary delighted in the prospect of a lengthy stay in Britain. Louisa and her husband had never intended to remain long in America, and as Henry had abandoned any fantasies about practicing law, he could continue as his father's secretary in London while finding time to visit his sister as she wandered about Europe. Charles Francis Jr. had no desire to go abroad but judged it a very good prospect for his parents. After thirty years in Boston, he thought, they "had grown into a rut." Although Abby had proved to be a superb Washington hostess, she "took a constitutional and sincere pleasure in the forecast of evil," Charles Francis Jr. supposed. In a passage harsh even by the family's standards, Charles Francis Jr. told his diary—and years later, the reading public—that his mother "delighted in the dark side of anticipation [and] indulged in the luxury of woe!" Breaking free "of the atmosphere of Boston," he suspected, would ultimately cheer them both "amazingly."[3]

For once, Charles Francis Sr.'s indecision on the appointment was no pose. As he pondered the positive and negative aspects of the position in his diary, Adams could find good reason to either accept or reject it. Should he remain in Massachusetts, he could hold his House seat for as long as he wished, and the previous session had shown him to be a congressman of growing influence. "Here [in Congress] my father had most memorably developed his great abilities," Adams remembered. "Here both Mr Clay and Mr Webster had laid the foundation of their political fortunes." With "the retirement of other prominent [southern] men from the House," Adams, wrote, he would have greater clout yet in the coming session. He assured himself that whatever decision he made, "one thing is certain, that no solicitation of mine has ever been the means of placing me there." Yet in the privacy of his journal, Adams quite nearly admitted a desire for still higher office, as he feared a long, "comparative retirement on the other side of the water" might cripple his political career. Even his own constituents might forget his service and grow loyal to whoever replaced him during his absence.[4]

In its favor, the appointment demonstrated "the growth of Mr Seward's influence," which Adams thought a "favorable sign." Most of all, Adams admitted, "it flatters my pride that I make the third in lineal descent in my family, on whom that honor has been conferred by his country, an unprecedented case in American annals." For a man who habitually measured himself against the successes of his father and grandfather, to become the third Adams to serve as minister to the Court of St. James was an achievement not to be denied, particularly as that diplomatic post had elevated his father into the State Department and finally the White House. To accept the position, he knew, would displease his wife, "involve great changes in our household," and carry him away from "his pursuits at home [and] literary labors." Yet as Adams put down his pen, his final sentence suggested that he had decided his course: "I turn my eyes away from these prospects of green fields and shady pastures, and strive to remember that I owe a duty to my own age and country too."[5]

Although he could not know it, Adams was not to see American shores again for seven years. His tenure in Britain would stretch to more than three times that of his father and longer than all but one of his twenty-two predecessors. Adams did anticipate that upholding "the honor of the country in the midst of its mortifying embarrassments" while keeping Britain from interfering in the American fray could pose nearly impossible tasks. Yet even before his return, all but a handful of critics—and more than a few dismayed Confederates—were to hail his service as exemplary. The personal traits that made him a less-than-faultless husband and father—his cold, controlled nature; his private and bookish personality; and his determination to uphold the family's name and memory—rendered him a nearly perfect diplomat. As Carl Schurz, Lincoln's minister to Spain, noted, Adams possessed "the clearness and exactness of mind, the breadth of knowledge," and the "serious and sober" demeanor for the job. As one anonymous writer in the normally staid *North American Review* observed in 1868, "Charles Francis Adams, at the Court of St. James, stands deservedly first among our ministers, and has attained the highest diplomatic honors."[6]

IF CHARLES FRANCIS SR. WAS HONESTLY SURPRISED BY THE AP-pointment, it was only because in true Adams fashion he was trying very hard not to hear what he dubbed "this noise"—that is, what his political friends were saying about him. Within weeks of his election, Lincoln had begun receiving missives from Adams's supporters, all urging the president-elect to find a place for him in the coming administration. Il-linois Congressman Elihu Washburne informed Lincoln that Adams "will be very strongly urged by N. England for either the State or Trea-sury," and Vice President-Elect Hannibal Hamlin, a resident of Maine, confirmed that "some of the best men here, whose opinions are entitled to high consideration, think Chas Francis Adams should be the man for New England." On January 3, Peleg Chandler and J. H. Mitchell, both members of the Massachusetts General Court, wrote to endorse Adams as a "gentleman of vast accomplishments and great industry," and Gov-ernor John A. Andrew hoped that "Adams might be among the possi-bilities." Henry Wilson, Adams's former coeditor and currently a senator from Massachusetts, assured Lincoln that Adams was "second to no man in either House of Congress in knowledge of American affairs." Even incoming Secretary of War Simon Cameron, a corrupt Pennsylvanian forced on Lincoln by a deal made at the Chicago convention, thought "no man in the whole U. States [would] bring to your adm. more weight of character, talent, and purpose." John Alley, another member of the Massachusetts congressional delegation, weighed in, as did the aged Francis Blair Sr., a founding member of the Republican Party. At length, the entire Massachusetts delegation submitted a joint letter insisting that Adams's "high character, spotless integrity, large experience & great attainments justify us in urging him upon your favorable consideration." In early January, Henry Adams heard rumors that Thurlow Weed, New York State's political boss, had journeyed to Springfield to suggest Adams for the Treasury Department. But "Lincoln seems jealous of C.F.A. as too Sewardish," Henry informed his brother Charles Francis. "He wants some one to balance Seward's influence" in the cabinet.[7]

Initially, Lincoln believed that by appointing Connecticut's Gideon Welles as secretary of the navy he had done as much as necessary for New England, a solidly Republican region that could safely be counted on to support him in 1864. On March 11, Lincoln wrote to Seward, recommending New Jersey Senator William Dayton for London, former Republican candidate John C. Frémont for Paris, Kentucky abolitionist Cassius Clay for Madrid, and Ohio Congressman Thomas Corwin for Mexico City. "We need to have these points guarded as strongly and quickly as possible," the president urged. Seward responded that afternoon. The New Yorker held Frémont's southern birth against him, however, and worried that he brought little more than prestige to the position. Instead, Seward recommended Drayton for France and Clay for Russia. Britain was the critical post, and "for England I am sure that Mr Adams is far above all others adapted to the British Court & society and infinitely more watchful, capable, efficient, reliable [and] everything." At length, Lincoln gave way and instructed Seward to notify Adams and the Senate.[8]

As late as March 19, newspapers were reporting that Adams had accepted the French mission or that he had lost his appointment to another New Englander. But the formal letter of invitation finally arrived, and Adams quickly caught the train for Washington. After checking into the Willard Hotel, he dressed and strolled over to Seward's office. The two breakfasted, and then Seward suggested they call on the president. After being ushered into Lincoln's office—a room Charles Francis associated with his own father's "trained bearing and methodical habits"—Lincoln entered and, Adams reported to his diary, "his much-kneed, ill-fitting trousers, coarse stockings, and worn slippers at once caught my eye." Adams stiffly thanked the president "for the honor conferred upon" him and "expressed the hope not to discredit his selection." Lincoln gazed down at his minister, artlessly admitting that he had "no great claim on you, for the selection was mainly Governor Seward's." A stunned Adams again tried to thank the president, who abruptly turned to Seward to discuss the appointment of the Chicago postmaster. "I respectfully took my leave," the "half-amused, half-mortified" Adams told his diary. He had hoped to discuss "the grave topic" of Britain with the president. But what he took to be a brusque dismissal was merely a harried president's way of saying that he had confidence enough in Adams and Seward to leave the matter to them.[9]

Adams waited until returning to Boston on April 13 to draft a reply. "I desire to express my grateful sense of this high rank of confidence reposed in me by my Government," he informed Seward. Privately, however, as he later confided to Dana, his interview with the president "filled [him] with the profoundest discouragement." Believing that even Seward could not save the administration from "the laxity in the system of administration," Adams "cheerfully acquiesced in the decision which removed" him to London, a safe "distance from all responsibility for the direction of public affairs."[10]

The press uniformly applauded the selection. "Although a comparatively young man, [Adams] has obtained an extended reputation from his course in Congress," remarked one Utah editor, "taking a place among the leaders in debate on all important topics." The *New York Herald* praised Adams as "one of the most talented and less pretentious representatives of his party," a "scholar of high order and a gentleman of fine social qualities." Most editors, of course, alluded to the Adams tradition of service abroad. The Washington *Evening Star* thought it noteworthy that as a boy Adams had been "obliged to fight his English school fellows in defense of the honor of America," perhaps expecting that as an adult he would have to do so again.[11]

Confederate journalists painted a darker picture, one that betrayed concern over both Adams's abilities and his opposition to slavery. The new minister's "patrimonial inheritance was an 'unrelenting hate' of the people and institutions of the South," the influential *Richmond Enquirer* worried. "Charles F. Adams figured as an anti-slavery agitator, and as a contributor to Abolition literature." A New Orleans editor condemned Adams as an "Abolitionist by education and by descent, prominent in the Abolition ranks long before that party assumed its present formidable proportions." Lincoln's haste in naming ministers to prominent foreign courts, the Louisiana editor correctly guessed, was designed to get his envoys into European capitals before Confederate President Jefferson Davis could do so "and procure the rejection of our claim to friendly recognition by the other powers of the world, if such a thing be possible."[12]

Charles Francis Sr. originally planned to name his son Henry as secretary of the Legation, a family appointment typical of an age in which the underfunded State Department attempted to supplement the meager salary accorded the minister. The Adamses were therefore annoyed to discover that Charles Wilson, a Chicago newspaper editor and unsuccessful applicant for the city's postmastership, had been granted the position by way of compensation. Adams was also to inherit Benjamin Moran, a Buchanan appointee, as assistant secretary. Vice President Hamlin had recommended Adams for the position in part because he "had a fortune of one or two millions of dollars" and the wealthy Adams could afford to bring Henry along as an unpaid, private secretary. (Two years before, on coming of age, Henry had inherited a princely $10,600 from grandfather Peter Chardon Brooks, and in London he would receive free room and board.) "As I suppose this to be one of Mr. Lincoln's selections," Henry complained, "of course there is no use in commenting on it."[13]

Lincoln was almost frantic about Adams reaching British shores before the Confederate envoys, but the sudden announcement of marriage between John Quincy II and Frances "Fanny" Cadwallader Crowninshield prompted Adams to delay his departure until May 1. As the eldest son, John Quincy had been pushed into the law, and if he was not inclined to pursue a political career, Charles Francis Sr. believed, his duty was to manage the family's business investments. But the genial John Quincy—unusually amiable for an Adams, anyway—longed for a rural existence.

"Boston is the most unutterably dull and stupid hole in this country," he informed his disappointed father, who sadly concluded that his eldest son was "not of the class to fight the hardest battles in life." But whereas Charles Francis Sr. failed to understand his son's wish to retreat into the rustic world of the previous century—the world of John and Abigail—John Quincy's enthusiasm for a landed estate was shared by his twenty-one-year-old fiancée, a wealthy descendant of John Winthrop, the first governor of Massachusetts Bay Colony. The two had been betrothed since June 1860, but the bride's mother judged the Adamses too poor for Fanny. When she finally relented, the couple chose April 29 as their date. Seward later remarked to Charles Francis Jr. that the postponement was the "greatest misfortune that ever happened to the United States," and Charles Francis Jr. himself agreed that it was "inexcusable" that his father was "allowed to dawdle away weeks of precious time because of such a trifle." Charles Francis's displeasure, perhaps, was caused in part by the fact that he had once hoped to court Fanny and because management of the family's business interests now fell to him.[14]

Preoccupied with the wedding and preparations for departure, Adams declined several offers to speak, especially as one of them bluntly urged him to discuss his "differences of opinion" with Charles Sumner. Adams did, however, deliver a brief "parting address" to his "neighbors and fellow-citizens" of the Third District. He again bemoaned "vacating a post more highly prized" in the House of Representatives, but he took solace that he was following in the path of his grandfather and his father when they left the "country on a similar mission under circumstances precisely similar to those which now surround him." What Adams had not yet realized, or perhaps simply did not care to acknowledge, was that he undertook this difficult task alone. John Adams had enjoyed the aid of Thomas Jefferson, while Henry Clay had joined John Quincy at Ghent. Charles Francis was assisted only by a morose twenty-three-year-old private secretary and two squabbling assistants.[15]

Adams booked rooms aboard the steamer *Niagara* for himself, Abby, Mary, and sons Henry and Brooks, the latter one month shy of his thirteenth birthday. Charles Francis Jr., John Quincy, and Louisa and Charles

At one point preferring a life as a gentleman farmer to governmental service, John Quincy Adams II married Frances "Fanny" Crowninshield, heiress to a wealthy and politically connected family. The death of two of their children, including eldest son John Quincy Adams III, just days apart in 1876 was a blow from which the couple never recovered. Upon her death in 1911, Fanny left an estate worth $1,200,000 to her three surviving children. *Courtesy National Park Service.*

Kuhn took a carriage to the East Boston docks to say their farewells, as did John Gorham Palfrey and Dana, who apologized for Sumner's absence. Adams attributed Sumner's nonappearance to "mortification at his not having had the mission" himself, an uncharitable assumption given Sumner's congratulatory telegram. Also aboard were Cassius Clay, his wife, and their five children, who would stop in Liverpool in transit to St. Petersburg. Just after twelve on May 1, the steamer left its moorings "amidst the firing of cannon." As the *Niagara* sailed below Fort Independence on Castle Island, the Adamses were saluted with cheers and the firing of thirteen guns. "My departure from my native land carries with it all the consolation which an honest man may desire," Adams mused.[16]

After thirteen days at sea, the steamer docked in Liverpool. The port's mayor and a large deputation from the American Chamber of Commerce were there to greet Adams, who felt compelled to offer a brief reply, but afterwards, several of the businessmen warned him that much of the "city sympathize with the secession party." Noting "the great anxiety" his hosts expressed regarding trade issues with America, Adams declined the mayor's offer to remain in Liverpool for several days and instead hastened to London. The next morning, May 14, Adams's predecessor, George Mifflin Dallas, met the Adams entourage at Euston Station. Dallas had reserved rooms at the Thomas Hotel in Berkeley Square until Adams's agents at the Baring Brothers, a London-based merchant bank, could find him a suitable rental home.[17]

As the departing minister, Dallas's final task was to present his successor to Queen Victoria. The two left for Buckingham Palace at mid-morning on May 16, but only after Adams decided to don traditional court dress—a black tailcoat with a gold, embroidered waistcoat, and ornate gold cuffs—rather than Dallas's plain dark suit. "Nothing can be more unwelcome than to figure in masquerade dress," Adams confessed to his brother-in-law Edward Everett. But regarding himself in competition with aristocratic southern envoys, Adams believed "that the interests of the United States would be better served by conforming to the customs of the country." Adams and Dallas had to wait their turn behind a delegation from Persia, and then they were ushered into the queen's presence. Victoria stood near a window in a room Adams thought surprisingly small. Adams judged Victoria to be "by no means handsome or imposing," and at only five feet tall, the queen was the rare leader to gaze up at Adams. But her "manner was favourable as sufficiently dignified and yet gracious." Victoria asked if Adams had been in Britain before, and he replied that he had when very young. "Thus terminated this ceremony," Adams wrote that evening, and the two Americans backed out of the chamber.[18]

Dallas departed London the next morning, and the Adamses moved into a rented home at No. 52 Grosvenor Square, an expensive "box about sixteen by forty [feet] and running up to the skies," the new renter complained. As a reminder that his nation paid attention to foreign affairs only in times of crisis, the American Legation had no permanent home, and four days after his interview with Victoria, Adams rented temporary quarters six blocks away at what he called the "obscure locality" of No. 7 Duke Street. Adams tolerated those rooms only ten days before moving the Legation to No. 17 St. George's Place, but he was unhappy there too, describing it as "fine looking outside but too small and cranky within."[19]

As best they could, the family settled in amid the chaos. Henry took an immediate dislike to London, detested the rented home, felt the Legation "confined," and derided the food as tasteless. "I feel in poor health myself and am easily tired and irritable," he reported to brother Charles Francis, yet despite recognizing his foul mood, he was surprised that nobody had invited him to dine. Henry also felt a bit guilty that each letter from Massachusetts spoke of Harvard classmates who had enlisted. Perhaps, he told himself, he might also do so if he could locate a regiment with "austere morality and the fear of God which pervaded all ranks." For Brooks, Charles Francis Sr. contacted the Wellesley House school, a private academy in Twickenham, a town close enough to London for Brooks to visit his parents on weekends. Most of Brooks's fellows hailed from aristocratic homes that favored the Confederacy, and so when not in class, Brooks resorted to hiding from the other boys and passed his time reading Walter Scott novels. Britain offered less in the way of female academies, but even so Charles Francis evidently did not inquire about schools or even a governess for Mary, choosing instead to educate her himself in his few moments of spare time.[20]

As Abby unpacked and organized their household, Adams faced his first diplomatic test. On April 17, even before Adams departed Boston, Confederate President Jefferson Davis issued letters of marque, empowering privateers to prey on Union shipping. Two days later, Lincoln responded by announcing a naval blockade of all southern ports, news of which reached London on May 4. Although an effective blockade would be the work of many months, the British government believed it necessary to warn its merchants of its existence and the possibility that their ships might be seized by Union cruisers. The so-called Queen's proclamation of May 13—issued on the day that the Adamses docked in Liverpool—announced a policy of neutrality but recognized the belligerent status of the Confederacy. The proclamation did not go so far as to diplomatically recognize the existence of the Confederate government, but it defied

Lincoln's insistence that the conflict was a domestic affair that foreign nations had no right to interfere with. Belligerent status came close to placing the newly organized Confederate government on the same footing as the eighty-five-year-old United States. Americans were outraged, and even Charles Sumner, normally the warmest advocate of cooperation with Britain, denounced it as "the most hateful act of English history since the time of Charles 2nd."[21]

Adams understood that London's first responsibility was the protection of its shippers, and he counseled a furious Seward that "such a measure was unavoidable." Yet he too feared the proclamation would have a negative "influence upon opinion here." Several members of Parliament were rumored to be preparing a formal motion to recognize the Confederacy. Only sporadic skirmishes had followed the fall of Fort Sumter; therefore, many in Parliament, Adams noticed, regarded it as likely "that there will never be any actual conflict." The Lincoln administration, they suspected, would eventually come to accept the loss of the southern states, so "our complaints" over the proclamation, Adams informed Seward, were regarded by the British government "as very unreasonable."[22]

Despite its royal title, the queen's proclamation was the work of the Palmerston-Russell ministry, a Liberal cabinet that had been in power for just under two years. The prime minister, Henry John Temple, the third Viscount Palmerston, was a vigorous seventy-six. His lengthy career included nearly twenty years as secretary at war, and since 1830 he had served three terms as foreign secretary, once under Lord John Russell, who now filled that role in his administration. Palmerston hoped to steer clear of the American conflict, despite the fact that his key constituents were cotton textile manufacturers. However, imperial consideration, given Canada's proximity to the United States and Ireland's desire for independence, prompted his desire for neutrality and his hopes of alienating neither side in the coming conflict. Yet Palmerston had little use for the North's democratic culture, and he particularly disliked Seward, who as both governor and senator had appealed to his state's Irish voters by routinely criticizing Britain. As early as the previous January, Foreign Secretary Russell admitted that "the principle of slavery" lurked beneath

This 1862 *carte de visite* by Manhattan photographer Edward Anthony, "The Great Surrender," portrays each nation yielding an important principle. Here, Foreign Secretary John Russell "surrenders [Britain's] great pretensions" by tearing up a document reading "Right of Search," as Secretary of State William Henry Seward "surrenders the [arrested] great commissioners," Confederate emissaries James Mason and John Slidell, while Confederate President Jefferson Davis "surrenders his great expectations." *Courtesy Library of Congress.*

southern secession, but Palmerston's hopes for impartiality were aided by Seward's April instructions to Adams, who was warned not to get drawn "into debate before the British government [over] any opposing moral principles which may be supposed to" divide the American states. Unable to draw on the moral capital of emancipation, Adams was to argue only the principle of "national self-preservation," and not abolition, Seward emphasized, when he met with Russell.[23]

On May 18, Adams traveled to Pembroke Lodge, Russell's country home in Richmond Park, ten miles southwest of London. The foreign secretary was fifteen years Adams's elder, but in other ways the two short, balding, whiskered men resembled each other. Even their cool, staid temperaments mirrored the other's reserved disposition. The meeting was cordial yet candid. Adams began by explaining Lincoln's position toward the southern states, insisting that secession was not sanctioned by the Constitution. The two diplomats agreed that no revolutionary nation deserved formal recognition until it demonstrated the ability to defend its independence, but Russell hinted that the Confederacy might well be doing so. In reply, Adams observed that foreign interference could shape that outcome and wondered whether the ministry planned "to adopt a policy which would have the effect to widen if not make irreparable a breach" between the North and South that he "believed yet to be entirely manageable by ourselves." Russell assured Adams "that there was no such intention," but he could not guarantee what his government might do if circumstances changed in America. Adams concluded the discussion by promising that on the day the ministry recognized "the pretended Confederate States, he would have nothing more to do with England." To that, Russell merely responded with what Adams described as a "provokingly diplomatic" nod.[24]

Russell took a step back from the precipice two weeks later, however, when on June 1 Palmerston's government announced that no privateers belonging to either side could sell their prizes in British ports. The ministry claimed that the decision was consistent with the queen's May proclamation, in that privateers were regarded as auxiliaries of established governments and the declaration of neutrality had not recognized the Confederacy as such. At about the same time, new instructions dated May 21 arrived from Seward regarding possible recognition and the potential acceptance of privateers. Even Henry, who deeply admired the New Yorker, thought the bellicose document "arrogant in tone and so extraordinary and unparalleled in its demands." Seward ordered Adams to let the memo's "spirit be your guide" when negotiating with Russell, but instead, Adams sought to soften its tone, explaining to Seward that Russell clearly intended his latest proclamation to diffuse northern anger. Southerners "were not a navigating people," he pointed out. "They had not a ship on the ocean." Because the United States controlled almost all of its prewar navy, a complete ban on privateers worked to the advantage of the North. "Her Majesty's Ministers have manifested a desire so far to modify the effects of their early precipitation as to render it a question in my mind, whether a corresponding modification of tone on our part would be deemed advisable," Adams suggested. Seward accepted the polite rebuke and withdrew his instructions.[25]

What Adams did not then know, however, is that Russell had already met with three Confederate envoys. Two months before, on March 16, Davis had appointed Pierre Rost, Ambrose Mann, and Alabama fire-eater William L. Yancey as commissioners to Britain, with instructions to negotiate for British recognition. The three met with Russell on May 4, nine days before Adams reached Liverpool, in what Russell emphasized was an "unofficial" discussion. In a meeting that lasted roughly one hour, Yancey emphasized the right of independent states to dissolve the federal compact, and despite his earlier advocacy of reopening the African slave trade—a move the Confederacy had shunned in hopes of appeasing Britain—insisted that the protection of slavery was not the cause of secession. When Yancey bluntly asked for official recognition, Russell blandly replied that such a step was a matter for the entire cabinet to decide. The envoys called on Russell again on May 9, but as an annoyed Yancey observed, the foreign secretary remained "cautious and non-committal." While he waited for an official response, Yancey dispatched Rost to Paris to argue their case to Emperor Napoleon III.[26]

Adams became aware of the commissioners' presence as early as May 17 and, shortly after receiving Seward's intemperate instructions, paid a second visit to Russell. This time, Adams was more inclined to support his superior's uncompromising position, warning Russell that any meetings, even unofficial ones, with "the pseudo-Commissioners could scarcely fail to be viewed" by his government "as hostile in spirit and to require some corresponding action accordingly." Because keeping the Confederate envoys at bay did not contradict the cabinet's wait-and-see approach, Russell somewhat disingenuously admitted that he "had seen the gentlemen once some time ago" but added that "he had no expectation of seeing them any more." That satisfied Adams, who assured Seward that Russell's unofficial meetings with the Confederates "did not imply recognition." In fact, Russell would never again meet with Yancey, who on July 15 informed Jefferson Davis that they had made no progress with Britain.

At about the same time, Russell announced that Britain had no intentions of challenging the Union's naval blockade. "I doubt whether anything short of a complete victory in the South" could revive the Confederate envoys' "prospects," Adams observed to William Dayton in Paris.[27]

WITH PARLIAMENT OUT OF SESSION AND THE CONFEDERATE EMISsaries momentarily checked, Adams had leisure to see to his family. Letters from Charles Francis Jr. regarding the uncertain nature of the American economy and the family's Boston investments were discouraging. "If a conflict with a handful of slaveholding states is to bring us to this," Charles Francis Sr. wondered, "what are we to do when we throw the glove down to all Europe?" The damp British weather did not agree with Mary, who spent most of the summer fighting a lingering bad cold, which made both of her parents quite "uneasy about her." Adams noticed that Mary "suffers a little from her solitude, which is almost as complete as if she were in the wilds of America." Yet it never occurred to Adams to hire a female tutor or companion to ease his daughter's loneliness. More curious still, for a family that traditionally approved of strong-minded women, Mary's parents never pushed her to make known her needs and desires, perhaps because they believed they already had a too-willful daughter in Louisa. But Adams was thrilled when Brooks captured his school's prize for history. However, Adams feared that the headmaster was trying to win favor with the American minister, at least until the teacher, Thomas Scalé, also "commented" on Brooks's social "backwardness," in response to which the offended if not terribly surprised father "had nothing to say."[28]

Britain's political climate also did little to lighten Adams's mood. "There never was any real good-will towards us," he warned one Massachusetts correspondent, "and the appearance of it [in] late years was only the effect of their fears of our prosperity and our growing strength." The Tories, a conservative and landed party, had no economic stake in the American contest, Adams suggested to another, but having fallen from power in 1859, they hoped to use any depression caused by a decline in cotton imports against Palmerston's Liberals. Even those supportive of the northern cause, Adams thought, regarded disunion as a fait accompli and had "long since made up their minds that the United States had ceased to exist." Despite his time spent in London as a boy, Adams concluded that an "American might live in England his whole life" without learning to understand its customs. On the whole, the New Englander groused, "America with all its faults has much better notions of humanity than this comes to." For all of Adams's complaining, however, honesty forced him to admit to Seward that within three weeks of his arrival, five members of the cabinet, including the prime minister, had invited the Adamses to dine "and have taken pains to express their sympathy with our struggle."[29]

Adams was particularly annoyed that British politicians could not grasp the nuances of Republican policy. "Because we assume that it is *not* our intention to declare emancipation," he grumbled to Dana, the cabinet "maintains that slavery has no part in the struggle." Neither party was inclined to go on the record in favor "with a cause based upon the extension of slavery," Adams told Seward, for the majority of British voters—the middle and upper classes only at this date—opposed human bondage. A few Liberal politicians even suggested to Adams that it was in the interest of abolitionism for the South to go in peace, as then the North would no longer have to compromise with cotton planters. Most galling for Adams was a lecture he received from Russell, who pronounced the struggle one "between Empire and Independence." The Lincoln administration, Russell remarked, was taking up arms against southern whites "who are fighting for their liberty." What the foreign secretary forgot, Adams observed to Palfrey, was "that this kind of liberty is of the sort that enslaves others in its turn."[30]

Once again, however, Adams was forced to agree with Russell that when any revolutionary government had "advanced so far as to prove its power to defend and protect itself against the assaults of enemies," it deserved the recognition of other nations. As the grandson of a diplomat who had advanced just that point in foreign courts eight decades before, Charles Francis could not object. "I come to the conclusion," he surmised, "that everything depends here upon the military results in America." When the contest began in earnest, he assumed, the populous, industrializing North would have little difficulty in putting down the planters' rebellion.[31]

THE ADAMSES HEARD NEWSBOYS SHOUTING IN THE STREETS EARLY in the morning of Sunday, August 4. A ship docking in Cork, Ireland, brought the first word of the July 21 debacle at Bull Run Creek, some twenty-five miles southwest of Washington. Confederate forces led by General Pierre G. T. Beauregard had routed US forces under General Irvin McDowell in what thus far was the bloodiest battle in the nation's history. Casualties were roughly even, with 400 Confederates killed and 625 northern men dead. But the raw northern troops broke and ran in retreat, shedding rifles and packs as they scrambled to cross the creek. The victorious Confederates were themselves too green and bloodied to march on Washington, but southern independence, for the time, had been up-held. "We are compelled to take the sceptre of power," crowed the editor of the *Richmond Whig*. "We must adapt ourselves to our new destiny."[32]

Having expected to be reading of a northern triumph, Adams was stunned. As the extent of the disaster grew clear, Adams realized that it signaled a "much longer struggle than I had anticipated." And as he had doggedly argued to Russell that the infant Confederacy could never uphold its sovereignty, he understood that "Bull Run has done us much injury." His tenure in London, he told Richard Henry Dana, "does not improve upon the news of our disasters." Adams had rented their house for a short period only, and he began to believe that he would soon be packing for home. In late August the *New York Tribune* reported that "let-ters from Hon. C. F. Adams state that England is about to recognize the Southern Confederacy," and while Adams had communicated no such thing, he feared that step likely, and if it came to pass, his work in Britain would be finished.[33]

The rumors were not far wrong. Taking advantage of the news, Yancey requested an interview with Russell and sent a note suggesting their two nations negotiate a treaty of recognition and commerce. Privately, Lord Palmerston doubted the ability of the Union to conquer the vast Confederacy. "It is in the highest degree likely that the North will not be able to subdue the South," he wrote in a memorandum, and Russell agreed. But despite the "valuable and extensive market for British manufacturers," the prime minister concluded, a single battle was "too indecisive to warrant an acknowledgement of the Southern Union." A treaty at this time could provoke war with the United States. Why, Palmerston reasoned, risk that when the South would most likely achieve independence on its own? On October 23, Russell informed a relieved Adams that for the present, the ministry's policy of neutrality was unchanged.[34]

As for Henry, his first inclination was to pack his bags for home and enlist in a unit commanded by some "Boston fellows." The Massachusetts Fifth had seen action at Bull Run, and Henry longed to join his Harvard friends in the fray. On August 5, the day after the news reached London, Henry wrote to Charles Francis Jr., requesting that he contact Governor Andrew about a commission, perhaps as a "second [or] third Lieutenant or Ensign, if you can do no better." The troops' lack of training had played a role in the Bull Run catastrophe, but Henry saw no reason why his legal background ill-suited him for the officer corps. Especially as his London acquaintances taunted him unmercifully about the loss, in the army he "would have only bullets to wound" him. Charles Francis's reply was brutal: "Like a coward, you want to run home because our reverses make the post abroad" very uncomfortable. Henry's militant mood soon passed, and he conceded that he was "hardly the material for a soldier." His father required his assistance in London, he rationalized, and in any case, convincing "the Chief"—as Henry increasingly dubbed Charles Francis Sr.—that any Adams should take up arms would prove a formidable task.[35]

Sunday, August 18, found Adams pondering the meaning of turning fifty-four, both for himself and his nation. "The darkness that draws over my country sheds its influence on my mind," he confided to his diary after attending services. "The country has at last come upon the rock which the father left barely protruding from the surface of the water, but which has risen up into a mountain," he added, in an apparent reference to slavery.

"The struggle against it may be successful, but I fear it will cost us dear." Two weeks later was his anniversary, which Adams spent alone as Abby and the rest of the family toured southern England. "Thirty-two years have gone by, the best of my life," Adams admitted, perhaps remembering his discreditable behavior as a young man in Washington. "If the prospect be now a little dark for my country, let me hope and pray that the lesson of humiliation may inure to our good."[36]

The prospects for his nation grew darker still that fall. In the early morning of November 12, Adams received a brief note from Lord Palmerston requesting a "few minutes conversation" that afternoon. Adams thought the invitation curious, as all his previous dealings had been with Russell. At one, he drove to Cambridge House, the prime minister's home in Piccadilly. As the two sat, Palmerston remarked that "he had been made anxious" by a rumor that a "United States armed Vessel" had put into Southampton, a port on the southern coast, for coal and supplies, and that while there, the captain had bragged that his plans were to intercept two Confederate envoys, James M. Mason and John Slidell. Adams replied that the captain in question, John Marchand of the *USS James Adger*, had called on him to discuss his instructions. Washington believed that the *CSS Nashville* had escaped the Charleston blockade "and was proceeding with these men on a voyage to Europe." Adams presumed that Palmerston's government could have no objections to the Union navy chasing a rebel vessel, and the prime minister agreed. Curiously, only days before, Adams had confided to one correspondent that little was likely to change with Britain unless an "unlucky blunder of some naval officer will set the people on a blaze."[37]

Adams thought no more about it. He and Abby were in Yorkshire visiting Monckton Miles, a member of Parliament, when a telegram arrived at the Legation with an update on the two Confederates. The *Nashville* had been unable to evade the five Union vessels blocking Charleston harbor, and instead Mason and Slidell had sailed on a smaller ship capable of navigating South Carolina's back channels. After reaching Cuba, the two boarded the *Trent*, a British mail packet. In nearby St. Thomas, Union captain Charles Wilkes of the *USS San Jacinto* read a newspaper account of their presence in Cuba, and on November 8, after firing two shots across the *Trent*'s bow, seized Mason, Slidell, and their secretaries as contraband of war. Wilkes intended to take his prisoners to New York, but on orders from Secretary Seward, the pair were imprisoned in Fort Warren in Boston Harbor. Charles Francis Jr. was there to witness the celebration. At a banquet at the Revere House, Governor Andrew lauded Wilkes for his "manly and heroic success" in arresting Mason, the hated author of the Fugitive Slave Act of 1850. Shortly thereafter, Congress unanimously approved a resolution thanking the captain "for his brave, adroit, and patriot conduct."[38]

Henry was at the Legation with Moran and Wilson when the telegram arrived. Henry judged the news a prelude not merely to his departure for home but as a declaration of war by Britain. The three "broke into shouts of delight." Britain, Henry argued, "was waiting only for its own moment to strike," so it was better "to strike first." Moran had the presence of mind to send his own telegram to Charles Francis at Monckton's estate on Wednesday evening, November 27. Adams hastened back to London the next day, and Russell fixed Friday afternoon for an interview with the American minister.[39]

Adams found the foreign secretary a "shade more of gravity, but no ill will." Russell himself evidently lacked all the details of the affair, as like Palmerston he asked about Marchand and the *James Adger*. To questions regarding Wilkes, Adams could only reply with the truth: "He was wholly unadvised both as to the occurrences and the grounds of the actions of Captain Wilkes." Russell left it at that, but only after making clear that the cabinet considered the matter to be most serious and that many felt "very sore and hostile about it." Upon his return to the Legation, Adams warned Moran that his tenure in London might not last the month. To Seward, Adams justly complained that all he knew of the affair was from Russell and the London newspapers. "Not a single word has yet been communicated to me officially or otherwise," he protested. "I am placed in a predicament almost as awkward as if I had not been commissioned here at all."[40]

While Americans feted Wilkes, Adams desperately sought to explain the enormity of the crisis to Seward, sometimes posting three dispatches a day. "The late news of the seizure of Messrs Mason and Slidell is so great as to swallow up every other topic for the moment," Adams warned in the first of several missives he wrote just after his meeting with Russell. In Liverpool, Adams noted, cotton merchants friendly to the Confederacy hastily organized a meeting to whip up "the public indignation" and drive the ministry "into some decided measure." Palmerston and Russell, Adams guessed, were not yet "desirous of pressing matters to a violent issue," but their hold on Parliament was fragile, he cautioned Seward, and "they are powerless in the face of public opinion." The London press, never friendly to the American cause, was uniformly hostile, "and now the dogs [of war] are all let loose in the newspapers." At the very least, he knew, the Lincoln administration would have to apologize and release the two envoys. "Yet on such a miserable issue is the peace of fifty millions of people to be staked!" he worried. "I can hardly conceive the madness which can have prompted the Administration for so paltry a prize as these two men to hazard a difficulty with any foreign nation." When two weeks passed with no word from Washington, Adams wrote again to Seward, saying that he was making arrangements to return home: "I may perhaps be permitted to add that I regret this prospect."[41]

For Adams, this was not merely a matter of alerting Washington to the depth of British anger. He was upholding his country's honor but, more profoundly, his family's as well. As a young diplomat, John Quincy Adams had argued for the right of neutral ships to sail the Atlantic unmolested by belligerents, and in large part James Madison had pressed for war in 1812 to prevent British warships from impressing American seamen. Although there might be some justice in pointing out that Captain Wilkes was doing no more than British officers had done during the Napoleonic wars, Adams argued to Seward, that did not change the fact "that the position taken by the United States from first to last has been one of resistance" to the long-standing British policy of searching and seizing neutral vessels. In private letters to Dana and Everett, Adams was blunter still. "Our record on this question as against [Britain] is like the Archangel Michael's against Satan," he lectured. "And now we are trying to prove that [England] was right" all along "because the sin has become inconvenient." Even Henry, after his initial bout of patriotic delight, recognized the historical problem in Wilkes's actions. "What in Hell do you mean by deserting now the great principles of our fathers," he fumed to Charles Jr. "What do you mean by asserting now principles against which every Adams yet has protested and resisted? You're mad, all of you."[42]

While Adams waited impatiently for clarification from Washington, events in Britain helped to decide matters. On the morning of December 15, Adams opened his newspaper to discover that Prince Albert, the queen's husband, had died at the age of forty-two. Adams was aware that Albert "was the most trusted advisor to the Queen," but what he did not know was that Albert had desired peace with the United States and had quietly pressed Palmerston to soften the British response to the *Trent* affair. Finally, two days later, the Legation received two dispatches from Seward, a short one dated November 27 and a lengthier one penned three days later. The first said little more than the seizure of Mason and Slidell "was done by Commander Wilkes without instructions and even without the knowledge of the Government." But that was enough. In the second letter, Seward again emphasized that Wilkes had acted on his own, and he expressed the hope that "the British government will consider the subject in a friendly temper." On December 19, in a meeting with Russell, Adams read both letters to the foreign secretary, who continued to insist that his government demanded "the surrender of the men and an apology." As they walked toward the door, Russell paused to remark "that if all matters were left between us, he had no doubt we should soon agree." Adams returned home in better humor than in weeks.[43]

After a series of cabinet meetings in late December, the Lincoln administration consented to release the prisoners and publicly admit that Wilkes had committed a grave error in boarding the *Trent*. To placate American public opinion, Seward's public statement slyly observed that the United States had "vindicated not only the consistency" of its principles and policies regarding neutral ships "while measuring out to Great Britain the justice which they have always claimed at her hands." At the same time, Adams took heart in the fact that British stocks had tumbled in value because of "the uneasiness of public opinion" about war with the

Union and that "the religious classes and especially the dissenters" were speaking out against hostilities. The supply of cotton already in British warehouses was as "yet quite large," Adams assured Seward, and with the release of the envoys, pressure from the merchant class to challenge the Union blockade would begin to dissipate. Shortly thereafter, at the lord mayor of London's annual banquet, Adams toasted to the "perpetual friendly relations between the two countries." When asked by a British correspondent if the crisis was at an end, Adams replied that he thought so, "unless our people are more insane than I give them credit for."[44]

THE FIRST MONTHS OF 1862 WITNESSED A PERCEPTIBLE REDUCTION of tension between the two countries. The *Trent* affair proved to be "somewhat in the nature of a sharp thunderstorm which has burst without doing any harm," the minister informed his son Charles Francis in February, "and the consequence has been a decided improvement of the state of the atmosphere." Adams noted that the politicians he encountered were decidedly friendlier to the American cause, and even the factory towns were "patient and uncomplaining." British honor had been satisfied, and a long-standing American position had been upheld. Even the release of Mason and Slidell had "done good in one particular," Adams suggested to Everett. Virtually all European countries now agreed that warring nations had no legal authority to board neutral vessels and remove passengers or crewmen. At least for the present, Adams added, "It suits [Britain] to uphold neutral rights."[45]

Henry also judged the "whole tone here so much changed." Benjamin Moran noticed the calm as well. "Our dispatches by yesterday's mail are very cheering," he noted in early May. Seward felt "less restrained than formerly," and the secretary urged Adams to press Russell for the removal of "belligerent rights to the rebels." Adams thought it unwise to damage the new sense of Anglo-American harmony by pushing the foreign secretary on this point, but he did assure Seward that any desire within Parliament "for interference has disappeared." The military news from home was favorable, Adams thought, although admittedly not decisive. But the overall intelligence from Washington convinced Adams "that the force of the rebellion is spent." The "game of secession looks as if it might be nearly played out," he informed Charles Francis Jr. The United States was "putting forth its power whilst the rebel armies [were] gasping for breath."[46]

The luckless Confederate envoys Mason and Slidell finally reached London by March, but their arrival coincided with news of the fall of Forts Henry and Donelson in the Trans-Appalachian Theater. Even the normally hostile *London Times* praised "the unexpected and astonishing resolution of the North." Several weeks later, Henry returned to the Legation after a stroll about the city to find his habitually staid father literally dancing across the floor, shouting: "We've got New Orleans." Aware of their weakened bargaining position, the two southern emissaries sent word to Russell that President Jefferson Davis was willing to offer concessions in exchange for recognition and a willingness to challenge the naval blockade. The commissioners promised to permit slaves to legally marry, to continue to prohibit the importation of African captives, and even to the gradual manumission of all slaves born after a certain date. "I have no faith in the sincerity of these professions," Adams observed to both Everett and Seward. A breakaway nation fighting to protect and extend slavery, Adams assured an interested Anglican bishop, was guilty of "fraud" in making such an offer. Palmerston's party had lost seats in the previous election, Adams knew, threatening the prime minister's hold on power. The cabinet declined to respond to the envoys. "President Jeff [Davis] will not enjoy much of his term if he has no better hopes to hold out to his friends," Adams joked.[47]

Stymied in London, Mason journeyed to several factory towns, where he sought to instigate popular demonstrations against the Union blockade, but with no greater success. Wealthy textile owners, Adams understood, were content to use the shrinking supply of cotton to justify higher prices for their cloth and also to drive smaller competitors out of business. Other manufacturers, long worried about the southern monopoly on the cotton trade, hoped the conflict would prod British shippers to pursue new sources of cotton, particularly in India and Egypt. Adams informed

Seward that the price of cotton stocks was dropping commensurate with supply, yet any talk of "intervention or even mediation in our affairs" remained muted. Even when mills closed or cut back on production, working-class Britons, who lacked the vote but identified with northern democratic ideals, peppered Adams with pro-Union resolutions passed in factory towns, together with requests that he forward their "simple expressions of goodwill" to President Lincoln.[48]

If Adams could not take seriously Confederate offers of internal reform, he welcomed the pretended concessions as they highlighted the southern dedication to unfree labor. Too many upper-class Englishmen, Adams complained to Everett, went to great pains "to misrepresent the facts" about slavery as the basic cause of secession. When liberal reformer Richard Cobden suggested that the European powers might jointly mediate an end to the bloodshed, Adams asked Cobden what the grounds for peace could be. The Confederacy would not accept a Republican in the White House, he observed, and the North "could not be asked to yield the [western] line of the slave states." It was "the failure to contemplate this truth," Adams remarked, "that clouded every judgment of our affairs." Adams was especially happy to remind his London friends that in April 1862, Lincoln had signed legislation banning slavery in the District of Columbia, just before endorsing a bill outlawing slavery in the territories. Adams thought these laws "the greatest step yet made in the struggle," although he guessed their "impact in Europe will probably be even more extensive than in America." Thanks to the Confiscation Act of the previous year, which recognized runaway slaves as contraband of war, "the fugitive can escape [any] which way he may turn," he told one correspondent, "and the fields must go uncultivated from when he flies." With the Confederacy seemingly on the verge of collapse, Adams informed Seward, he had received numerous "letters and communications from people in all classes" who wished the minister to know they were opposed to any British policy "which will sustain the slaveholding system in the Southern States."[49]

On March 24, 1862, Adams was reading the *Times* when he spied an advertisement for a rental property in Ealing, a district in West London, and realized it was the home the Adamses had lived in during his father's tenure as minister. Henry, Mary, and Abby accompanied Charles Francis to visit the empty house. "There was my mother's Drawing room, my father's study, my brother George's chamber, and that occupied by John and myself," he marveled. "And every person in the family gone but myself." Like many an adult revisiting a childhood home, Adams was surprised to find the house so small, especially "modest for the minister of the United States to live in." Gazing back almost fifty years, Adams also recalled his "dismal school experience at Dr Nicholas's" with its "dismal iron gate." Charles Francis's family quietly strolled behind as he examined the grounds. "I remember nothing since that [time when he lived in the Ealing house that] comes back quite so sunny to my heart," Adams reflected that evening in his diary, "although my life has not been unhappy." Despite his many accomplishments, the health of his family, and the success of his sons, Adams could never be content with his role in history. "The future which then seemed illimitable is now little or nothing," he concluded. The day was but a "cheering vision of the distant past, as one of the compensations of my in some respects painful present state."[50]

THE MINISTER WAS ABOUT TO DISCOVER JUST HOW PAINFUL THE present could be. In early March, Major General George B. McClellan sailed down the Chesapeake with his Army of the Potomac, 75,000 strong, landing his army at Fort Monroe in Hampton, Virginia, where he rendezvoused with another 50,000 men. The drilling of McClellan's vast invasion force had been no secret, even abroad, and on March 7 Adams had prayed for "success in the field," as "without it we were at the mercy of the wind." The minister initially guessed that Jefferson Davis would be forced to evacuate the Confederate capital of Richmond "and retreat to the far South." The Union force, the largest ever raised, began to march northwest up the Virginia Peninsula, forcing Confederate General Joseph Johnston to slowly retreat toward Richmond with his smaller force of 60,000. After the cautious Johnston was wounded in late May at the Battle of Seven Pines, President Davis handed the command to the aggressive General Robert E. Lee. Despite McClellan's superior numbers, Lee went on the attack. Confederate casualties outnumbered Union losses, but the timid McClellan, claiming that he faced a Confederate force 200,000 strong, retreated twenty-five miles toward the James River before demanding another 50,000 reinforcements. Disgusted Union soldiers claimed they had been close enough to the Confederate capital to hear church bells tolling.[51]

The grim news trickled into Britain only slowly. In late June the *Persia* brought word, as Adams put it, that McClellan had experienced "another surprise, which though not serious is mortifying." Two weeks later, Adams could not imagine why the Army of the Potomac allowed itself "to be put on the defensive, which is not a favorable symptom." After another week passed, Adams wrote to Everett, bemoaning the fact that July "is not a lucky month with us." The war, he fretted, would now drag on for at least another year. "I can not help feeling some little doubt whether McClellan is quite equal to the enormous task imposed upon him," he added. Struggling to find a silver lining, Adams took some solace in the fact that McClellan, a conservative New Jersey Democrat, "will never make a Napoleon [and] perhaps it is well that he should not."[52]

Adams knew what was coming next. The British press, and especially the influential *London Times* and the *Post*, returned to their earlier view that the Union could not be maintained through force of arms. "At present the momentary slackening in our progress has revived the hopes of the friends of the insurgents," Adams warned Seward. The *Times* went so far as to report that McClellan had surrendered his entire force and that, like Bonaparte after Waterloo, had abandoned his army and fled aboard a steamer. For a moment, Henry believed the report, which caused the Legation "great anxiety," as he reported to his brother Charles Francis. "The current here was rising every hour and running harder against us than at any time since the Trent affair," Henry added. Charles Francis Sr. was convinced that for some years the British had feared the rising power of the United States, so the failed Peninsula Campaign was not the cause of their "desire for division" but merely a pretext for action. "How much longer my term may last does not depend on my will," Adams confided to former Congressman John Gorham Palfrey. "Thus far I have only repeated the experience of my grandfather and my father with exactly the same result: profound disgust."[53]

Still in Britain, Mason was able to take advantage of the upturn in British sympathy to renew his previously failed efforts to purchase a navy. Assisting in his efforts was George Bulloch of Georgia, who had served in the US Navy for fifteen years before taking a position with a private shipping firm in 1854. Based in Liverpool, Bulloch had long-standing ties to British shippers, factory owners, and trade officials. In the late summer of 1861, Bulloch had purchased the steamer *Bermuda*, owned by Fraser and Trenholm, a commercial house run by Charleston natives George Trenholm and Charles Prioleau. The Confederates, Adams informed Seward, were "straining every nerve in the purchase of arms and ammunition," and their hope was to purchase a number of ships through Bulloch, gather their armada in Nassau, and then blast their way through the Charleston blockade. The British Foreign Enlistment Act of 1819 prevented the construction of warships for belligerent nations, but provided that the ships were armed outside of British waters, Russell argued, the Confederates did not violate the letter of the law. However, so long as British admiralty courts, tribunals that exercised jurisdiction over maritime contracts, were favorable to American interests, Adams was typically able to prevent any further sales to Bulloch.[54]

By the Peninsula debacle, however, the Confederates had devised a new and far-more-dangerous strategy. Bulloch—whose half-sister Martha had given birth to Theodore Roosevelt four years before—arranged for a French firm to order the construction of a huge vessel, known only as No. 290, from Laird Brothers in Birkenhead. Despite the alleged French ownership, even the artisans constructing the ship knew it was intended for the Confederacy, as its sides were pierced for cannon. To Russell, Adams penned his strongest protest yet, expressing "the deepest regret" that "nearly all of the assistance that is now obtained from abroad by the persons still in arms against their Government comes from the kingdom of

Great Britain." In June, Lord Richard Lyons, Britain's minister to the United States, suddenly left Washington. Although Lyons insisted he was simply trying to escape the sweltering heat, both Mason and Slidell regarded it as a signal that Palmerston was preparing to abandon neutrality. Seward counseled Adams of the "probability of recognition and of meeting the question of your withdrawal" from London. "The suspense is becoming more and more painful," Adams admitted. "I do not think since the beginning of the war I have felt so profoundly anxious for the safety of the country."[55]

While in search of documents to take to the admiralty court, Adams uncovered a statement from the French firm, the Bravay Brothers, indicating it was merely acting as agent for the real buyer of the ship, the Egyptian government. That forced Russell to ask the British consul in Cairo to make inquiries, and he wired back that the French firm's claim was untrue. Armed with that, Adams submitted his evidence to the court, which on July 24 ruled that "it appears difficult to make out a stronger case of infringement on the Foreign Enlistment Act." The judge, Henry thought, came close to implying collusion between the British government and "the rebel agents." Despite this, the documents supporting the ship's detention sat on the queen's advocate's desk for five days while the Liverpool Collector of Customs, a southern sympathizer, chose to do nothing. Russell finally stepped in, only to discover that the 220-feet steamship, rechristened the *CSS Alabama*, had slipped away from the docks on July 29. "We are drifting towards a war with Great Britain," Seward advised Adams.[56]

Lyons's June departure from Washington, Seward discovered, was not a vacation to cooler climes. Ever since McClellan's failure to capture Richmond, Lyons had advised his superiors that if the summer ended without a significant Union victory, Lincoln would have no choice but to accept mediation. Russell was not yet persuaded, remarking in late August that he expected "the President to spend his second batch of 600,000 men before we can hope that he & his Democracy will listen to reason." The foreign secretary did not have long to wait. Even as he penned those thoughts, General Lee engaged Union Major General John

Pope on August 28 at the Second Battle of Bull Run. Once again, the smaller Confederate force battered the Army of the Potomac, inflicting casualties of 14,462, roughly double the number of Confederates killed and wounded. Although unable to march on Washington—by this time heavily fortified from the South—Lee planned to invade and "liberate" Maryland. "The next news was expected by the Confederates to announce the fall of Washington or Baltimore," a glum Henry observed, adding that if Maryland fell, "no one could have blamed Palmerston for offering recognition."[57]

Just how close Britain was to that step became clear on October 7, when William Gladstone, the chancellor of the exchequer, addressed a public dinner in Newcastle. Speaking from prepared remarks, Gladstone concluded with "We may have our own opinions about slavery; we may be for or against the South; but there is no doubt that Jefferson Davis and other leaders of the South have made an army; they are making, it appears, a navy; and they have made what is more than either, they have made a nation." Afterwards, Russell gently chided Gladstone for appearing to announce a decision for which "the Cabinet is not prepared," and reformer John Bright condemned the secretary as coming from a "family long connected with slavery." But nobody in the Legation doubted the seriousness of Gladstone's words. Gladstone "makes an insulting attack upon us," Moran fumed, "and is applauded." Henry noted the hypocrisy in Gladstone's praise of a Confederate navy. "No one knew so well" as Gladstone that "he and his own officials and friends at Liverpool were alone 'making' a rebel navy," Henry complained, "and that Jefferson Davis had next to nothing to do with it." Charles Francis Sr. thought it revealing that Gladstone had "ventured to touch upon the slave portion of the controversy," as if reasonable men could disagree on its role in secession. But he guessed that Gladstone had exposed "the course that may be taken by [his] Government as soon as Parliament meets." Adams supposed, yet again, that he would soon be taking his family home. "The only thing now likely farther to retard [recognition] in my opinion," he counseled Seward on October 10, was "any serious change in the character of the war."[58]

Once more, events in America outpaced the slow arrival of news abroad. On September 17, three weeks before Gladstone's speech, Lee's invasion of the United States was repelled at Antietam Creek near the town of Sharpsburg, Maryland. On what became the single bloodiest day of the conflict, McClellan struck Lee's army after two Union soldiers discovered Lee's mislaid battle plans—Special Order 191—wrapped around three cigars. The Union's 12,410 casualties were slightly higher than Confederate losses, but Lee lost a higher percentage of his smaller army, and despite the Confederate draft of the previous spring, southern manpower reserves were increasingly depleted. Lee's Army of Northern Virginia limped back south, his objective of adding Maryland to the Confederacy having failed. The particulars reached London slowly, but for once Adams had cause to rejoice as the details became clear. "At all events the northern invasion has come to an untimely end," he exalted. "God be thanked for all his mercies."[59]

So sure had the British press been that Lee would again best McClellan, and that Washington would have to be evacuated, that the *Edinburgh Review* confidently predicted that "the merchants" of New York City intended to replace Lincoln with Jefferson Davis in the White House. McClellan's victory "has done a good deal to restore our drooping credit here," Henry assured his brother Charles Francis. "As a consequence" of Antietam, the senior Adams guaranteed Seward in early October, "less and less appears to be thought of mediation or intervention." His guess was correct. The prospect of recognition "seemed ten days ago to be approaching," Palmerston remarked to Russell on October 2, but now "the whole matter is full of difficulty." Several weeks later, Palmerston made his views clearer still when he instructed his foreign minister "that we must continue merely to be lookers-on till the war shall have taken a more decided turn." The only part of this positive news that "puzzled" Adams was the reports that McClellan had not chased retreating Confederates into Virginia. "Our West point graduates appear to have been taught caution in warfare until there is no enterprise left," he sighed. "They do not well understand an aggressive policy."[60]

Five days after the battle, Lincoln called a special cabinet meeting. Two months before, the president had proposed issuing a proclamation of emancipation, but Seward had pressed Lincoln to wait upon better war news so that the administration did not appear to be acting out of desperation. However, the secretary of state had hinted to Adams of the possibility, as in late July the minister privately commented on news from Washington "as intimating the suggestion of a policy of emancipation by the President." During Lee's invasion of Maryland, Lincoln told his cabinet in September, "I determined, as soon as [Confederates] should be driven out of Maryland, to issue a Proclamation of Emancipation." Aware that northern Democrats would bitterly oppose any attempt to transform the conflict into an antislavery crusade, Lincoln wished to give the appearance of moderation. His proclamation provided the Confederate states with a window in which to surrender. If they did not return to the Union by January 1, 1863, Lincoln warned, their slaves "shall be then, thenceforward, and forever free."[61]

Even more than the failed Antietam campaign, the Emancipation Proclamation rendered it nearly impossible for Palmerston to sell Confederate recognition to his antislavery public. "Since the President's latest step," Adams wrote to William Dayton in Paris on October 5, the ministry "seems to be rather in favor of letting things take their natural course, at least until the meeting of Parliament." Adams had long believed that the chaos of war, regardless of its outcome, could not "pass away without leaving slavery a wreck." The "adoption of such a policy," he mused, had been a "mere question of time," and while the Union might in the end lose the contest, "the very existence of the war renders a retreat from it impossible." Henry took particular joy in the fact that Lincoln's decree infuriated the *London Times*. "The Emancipation Proclamation has done more for us here than all our former victories and all our diplomacy," Henry informed his brother Charles Francis. The elder Adams took pains to personally thank British reformers who wrote in support, even while reflecting that few Americans were innocent of involvement in the nation's greatest sin. "This terrible series of calamities appears as a just judgment upon the country for having paltered with the evil so long," Adams feared. "God have mercy on us, miserable offenders."[62]

The entire Legation, according to Henry, was in "high spirits." The only unhappy news from home was the deepening estrangement between Charles Sumner and Secretary Seward and, by extension, Adams as well. Sumner had long been critical of what he regarded as the president's lethargic pace in embracing abolitionism as a war tactic, and he blamed that slowness on Seward. At least initially, the Massachusetts senator had hoped to win Adams back as a friend and supporter. In the fall of 1861, Sumner had delivered a speech critical of Seward, a copy of which he sent to Adams. "I read it without the smallest remnant of pity," Adams observed. Sumner's behavior "opened up such a view of human weakness, that it awakens my pity rather than any other emotion." Shortly thereafter, Thurlow Weed, Seward's longtime political handler, arrived in London, and over dinner the two discussed Sumner's "efforts to destroy Mr Seward's public and private character." Adams replied only that he was sorry he "should have been so deceived" by Sumner in their earlier days. Rather more serious than any trouble Sumner made at home within the Republican Party, Adams believed, was his correspondence with British friends. "Sumner has done us some harm by giving currency to the notion among Englishmen that Mr Seward is their enemy," Adams complained to Everett. A few of Sumner's correspondents went so far as to alert Adams to the harm that Sumner was doing regarding public opinion in Britain. "My feelings are more those of compassion than of anger," Adams insisted to Dana. "Though I neither expect *nor even desire* any future intimacy with him."[63]

Apart from quietly dissuading any of Sumner's British friends as to Seward's alleged Anglophobia, Adams sought to avoid the intraparty spat. That became difficult in the weeks just before Antietam, however, when it appeared that British recognition of the Confederacy would lead to his withdrawal from London. Should that happen, Seward suggested, Adams should stand as a candidate for the Senate against Sumner, whose term was up that fall. That had the virtue of allowing the administration to make continued use of Adams's talents while silencing a persistent critic in the Senate. Sumner had, in fact, become increasingly unpopular among Lincoln loyalists and party moderates in Boston. Several Republicans alerted the Legation of a move to replace Adams with Seward, depriving Sumner of a chance at the position in London. Adams tried simply to ignore the talk, but that became untenable when four leading Massachusetts newspapers united in endorsing Adams for the seat. In late October, a breakaway Republican group calling itself the "People's State Convention" met in Springfield and formally nominated Adams as a candidate. Even Dana, once a close confidant of Sumner, labored behind the scenes to secure Adams's election. But believing that events had finally turned in favor of the Union, Adams wished to remain in Britain. Certainly, he had no desire to win a seat in the Senate through a brutal Republican coup against one of its own. Adams hurried word to his son John Quincy in Massachusetts to make it clear that he refused to accept any nomination, a disavowal accepted with regret by one Vermont editor, who thought "the Adams stock is good blood and always was." At about the same time, Adams also swatted away any discussion of his either replacing Seward in the State Department or swapping places with the New Yorker. To Dana, however, Adams privately conceded that he thought Sumner a "fanatic" lacking in the principles of "practical statesmanship." Perhaps, Adams supposed, the "outrageous assault of Brooks has had a most unfortunate effect on his mind and heart."[64]

That done, Charles Francis Sr. settled in for the winter holiday with Abby, Mary, and Henry. To celebrate the season, Adams read aloud to them from *Somebody's Luggage*, Charles Dickens's latest Christmas story, which he judged "on the whole mediocre." But he could take great satisfaction that in his nineteen months in Britain, he had developed a solid working relationship with Lord Russell, checked the efforts of the Confederate envoys to win recognition, and injured Mason's attempts to build a navy in English ports. If the greatest blow to Confederate hopes abroad had nothing to do with Adams's diplomacy but rather to the curious fate with Robert Lee's misplaced maps and the timing of Lincoln's proclamation, his numerous dispatches home had alerted Seward and Lincoln to the depth of British anger over the *Trent* affair, and at a time when the Union could ill-afford to take on yet another dangerous enemy. His relations "with the Court of St. James," he assured his son John Quincy in early January 1863, "were never more cordial or pleasant than now." But the *CSS Alabama* remained at large, and his greater worry, he admitted to the privacy of his diary, was the well-being of Charles Francis Jr., who had defied his will and enlisted in the First Massachusetts Volunteer Cavalry.[65]

6

"NOT PARTICULARLY WELL FITTED FOR THE ARMY"
The Officer

"I PLAYED AT SOLDIER AT FORT INDEPENDENCE," CHARLES Francis Jr. admitted, months before he actually became one and realized that war was "no plaything." In the days before Fort Sumter and just prior to his twenty-sixth birthday, Adams enlisted in the Fourth Battalion—the Quincy company—of the Massachusetts Volunteer Militia, a home guard of sorts. Young recruits poured into Boston from the western counties, but few thought a war or even a battle to be likely. President Abraham Lincoln had yet to issue his call for troops, and Adams's fellows wore clothes from home, all "pluck [and] outer gaiety." Half of the battalion were farm boys, the other half sons of privilege. Most "had never handled a musket," Adams acknowledged, "nor was there a single uniform amongst us." Charles Francis guessed they would drill on weekends, provide a show of force sufficient to unnerve southern secessionists, and be safely home before the summer began.[1]

On April 24, 1861, eleven days after the fall of Fort Sumter, Massachusetts Governor John A. Andrew ordered the militia to perform garrison duty at Fort Independence on Castle Island in Boston Harbor. "A pleasanter or more useful five weeks in the educational way, I do not think I ever passed," Charles Francis reflected. Apart from a brief leave to attend his brother's wedding and to see his family off to Britain on May 1, Adams remained with his company over the period. Because of the filth, Adams shaved his head and was "just about as bald as our worthy father the Minister," he laughed to his brother John Quincy. Upon returning home, Adams glanced in the mirror and was amazed by what he saw: "My face was brown and tan, my hair was cut close to my head, my loose coat and blue shirt gave me a brawny reckless bearing, and I thought I had never looked so rollicking and strong, or felt so well, in all my life." But it was "only a military kindergarten," he conceded, and unless a Confederate privateer somehow arrived in Boston Harbor, the militiamen would never see action. As young men his age caught the train for Washington and enlisted in the US Army, Adams returned to his law practice and to managing the family's financial affairs, both of which he "loathed." No Adams had ever picked up a musket. Adams men negotiated treaties, crafted legislation, and argued important cases before the Supreme Court. They were not warriors. As he confided to his diary, "I lacked the spirit of adventure and the daring to throw myself into the new life." Instead, Charles Francis agreed to serve his city by helping to raise funds for enlistment bounties and "to procure uniforms and revolvers" to equip other men who were, he reasoned, better suited for a martial life.[2]

Over the course of the summer, Charles Francis "fostered a delusion" that his presence in the office was "essential to the conduct of [his] father's affairs." At the close of each day's business, a conflicted Adams "argued the matter continuously" with himself. Duty to family, almost as much as duty to nation, had been drilled into every Adams for decades. But perhaps duty to America's first dynasty, he rationalized, was synonymous with obligation to country. He believed that "one at least of the family ought to be with the colors," and he felt "ashamed" to be safely at home while his Harvard classmates enlisted. Before the year was out, Charles Francis Jr. would defy his father and enlist. Over the course of the next four years, Adams was to rise in the ranks, eventually becoming the second colonel in his state's pioneering black cavalry regiment. While his father waged his own kind of battle at the Court of St. James, constantly wishing that his superiors would hasten in transforming the conflict into a war against slavery, Charles Francis Jr. helped make it so in South Carolina, Virginia, and Maryland. Both sought to save the nation forged by their ancestors. Yet leading a black cavalry unit also, ironically, solidified his disdain for African Americans. The brilliant, caustic son was to fight the good fight, but rarely as a good man.[3]

ON JUNE 10, 1861, CHARLES FRANCIS PREPARED THE GROUND IN A letter to his father: "About this war business, a great change has come over my feelings since you left," so much so that Adams felt "not only a strong inclination to go off, but a conviction that from many points of view I ought to do it." Charles Francis explained that he had recently talked to Governor Andrew, who assured him that if the state raised another regiment, he could be given command of it. "I wish to go in it, and I think I have a right to almost demand your assent to my doing so." How did posterity judge young men who, during the American Revolution, had "sat at home reading the papers?" Their own family, Charles Francis reminded, had long stood against "slavery and the South, and been most prominent in the contest of words." But now, after Sumter, it was a contest of armies, and "does it become us to stand aloof from the conflict?" The married John Quincy could take control of the family's investments, with Henry remaining as secretary in London. Brooks was too young. That left only Charles Francis. "It seems to me almost disgraceful that in after years we should have it to say that of them all not one at this day stood in arms for that government with which our family history is so closely connected." Not that it much mattered to his father, Charles Francis guessed, but he thought himself a "failure as a lawyer," a mere "real estate agent." Perhaps the war would last but one summer, he concluded, or there might be no new state regiment. But "great events were transpiring," and Charles Francis prayed that his father "will make no objection" to his accepting a commission "and going forth to sustain the government and to show that in this matter our family means what it says."[4]

The senior Adams declined to reply, perhaps hoping that if he did not provide a blessing, Charles Francis Jr. would abandon his quest and return to the law. Henry finally responded in early July, informing his brother that their father yet believed "the war will be short and that you will only destroy all your habits of business without gaining anything." Henry's advice was to "say no more about it" and return to his family obligations. Should, in the end, Charles Francis decide to enlist, he added, the best policy might be to stop asking their father for permission and "just write and notify him." The senior Adams would be irate, of course, but he "will consent to that as a fait accompli."[5]

Independence Day arrived, and amid the speeches and celebration, the Second Massachusetts Infantry departed Boston. The Fourth Battalion of militia escorted the regiment to the station, a task that initially pleased Adams, for many of his oldest friends filled its ranks. "Off they all went," he wrote his mother, "and apparently in good spirits and full of life and hope." Wilder Dwight spied Adams on the platform and waved his hat. Another, Hal Russell, caught Adams's attention "and went through a war dance." As the crowded train pulled away, Adams realized just how much he envied his friends. "Then, after seeing others on their way to the real strife," he observed with considerable irony, the militiamen "quietly marched back to our armory—and were not ashamed!" Reading the letter, Abby could scarcely fail to miss this latest warning that her son was preparing to abandon the home guard for the army.[6]

A few days after the departure of the Second Infantry, word reached Boston of the July 21 debacle at Bull Run Creek in Virginia. Charles Francis had just reached his office when he heard newsboys in the street crying "Retreat of the federal army!" Adams hastened to the telegraph office and "turned pale" as he listened to the "frightful tale of running men, abandoned arms and blasted honor." Rumors circulated that Washington was in danger of being captured. "I then began to realize the mistake I had made in not going earlier," Adams reflected. Had he enlisted in April, he "too might have been found ready, when to be ready was the duty of every man." Charles believed that he "could fight with a will and in earnest." Confederates "were traitors, they war for a lie, they are the enemies of morals, of government, and of man." He had recently mocked Henry's desire to enlist, pointedly observing that Henry was "not particularly well fitted for the army." But with the brutal honesty so typical of his family, Charles Francis admitted to his diary that he was not much suited for that life either. The army was not his "vocation; and that, in deserting the law for it," he was abandoning a profession for which he was "little adapted for one to which I was adapted even less." Charles Francis then wrote to his father, devoting most of the letter to a discussion of how the news would bolster the Confederate cause abroad, but ending with the cryptic "In any case I no longer see my way clear."[7]

Charles Francis's mind was nearly made up when John Quincy unexpectedly announced that, as the eldest brother, it was his duty to enlist. Charles Francis dissuaded him from doing so and then dashed off to their father a letter revealing their "gloomy" conversation, perhaps to alert him again to the fact that one Adams son planned to serve. Two weeks later, on November 26, Charles Francis again sat down to write his father. "I don't know whether you will be surprised or disgusted or annoyed or distressed by the information that I have gone into the army," the lengthy missive began, "but such is the fact." Governor Andrew had announced the formation of the First Massachusetts Cavalry, and when Charles Francis Jr. discovered that Caspar Crowninshield—John Quincy's brother-in-law— was to be a lieutenant, he contacted Andrew about a commission. Generations of Adamses had built America, and "it cannot be otherwise right for me to fight to maintain that which my ancestors passed their whole lives in establishing." The dissatisfied attorney again insisted that he had "completely failed" in his profession and longed to be free of it. His future, Adams guessed, "must be in business or literature," and the army might prepare him for either. "It will go hard if my pen is idle while history is to be written or events are to be described," he noted. The decision was final: "You know it now and I am glad of it!"[8]

Charles Francis Sr. once again declined to reply. Instead, he poured his emotions into his journal: "My son Charles after long doubt and hesitation has at last accepted a commission as an officer in the cavalry regiment now forming in Massachusetts," adding that he had "feared this, because of all my sons he is the one I lean upon the most." One month later, Adams again indicated to his diary that he would never comprehend his son. "I fear he has thrown himself away," and "simply from family pride." Because "none of his predecessors have been soldiers," Adams wondered, "why should he?" Adams regarded his son as poor material for a soldier, a point Charles Jr. had already conceded, and like all parents in wartime, he feared for his son's life, although his journal entry only hinted at this possibility. But he finished his entry that evening with a blessing his son longed to hear: "Yet as he has decided upon high grounds of duty I am content to abide by it. God protect him in the midst of this agony." Instead of conveying his approval, however, three days later he posted a letter to Charles Francis Jr. commenting only on the *Trent* affair.[9]

After receiving that curious missive, Charles Francis Jr. mailed off several inquiries to Henry: "How do they like my going into the army in London? Did they expect it? Were they pleased or disgusted?" Their father was little inclined to say much about the matter to either son, realizing that he and his second son would never understand the other. Since the day decades before when John Adams had complained that George Washington was but a "lucky soldier" of modest intellect, Adamses had regarded warfare as unworthy of their talents. For his part, as Charles Francis Jr. much later announced to the world in his autobiography, his father, "with the coldness of temperament so natural to him, took a wholly wrong view of the subject, did not believe in anyone taking a hand in actual fight." The younger Adams thought it unfathomable that "his family, of all possible American families," should be unrepresented in the field. He was young, single, healthy, and bored, so he "was the one to go!"[10]

"You are going into the army," Henry responded in late December. "I do not think it my duty to express any regrets at the act, or at the necessity for it." Although he admitted that he thought it would be wiser for John

Quincy to enlist—nobody in London had any great confidence in the eldest son's financial wizardry—Henry did not wish to burden Charles Francis "by mourning or maundering about it." Perhaps it was "the strange madness of the times," Henry mused, that no longer allowed for "settled lives and Christian careers." Henry promised to stand by his brother and support his decisions. Yet he could not help adding that while he had grown "callous and indifferent" regarding his own fate, part of him was "vehement against throwing yourself away like this." A furious Charles Francis penned a blistering reply: *"You* [are] tired of this life! Pray how old are you and what has been your career?" After Harvard, Charles Francis observed, Henry had wasted two idle years in Europe but was now abroad again and in a position to play a role in the outcome of the "great questions" of the age. "Fortune has done nothing but favor you and yet you are 'tired of this life.'" Henry was about to turn twenty-four, Charles Francis noted. "What do you mean by thinking, much less writing such stuff?" Far from throwing his life away, Charles Francis added, "Isn't a century's work of my ancestors worth a struggle to preserve?" "Excuse me if I have been rough," he concluded, "but it will do you good." When the contrite Henry found the courage to reply, he did so with a simple apology: "I've disappointed myself."[11]

Before departing for camp in early December 1861, Charles Francis turned over all the records of the family's finances to John Quincy, but only after leaving detailed written instructions and signing over power of attorney. For collecting rents, keeping tabs of investments, and paying stipends to their cousins and other Adams relations, John Quincy was to receive $3,000 each year. Far away in London, Charles Francis Sr. doubted that his eldest son was up to the task. "I am haunted by an indefinite apprehension that he is charged with too great a responsibility in money matters," he fretted, "by the departure of Charles, whose judgment on such subjects is better." But Charles Francis Jr., discontented with his old life and drawn to romanticized notions of battle, Adams groused, "seems to have an idea that management of another's property is derogatory to the dignity of an independent citizen."[12]

ALTHOUGH CHARLES FRANCIS JR. WAS ANXIOUS TO SERVE IN ANY capacity, a posting in the First Massachusetts Cavalry pleased him immensely. In both Confederate and Union forces, as Caspar Crowninshield once bragged, the cavalry was a "sort of elite corps." Troopers rode while infantrymen tramped dusty byways, and although both branches expected to see action, cavalrymen were the eyes and ears of the army. Crowninshield insisted that recruits came "from all ranks of life" and from a variety of civilian occupations, but Adams admitted that the regiment "was essentially a body of picked men," all of them "young, athletic, ingenious, surprisingly alert and very adaptive." Many represented old money. Harvard populated the officer corps; three out of ten majors and seven of twenty-eight captains had attended the college. Crowninshield had entered Harvard in 1856—where he was the roommate of Robert Gould Shaw, soon to lead the North's first black regiment—the year Adams graduated, and Lieutenant Colonel Horace Binney Sargent was of the class of 1843. Adams had supposed he would begin his service "as a simple sergeant" in Crowninshield's company, but rather to his surprise, a commission arrived on December 19 bearing the rank of first lieutenant. "This is all I hoped for and much more than I expected," he assured Henry.[13]

As was the case with an infantry regiment, Adams's unit numbered one thousand men, organized into ten companies of one hundred each. Before the war's end, roughly twelve hundred men would serve in the regiment, and Adams later boasted that no "better men got together than those" who filled the ranks of New England's first-ever cavalry regiment. For Governor Andrew, it was fortunate that so many recruits came from wealth. Outfitting the regiment cost nearly $300,000. Northern cavalrymen, unlike their Confederate counterparts, typically owned their own horses, but US cavalrymen carried superior arms and equipment. Each soldier was outfitted with three days' rations for himself and his horse, a saddle and bridle, a carbine and revolver, ammunition for both, and a saber and belt. Weighed down by their gear, Crowninshield fretted, new recruits experienced difficulty getting "in and out of the saddle, and a derrick, sometimes, would not have been a bad thing." Privates in the regiment drew $13 each month, but as a first lieutenant Adams received $105.[14]

Somewhat to his surprise, Charles Francis liked most of the men under his command. "We were kith and kin," he remembered. Being an Adams, the new officer thought it only proper that he was neither especially "popular or adored by them," not the way that Crowninshield was. Adams was less fond of the regiment's colonel, Robert Williams. Although a West Point graduate and a career soldier, Williams was a southerner and, as Adams put it, a "gentleman of the Virginia school." That was not a compliment. Williams was a strict disciplinarian, Adams charged, "severe to [the point of] brutality." He ordered the men to devote a "full stable hour" to their horses, grooming and preparing their steeds with "military precision." Although loyal to the Union, Williams detested New Englanders. "He had a set of us young Harvard fellows for officers," Adams insisted, "who served him like dogs, who bowed before him in blind, unquestioning obedience." But Williams simply did not understand "our" Massachusetts men. And even in a time of hard drinking, Williams enjoyed his whiskey and was a "drunken beast" when in his cups. Williams "got drunk before" the regiment shipped south, Charles Francis complained to Henry in early January, "and has continued so ever since." When sober, Adams admitted, "Williams did know his business," but those times were rare, "and in moments of emergency, [was] invariably drunk."[15]

In the months after Bull Run, there was little time for training. Adams drilled at Camp Brigham in Readville, just southwest of Boston. "I was never properly trained as an officer," Adams once remarked. "All I ever learned was from rough experience and as an outcome of my own blunders." Three days after Christmas, on Sunday, December 28, 1861, Adams and the men of Company H shipped south, first by rail to Manhattan, which gave him the opportunity to dine with his brother-in-law Charles Kuhn, and then down the coast for Port Royal, South Carolina, which had fallen to Union forces the previous November. While in New York, Adams also discovered that Governor Andrew wished John Quincy to join his staff as aide-de-camp. Although he was granted the rank of

Embarrassed that most of his Harvard classmates had enlisted in the days after the attack on Fort Sumter and believing that a member of his family should fight in the conflict, twenty-six-year-old Charles Francis Adams Jr. (far left) enlisted in the Massachusetts First Cavalry before informing his parents of his decision. Although later proud of his son, the elder Adams never agreed with the decision. *Courtesy Library of Congress.*

lieutenant colonel—a title the genial John Quincy little cared about—his role was wholly advisory. John Quincy had been the only person to brave the bitter winds and see Charles Francis off, but that suited Adams, as he was "cross and hungry rather than [in] the sentimental mood." Adams's company reached the Carolina coast by mid-January and marched into Beaufort. "As for being cooped up on Hilton Head all winter," Adams complained to Henry, "I don't relish the idea much." But the hiatus provided them with time to work with their mounts, which remained terrified by the sound of guns.[16]

Williams detailed Adams and Crowninshield as field officers in charge of checking pickets—soldiers positioned in a line forward of the regiment's main position to watch for enemy movements—a task that

Adams described as hellish. The farthest picket was fifteen miles away from camp, with each subsequent group placed at five-mile intervals. "I was fourteen hours in the saddle through the bedamnedest country that ever man saw," he told John Quincy. At one point, while galloping toward the next group, Adams's horse tripped over a stump, and both went down. After a long day, Adams finally returned to Beaufort, "to sleep on the soft side of a board with my coat-cape for a bed and my boots for a pillow, after a cup of water for my supper."[17]

Adams did not long survive on water only. Despite his complaints about his colonel's drinking, Charles Francis and his Harvard friend Henry Davis fell into "horrid habits," he confessed to Henry Adams. Before riding out each morning, the two imbibed a "cocktail before breakfast," which he rationalized as "medicine." Adams also wrote to John Quincy to request a "continuous supply" of cigarettes and a new pair of high-topped riding boots. The dutiful brother shipped those and more, ordering a "devilishly handsome pistol" and a trunk of custom-made uniforms from the exclusive company Jacobs & Deane. Either John Quincy or the clothier thought to toss four bottles of whiskey into the trunk. "Whoever sent the whiskey," Adams wrote to John Quincy, "it came just in time," for the regiment's pay was late and they had no cash for local stores. "You should have heard Caspar [Crowninshield] howl and seen Davis' eyes light up as the bottles came out."[18]

As was true for many northern soldiers, the voyage south provided Adams with his first view of the region and of plantation slavery. The United States controlled Port Royal Island, but Confederates occupied the land just across the Broad River, and "our pickets stand and gaze placidly at the pickets of the enemy on the shore opposite," Charles Francis informed his mother. The senior Adams had to consult a map to locate his son's position, and realizing that the First Cavalry was stationed between Charleston and Savannah, he worried that he might "never see him again." For his part, Lieutenant Adams dreamed of taking part in the capture of Charleston, regarded by Republicans as the heart and soul of secession. "Ah," he wrote to Henry, "wouldn't I like to ride into Charleston!"[19]

On February 2 Adams rode north to Barnwell Island to check on his pickets and realized they were on the estate owned by William Henry Trescot, a slaveholder, former minister to Britain, and assistant secretary of state under James Buchanan. Dismounting, Adams strode into the abandoned house. "It isn't a pleasant picture," he told his mother. The house itself was new, but the rooms were filled with "broken furniture, scraps of books and letters." Trescot had amassed a "fine library of books of many languages," but now they lay piled up in corners, evidently in preparation for shipment before Trescot was forced to flee. Most of the windows were shattered. As he stared out toward the river, Adams "wondered why this people had brought all this upon themselves." Two months before, Charles Francis had been anxious to do battle with Confederates, yet now he "couldn't but pity them." How might he feel, Adams mused, if he witnessed "such sights at Quincy?"[20]

Charles Francis's months in Beaufort also brought him into contact with large numbers of African Americans. More than seven thousand runaway slaves had crowded into the town, and Adams expected that thousands more would soon arrive. Charles Francis realized that he was observing the dawn of emancipation or, as he indelicately remarked, "This little island has begun the solution of this tremendous 'nigger' question." Precisely what the government was to do with liberated slaves was a mystery. "I have not thought sufficiently to express an opinion," he told his father. Not that that prevented him from doing so. Freed people might be placed under military jurisdiction, he thought, so that children could be educated and adults could be taught "the first great lesson, that they must work to live." Pay them "low wages and let the blacks support themselves or starve." It evidently did not occur to Adams, a young man of inherited wealth, that South Carolina's black population had been laboring since childhood far harder than he ever would. "My views of the future of those I see about me here are not therefore encouraging," he warned Henry. Federal emancipation "would be a terrible calamity to the blacks as a race," for "their freedom will be the freedom of antiquated and unprofitable machines."[21]

Adams's inability to recognize the precarious position of the African American refugees betrayed the first hints that he would never truly come to understand the black troops he would one day lead into battle. The federal Confiscation Act of August 1861 recognized runaways only as "contraband" of war, not as liberated people. Trained from infancy not to trust the master class, few runaways believed that the army would ferry them north if it were forced to evacuate the coast. Unable to grasp that the refugees were biding their time, Adams assured his father that they were "dreadful hypocrites" who "tomorrow would say to their masters, as a rule, what today they say to us." Again and again, Adams complained that Carolina blacks were "fearfully lazy," yet in the same letter he conceded that "they will work for money and indeed are anxious to get work." African Americans, he supposed, were "intelligent enough," although he suspected their "intelligence too often takes the form of low cunning."[22]

Adams's acerbic opinions on black abilities were endorsed by some of his fellow officers, including John Quincy's brother-in-law. While riding picket with Adams, Crowninshield, who had briefly served with his state's Twentieth Infantry and been stationed in Washington, launched into a discussion of the differences between South Carolina bondmen and "the Virginia negro." The contraband in Beaufort, Crowninshield observed, were "intensely black, uncouth, and unattractive in their appearance." As the two officers debated the issue, they came across an "immensely powerful, jet black man" who was "bewailing" the loss of seventeen children under his care. They had recently been sold inland, he explained, to get them away from Union liberators, and for a very low price. "Well, our family is pretty well on record as abolitionists," Adams smirked, "but if niggers are as cheap as that, I shall have to think about buying some." Neither officer bothered to record the fate of the children.[23]

Nor did Adams think much about the prospect of arming runaways. Shortly after the First Cavalry arrived in Beaufort, General David Hunter, commander of the Department of the South (comprising Georgia, South Carolina, and Florida), requested that the War Department ship him 50,000 rifles and uniforms enough to clothe "such loyal men" as he could find along the Carolina coast. Although the New York–born abolitionist did not explicitly say so, he clearly intended to liberate and arm African Americans. Some blacks enthusiastically signed on, but others, fearing white retribution if captured, proved so reluctant that Hunter resorted to conscripting men from the countryside. "Our ultra-friends, including General Hunter, seem to have gone crazy," Charles Francis informed his father, "and they are doing the blacks all the harm they can." The young lieutenant was particularly incensed that Hunter exempted his black recruits from fatigue duty, so "while our Northern soldiers work ten hours a day in loading and unloading ships, the blacks never leave their camp." With his next breath, Adams conceded that Hunter drilled his men incessantly, trying to accomplish in a matter of weeks what the First Cavalry had spent more than six months learning. In August, when Secretary of War Edwin Stanton ordered Hunter's unit disbanded, Adams celebrated the moment with "great joy," telling his father that "our troops have become more anti-negro than I could have imagined." Very few African Americans were capable of bearing arms, Adams believed. "What God made plain we have mixed up into inextricable confusion."[24]

While Charles Francis's letters slowly made their way north and then east across the Atlantic, a missive from Henry reached his brother in Beaufort. "I congratulate your General Hunter on his negro-army," he gushed. "We *all* here sustain him and I assure you that the strongest means of holding Europe back is the sight of an effective black army." Perhaps, Henry suggested, if enough blacks enlisted, Charles Francis might volunteer to serve as their colonel. Charles Francis was having none of it. "No! Hunter and you are wrong, and, for once, the War Department was right," he shot back. Contrabands might be used on fatigue duty, he argued, driving wagons, cooking rations, and digging latrines. But the time had not yet arrived that "they could be made to stand before their old masters" and face Confederate guns. With effective white officers, Adams lectured, black troops "might make soldiery equal to the native Hindoo regiments" used by the British in India "in about five years." But never with him as their officer, Adams scoffed. "I smiled audibly at your idea of my taking a commission in one of them," he told Henry. He had no interest in becoming a "nigger driver," for that, he believed, was what was necessary, "seeing that they don't run away, or shirk work or fatigue duty." Charles Francis suspected that Henry had underlined the word "all" in his letter to suggest that their father agreed with him. But if so, Charles Francis wished the entire London household to understand that "the idea of arming the blacks as soldiers must be abandoned."[25]

Rather than engage his second son in a transatlantic debate or confront his growing racism, Charles Francis Sr. retreated to his diary, fretful as ever that his son "has sealed his own fate." Even if he survived the war, Adams worried, "he will scarcely recover from the dislocation of mutual and moral habits consequent upon such a change of life at his years." Although he had no reason to suspect that camp life in Beaufort was in itself depraved, Adams believed that of all of his children, Charles Francis Jr. was the most likely "to acquire distinction in civil life." His single flaw was "the want of perseverance in one direction, which materially contributed to impel him" into the army. As a civilian who had no desire to understand military culture, Adams pondered how rising in the ranks in the cavalry might instill just that trait he thought his son lacked. "As a subordinate officer of cavalry his powers are all thrown away."[26]

Far away in London, the elder Adams did not know the half of it. While Charles Francis Jr. regarded the junior officers of his age and social status as brothers, his relationship with the senior officers in the First Cavalry continued to deteriorate. Colonel Williams, Charles Francis grumbled to John Quincy, "drinks like the devil whenever he particularly ought to be sober." Worse yet was Adams's view of the two brothers immediately above him in rank, Lieutenant Colonel Horace Binney Sargent and the younger captain, Lucius Sargent. Adams viewed Horace as "ludicrously incompetent" at his job, while Lucius, he assured John Quincy, was "ugly as the devil, crazy as a coot, and, half his time, drunk as a lord." For the most part, the three men attempted to keep their distance, but given the chain of command, that was not always possible. After each "bloody row," Horace was forced to serve as a "sort of umpire," and while Adams conceded that the lieutenant colonel tried to act professionally, he was not "much pleased by the young gentleman who made such an unpleasant exposure of his brother."[27]

Adams's use of the term "gentleman" to describe himself was revealing. Although both Sargent brothers had attended Harvard, with Lucius first serving as surgeon with the Massachusetts Second Volunteer Infantry, Adams regarded them as no true Brahmins. Tempers finally boiled over in early March. Rather to the annoyance of officers, cavalrymen were notorious for wandering off, usually in search of a nearby smokehouse or orchard to plunder. Adams had ridden away from the pack to check for stragglers when Captain Sargent realized he was missing. Upon Adams's return, Sargent ordered him arrested, shouting: "By the Almighty Jesus Christ I will make you do your duty, Sir, or I will disgrace you! Go do your duty!!" Once again placed in the middle of a feud that he little needed, Horace privately dressed his brother down for bringing up charges. Unwilling to leave it at that, Adams complained to the lieutenant colonel about his brother's harsh language. Infuriated with them both, the senior Sargent, Adams grumbled, no longer regarded him "with favor and [was] disposed to treat me roughly." Adams expected no help from Colonel Williams, who "on general principles supports the superior officer against the inferior." Perhaps, Charles Francis encouraged John Quincy, he might contact Governor Andrew about a position in a new regiment. "I am fully fit for a Majority now," Adams added, "but if I can't get that, a Captaincy, but a transfer at any rate and at once."[28]

IN EARLY JUNE 1862, BEFORE JOHN QUINCY COULD TAKE ANY ACtion, Company H was ordered north to support McClellan in the aftermath of his failed Peninsula Campaign. Adams had fallen ill and was hospitalized in one of the elegant Beaufort mansions confiscated by the army for wounded and sick soldiers. At the time he regarded his hospital stay as "most unlucky," as he preferred to accompany his men. Instead, he was assigned as an aide to Colonel Williams, a position he held until September. Several days later, he was well enough to return to camp, and it was then that he received his "baptism of fire," or "seeing the elephant," as many soldiers dubbed it after their first firefight. Having already captured Hilton Head and nearby Tybee Island, American forces hoped to expand their control of the coastline by advancing on Charleston. It was a formidable task. Fort Sumter guarded the harbor's mouth, while Fort Moultrie sat just north across the channel, its seaward wall protected by bags of sand. Just south of the harbor's entrance stretched Morris Island, home to Confederate batteries Gregg and Wagner. North of Morris Island and to Charleston's west, just across the Ashley River, was James Island, the most obvious land route into the city. But the large island was latticed by swamps and streams, and the Confederates counted on a salty marsh that lined James Island's border with Morris Island, together with Confederate artillerymen under General Thomas Lamar, to keep invading forces at bay. Despite these odds, it was there that General Henry Benham—an "old hen," in Adams's estimation—determined that six thousand soldiers from seven northern states, including the Twenty-Eighth Massachusetts, would launch their attack.[29]

As a member of Williams's staff, Adams knew what was coming. Their camp on the Stono River was close enough that shells shrieked overhead every few hours. "We might soon have hard fighting and a hard time of it," he warned John Quincy. In preparation for his first fight, Adams took the necessary precautions that had become all too common for soldiers on both sides. Charles Francis asked John Quincy to drop a line to Louisa but to "draw it up mild so as not to scare her." Should he be wounded or killed—Adams preferred the euphemistic "in case of accident"—he alerted his brother that he had left his trunk of personal possessions with the Adams Express Company Office at Hilton Head. Gazing across the river at the swamps, Adams thought the attack "decidedly premature" and feared "we may be in a scrape."[30]

Orders to saddle up arrived at one in the morning on June 16. As he rode through the gray dawn behind Williams, Adams remembered feeling "in no way heroic." After wading through creeks and bogs, they came to an open field, and Adams could see Lamar's works directly before him. A shell landed but a few yards away, although it did not explode, instead bouncing and rolling through the ranks. "It impressed me un-pleasantly," Adams remembered thinking. Confederate forces numbered only two thousand, but rifle companies from South Carolina and Georgia were dug in near Lamar's cannon. Shells shrieked over the First Cavalry, and the roar of artillery was so deafening that Adams could not hear the muskets but only spy "puffs of dust" raised about him as the balls dug into the earth. Williams led his staff—most of the regiment being held in reserve—to the extreme left, and as they galloped, Adams thought it curious that he "had lost all sense of danger." Thanks to months of drills, his mare was equally calm: "Nothing scared her; not even the explosion of shells close by." As he galloped behind Williams, Adams drew the expensive pistol that John Quincy had sent him, but, evidently damp, it refused to fire.[31]

Union infantrymen made three attempts to overrun or flank the Confederate artillery, but at great cost. "We tried the front and got hell," Adams told John Quincy, "and then left and its back-kitchen." Benham finally ordered a retreat at 9:45 A.M., after four hours of combat. "We retreated in perfect order," Adams observed, and the equally weary Confederates left them "wholly unmolested [and] did not even try to shell" them. Northern casualties approached 700, while Confederates lost but 204. After Union forces pulled back, Lamar ordered his soldiers to bury the 341 northern dead in front of his lines. "The affair was badly managed," Adams fumed, "and it was a wonder we were not all killed." Basking in the radiance of his unexpected survival, however, Adams thought little about the soldiers lost, most of whom were not from the First Cavalry. "It was a pleasant feeling, that of riding out of my first battle, having done well in it," he remarked to his journal. "I don't think I ever experienced so genial a glow." As he dismounted, Adams felt a "new and exalted sense of my own importance" and reflected that he did not believe he had "ever passed a more pleasurable morning." Williams was equally effusive, praising his staff for riding "through the hottest of fire with the utmost coolness." Less enthusiastic about the battle's outcome was General Hunter, still in command of the Department of the South, who ordered Benham arrested and held for court-martial for disobedience. So ended the first and only attempt by US forces to capture Charleston with an overland thrust.[32]

Adams was still trying to sort out his emotions ten days later when he admitted to John Quincy that he was "not above wishing to have the credit of it," and he hinted to his brother that he might want to write to Governor Andrew, as all of Williams's staff were "Boston men." Aware that news of the skirmish might reach his sister in Newport or his parents in London before he could write, he also asked John Quincy to "immediately notify the Governor and Lou of my safety." In fact, newspaper accounts of a "very severe action at Charleston" had arrived in Britain just prior to a letter of Charles Francis's dated June 18, and as Charles Francis Sr. told his diary, the family had been filled "with private uneasiness." Charles Francis Jr. made no effort to soften the blow. "We had a severe action and were repulsed with very heavy loss," he bluntly told his father, adding that he himself "was in the advance of one of the attacking columns." The thrill of survival had cooled since June 16, as he confessed that he had been frightened. But his mind had been clear: "the machine worked with a vigor and power" he little suspected that he possessed. Perhaps the groans of the nearby wounded gave Adams pause, as he warned his family that he "would rather not run its risk" of ever again seeing action. Yet as before, Adams concluded that he would not have missed the experience "for anything," insisting that "it was one of the most enjoyable days I ever passed." Upon receiving the letter, the worried minister again fretted in his diary that Charles Francis Jr. was "not fitted for such business."[33]

In the weeks after the battle, it became clear to the cavalrymen that their services on the Carolina coast were not required. "They tell us we are to see Charleston," Adams recorded on June 28, "but not now to enter it." General Hunter intended to make Benham "the scape-goat of all our misfortunes," which was the only news that provided Adams with any satisfaction. The only new fighting, he discovered, was with the heat and insects after their return to Hilton Head: "Dust, sand, government warehouses and fleas, constitute all its attractions." Colonel Williams watched as his regiment grew increasingly filthy, and he tasked his officers with the "responsibility for the cleanliness of their men." Following a surprise inspection, Williams found the men's clothing, arms, and equipment to be in a "very dirty state." He ordered the men to bathe or swim as often as possible, cut their hair, trim their beards and, in a directive that would have infuriated General Ambrose Burnside, shave off all "side whiskers."[34]

By mid-July, rumor had it that the remaining companies of the First Cavalry, together with roughly nine thousand other soldiers, were to be shipped to northern Virginia to join Company H in protecting the capital and shoring up the battered Army of the Potomac. "Our poor regiment seems likely to go into garrison duty in the midst of an active war," Adams informed his father. He agreed with the decision to pull the cavalry out of the Charleston fight, as in the coming months the US Navy planned to bombard Sumter and Wagner from just outside the harbor. But Charles Francis wondered about the political consequences of trying to subjugate Virginia while much of the Confederacy remained intact. Should the army succeed in capturing Richmond, he saw "only an immense territory and a savage and ignorant populace to be held down by force." The North, "right or wrong," would have to liberate the slaves in that region, followed by a "spirit of blind, revengeful fanaticism," about which Adams thought Charles Sumner was "typical, utterly lacking in practical wisdom." But junior officers followed orders, and August 20 saw Adams embarking on the inaptly named steamer *McClellan*.[35]

THE RELOCATION BROUGHT OTHER SORTS OF CHANGES AS WELL. Although Adams had learned to tolerate Colonel Williams, and even to admire his bravery on James Island, few of the men thought highly of the Virginia native. Nor did he much care for them. In the early fall, Williams announced his intentions to resign his commission and accept a desk job in Washington with the adjutant-general's office. Lieutenant Colonel Horace Binney Sargent was given command of the First, which signaled a promotion for his brother Lucius as well. That in turn prompted Adams to renew his efforts to obtain a transfer and promotion. He had long feared that his "utter lack of a nice, ingratiating tact in my dealing with other men" might prevent him from rising in the ranks. "It is an inherited deficiency; a family trait," he observed, a "hindrance in life, and never so much as in the army." Having the Sargents leading the regiment meant he would finish the war as he began, a first lieutenant. Even before shipping north, Adams contacted John Quincy, imploring him to use his connections and intercede with the governor. John Quincy "lost no time in going to work," but with little success. Andrew deemed it "unjust to many older and ranking candidates who were anxious for promotion." John Quincy then "stirred up" influential family friends John Gorham Palfrey and Richard Henry Dana to lobby Secretary William Seward, and he even "incited Lou to do so." In response, Seward urged John Quincy to travel to Washington "and try to engineer it" with the War Department.[36]

John Quincy's enlistment of his sister Louisa may simply have been an attempt to recruit a female voice when lobbying an old family connection. Or perhaps he hoped to persuade the brilliant Louisa into making herself useful in the Union cause, and in the process dragging herself out of her lethargy and emotional distress following the death of her infant daughter in October 1857. Louisa had initially fretted that she was "not good enough" for motherhood, but after her brief trip to Europe, she rationalized that losing the child might prove a "blessing in time." Many Brahmin wives and mothers devoted long hours to rolling bandages or organizing fund-raisers for care packages to the front or to underemployed British textile workers, but apart from writing a brief letter to Seward in her brother's behalf, Louisa was content to play the role of Newport socialite until finally fleeing again to Europe in 1864.[37]

At length, John Quincy secured his younger brother a position on the staff of Major General John Pope, commander of the Army of Virginia. President Lincoln was clearly displeased with McClellan, and as John Quincy put it, "Pope is a coming man and you will probably have as much fighting and as much devilish hard work as you can wish." In London, Charles Francis Sr. was gratified to hear of the offer as, unlike John Quincy, he assumed that the position would keep his son far removed from Confederate guns. But even as the *McClellan* steamed up the coast, Charles Francis decided to remain with the First. The army had "grave fears for the safety of Washington," he informed a stunned John Quincy, "so that evidently this regiment is soon to see severe service." The only twist that might now compel him to transfer was if he and his friend Caspar Crowninshield could move in tandem. Otherwise, did not his duty to his old regiment, he wrote his father, outweigh service "on an ornamental staff?"[38]

The normally affable John Quincy was understandably irate upon hearing of his brother's indecision. "I am as you know very anxious to do all in my power for you, but when you change your mind every day I have no ground of surety on which to act," he snapped. "The last three letters from you have each contained a different plan entirely incompatible with my previous efforts for you." Charles Francis's latest scheme, that he and Crowninshield might be transferred together, John Quincy added, "is perfect in all but feasibility." Wanting it clearly understood that he was done contacting governors and cabinet secretaries on his brother's behalf, John Quincy concluded his blunt missive by remarking that he was aggrieved "to find that my successes" in procuring an appointment for Charles Francis were somehow a "mortification for you, but you *must stand by it*."[39]

For once, Charles Francis was contrite. "You are quite right in blowing me [up] for changing my mind in this business," he agreed. "Like a trump you stood by me and got me a higher transfer than I could have hoped for." Charles Francis admitted that he had been an "ass" and a "knave" to a brother who had performed nearly herculean efforts to remove him from the entanglements of his regiment. The lengthy letter was a thoroughly abject apology, but also one that revealed that Charles Francis's relationship with John Quincy was quite unlike that with the younger Henry. As John Quincy had demonstrated that he desired nothing more in life than the pleasant existence of a gentleman farmer, and Louisa not a consideration as an heir apparent, Charles Francis did not feel the need to compete with them over who was the ascending member of their generation. He and John Quincy rarely even discussed politics in their weekly correspondence. But the brilliant Henry was an altogether different matter. Only three years Charles Francis's junior, and now meeting prime ministers and foreign secretaries in London, Henry might achieve greatness, relegating Charles Francis to the shadows. Their prickly, political, and often caustic missives were a world apart from those posted to each other by the two eldest brothers. Unfortunately, Charles Francis and Henry would carry their rivalry to their graves.[40]

As strange fate would have it, shortly after Adams arrived in Washington and reluctantly prepared to report to Pope, Lee struck the US Army of Virginia on August 28 before McClellan could bring up the entire Army of the Potomac. Fought on the same ground as the first Battle of Bull Run the year before, Lee's smaller army inflicted enormous damage on Union forces, resulting in roughly twice as many casualties as the Confederate losses of 7,300. "All army officers say that [Pope] is a humbug and is sure to come to grief," a prescient Charles Francis informed John Quincy earlier that morning. "He has already played himself into such a position that he will be crushed and Washington lost." Then, shortly before Pope was relieved of his command on September 12, the retiring Colonel Williams simplified matters by reminding Adams that the Revised Army Regulations proscribed cavalry officers from detachment for staff duty. Worried that he might yet be transferred to an infantry regiment, Adams opted to return to the First. "You must take it out in cussing my instability," he laughed to John Quincy. This time, his elder brother understood. "I entirely concur in your decision if the facts are as you think," he replied, adding that he would explain matters to a disappointed "Lou [and] the Governor." Although he would not know it for several months, Charles Francis's luck further improved on October 30, when he was promoted to captain in the First.[41]

By then, Adams was again in the midst of battle. Emboldened by his victory at the second Bull Run, Lee convinced President Davis to carry the war into the United States. On September 3, Lee's Army of Northern Virginia—fifty-five thousand strong—crossed into Maryland, hoping to "liberate" the loyal slave state and force Lincoln to abandon an encircled Washington. McClellan's Army of the Potomac, including the First Massachusetts, marched north to intercept the invaders. Adams's regiment was ill-prepared. The troopers were down to seven hundred horses, so many of the cavalrymen were forced to tramp alongside those mounted. Orders to ride gave them little time to stock up on rations for themselves and forage for their horses. As they rode, Adams's company fed on green corn and apples and whatever they could steal from nearby farmhouses, thefts that did little to endear the Union to Maryland farmers. The horses fed almost exclusively on green cornstalks, a "very poor food," Crowninshield remarked, and probably responsible for the epidemic of "greased heel"—cracked and inflamed skin on lower limbs—among their mounts. By the time they reached Frederick, Maryland, on September 13, Adams's mare was "fairly done up," so he left her there, together with his last clean shirt and bar of soap, after commandeering another mount.[42]

Adams caught up to his regiment about three miles outside of Frederick after it paused because of artillery fire to its front. Some of the shells landed "disagreeably near" the troops, and Adams urged an infantry captain to clear his men from the road. Just then a ball hurtled through the trees, narrowly missing Crowninshield but shearing off the legs of three resting infantrymen. The First galloped into the hills to discern Confederate movements. "The bullets sung over our heads in a lively style," Charles Francis later told his mother, but as they approached a field, they blundered into Illinois cavalrymen in a "sharp engagement." Adams dismounted and drew his pistol, only then noticing loyal Maryland women waving their handkerchiefs at them, passing out water and hailing them as "liberators." He thought it curious that the women were so close, especially as carbines on both sides were blazing away "like crackers on the 4th of July." Adams shouted to press ahead, but retreating Confederates burned the bridge before them, hindering their advance.[43]

Over the next two days, McClellan wasted his cavalry. The First "moved aimlessly about," Crowninshield complained. At one point on September 14, they found themselves in a cornfield caught between Confederate and Union batteries, "the shells hurtling over us like mad," Adams remembered, "but fortunately doing us no harm save ruffling our nerves." Finally, early in the morning of September 17, the First was posted in the trees above Antietam Creek in support of General Fitz-John Porter's battery. The woods shielded the First from the sight of Confederate batteries, which blindly shelled the hillside. "It seemed as if we were doomed," Adams recalled, so incessant was "the hurtling of projectiles as they passed both ways over us." At any moment, Adams assumed, the order to charge would arrive. It never did. The weary Adams dismounted and fell asleep, deaf to the "storm of artillery [and] the crashing of shells." He awoke briefly to tend to his horse, "who was grazing somewhat wide." Despite the carnage of the morning— combined casualties of 22,726—the First did not lose a single man or, as Adams drolly added, "scarcely a horse."[44]

The next morning, Lee retreated across the Potomac. The First rode to his rear, collecting a "few abandoned wagons, a caisson or two, and other worthless trash," as a disgusted Crowninshield sighed. Having lost his pen and papers several days before, Adams scribbled out a note to John Quincy with a borrowed pencil to let him know that he was "so far well and hearty." But he had not washed his face in four days, had no toothbrush, and owned just the uniform on his back. "In 22 days I have undressed twice and changed my clothes once," he complained in late September. Adams had now survived two major battles and been under fire "for five consecutive days" but had yet to draw his sword or fire his pistol. Most distressing, he thought, was that while he had played a small role in running "the rebels out of Maryland" and had now been in the cavalry for nine months, "I don't see that I am any nearer my desired result than I was the day I came into it."[45]

Mid-October found Adams near McConnellsburg in southern Pennsylvania. They were still in pursuit of Confederate raiders and had spent nine days in the saddle, searching much of western Maryland. One day, the sore Adams recorded, they covered fifty miles, and another twenty and thirty over the next two days. But the exhausted cavalryman remained a child of privilege, despite the fact that, once again, the paymaster had not appeared in weeks. "I must have a servant, and have one at once," he implored John Quincy. He required a young man who knew not only how to groom a horse but also "how to take care of himself and me too." A number of displaced-persons camps had appeared in both Boston and Washington, and Adams suggested that his brother inquire at the stables of the Somerset or Temple Clubs. "Do not send a green boy," he added unhelpfully, "unless you know him to be smart." It would be permissible for his servant to "drink in moderation," and he guessed twenty dollars per month to be a fair rate. For lack of a proper servant, Adams fretted, "I now starve, freeze, soak, lose my property, my reputation and my temper."[46]

The remaining months of 1862 did not go well for Adams. By the end of October, the epidemic of "greased heel" had spread to the point that the regiment was down to just two hundred mounted men ready for duty. Confederate cavalrymen led by the flamboyant J. E. B. Stuart made off with roughly one thousand Maryland horses, serving to further demoralize Adams's men. Black refugees poured into the camp, cutting into their already-stretched food supplies. Nor did his search for a manservant go as hoped. John Quincy hired a young Bostonian named Morris White, but Charles Francis, despite his own disposition toward morning cocktails, dismissed him for heavy drinking. Adams immediately thought better of it. Perhaps, he instructed a frustrated John Quincy, he might track him down and hire him again, provided that "he has not yet become a sot." White had proved an admirable groom and an attentive servant, at least when sober. "As it is," Adams complained, "my life is worn out of me by the stupid negroes who ruin my things and sour my temper."[47]

By Thanksgiving, Adams's company was camped near Potomac Bridge, Virginia, wading "through mud and mire and rain" in winter quarters. The Quartermaster's Department was as delinquent as the paymaster, and those men who could not obtain shipments from home still wore "the lightest clothing," which they had been issued along the Carolina coast. Crowninshield reported to superiors that the entire regiment was in rags and freezing. Charles Francis begged his brother to ship him tobacco, underclothes, boots, and blankets, not just for himself but as many as John Quincy could procure. Safe in Boston, John Quincy chided his brother for losing so many things, prompting Adams to reply that "regular pilfering" was a way of life in the unit. To Henry, also snug in an elegant London home, Charles Francis lamented that they had "not a drop to drink, save water," especially after his latest servant discovered the brandy Adams carried in his flask and polished that off. The water was foul, and Adams suffered a "smart attack of [his] friend the dysentery," which the army treated with opium, a drug that left him "cross and disgusted."[48]

After Governor Andrew received word of the regiment's distress, he dispatched John Quincy to Washington to see to the unit's needs. He hoped to locate Charles Francis, who had been allowed a few quick visits to the capitol, and when that failed, he and several other aides rode out into Maryland, unsuccessfully asking about the location of the First. They reached a dark and shuttered Frederick just before midnight. "At last I managed to rouse an old nigger," John Quincy wrote, easily falling into his brother's habit of employing racial epithets, despite the fact that the kindly freeman fed and watered their horses and provided them with "nice beds and a nice breakfast." Charles Francis missed his brother by only four days, arriving in Washington on November 14, but he collected the bundles left for him, fell into a soft bed at Willard's Hotel, and enjoyed a "feast daily at Butler's."[49]

"We are having a devilishly hard time here," Adams reported to his parents on December 8 from Brooks Station, Virginia. Their tents had no heat, so the new captain ordered his men to construct a stone fireplace at the rear of his tent. The region had been hit with an ice storm, and the season was as bad as in Boston. His latest servant was ill, so Adams paid to have him shipped back to Massachusetts, as he judged it wrong "to expose a boy of his age to such hardships as we now have to endure." Despite the ice, Adams was still obligated to ride picket duty, spending several twenty-hour periods in the saddle. Rather than express sympathy to his cold, grimy brother, John Quincy reached the end of his patience. "What in hell is the use of troubling yourself to write when you are so damned ugly?" he exploded. "Can't you hold it in till you feel a trifle more serene?" Both brothers were aware that at that moment, General Ambrose Burnside, the latest commander of the Army of the Potomac, was approaching the hamlet of Fredericksburg and more young men were about to die. "Nor do I agree with you in thinking our people unmindful of your difficulties and sufferings and privations," John Quincy continued. Other soldiers, lacking wealthy families to ship them boots and hams and whiskey, had it worse. A man "has made an ass of himself when he puts his tantrums on paper," John Quincy concluded, pouring out his ire. This time, taking a cue from their father, Charles Francis simply declined to reply.[50]

On both sides of the Atlantic, the holidays ended in despair. In London, Charles Francis Sr. found little solace in *Somebody's Luggage*, Charles Dickens's latest Christmas offering, although a letter from Charles Francis Jr. assured him that he was safe and that no cavalry had been engaged at Fredericksburg, the latest Union debacle. "I fear there are many parents who have not been able to cheer themselves in a like manner," the elder Adams reflected. But his apprehensions about his son were not diminished: the conflict, despite Lincoln's Emancipation Proclamation, was sure to drag on for several more years. "Much more blood has been shed, but without materially changing" the balance of power between the North and South, he fretted. "I am filled with anxiety about my son, whom I [am] strongly reluctant to see sacrificed," even in a cause they all shared. At least, he mused, letters from his son John Quincy— who had not corresponded with his brother in weeks—were "unusually cheerful."[51]

On Christmas Eve, Charles Francis Jr. was arrested yet again, this time by Colonel Horace Binney Sargent rather than his younger brother. As before, the charge was abandoning the column while on march. Having led a patrol out to check pickets, Adams had returned to discover that Colonel Robert Buchanan was quartered nearby. Adams wished to see him and, obtaining the permission of Major Henry Lee Higginson to do so, rode over for a discussion of about ten minutes. Upon his return, Sargent demanded to know where he had been. "I pleasantly informed him, in that airy manner which makes me a universal favorite," Charles Francis told his father, and Sargent ordered his arrest. Adams strode away, "winking pleasantly" at Sargent's orderlies. He had the consent of Higginson, his own "immediate superior," and word had finally arrived of his promotion. "Now if I am Captain he *may* go to Hell," Charles Francis laughed to John Quincy. As Adams anticipated, the matter was dropped.[52]

On Christmas afternoon, his makeshift fireplace warming the tent, Adams and Henry Davis enjoyed a dinner served on battered tin plates. Louisa was with her husband, Charles Kuhn, in Rhode Island, and the rest of the Adams were divided between Massachusetts and Britain. "Your dinner in London and John's in Boston will not taste better than ours," Charles Francis informed his father, "though we do eat tough beef and drink commissary whiskey." Toasts to his good health, Charles Francis Jr. was confident, "will be drunk [in] Boston and Newport and London." Unlike his dour father, Captain Adams expected that Lincoln's new war of emancipation would quickly turn the tide and that this would be his last Christmas in the field. Perhaps, however, his dislike of his father blinded him to the elder Adams's wisdom on this score, as the coming two years would put both men to the test.[53]

7

"YOUR LORDSHIP, THIS IS WAR"

The Combatants

"A TELEGRAM FROM AMERICA BROUGHT US THE NEWS OF THE
President's proclamation," a relieved Charles Francis Adams Sr.
confided to his diary on January 13, 1863. Especially in New England,
abolitionists had feared that at the last moment, Lincoln might withdraw
his promise of emancipation in hopes of winning back portions of the
Upper South. But the president's course, Adams observed, was "now no
longer in doubt." The "mighty revolution" against human bondage continued, and Adams prayed that "the mark of Divine providence" had taken a
hand in his nation's fate. The contest was far from over, he conceded. But
freedom was "coming," and all "the more rapidly on account of the war."
As ever, Adams feared for the life of his son, but it was of little use, he
reflected, "for us feeble mortals to waste ourselves with public anxieties,
when we see not as He seeth."[1]

Adams had been in Britain for nearly two years, and he hoped the
day was not far distant when he might return home. The family had
moved into more spacious quarters at 54 Portland Place, where they were
cared for by a staff of nine, including two footmen, two housemaids,

a coachman, a butler, a lady's maid, a cook, and a kitchen maid. But his daughter Mary's health concerned Adams, and doctors warned him that her lungs suffered from the damp British weather. If returning to Boston or Washington would not draw his son Charles Francis out of harm's way, it had the virtue of dramatically shortening the arrival of news from the front, and the endless waiting to hear of his son's safety was a constant source of emotional pain. The next sixteen months, however, were to prove the most critical yet for the minister, for his son's regiment, and for the American nation they both served. The two men, both warriors after their own fashion, were far from finished with their respective tasks and nowhere near returning to the quiet of hearth and home.[2]

Two days later, on January 15, Adams notified Seward that as the Lincoln administration hoped, the proclamation "had a decided effect in concentrating the opinions" of those in Britain already sympathetic to the Union cause. Having eradicated slavery in their Caribbean empire in the 1830s, the British public was staunchly antislavery. So long as prominent Republicans insisted that the war was one of reunion, while Confederate envoys discounted the role that the expansion of slavery had played in secession, Palmerston's government could balance his nation's opposition to slavery with a quiet desire to see the South victorious. Lincoln's transformation of the conflict into a war for human liberty changed all of that. "The current of opinion continues to set strongly in favor of the President's Proclamation," Adams again assured Seward later in the month. At the same time, Jefferson Davis had damaged his standing abroad by announcing that "all negro slaves captured in arms" were to be treated as rebels and runaways, while white officers "found serving in company with armed slaves [were] criminals deserving death." The "first fruits of that barbarous edict tend to dispel all motions heretofore so industriously propagated in Europe of the superior civilization and refinement of slave-holding society," Adams observed. "Some military successes at home" could settle the matter in Britain once and for all. But with his own state preparing to raise a pioneering black infantry regiment, Adams suspected that "the principle of emancipation has got such hold that it cannot again be eradicated."[3]

The proclamation was particularly popular among Britain's industrial working class. Although as yet unable to vote, working-class urbanites found numerous ways to express their political views, and had they united with their employers in opposing Lincoln's naval blockade, which bottled up southern cotton, Palmerston's ministry would have enjoyed far greater freedom in pursuing a disunionist agenda. Adams persisted in thinking that "the higher classes" remained opposed to the United States, but the proclamation, he told Edward Everett, "has produced meetings the like of which have not been seen since the days of reform and the Corn-Laws" (the post–Napoleonic War tariffs on foreign grains that kept bread prices high). Adams and his secretaries suddenly found much of their days devoted to answering "addresses and resolutions" submitted by working-class groups which begged that their expressions of sympathy be forwarded to President Lincoln. For the present, the determination of working men to stand by the Union deterred any discussions of recognition of the Confederacy in the House of Commons. Adams thought it fascinating that while British aristocrats claimed Confederates were "struggling [against] oppression," the undereducated factory workers grasped the essential truth "that on the contrary [slaveholders] are fighting only to establish it."[4]

One morning in mid-January, Adams opened the door of the Legation to find a "large deputation of the Executive Committee of the Emancipation Society" waiting to present him with a series of resolutions. The normally dour minister was thrilled by the "strong manifestation of good feeling" and delivered a brief, impromptu speech of thanks. Public meetings at Aberdare in Wales and Bradford in Yorkshire submitted "similar manifestations of the public sentiment," and members of the Manchester branch of the Emancipation Society addressed "public meetings throughout the manufacturing districts." Working-class Britons, who had been demanding the right to vote since being left out of the Reform Act of 1832, believed that the Union was fighting their fight and that southern slaves were their brothers in labor. "The aristocracy are decidedly against the continuance of the Union," Adams complained to longtime friend and Republican activist Richard Henry Dana. But the "working and the religious classes," and especially the dissenting faiths, supported "our struggle."[5]

When in January 1863 British reformers held an "Emancipation and Reunion" rally in London's Exeter Hall, Henry strolled over to see for himself whether the support of industrial towns held true in England's shipping center. By the time Henry arrived, the hall was packed and the crowd spilled down the street and blocked all traffic. Organizers quickly secured a second, nearby hall, where author and evangelist Tom Brown took the podium. "Every allusion to the South was followed by groaning, hisses, and howls," Henry reported to his brother Charles Francis, "and the enthusiasm for Lincoln and everything connected with the North was immense." Henry had expected the Proclamation to solidify support behind the Union, but what he witnessed revealed abolitionist fervor to be even "stronger than we ever expected." Those members of Parliament already supportive of the United States knew they had the middle and working classes firmly on their side, while those representing manufacturing districts, Henry crowed, "have fairly been thrown over by their people."[6]

That March, the American cause received an even greater boost when the trade unions of London held a huge meeting at St. James Hall. Organized in part by Karl Marx, who had been expelled from Paris by city authorities more than a decade before, the convention's keynote was delivered by John Bright, a Quaker and longtime Corn Laws opponent who had sat in the House of Commons in the early 1840s. Bright reminded his audience that the American struggle for democracy was their own. "Do not," he shouted, extend "the hand of fellowship to the worst foes of freedom that the world has ever seen." The conservative London press did its best to belittle the meeting. The *Saturday Review* sneered at Bright's "carnival of cant," and the *Times* sniffed that the enormous convention had been peopled only by middle- and working-class "nobodies." However, Adams took especial care to personally thank Bright, assuring him that the president was "profoundly impressed by your liberal sentiments" and that he himself firmly believed that "the Trades Unions have spoken in the voice of the people of Great Britain."[7]

The only sour note was expressed by Benjamin Moran, the assistant secretary of the Legation, who believed that he was spending too much time responding to delegations of supporters, a task that he thought far better suited for Henry. When Charles Sturge, the mayor of Birmingham, arrived unannounced at the head of a large delegation, Moran let them know that he was annoyed by their lack of warning, and he privately complained that Adams should somehow have known of their plans. Adams, however, invited them all inside and delivered yet another short address of thanks. Apart from the desire not to alienate any potential supporters, Adams honestly thought it "remarkable" that the same textile workers who had endured pay cuts and a reduction of hours because of the shortage of cotton resolutely sided with the North: "The people who have the greatest cause to complain of us are the most unequivocal in their expression of sympathy."[8]

FAR AWAY TO THE WEST, NEAR POTOMAC RUN, VIRGINIA, THE NEW year began calmly, if hardly as encouraging as it was perceived in London. In the wake of the Fredericksburg debacle, a frustrated Lincoln decided to replace Ambrose Burnside with yet another commander of the Army of the Potomac, Major General Joseph Hooker. While the new commander made a number of high-level administrative changes, the cavalrymen of the First Massachusetts spent the first months of 1863 caring for their mounts and scavenging for food and supplies. Rumor had it that Hooker intended to improve his army's quartermaster system and daily diet, and Charles Francis Jr. was all for that. "The men are fearfully in want of boots," he informed John Quincy in late January, begging his brother to ship him five hundred pairs. The quality provided by the army had degenerated to the point that what they received did "not last three weeks." Marching about on the frozen ground with feet wrapped in rags was something only Confederates should do, he groused. Hooker was a Massachusetts man, and Adams expected better of him.[9]

Adams also remained out of sorts with his colonel. The regiment's lieutenant colonel, Greeley Curtis, five years Adams's senior and a member of the Harvard class of 1851, was one of the few senior officers Adams respected, but Curtis had been dispatched to Hooker's camp near Falmouth, Virginia, while the general considered reorganizing the cavalry. Curtis "alone stands between us and the mad incapacity of Col. Sargent," Adams fumed to his brother, who declined to take the hint that he should again inquire about a transfer for the disgruntled captain. Charles Francis did not hide his feelings from his parents, and his complaining missives left his father feeling "very anxious." But the elder Adams was not one to abuse his friendship with Seward by requesting a transfer for his son, assuring his diary that it was "not in his power to extricate him" from a predicament largely of his own making. "I feel more than ever that he is in danger of being sacrificed to no useful end," he worried. "My whole life here has been shaded by this case."[10]

If Charles Francis Jr.'s influential relations refused to secure him a new appointment, John Quincy was willing, at least, to ship him boots, cases of whiskey, and, most of all, an English bulldog. Most cavalry officers kept a pet, Adams noticed, which naturally meant that he also desired one. John Quincy found a bulldog "with a very open countenance," but, judging him fairly stupid, he named the dog McClellan. "He has not had any advantages of education and his manners are rough from long association with the lower classes," John Quincy wrote, only partly in jest, but he had the making of a "very savage and dangerous enemy." Charles Francis adored Mac, but his brother officers and nearby Virginia civilians were less enthusiastic. Mac tried to kill several of their pets and succeeded in catching and devouring a farmer's pig, forcing Adams to keep him chained up when in camp. While on patrol, the "magnificent beast" trotted along beside his horse.[11]

The war returned with a vengeance on the morning of March 17. Hooker ordered General William Averell to lead his reorganized cavalry division of 2,100 troopers across the Rappahannock to attack the Confederate cavalrymen detected near Culpeper Court House. The Union riders reached Kelly's Ford, only to discover that a smaller force of Confederates under General Fitzhugh Lee—Robert E. Lee's nephew—had felled trees and positioned sharpshooters along the river. Averell ordered Rhode Island and Pennsylvania regiments to ford the swiftly flowing river, forcing entrenched Virginians to fall back. The First Massachusetts was ordered not to cross but instead to guard the approaches to the ford against potential flanking maneuvers, and all day, Adams "anxiously expected an attack on ourselves." Late in the afternoon, after hearing railcars approaching and fearing that Confederate infantrymen could trap him against the Rappahannock, Averell ordered his troopers to withdraw. Confederate losses were higher, but among the six Union dead was Second Lieutenant Samuel Bowditch, taken by a sniper. "We were all very fond of him, and his death cast a sharp gloom over our return to camp," Adams wrote John Quincy. Foolishly, Charles Francis also told his father of the skirmish, and the elder Adams lamented that his "uneasiness is not likely to be soon relieved."[12]

Upon reading his brother's letter, Henry reflected that both were changed men. "And so two years have passed and gone, and still I am abroad and still you are a Captain of cavalry," he wrote. After what the pair had witnessed in London and in battle, he mused, how could either return to the dull life of a solicitor? "In short, we have both wholly lost our reckonings and we are driven at random by fate." Henry professed to have no clue what awaited them at war's end, but it would not be their former lives. "Let us quit that now useless shelter, and steer if possible for whatever it may have been that once lay beyond it," Henry urged. "Neither you nor I can ever do anything at the bar."[13]

It was not simply the terrifying prospect of his brother facing Confederate snipers that prompted Henry's musings. By the early spring, it was clear that Charles Francis Sr.'s hopes of having achieved a final resolution to the issue of Confederate shipbuilding and purchases

were premature. Despite Lee's failure at Antietam, British banks had continued to loan the Confederates money; Adams estimated a staggering
total of fifty million pounds (roughly £5.5 billion or $7.3 billion today).
Confederate purchases of British arms and munitions, he feared, "were
growing more [rather] than less" since 1861, with most of the weapons being shipped to Nassau in the Bahamas, "now a perfect storehouse of every
article needful for war." Francis Lawley, a former member of Parliament
turned foreign correspondent for the *London Times*, returned home from
America to give speeches promising the ultimate success of the South. "I
have reason to believe that he has had interviews with Lord Palmerston,"
Adams warned Seward.[14]

For his part, the prime minister demonstrated his coolness to the
Union by discouraging his wife from inviting the Adams household to her
evening parties, and even from returning Abby's calling card, a studied
insult in diplomatic circles. When Parliament resumed in February 1863,
Adams took solace in the fact that opposition leader Benjamin Disraeli
urged caution for the present: "On their minds the effect of the President's
proclamation on public sentiment here has not been lost." But watching
the debates in the Commons, Adams also observed Palmerston's stony
silence. "At heart he has been against us from the first," he groused,
suspecting that only opposition within his cabinet prevented him from
speaking in behalf of the South. Echoing his father, Henry agreed that
Palmerston was a "bad man [who] detests everything American." But
having witnessed the mass workers' meetings of support, Henry remained optimistic; he predicted to Frederick Seward, the secretary's son
and clerk, that Britain was facing a democratic revolution as "the upper
classes have been pledged to a cause hateful to the working men."[15]

Charles Francis Sr.'s mood worsened on March 14, when he received
two notes from Russell, "each of which [was] a little irritating." Some
of their exchanges over the *Alabama* affair had leaked and appeared in
newspapers in both Manhattan and London. Although their contents
were hardly news to the foreign minister, Adams's sharp tone offended
British pride. "I am not aware of having done more than to repel with
spirit the very improper and irrelevant attack of his Lordship, on myself

as well as my government," Adams huffed. Even so, he thought it prudent to craft a limp apology, in which he expressed "profound regret" at any pain that the leak had caused Palmerston's government while also taking pains to applaud the general conviction in the North "that the war has been continued and sustained by the insurgents for many months mainly by the cooperation and assistance obtained from British subjects." The queen's 1861 proclamation of neutrality still stood, Adams complained to Seward, yet Russell simply pretended that he lacked the authority to check the actions of British banks and shippers: "the latest example is the rebel loan of £3,000,000," which was "openly negotiated without a comment from the ministerial press!"[16]

Whether it was bluffing or not, an irritated Congress assisted Adams's efforts in March by passing a bill authorizing Lincoln to commission pro-Union privateers. Late that month, Adams paid yet another call on the foreign secretary, presenting him with a list of American ships that had been sunk or burned by the *Alabama*. Russell insisted that his country also wished to avoid conflict with the United States, but on this matter "the law was difficult to execute." He had recently made a speech to the House of Lords endorsing neutrality, Russell reminded, noting that Palmerston sent him a note "entirely approving of it." Adams drolly replied that had the speech "been made two years ago, we should not have been where we are now," adding that he wished Palmerston might "say the same thing in public." Adams then played his trump card. A good number of Irish nationals had approached the Legation, offering to "enlist in the service of our Government." One day, perhaps, those same émigrés might wish to construct a navy in foreign ports. What then, Adams wondered, would be England's position regarding this precedent?[17]

Adams wisely continued to court Britain's political radicals. After being prodded by Senator Charles Sumner, manufacturer and Liberal Party politician Richard Cobden called on Russell, pressing him to use the authority of the government "in enforcing the law respecting the building of ships for the Confederate government." On May 2, Adams received thirty "working men of London" led by chairman John Bright. "I saw in them a class of persons associated for the protection of the rights of labor,"

Adams noted. "It was natural in them to feel alarmed upon discovering an attempt to set up in America a new government upon the basis of a denial of the existence of any such rights." At about the same time, Adams also hosted a "large breakfast party" designed to introduce Cobden and Bright to John Bigelow, Lincoln's minister in Paris. Unhappily, the otherwise successful affair served to worsen the animosity between Secretary Moran and the Adams family. "His son [Henry] was of course present," Moran grumbled, "but not his secretaries." Although Henry Wilson and Moran were the Legation's formal secretaries, Moran complained that the unpaid Henry enjoyed too much authority. "I find Mr. Adams has two Legations in the house," he fumed. "It all comes from having his son here."[18]

Moran's fury grew in the following weeks after he failed to receive an invitation to dine with the family when Adams hosted authors Charles Dickens and John Forster, along with French socialist Louis Blanc. Moran was then both irritated and gratified when Charles Francis, Abby, Mary, and Henry Wilson—but not he or Henry—were invited to a ball in honor of the Prince of Wales. "I have been left out in the cold," Moran whined, even as he thought it justice that Henry, "who ridiculed the family pictures of his English host and sneered at their hospitality," also remained behind. But having taken exception to Henry's "impertinent meddling" with professional correspondence, Moran then complained that as the summer approached, Henry and Mary devoted two hours each afternoon to riding in a nearby park: "Ye gods! after all an inward contempt for honest labor is as deep in the republican heart as that of the aristocrat."[19]

The minister was either oblivious to the personal divisions within his official household or simply thought the matter unworthy of mention. Or perhaps instead he was simply too pleased that his efforts with the British public had proven effective. Worried that the American government was about to unleash a flock of privateers to prey on British shipping, London's commercial interests joined with working-class organization to lobby the ministry to enforce neutrality. Russell informed Adams that his government intended to seize the *Alexandra*, a wooden screw steamer then being constructed in the same Laird shipyard that had produced

The first Adams to abandon the Republicans for the Democratic Party because of his disaffection for Reconstruction reforms, John Quincy Adams II found his path to high office blocked by his conservatism in a progressive state. Although elected to the state legislature four times, John Quincy's repeated and unsuccessful bids for the governor's chair became the subject of national humor. *Courtesy National Park Service.*

the *Alabama*. At the same time, Russell withdrew his earlier protest over the US Navy's seizure of the British-owned *Peterhoff*, which had been captured by now-Admiral Charles Wilkes while attempting to run the Union blockade. "It is so favorable a sign that my hopes revive of maintaining peace," Adams rejoiced, assuring Everett that while Russell was "not always courteous," the two diplomats invariably "harmonized." Adams again ventured the hope that his tenure in London was coming to an end, and with this latest reduction of tensions, he "began to count the months of [his] remaining term under the most favorable view."[20]

Adding considerably to Adams's satisfaction was the April birth of his second grandson. John Quincy's wife, Fanny, had given birth to a son, John Quincy III, the year before in February 1862, so the second son was christened George Caspar Adams after Charles Francis Sr.'s unfortunate eldest brother. "And the political news is quite favorable," a delighted Adams observed. "So with the exception about Charles's position, things were very encouraging." Charles Francis Jr. took the news with less equanimity. Hoping to finish his service and father the next generation of Adams men, he adopted the attitude toward females typical of his family. "I congratulate you on your increase of family and hope that next time it will be a girl," he wrote from Potomac Run. "But don't have too many, or I'm damned if I come to pass my Sundays with you."[21]

"WE HAVE BEEN VERY QUIET HERE," CHARLES FRANCIS SR. REPORTED to Everett on May 15. Following the seizure of the *Alexandra*, the influential *Times* had moderated its tone, and that in turn calmed the agitation of the city's conservative political clubs. "Yet the main idea of effecting a division in America is never lost sight of," Adams sighed. He ended almost every letter to America by noting that one great success on the battlefield might put an end, once and for all, to British dreams of disunion. George McClellan, Adams had come to understand, scarcely possessed "the materials out of which to make a hero." The Military Academy at West Point, he groused, "has furnished education but nothing more." As a former secretary of war and an officer in the Mexican conflict, Jefferson Davis was "perhaps in some respects superior" to the northern commander-in-chief, but he was hardly a "superior man." Adams was correct in thinking the war had become a "struggle [of] which side can hold out the longest, or chooses to give up the first." What Adams could not know from his remote post was that General Hooker was at last on the move.[22]

On April 27, Hooker's Army of the Potomac, nearly 134,000 strong, began to cross the Rappahannock to the north of Fredericksburg, where Lee's far smaller forces had constructed a vast network of trenches, before shifting south toward Chancellorsville. After nearly encircling the Confederates, Hooker expected Lee to "ingloriously fly." Instead of retreating, Lee sent General Stonewall Jackson's entire corps on a flanking march that so unnerved "Fighting Joe" Hooker—a nickname he had bestowed upon himself—that he withdrew his men to defensive lines around Chancellorsville, ceding the initiative to Lee. After suffering 17,000 casualties to Lee's 13,000, Hooker retreated back across the river on the night of

May 5. In London, successive reports of the invasion and then the defeat filled Adams "with great uneasiness," although that lessened somewhat when letters from John Quincy indicated that the First Massachusetts was not part of the incursion. But pro-southern London papers initially reported that Hooker "had capitulated with his large army" and that Lee was marching on Washington. Subsequent reports cheered Adams somewhat, as he believed the battered Army of Northern Virginia was "crippled" by its losses, and while wrong on that account, he was right in thinking the May 10 death of Stonewall Jackson a "great loss to the rebels." Even so, "Hooker's reputation [was] now reduced" in status, and the nation had sustained another blow to its morale, "which it can ill afford just now."[23]

Charles Francis Jr. was nearly apoplectic, in part because his regiment had not been part of the invasion force, but also at Hooker's timidity. "Do people know what a lying, drunken, low, lewd humbug Josephus pugnacious is?" he stormed. "Those who saw much of Hooker during the fight tell me that until his plan went wrong he was boastful and blasphemous," Charles Francis Jr. informed John Quincy. Most soldiers in the Army of the Potomac, rumor had it, believed that they could have achieved the great and final victory of the war, but "Hooker threw it away." However, the furious captain was almost prescient in thinking that Lincoln should stop appointing self-professed "geniuses." What the army required, Adams believed, was an "honest, faithful, common-sensed and hard-fighting" general, adding that in his campaign against Vicksburg, Mississippi, "Grant seems to be doing well." John Quincy was sympathetic, wishing his brother was with him in Massachusetts, "sucking on your liquor all the day long and dozing under the shade of the chestnut." Yet John Quincy, pondering "solitary life" while drinking to his brother's health, and Henry, far away and dining with Charles Dickens, could hardly fathom what the First Cavalry was about to face.[24]

Emboldened by his victory at Chancellorsville, Lee prevailed upon President Davis to permit a second invasion of the United States. Rather than again invade into Maryland, Lee determined to march up the Shenandoah Valley into Pennsylvania, obtaining badly needed supplies and further damaging northern morale before swinging southeast toward Washington. Hoping to punch through Confederate cavalryman J. E. B. Stuart's protective screen and discover the precise location of the Army of Northern Virginia, Hooker ordered General David McMurtie Gregg to lead his division, which included the First Cavalry, north from their base camp at Potomac Creek, just outside of Fredericksburg. The regiment broke camp on May 24 but rode north very slowly, stopping often in search of Confederate pickets. The alarm came around noon on Wednesday, June 3. Virginia cavalrymen were galloping east toward Sulphur Springs. "We gathered in haste," Charles Francis Jr. wrote. Ordered to collect Union pickets as he moved, Adams worried that he led only fifty men, and one of the officers was an eighteen-year-old recruit fresh from home, "worse than nothing."[25]

As they rode, Adams's men gathered up the exhausted remnants of a few companies spread across the county, but a handful of Virginia runaways warned them that they faced three hundred Confederates. In hindsight, Adams later reflected, he should have organized a "slow, ugly retreat," but instead when the Confederates charged, the First bravely waded into the head of their column. Surprised by the resistance, the Virginians retreated up the turnpike. "The rebs found a wolf where they looked for a hare," Adams proudly told his father.[26]

The First spent most of the following week tending to their mounts. "Our horses were thin and poor," Adams reported. "They needed shoes, [and] our baggage needed overhauling and reduction." Mac also fell ill with a strange swelling, and Adams packed him aboard an ambulance for Warrenton Junction; the surgeons cared less for a bulldog than wounded soldiers, and Mac was heard from no more. "However, in campaigning we risk and lose more than the company of animals," Adams conceded, and "I could not let the loss weigh on me too heavily." Within moments, buglers issued the call to mount, and the First found itself on June 9 in a fight at Brandy Station. Scouts had discovered Stuart's cavalry, and General Alfred Pleasonton ordered a surprise dawn attack. Adams's company "was not very actively engaged" and was ordered to flank "the enemy's right and rear." After a long day of heavy fighting, the Union cavalry pulled back. Confederate casualties were slightly lighter than the Union killed and wounded, although among those wounded and captured was Rooney Lee, Henry Adams's old classmate. For the first time, however, federal cavalrymen had fought the celebrated Stuart to a draw, and Caspar Crowninshield judged it to be "the turning point in the war" for the northern troopers. Adams thought it a lost opportunity. "I am sure a good cavalry officer would have whipped Stuart out of his boots," he swore, "but Pleasonton is not and never will be that."[27]

Two weeks later, the fighting grew worse. Around 4:00 P.M. on June 17, the First Cavalry approached Aldie, Virginia, a strategically important hamlet thirty-five miles northwest of Washington that was intersected by two major turnpikes. As the Massachusetts troopers— together with riders from Maine, New York, and Rhode Island—rode into the little village, they were fired upon by Virginia cavalrymen who had been sent on a forage mission. Union forces slightly outnumbered the fifteen hundred Confederates, but the Virginians had taken cover behind two stone walls and had posted sharpshooters along a ridge that sat above roads leading out of town. Lieutenant Colonel Greeley Curtis ordered one squadron from the First to charge up the narrow road leading to Snicker's Gap Turnpike to discover the Confederates' strength, and ordered Adams to lead the assault on what he believed were retreating Virginians. But the first unit was cut down by murderous fire from behind one of the walls, and Adams realized that the order to advance was suicidal. "What with men shot down and horses wounded and plunging, my ranks were disordered," Adams wrote, "and then I fell slowly back to some woods." Adams shouted for his men to dismount and fight on foot with their sabers and pistols: "The men fell right and left and the horses were shot through and through." As Confederate riders charged, the New Yorkers to his right broke and ran. Major Henry Lee Higginson went down with a cut to his forehead and a bullet near his spine, and Adams spied his rival Captain Lucius Sargent lying in the road, apparently dead. Curtis bellowed a retreat, and those who could mounted and galloped for the Ashby Gap Turnpike. "How and why I escaped I can't say, for my men fell all around me," Adams told John

Quincy, "but neither I nor my horse was touched, nor were any of my officers or their horses."[28]

As they raced out of town, the survivors were met by fresh Ohio cavalrymen. The reinforcements, together with the fading light, prompted Confederates to withdraw around eight o'clock. "I went into action with 94 men in my squadron and 57 in my Company, and came out with between 30 and 40 in my squadron and just 25 in my Company," Adams tallied. "My poor men were just slaughtered." Casualties for the entire regiment amounted to 161 men killed, wounded, or captured. Both Higginson and Sargent lived, although their wounds kept them from the regiment for some months. Adams admitted that while he felt "little stomach enough" for what he guessed was a coming clash between Lee's army and the Army of the Potomac, he supposed he had some "fight left." Higginson's battered unit was consolidated into Adams's squadron of forty men, "so if we have to smash the machine," he assured John Quincy, "we'll smash something else first and go up in glory." Adams had the presence of mind, however, to urge John Quincy to "ease Lou's mind" and hurry word to London that he was well. John Quincy's missive arrived only after a newspaper account of the battle reached London. Quickly scanning the story, Charles Francis Sr. saw Higginson's name but not his son's. "I thank God he is yet safe," Adams rejoiced.[29]

John Quincy's comforting words did little to ease their father's mind. Telegrams from Washington carried the grim news that Lee was "well on his proposed advance into Pennsylvania." Henry prayed that Lee might swing west and march toward Ohio's wheat fields, putting Charles Francis out of harm's way and even free to ride toward Richmond. American newspapers predicted that Lincoln was preparing to remove Hooker from his command, and the senior Adams thought it likely that "in spite of all his shortcomings [McClellan] may be recalled to do the same thing that he did last year, repulse the attack." The Army of the Potomac, Adams complained to Everett, appeared doomed to sink "under the struggle about its commanders." Unlike Henry, Charles Francis Sr. assumed that the First Massachusetts was even then riding north, shadowing Lee's invasion force of seventy-five thousand. "My spirits are now habitually depressed by the constant anxiety about my son," he told his diary.[30]

Adams was cheered a bit by letters informing the Legation that Lincoln had replaced Hooker with General George Meade. Meade's division had been the only one to punch through Confederate lines at Fredericksburg, and he had made his fury known at having his men held in reserve at Chancellorsville. "The nomination evidently is welcome to the army," Adams observed, although he understood that Meade had only days "to put a stop to Lee's progress." The thought of the coming clash made him all the more anxious "for the fate" of his son. Adams had hoped that the most recent batch of letters would also carry news of Vicksburg's fall, and although it did not, "General Grant's previous successes have been great."[31]

As the elder Adams supposed, the First Cavalry was on the move, although several days behind Lee's forces. Riding and sleeping in drenching rains, Adams left Aldie only on June 26 and took two days to reach Frederick, Maryland, forty miles north. Two days more found them near Taneytown, but that was July 1, and roughly twenty miles to his north, fighting had already begun outside the small Pennsylvania town of Gettysburg. That night, rumors of heavy fighting reached their camp, and before dawn the First Cavalry joined with General John Sedgwick's Sixth Corps. "All that day we marched to the sound of cannon," Adams remembered. As the day wore on, the riders passed to the head of a column of hurrying infantrymen, and "the roar of battle grew more distinct." Riding over a crest into the valley, Adams spied puffs of white smoke from bursting shells in the distance. The road before them was choked with ambulances, caissons, ammunition trains, and "tired, footsore, hungry, thirsty" infantrymen. The First paused inside Union lines at Rock Creek to water their mounts and await further orders. "At sunset we were whipped and night saved the army," Adams wrote. "I never felt such sickening anxiety."[32]

The next morning, July 3, Adams found himself perched on a patch of high, wooded ground near the right of the Union's long line, protecting the army's flank and rear. Even from his elevated position, Adams could see no Confederate movements. While awaiting further orders, the cavalrymen dismounted and found shade in the trees. Just around one o'clock in the afternoon, they heard Confederate guns begin to fire. The Massachusetts men could see nothing, but Adams was later to understand that the artillery was designed to cover General George Pickett's advance on Meade's center. "Lulled by the incessant roar of the cannon, while the fate of the army and the nation trembled in the balance," the weary Adams fell fast asleep. "It was not heroic," Adams admitted, "but it was essentially war." And that day, he told his father, "The enemy were fairly whipped out."[33]

Adams spent the next three days helping to bury the dead, a ghastly task that received but a single, terse line in his daybook. By July 8, he was back in Frederick, drawing "up final statement papers of my killed & wounded," when word reached his company that Vicksburg was "at last captured, thanks be to God!" The Army of the Potomac had performed "nobly and is in fine condition," he promised John Quincy. But he understood also that Lee had "lots of fight left and this war is not over yet." Ten days on, Adams was near Harpers Ferry, arresting Confederate stragglers. "My horse has been unsaddled eight hours during the last three days," he reported. Yet while he was "tired of fighting and campaigning," peace could be achieved "only in complete victory," and he was furious that Meade had not pursued Lee into Virginia. "While I have a horse left I want to see no pause," Adams groused. "For God's sake, let's strike when the iron's hot and finish this job up." He was even more irate after reading about the mid-July antidraft race riots in Manhattan, which had left more than one hundred murdered—most of them black—the Colored Orphan Asylum in ashes, and the *New York Tribune* besieged. "Is this the way the country supports the victories of its army?" he fumed. The Army of the Potomac, he believed, should march into New York to deal "with rioters and copperheads [conservative Democrats]. You would see a very clean piece of work done in the Cromwellian style."[34]

In London the hostile press was confident that the Army of Northern Virginia, as ever, would again best whatever hapless northern commander

Lincoln threw against it. Confederate envoy James Murray Mason was again in the city, and at a public dinner he promised the assembled that Lee had marched on Washington and "taken possession of the Capitol." The *London Times* reported Mason's boast as fact and added that Grant's army in the West was "in extreme danger of having itself to capitulate." On Sunday, July 19, a telegram arrived at the Legation, which Adams opened "with trepidation," fearing ill news about Charles Francis Jr. or Meade's army. Instead, it was from Seward, announcing that Lee was in retreat and that Vicksburg had surrendered, so "control over the Mississippi is practically restored to our hands." At about the same time, a letter from John Quincy told that Charles was "still safe, well and sound." The entire Legation rejoiced, even the ever-sour Moran. Just to see "how unpleasant the news" was for conservative Englishmen, Henry wandered down to the Cosmopolitan Club, "where the people all looked at me as though I were objectionable." Henry mostly refrained from discussing war news at the club, he assured Charles Francis Jr., although the diminutive secretary was in a mood "to fight some small man and lick him." Although the overjoyed Henry meant that in jest, it was also probably as close as he could come to telling his soldier brother that he was proud of him.[35]

Official Britain grasped the significance of the two battles only slowly. Late in the month, the Adamses attended a reception hosted by Lady Palmerston. The minister and the prime minister spoke about the war, and Palmerston appeared "surprised and incredulous" that Adams "considered the invasion over" after Gettysburg. Even after the London press conceded that Lee had failed in his objectives, it refused to believe that Vicksburg had fallen, Adams observed, "and especially that it should have happened on the fourth of July." Finally, on July 30, the *London Times* published the truth about Vicksburg in a "depressed" tone that betrayed "the profound disappointment and mortification of the aristocracy as a result." In the city's stock market, holders of Confederate bank loan notes hurried to sell their discounted stocks at any price. "I should not be surprised if some bankruptcies were to follow," Adams gloated. "People here must pay something for their pro-slavery sympathies."[36]

Despite all his disdain for professional soldiers, Charles Francis Sr. revealed an instinctive understanding of the art of warfare. In the weeks after Gettysburg, Charles Francis Jr. came to believe that Lee's Army of Northern Virginia "was in every respect superior" to Meade's army, and certainly "better officered." The minister disagreed. "Neither am I disposed so much as others are," he lectured Dana without mentioning his son's opinion, "to extol the skills of rebel generalship at the expense of our own." Lee had bested previous Union generals by adopting aggressive tactics, but what that amounted to, Adams suspected, was a reliance on "the massing [of] all their force to attack a part of ours, an operation always carried on with great disregard for life." American newspapers circulated in London stated that Pickett had suffered a 50 percent casualty rate on July 3, which Adams regarded as a "suicidal act." Even had Lee won at Gettysburg and marched on Washington, Adams observed, forces held in reserve would not have surrendered "without another fight quite as continued as that which saved Richmond from our grasp." With Lee's army shrinking and his artillery spent, how many more such campaigns could he endure?[37]

Despite the promising news from Pennsylvania and Mississippi, the potentially explosive problem of Confederate shipbuilding, rather to Adams's surprise, did not go away. In Liverpool, Charles Prioleau, a senior partner of Fraser and Trenholm, persisted in finding new ways to evade the queen's neutrality proclamation. A naturalized Englishman, Prioleau had been raised in Charleston and still had family there; two years before, he had attempted to sell the *Bermuda* to Confederate agents. In July, Prioleau held a grand party aboard the *Southerner*, and his guests, including delegates from Savannah and the loyal slave state of Delaware, drank toasts to "the health of the President of the Confederate States of America." Adams was also concerned about the ironclad steamer *Japan*, then being constructed by the Laird Brothers, ostensibly for Thomas Bold, a British subject. Adams fired off yet another complaint to Russell. But while the British government made it clear, Adams observed to Seward, that it would not allow the sale of an "armed belligerent vessel" to a neutral nation, the ministry "quietly permitted the act to be done" when the sale was ostensibly to a British subject. In the past, pro-southern builders had been thwarted in their alleged sales to the Egyptian government. But if the buyer was a British national, Adams worried, proof that Bold intended to transfer ownership to the Confederates after putting out to sea was difficult to obtain.[38]

On July 16, Adams forwarded two depositions regarding the Laird ship, both providing testimony that George Bulloch, the Georgian who had arranged the *Alabama* deal, was seen supervising the layout of the vessel's keels. But even then Russell, Adams complained, shrugged off "the sufficiency of the evidence to establish intention in this case." Adams quickly responded that "any failure to act might be attended with the most serious consequences." Adams also thought it prudent to again consult with the supportive Richard Cobden. The two spoke of "the grave nature of the question," with Adams knowing that Cobden desired peace with the United States above all else. Ever since the launch of the *Alabama*, Adams added, his government had been "in process" of keeping a tabulation of damages inflicted by British-constructed privateers, a warning that shocked the English radical and one that Adams safely assumed would be repeated to the foreign secretary.[39]

Despite Cobden's best efforts, and that of an "earnest memorial" presented to the ministry by the Union and Emancipation Society, Adams had no reason to believe that his flurry of missives had goaded Russell into action. On September 3, he notified Seward that the *Japan* was "prepared for departure." In Washington, Gustavus Fox, the assistant secretary of the navy, warned the president that there was "no evidence in Mr. Adams dispatches, that these vessels are to be arrested." General Thomas Ewing counseled Lincoln to "consider it an act of war" if Britain permitted the ironclads to sail. A frustrated Seward sent Adams what he emphasized were "explicit" instructions. If any further ships left British ports, the "partial war" against such ships might "become a general one between the two nations," and, if so, "the President thinks that the responsibility for that painful result will not fall upon the United States."[40]

Thursday, September 3, was also Charles Francis's thirty-fourth anniversary, but he was back at his desk following a hasty celebratory dinner with Abby. In the wake of Gettysburg and Vicksburg, Adams suspected, "the rebellion would collapse" before the New Year were it not for British interference. "My duty therefore is a difficult one," he reflected. "Without indulging in menace I must be faithful to my country in giving warning of its sense of injury." Once again, he dashed off a short note to Russell, assuring the foreign minister that the Laird steamers "would be at once devoted to the object of carrying on war against the United States." The next morning, a weary Russell replied, saying that in response to the documents and evidence forwarded to his office, the matter was "under the serious and anxious consideration of her Majesty's government." That was hardly the firm commitment Adams hoped for. But then, he did not actually expect to receive one.[41]

Late in the afternoon of September 4, word arrived from consul Thomas Dudley in Liverpool that the *Japan*, rechristened the *Virginia*, was about to depart. At almost the same moment, a note from Russell arrived at the Legation announcing that his government "could find no evidence upon which to proceed in stopping the vessel." Although deeply shaken and grimly aware "that a collision must now come out of it," Adams sat down to draft the most important letter of his life. His missive of five terse paragraphs began by quoting from a Richmond newspaper, which boasted that an ironclad could inflict a "vital blow" against under-defended northern seaports, particularly Adams's Boston, assaults "worth a hundred victories in the field." Should that happen, Adams coldly observed, any third party that allowed weapons of war to be constructed in its harbors effectively "ceases to be neutral." Then followed sixteen precise words: "It would be superfluous in me to point out to your lordship that this is war." Adams's father and grandfather had penned their share of eloquent documents, but both tended toward the verbose. His own succinct phrasing was brilliantly crafted in that it invited no disagreement, no debate. The "matter-of-fact statement," Henry marveled, "without passion or excitement," rendered it unnecessary to explain what actions his nation would be forced to pursue. "The war was Russell's war," Henry observed. "Adams only accepted it."[42]

Adams waited impatiently. "We are now all in a fever about Mr. Laird's iron-clads," Adams wrote John Murray Forbes, an advisor to Governor Andrew. Should Russell fail to act, Adams mused, he was "prepared to make my bow to our friends in London, as soon as the papers" for his return to America could be drawn up. Adams confided much the same thing to Dana, saying that he was resigned to the fact that the ships would sail, "such is the feebleness of this Ministry." He had tried to warn Russell of "the consequences," and he was secure in the knowledge that his threat did not exceed his instructions from Seward. But on September 7, the normally hostile *Times* advocated the seizure of the ships, and the *Post* carried a short article claiming that the government had decided to detain the vessels. "And yet I could scarcely put faith in it while I had no notice myself," Adams worried.[43]

Verification arrived the next morning. In the briefest of notes, Russell wrote to inform Adams "that instructions have been issued which will prevent the departure of the two iron clad vessels." Adams hurried a response to the Foreign Office, assuring Russell that he would "take great pleasure" in informing Seward and Lincoln of his decision. Adams posted a lengthy missive to the State Department that evening. Although Seward's instructions had been both explicit and bellicose, Adams felt the need to explain his course of action, if perhaps only to himself. He had not resorted "to intimidation," Adams remarked, although he attempted "to convey, in its full sense," how such an "extraordinary and unjustifiable violation of neutrality" would be regarded in Washington. To his diary and to his brother-in-law, Adams expressed only a deep sense of relief, greater even than he felt after the *Trent* affair. In true Adams fashion, he assured himself that he "shall not venture to claim any such victory" for his adroit diplomacy and perfectly chosen words. Rather, his sole object, Adams informed Everett, was to prevent the "difference between the [two] countries from maturing into an open quarrel."[44]

If the dour minister refused to celebrate his success, Henry was ecstatic. "To us this is a second Vicksburg," he informed Charles Francis Jr. "If our armies march on; if Charleston is taken; above all if emancipation is made effective, Europe will blow gentle gales upon us." The value of Confederate bonds in Britain sank yet again, and best of all, from the Legation's viewpoint, James Murray Mason abandoned any further attempts to court Palmerston's government, and he quit Britain for Paris. The news merited a second letter from Henry to his "dear Lieut-Col-Major-Captain." For two years, Mason and other Confederate envoys had sought to win favor in Britain, and for two years, Henry gloated, his father had "battled and marched" against their efforts. Mason has "sullenly retreated before the frowning batteries" of their father, who "had his usual luck in enemies." For all his failed tries, Henry thought, Mason might have been wiser "to rot at Fort Warren."[45]

Adams immediately noticed that the sudden "relaxation in the fierceness" of the *Times* was not a temporary lull but rather a permanent change of attitude. Neither did Mason's departure for France and the court of Napoleon III illicit "any sympathy" in Britain, even among the landed and commercial classes. "The lower classes are most generally with us," Adams promised his son Charles, and the "only mob that could be raised here in sympathy with the rebels would be among the nobility." But aristocratic affection for the South, he suspected, largely depended "on the ability to do mischief to us," as their "dislike and jealousy of America is general." However, Lord Palmerston could not resist trying to diminish Adams's achievement. The prime minister waited until Russell left London and then instructed William Stuart, the chargé d'affaires in Washington, to inform Seward that the ministry had decided to seize the ironclads moments prior to receiving Adams's warning, despite what the State Department might have heard "from other quarters," that of course being the Legation.[46]

Seward knew better, of course, and Adams was content to ignore the prime minister's petty act of gamesmanship. Although the order to halt the ships was officially "temporary," that too was but a face-saving gesture on the part of the ministry. Upon his return, Russell hinted that the ships would be sold to the Danish government, while the *Alexandra* was sold to a foreign agent who provided Adams with "satisfactory assurances" that it would not be transferred to the Confederacy. In Paris, Napoleon III was rarely inclined to defy British policy, and he also detained several vessels being constructed in Nantes. The Crimean War, which had pitted France and Britain against Russia, had ended less than a decade before, and Alexander II, the new, reform-minded tsar, sided with the Union, largely because San Francisco Bay provided a safe haven for his navy. "The fear of a continental war is becoming general," Adams observed. "The state of things all over Europe is becoming so alarming as to render every nation careful not to multiply complications."[47]

Even so, Adams remained vigilant. Confederate agents in search of ships abandoned Liverpool for Glasgow, a fact Adams promptly brought to Russell's attention, together with the anticipated gratitude of President Lincoln for the foreign secretary's actions. A group of Richmond ministers published an *Address to Christians throughout the World*, which southern lecturers in Britain circulated to Anglican ministers, but Adams already judged their aristocratic flocks the enemies of his republic and dismissed any impact that the pamphlet might have on the dissenting faiths. More worrisome was that shipbuilder John Laird had recently been elected to Parliament as Birkenhead's representative, but after a series of late-fall meetings with Russell, Adams was confident that the problem of Confederate shipbuilding was at last resolved. When pressed about Confederate agents and their business partners "systematically abusing the neutral position" established by this ministry, Russell conceded that the issue had somewhat taken him by surprise "as a wholly new feature in this history" of his nation. As an indication of how thoroughly Adams had beaten the Confederate cause, George Trenholm quit his Liverpool business and returned to his native South to serve as Jefferson's Davis's secretary of the treasury. Finally, in May 1867 Fraser and Trenholm would declare bankruptcy after being owed £170,000 by the defunct Confederate government and having itself purchased Confederate bonds.[48]

During his last interview with Russell that December, Adams was given to understand the British government realized that the Confederates might fight on for another season, but that they were sure to eventually lose. It no longer seemed worthwhile for Britain "to hazard a permanent alienation merely for the sake of sustaining a foreign cause," he explained to Everett. So calm was the political atmosphere in London that Adams leased a house at the coastal resort of St. Leonards. "The climate is mild and the atmosphere generally less foggy" than in London, an important consideration for Mary's health, and his duties were suddenly light enough that he needed to return to the Legation only every few weeks. Adams realized also that he had served his country in Britain for "two years and a half," a longer residency at the Court of St. James than that of either his father or—unless he returned home soon—his grandfather. For a man who longed to equal, and perhaps even to best, his illustrious ancestors, the number of months abroad meant a great deal. "I find mine has already exceeded the former and is only four months short of the latter," Adams tallied, "so that the account averages well as it is."[49]

Adams's only causes for concern were personal. The First Cavalry was again on the march, and the worried father "tremble[d] on the receipt of any mail" about the Virginia campaign. His daughter Louisa wrote to Abby "from a bed of sickness, in a rather suffering vein." As ever, no doctor could precisely identify the source of her "distress." At least the rest of his family was well, he reflected, and "by the blessing of God" Charles Francis Jr. had "escaped in safety from many perils dire." His son John Quincy had turned thirty and was well "established in life with a Wife and two children." Having himself celebrated his fifty-sixth birthday the previous August, Adams believed himself "advancing toward the end," although his father had lived to eighty. But the year had been a good one, both for himself and his nation. "Heaven has been merciful and bountiful to me," he admitted.[50]

The holiday season ended with the quietest weeks Adams had witnessed since his arrival in Britain. Henry, forever failing to consider how his stories of leisurely enjoyments were met by a far-away brother huddled in a damp tent, assured Charles Francis Jr. that he had "been worried half to death" by the problem of purchasing just the right Christmas presents for the family. Brooks, he added, was home from his boarding school, having adopted an upper-class British accent. "I think that with good luck and a copious licking, something may be made of him yet," Henry joked.

The Adamses hosted a large party for visiting Americans, and Charles Francis Sr. read aloud the proclamation issued by the president, which he pronounced "very good" and assumed was written by Seward. As the president had no formal education, Adams much doubted the eloquent statement "emanated from Mr. Lincoln's pen." Yet as he pondered the political and military successes of the previous year, Adams conceded that Lincoln possessed an "organizing mind" and that this "raw, inexperienced hand" had performed miracles "in the face of difficulties that might well appall the most practiced statesman! What a curious thing to History."[51]

While Henry was agonizing over proper Christmas purchases, Charles Francis Jr. was on the march in northern Virginia, chasing J. E. B. Stuart's cavalry and enduring an unusually damp, cool fall. "Where [went] the beautiful summer?" he wondered. A week of picket duty while searching for Confederates went awry, with a sergeant, two corporals, and four privates captured by Confederate guerrillas. "The only shot fired while we were out," a disgusted Adams reported to John Quincy, "killed a poor negro girl who was seeking by night the precious boon of liberty within our lines, bringing with her a little child of five." For once, the tragedy of the situation prompted Charles Francis to spell "negro" using only five letters.[52]

On September 12, the First Cavalry, together with nine other cavalry regiments, yet again forded the Rappahannock and attacked Stuart's headquarters at Culpeper Court House. The outnumbered Confederate forces scattered, and the Union cavalrymen, led by General George Armstrong Custer, captured one hundred prisoners and a number of artillery pieces. That night, Adams wrote, "we went into camp in a drenching rain." It was a "wretched business," and once again, Adams had no manservant to prepare his dinner, so instead the company took care of him. Two days later, Confederate pickets approached but were easily driven off. Even so, it was a "terrible experience, & I have had such a strain on my nerves," Adams admitted. He was especially disheartened by the fact that his regiment was marching over the same "ground of last June & now where was our progress?" October 13 and 14 found the First engaged at Auburn in Fauquier County, again forcing Stuart's unit to withdraw.

But the seemingly endless string of skirmishes frustrated Adams. "A hard fight with utter demoralization," he snapped. "I cannot give up!"[53]

Adding to Adams's unhappiness was his ongoing feud with the Sargent brothers, especially after Captain Lucius Sargent recovered enough from his wounds to rejoin the regiment. "You always chose to repudiate friendships," John Quincy reflected in a letter to his brother, although he was unsure as to whether that was wiser than his own tendency to "cultivate them to my own expense." Despite his dislike of the regiment's senior officers, however, Adams declined the offer of a promotion to lieutenant colonel in a New Jersey cavalry regiment, as it meant leaping over several junior officers who had endured a longer tenure in the military. That rare moment of selflessness impressed his father, who felt "very proud of him," not that the elder Adams actually told his son so. Instead, the minister poured his pride and his worries into his diary, "trusting that Heaven may lead him hereafter as heretofore safe through the immediate trial." Unfortunately, John Quincy was as thoughtless as Henry, and apart from his ruminations on their shared inability to get along with their fellow men, his tone-deaf letters told of the "damned pleasant life" he led as a "country gentleman," planting as "many little trees across [his estate] with every hand I can muster." But small joys meant a good deal to soldiers on march, and John Quincy at least thought to send his brother a warm coat. Just days before, one junior officer reported, Adams had been "in a great state of despair," but the next time he saw him in early November, "he had a new jacket on, and Adams was himself again!"[54]

Charles Francis Jr. had also undergone a major change of heart on the issue of black military service. Just fourteen months before, he had assured Henry that African Americans were good for little more than fatigue duty or driving wagons. But since his disparaging comments of July 1862, his own state's pioneering black infantry regiment, the Massachusetts Fifty-Fourth, had assaulted Battery Wagner, just south of Charleston Harbor, bravely marching into withering fire. That attack had failed, but after considerable shelling by the Union navy and ground artillery, the Fifty-Fourth captured the fort on the morning of September 7. "The freedom and regeneration of the African race," a now-convinced Adams lectured his father in late October, "can only be wrought out through the agency of the army—the black soldiers." The marching and remarching over old ground, "every disaster and every delay," made the wholesale recruitment of black men a necessity. "I want to see 200,000 black soldiers in the field," he insisted. Political rights for African Americans could not advance if the "final success [was] won by white soldiers." But everything would be different "after that success to which 200,000 armed blacks have contributed." Although Adams did not say he had changed his mind about leading black troops, neither did he assure his family, as he had in the past, that he would never consider doing so. And in the wake of the Fifty-Fourth's triumphs, both Lincoln and Massachusetts Governor Andrew were preparing to raise nearly as many men as Adams advocated.[55]

On Christmas Eve, as his far-flung family celebrated the holidays, Charles Francis Jr. wrote to his father from his regiment's winter quarters in Warrenton, Virginia, only just west of Washington and not far south of Aldie. He and another officer had constructed "comfortable, finished quarters" by placing part of a roof from an abandoned house atop their tent, "the front and rear [openings] logged up, with an open fireplace in the rear" and a wood floor. The dwelling was snug enough, Adams assured his father before adding, in a brutal aside on the level of emotional support common in the family's Beacon Hill mansion, that he enjoyed "more real, positive, healthy comfort here than ever I did in my cushioned and carpeted room at home!" Having fired that shot, however, Adams noted that he had just ended his "second year of field duty," and for all their faults, he missed his family. Dipping his pen again into the inkwell, he set to work at once on his "application for leave to go to Europe."[56]

Adams requested a leave of absence for seventy days for himself and thirty-five days for the troopers in his company, which because of injury and illness had fallen to less than half strength. In thanks, his entire company promised to reenlist after their furlough, the only unit in the regiment to do so. "They seem to think that I am a devil of a fellow," he bragged to his father. The enlisted men, not having had the virtue of a Harvard education, "come to me to decide their bets and to settle questions in discussion." Being captain of forty men was not quite the same as serving in Congress or even the Massachusetts statehouse, but at twenty-eight Charles Francis took pride in his leadership abilities. "To be egotistical, I think I see the old family traits cropping out in myself," he added. However, Adams was not above using his family name to curry favor with the War Department or adding that he had secured the approval of Governor Andrew. "My father and all the members of my family have, as is well known," he wrote in his application for leave, "for two years & eight months been abroad in the service of the country, and I am most desirous of visiting them." Yet he was right enough in pointing out that he had amassed more than two years of campaigning "and during that time, alone of all the officers of the regiment, have never visited my home."[57]

The prospect of seeing his son thrilled the elder Adams, although, as ever, he restrained himself from revealing that to anybody but his diary. Despite the approval of Andrew and the Adams name, the machinery of the army moved slowly. Over the next weeks, the minister impatiently awaited each bag of American mail, with each being "not very encouraging to our hopes of seeing" Charles Francis. He blamed the delay on a "fit of caprice" on the part of Secretary of War Edwin Stanton, although such applications never reached that high in the War Department. In the meantime, Henry and Brooks escorted their mother and sister Mary to Paris. "Occupation is the only the thing that makes [the waiting] tolerable," Adams grumbled. Finally, Louisa wrote to London, assuring her father that the army had granted Charles Francis his requested seventy days. "This brightens me up," Adams admitted.[58]

The order, dated January 18, 1864, arrived at Warrenton the next day. Adams mustered his company, saw to it that his men were paid, and then, with true army efficiency, "another muddle" emerged, and they were ordered to wait. "Disgusted & alarmed," Adams went in search of General David McMurtie Gregg, who promised to countermand any glitches, and Charles Francis returned to his tent a contented man. The next morning, his men were packed and ready to move, but then came yet another "terrible day of waiting for authorization." Gregg's order arrived at sunset, and Adams and the forty men remaining in his company left camp, passing forty-five new recruits riding in to fill his depleted ranks. Adams and his men reached the train station in Alexandria, Virginia, that night and finally arrived in Boston on January 23.[59]

As was the case with many soldiers on leave, Adams found the polite society he had once enjoyed suddenly dull. For all the advantages he enjoyed as a cavalry officer, from his whiskey to his bulldog, the war had altered Charles Francis, and he thought it most curious that New England, so distant from the front, had not been altered with him. "I am much struck by the absence of change," he marveled. Having roughed it for the past two years and shared his tent with other men, the company of elegant young women was especially unfamiliar. Drinks and cigars on John Quincy's porch were one thing, and the young captain was flattered to be invited to a public reception hosted by Governor Andrew. But when he dined in Boston with several old friends, he found them "wholly unchanged, almost unpleasantly so." Two women of his acquaintance, a "Miss Mary & Miss Ellen," no longer interested Adams, yet he felt "no inclination to query as to why."[60]

All of that changed only days later when Adams journeyed on to Newport to visit Louisa and Charles Kuhn. Among Louisa's circle was twenty-year-old Mary Ogden—Minnie, to her friends—the daughter of New Yorkers Edward Ogden and Caroline Hone Callender, both descended from colonial shippers who had amassed vast wealth. From their first meeting over dinner, Adams was smitten. "I was charmed," and she was "as pretty as a French picture," Adams thought. "I regularly gloated over her." Part of the attraction was that Minnie was not just rich but pleasant and kind, and Adams admitted that he saw in her a natural contrast to his own prickly personality: "I thought I had never met so charming and attractive a person as she." Unlike his Boston acquaintances, Minnie instinctively understood Adams's experiences of the past two years. Her brother Frederick was then fighting in Virginia, a lieutenant in the First Regiment of Cavalry. "She runs in my head infernally!" he assured Henry several weeks later. "She persuades [me] that my sensibilities were not played out."[61]

Charles Francis's ship landed on February 16 in Liverpool, where he was surprised and pleased to be met by Henry. In an indication of how splendidly the elder Adams was faring with the British government, Russell sent word to port officials to treat the minister's son with deference, and Charles Francis was allowed to disembark first and glide through customs. The official, Adams noticed, expecting a man of importance, gazed at the diminutive soldier and his single carpetbag "with undisguised contempt." The brothers caught the afternoon train to London, where Adams was bemused by the formal greetings and bows of the household staff. Charles Francis's father was pleased to see how healthy he looked, and while he wished his son did not have to return to the front, he understood "there was little prospect" of the conflict ending anytime soon. That night, the minister's diary was a scrawling tribute to contradiction. Having heard of the governor's reception, Adams found it a "great source of satisfaction" that his son had "acquitted himself creditably in his undertaking." But Adams still refused to understand why his son had enlisted. "Our family has not been of the warrior class," he insisted, and while that thought might have prefaced a statement of pride in his son changing that tradition for the better, it did not. "Neither do I much fancy the honors that come from the knowledge of the arts of destruction."[62]

Charles Francis Jr. promptly reported back to John Quincy about how the family was surviving Britain. Henry, he believed, was "indispensable to the Minister" and handled all of the confidential correspondence. But going to the office, he worried, was Henry's "only routine." He appeared healthy enough but acted "123 years old mentally and [was] becoming a regular recluse." However much he was needed at the Legation, Charles Francis thought, "as soon as he can," Henry should "go back to America" and make himself useful in his own right. As for Mary, the two years in London had changed her not at all. But Charles Francis did not think about the fact that of all the family, she was the most tied to the parlor, so whether she was in Boston or London was of little consequence.

"She still has that same wonderful composure of temper and equanimity of disposition, which she never got from her Mother," Charles Francis drolly observed.[63]

The minister was most anxious to introduce Charles Francis to those in power, squiring him to receptions held by William Gladstone, the chancellor of the exchequer, Henrietta Robinson, the Countess de Grey, and John Russell. The round of parties infuriated the ever-irritable Benjamin Moran, who fumed that the elder Adams failed to "introduce his secretaries to their rights," while he and his family went "out of their way to *stuff* their son into every possible house in London, when he really has no business there." Moran derisively dubbed Charles Francis "Captain Adams" and characterized the minister as a "cold hearted fellow, saturated with utter selfishness and incapable of doing an honest action." What Moran failed to grasp, however, was that Adams wished Britons of influence to see that his son was risking his life for his nation. Although he himself had scant regard for battlefield heroes who leveraged their fame into political office, Adams well understood that the British, who had twice elevated the Duke of Wellington into the prime minister's chair, were every bit as enamored of successful soldiers as were American voters. As much as he wished Charles Francis out of harm's way, his son the captain was far more politically useful than the dour, civilian Henry ever could be.[64]

Ironically, the jealous Moran might well have been a member of the Adams family, in that he shared their tendency to complain about life even when things went well. Just before Charles Francis had to sail for home, the Adamses hosted a farewell dinner and invited the minister's two senior clerks, together with secretary Charles Wilson's wife. Moran thought the guest list inferior and groused that the "patched up affair" was not worth the cost of his cab and gloves. "The valiant captain showed himself an ass by bawling across the table that he considered himself as good a specimen of a well educated American" as any man, Moran complained, while "Mrs. Adams made herself ridiculous by her senseless tattle." Evidently, the Legation's official family was every bit as unhappy and dysfunctional as the Adams clan itself often was.[65]

"My son sails from Liverpool today," Adams wrote on March 26. "For he must return, and with [it] our anxiety." Over their last meal together, Charles Francis Jr., as he later scribbled into his journal, tried to remain cheerful and "kept up the spirits of all tolerably." After his sons boarded the train for Liverpool, Adams retreated to the solitude of his office and his coin collection. He already missed his son a "good deal," Adams confided to his diary, and as did every parent ever, he fretted that it "seems scarcely a moment since he came." But no evidence suggests that he said as much to Charles Francis, who concluded his journal of his travels with a enigmatic comment: "At 9:50 on board the steamer & soon, Henry nodded me good-bye from the dock &, with a bitter taste in my mouth, was off for home."[66]

Adams's arrival in Boston allowed for a quick return to Newport before having to report to his regiment in Virginia. He was surprised to find "Lou sick and suffering," if only because her husband was out of town, and both Charles Francis and Henry were convinced that her troubled marriage was the source of her illness. Even so, Adams thought that his brother-in-law should be apprised of her condition, although when he "wrote to Kuhn about her," this itself left Louisa "much distressed." But the real reason for his visit was to see Minnie once more: "Miss Ogden dined with me & we had a quite charming talk, lively & pleasant." Before they parted, it seems, the two had an understanding. With enormous regret, Adams caught the southbound train and upon reaching Washington was greeted with news that his squadron was ordered to ride for the main Army of the Potomac, to act as guard and escort for General Meade.[67]

The previous sixteen months had seen the elder Adams victorious, and with Palmerston's government at last determined to avoid American entanglements and animosity by not allowing its docks to be used by Confederate agents, Adams began to hope that his tenure in London was winding to a close. Lincoln, he suspected, would be reelected that fall, and although he dared not mention it even to his journal, the last secretary of state to serve two complete terms had been his father. Should Seward also decide that his job was done and return to upstate New York, as his wife so badly desired, who was better suited by name and experience to step into the cabinet? As for Charles Francis Jr., his victory was not yet won, and he understood that there was hard fighting ahead. Neither his feud with his colonel nor his change of heart regarding black troops was a secret kept from Governor Andrew, thanks to John Quincy's occasional duties as advisor to Andrew, who was beginning to consider raising the country's first-ever regiment of black cavalrymen.

8

"THE EVENT OF MY LIFE HITHERTO"

The Colonel

A S AN AVID READER OF NEWSPAPERS, CHARLES FRANCIS JR. surely knew what was coming next. "Pursuant to authority received from the U.S. Department of War," the *Liberator* and the black-run New York *Weekly Anglo-African* proudly announced in January 1864, a "regiment of Cavalry Volunteers, to be composed of men of color, is now in process of recruitment." Having shepherded the pioneering Fifty-Fourth Infantry into existence the year before, Governor John Andrew now wished black troopers to "illustrate their capacity for that dashing and brilliant arm of the military service." The infantrymen of the Fifty-Fourth and its sister regiment, the Fifty-Fifth, shared pride of place as the first black units with the soldiers of the First Kansas Colored Volunteers and the First South Carolina Volunteers, which had been reorganized as the Seventy-Ninth and Thirty-Third US Colored Troops (USCT), respectively (although early on both regiments had been hidden from the eyes of official Washington). Andrew wanted it known that Massachusetts would raise the first black cavalry regiment in the nation. The "destiny of their race is in their own grasp," the governor proclaimed, urging black riders to enlist "and annihilate the rebel power." As with the Fifty-Fourth and Fifty-Fifth, its senior officers were to be white.[1]

The offer, as Adams anticipated, arrived by way of his brother John Quincy. "The Governor wishes me as his Aide to consult you in regard to the Lieutenant-Colonelcy of the 5th Cavalry," he wrote. Having endured Charles Francis's endless requests and annoying indecision of the previous year, John Quincy opted for bluntness. Andrew had "long destined this position for you," he insisted, and the governor expected an "immediate answer." John Quincy had been embarrassed by his brother's earlier behavior, so he laid out the many reasons why Charles Francis simply could not decline the offer. He played on their family's traditional hopes of obtaining advancement without appearing overeager. A good number of white officers coveted the second position in the new regiment, John Quincy observed, yet Andrew thought first of Charles Francis even though "no soul" had suggested his name. The promotion would free him "most honorably" from his current regiment, allowing him to rise in ranks and, as an Adams always charted careful political paths, placing him "on vantage ground for your future plans." John Quincy concluded with the hint that this was his final effort on behalf of his younger brother. "Pray let none but the most cogent reasons prevent an immediate and handsome acceptance."[2]

When Charles Francis failed to respond immediately, John Quincy fired off a second missive. Reminding his brother of his current unhappiness with his colonel, John Quincy emphasized that he would be serving under Henry "Hal" Russell, a Harvard classmate of his friend Caspar Crowninshield and a cousin of the late Robert Gould Shaw, the first colonel of the Fifty-Fourth. The Adams family, John Quincy observed, as he compiled yet another list of reasons why Charles Francis should accept, was long associated with antislavery. Because Charles Francis had recently dropped his earlier opposition to black military service, helping to lead the first-ever African American cavalry regiment would "work strongly upon your new nigger notion." Even more than in his previous letter, John Quincy signed off with an angry conclusion. "I do not know whether his Excellency has tired of waiting to hear from you or not," he warned. "For God's sake, send an immediate answer."[3]

His tardy reply notwithstanding, Charles Francis had no intention of declining the offer. Upon his return from furlough, Adams found his "squadron dirty & disconsolate, deep in mud and filth." Initial orders instructed the unit to prepare to serve as guard for General George Meade, but as ever, no clear directives followed. "Nothing going on," Adams confided to his diary. "We have gotten into a state of such constant expectations & daily expecting to ride & yet not riding." Adams promptly renewed his feud with the Sargent brothers, assuring Henry Lee Higginson that his longtime "fears of incompetence" in those above him in rank were "more than justified." Life in the First Cavalry, he sighed, was "bad, very bad." Andrew's offer was the obvious solution.[4]

Captain Lucius Sargent's wounds had healed enough so that he had rejoined the First, and that alone, Charles Francis assured his brother, led him "to look with more favor on the 5th Cav'y." Adams wished it understood that the offer was "unsought" and that he cared little "for the increased rank, still less for the pay." But he fretted that the First was doomed to long months of orderly duty and that leading a "colored regiment would prove an interesting study." Many junior officers had grown to regard their fellows as a band of brothers and often resisted promotion if it meant a new posting. Not Adams: "There are few [in the First] who know or care for me and my whole life in the regiment was embittered and poisoned. You may accept for me the Lieut. Col'cy of the 5th," he instructed John Quincy on May 31.[5]

"My connection with the 1st Massachusetts Cavalry draws toward its close," Adams informed his mother. But as he was already in Virginia, neither Andrew nor the War Department thought it necessary for him to return north and assist in the training of the black troopers at Camp Meigs outside of Boston. Before he could join his "colored brethren," he added, he had one final task for the First: to carry orders to Meade at Spotsylvania Court House. With Meade was Ulysses S. Grant, recently named commanding general of the United States Army. Hoping to advance on Richmond, Grant had ordered his forces to shove through the dense underbrush outside of Spotsylvania. Adams arrived just as what came to be known as the Battle of the Wilderness erupted on May 5. By the time he reached Meade's headquarters, what had started as a "mere rumble" had escalated "into a perfect tempest of explosions" just miles to their front. Adams handed the orders off and then, "for lack of other things to do," watched the two generals plot strategy. "I am immensely impressed with Grant," Adams wrote John Quincy. "He is the coolest most imperturbable man I ever saw." After two days of fierce combat, Grant disengaged his forces yet refused to retreat. Despite Union casualties of 19,000, Adams believed that under Grant's leadership the Army of the Potomac was "just on its second wind." With well above 100,000 men present for duty, Grant's army, Charles Francis promised his father, was "more formidable than it ever was before."[6]

For his part, the elder Adams was pleased by his son's decision and by his advancement in the ranks. But Adams had yet to develop any confidence in the president: "That original inherent weakness so long ago perceived by me is now becoming palpable to the people at large." He also worried that Lincoln might yet backtrack on his promises of emancipation. "Every consideration of honor and policy should prevent the Government from retracting the pledge of protection that has been given to every negro who has exercised his right to freedom," he wrote to John Murray Forbes, a Massachusetts railroad magnate and advisor to the governor, knowing that his sentiments would quickly reach Andrew. Beyond his general lack of faith in Lincoln, Adams had little reason to think emancipation in danger, but he agreed with his son that the existence of black troops made any retreat on civil rights impossible.[7]

Initially, Adams hoped that his party might decide to nominate another in place of Lincoln, a not unreasonable assumption in an era that had not seen a president reelected since 1832. "We have had enough of merely available men," he lectured Richard Henry Dana. If the Republicans dropped Lincoln, Adams supposed, they would most likely nominate Seward, and that in turn surely meant his own elevation into the State Department, the traditional stepping-stone for presidents. Adams correctly guessed that the Democrats would nominate the fired George McClellan, whose military career, Adams thought, "implies a want of some qualities which a Chief [Executive] ought to possess." When Dana replied that the Republicans, who in early June were to meet in Baltimore, would again nominate Lincoln, whom Dana also believed would be re-elected, Adams was dismayed, fearing Lincoln's "defects" would become more pronounced "in the second term than the first."[8]

Either way, Adams prayed that Lincoln's reelection would not lengthen his own stay in London. "I will frankly confess that I am quite weary of the war as well as of my place," he warned Dana, "the tenure of which depends on it in a degree." Yet he wished to return home on his own terms. When Salmon Chase resigned as secretary of the treasury in late June 1864, Adams had a "very slight apprehension" that Seward's ally Thurlow Weed would advance his name as a possible replacement. Serving in the cabinet under a President Seward was one thing; overseeing the nation's finances for the rustic Illinois attorney was something else. "Mr. Lincoln is not on that level," he mused. "He is honest, but trite and commonplace; well intentioned but not great."[9]

The minister remained equally exasperated with British attitudes toward Lincoln's newest general. Despite his son's insistence that he placed "much faith in General Grant," London's well-heeled residents continued to openly praise Lee. While attending a dinner party in late June, Adams overheard one guest assuring another that Lee had driven the Army of the Potomac back toward Washington and that Union General William T. Sherman "had been beaten with a loss of seven thousand men." Neither was true, and Adams chose to ignore the exchange. But his "annoyance of the situation in the midst of people perceptibly exulting in our supposed calamity [was] considerable," and Adams promised himself that he and Abby had "attended the last Drawing room of the season" and, he prayed, "the last in my term of service."[10]

WHILE HE AWAITED THE ARRIVAL OF HIS COLONEL AND HIS MEN, Charles Francis Jr. passed the time with leisure activities. Judging Shakespeare's *Love's Labours Lost* to be "poor stuff," Adams instead picked up a "very trashy novel." The days were hot, but he bathed often in a nearby stream and enjoyed dinner and surprisingly decent wine with a nearby regiment. As was too often the case with soldiers housed in close proximity to thousands of others, the unsanitary conditions of camp plagued him with diarrhea; on the sick list for a week, he lounged in "bed all day taking blue pills."[11]

He did not have long to wait. Sailing down the coast, the men of the Fifth Cavalry Regiment reached Point Lookout, Maryland, in early June. Uncharacteristically, Adams immediately liked his commander, in part because Russell treated him "with the utmost consideration" and consulted with him "very freely." The two got "on together like a couple of mice." But for the twenty-nine-year-old Adams, meeting the recruits was an unhappy shock. If he expected them to resemble the gifted black orators who had shared the Boston stage with his father in decades past, he was much mistaken. Although the recruits who had filled his state's two infantry units were largely northern-born freemen, roughly two-thirds of the black troopers had been born into slavery. Frederick Douglass's son Charles served the Fifth as a sergeant, having transferred from the Fifty-Fourth, but he was atypical in a regiment comprised of Virginia contraband who had enlisted after escaping to Washington. Many had cared for their masters' steeds and racehorses in their previous lives, and so while few were field hands, the cultural gulf between them and their Harvard-educated officers was far greater than that between the enlisted freemen and the white officers of the state's other black regiments. While Adams and the Fifth were to achieve considerable acclaim and witness the war's end in the Confederate capital, the final year of fighting ultimately served to deepen the young officer's mounting racism.[12]

Not yet in possession of mounts, the cavalrymen were tasked with guarding roughly 14,000 Confederate prisoners of war. No runaway had enlisted for the purpose of serving breakfast to Confederate prisoners, who despised them every bit as much as the black troopers loathed their charges. Within the week, Colonel Russell received orders to move into Virginia and join General Edward Hincks's Third Division in its assault on the outer defenses that circled Petersburg, south of the Appomattox River. Hincks's two brigades also included six USCT regiments, all more experienced than the Fifth, which was instructed to march in reserve. On the morning of June 15, the soldiers were within five miles of Petersburg. "Buggies, hacks, and vehicles of every description were in use, carrying off the women and children," one soldier reported. The Confederates had constructed elaborate earthworks, with breastworks twenty feet thick and backed by four cannons. Thick woods lay before the defenses, and as the first black infantrymen snaked into the clearing on June 15, Confederate gunners rained shells down on the Fifth, still marching through the trees. "But we kept on," one trooper wrote his father, "while the shell, grape and canister came around us cruelly." As Confederate pickets retreated into their fortifications, one shouted: "Lincoln's Massachusetts niggers are on us. They are coming, the damned black bastards, but we'll give 'em hell."[13]

As the Fifth reached the edge of the woods, its troopers fired a volley into the Confederate lines. The USCT units fell back in disarray, and Russell and Adams pulled their unit back into the trees to reform before advancing again. A ball snapped off Russell's strap, and a second pierced his upper arm. With the First and Fourth USCT taking the lead, the regiments charged a second time, many of the soldiers bellowing "Fort Pillow" as they ran forward, a reference to a Confederate atrocity in Tennessee and a warning, as one soldier put it, that they planned to "show the rebs no mercy." The Fourth took heavy casualties, with nearly half the regiment killed or wounded. While their officers desperately bawled for them to advance, wounded infantrymen shouted for retreat. Fearful that his untested troopers might join the flight, a bleeding Russell cried, "No cowards in the Fifth! Rally, boys, rally." As the Fifth poured into the Confederate trenches, the defenders, many of them boys and old men, threw up their hands in surrender. The victorious Fifth "gave three cheers for our victory" and celebrated the capture of nine artillery pieces and two hundred prisoners. Only then did Russell quit the field; Sergeant Charles Douglass helped him stagger toward surgeons in the rear.[14]

Unduly fearful of Confederate reinforcements and doubting, even then, the ability of black soldiers, General William Smith, Hincks's superior, refused to allow the Fifth or the USCT regiments to advance closer to Petersburg. Grant was furious with Smith's hesitancy, believing he had bungled a perfect opportunity to capture the city that stood between his armies and the Confederate capital. "There was nothing—not even a military force," he fumed, "to prevent our walking in and taking possession." An irritated Adams agreed, complaining to John Quincy that "there does not seem much chance of our getting into Richmond as yet." Worse yet, news reached Adams that just days before, on June 11, Minnie's brother Frederick Ogden had been killed not far away at Trevilian Station, Virginia, in what was the bloodiest cavalry fight of the war. Frederick had recently turned twenty-five.[15]

While the Fifth awaited further orders, Adams decided the time had arrived for his men to obtain proper mounts. Because of improvements in weaponry—rifled muskets were now able to reach three hundred yards—traditional cavalry charges had become anachronistic. In the wake of disastrous cavalry assaults at Gettysburg, US General John Buford had begun to advocate transforming cavalry regiments into mounted infantry units armed with carbines—which could be fired at twice the speed of muskets carried by infantrymen—so that they might ride quickly into battle but also dismount and fight on foot. Requesting leave from the recovering Russell, Adams traveled to Washington, where John Quincy was doing business for the governor. If the War Department would not provide his regiment with fresh horses, he hoped to locate "enough old horses unfit for present service, owing to severe work in the present campaign," and allow his men to care for the animals "and build them up" for the coming assaults.[16]

Upon reaching Washington on August 19, Adams discovered the byzantine vagaries of wartime bureaucracy. He began by making his case to a Major Williams, who suggested he instead talk to his superior, Colonel James Hardie. The colonel recommended that he try Charles Dana, the assistant secretary of war. Despite Dana's being kinsman to Adams family friend Richard Henry Dana, the secretary, Adams complained, "suggested Colonel This or General That." Despite being a late convert to the use of black troops, Adams believed that if the government intended to pursue the experiment, it must do so seriously, and he was irritated to find so many Republicans who simply wanted to refer the question up the chain of command. The stubborn Adams returned to Hardie's office and refused to leave until he could speak with Secretary of War Edwin Stanton himself. Hardie insisted that Adams might have better luck taking up the matter with General Henry Halleck, the general-in-chief of all US forces. But Halleck, a "rough old coot," made clear his "emphatic disapproval" of both Adams and his proposal. Snapping that "he wouldn't give Adams a single horse," he then slammed his door in Adams's face. That evening, the lieutenant colonel "dined alone, [had] diarrhea again," and was "homesick, unenergetic, & discouraged."[17]

The next morning, Adams determined to make one final effort. General Meade was then in the capital, and rather to Adams's surprise, the general not only approved of the scheme but scribbled out a note of introduction to Grant. Adams galloped off and presently found Grant sitting beneath a tarp chatting with his staff. "I stated my business and presented my letter," Adams wrote his mother. Grant read the letter several times, "puffing at his eternal cigar and stroking his beard." Looking up, the general stunned Adams: "I will approve your plan and request the Secretary to issue you the horses and have an order made out for you to go to Washington and attend to it yourself." Adams "at once became a violent Grant man." As Grant wrote the brief order, he spoke easily to Adams, just as if Grant "had been another Captain of Cavalry." Unable to gaze into the future, Adams could not know that Grant would one day stand in the way of his father's success or that he and his brothers would come to loathe the man for his supposed ignorance and corruption. For the moment, Adams thought only that Grant possessed "all the simplicity of a great man, of one whose head has in no way been turned by a rapid rise."[18]

When Adams returned to Stanton's office, the secretary barely glanced at him, but he paid attention enough to Grant's missive. "Grant's endorsement was too strong to be overlooked," Adams recalled, "and I had gotten my horses." Before catching the steamer back to Point Lookout, Adams spent several days with John Quincy and dined with Governor Andrew and advisor John Murray Forbes, informing them that we "have got an order for 1,000 horses now, as fast as we can receive them." Charles Francis and his brother also stopped by the State Department to visit Seward but found him deeply worried about Lincoln's election chances that fall. "His tone was very different from that of last spring," Charles Francis reported to his father, "when he seemed to me so buoyant and confident of the future."[19]

It took more than a week for Adams to secure transportation for the horses, but he finally returned to Point Lookout on September 11. "Here I am at last," he wrote John Quincy, "up to my chin in nigger." A good many white officers dubbed themselves "nigger colonels," in part to lessen the sting of the slights they received from more-conservative soldiers after consenting to lead black regiments. By comparison, Adams simply used the word as synonymous with "negro" or "colored," and his tone suggested disdain for his troopers' working-class origins as well as their pigmentation. "I'm sick and out of sorts and hearts," he told John Quincy on another occasion, as "the niggers bore me." Aware that a majority of his men had begun life in bondage, Adams even found humor in the fact that he was now in charge of so valuable a commodity. "Nigger driving seems to be a good business, and I think I shall turn my training here to practical advantage on a small well-stocked plantation as soon as this cruel war is over," he joked to his brother. "These men are worth any day a thousand dollars apiece right along. Am I fit to be trusted with the care of $1,200,000 in niggers alone?" As they led black troops into battle, most Brahmin officers quickly shed their genteel racism, but it was never in an Adams to change.[20]

When writing to John Quincy or Henry, Charles Francis habitually referred to his "nigs," but as he watched the recruits strive to master the complicated mounted maneuvers that required long hours of training, Adams praised them as "eager to learn." Never pausing to consider how his recruits had survived growing up in slavery, however, he was surprised to find them "docile and naturally polite." And not considering that enslaved groomsmen stole sleep when they could, he complained to Henry that he routinely found entire companies "all asleep and the Corporal leading the snore." The short, fastidious Adams also thought their bodies curious. "They're built so much better than white men," he mused. "Their feet—you never saw such feet." But at least initially, Adams suspected that the freedmen possessed "immeasurable capacity for improvement," and he reminded himself that while decades of brutalization had "crush[ed] them into slaves," it would require "kindness and patience" to elevate them "to our own standard." Unhappily, he admitted, with considerable self-reflection, to Henry, "patience, kindness and self-control have not been my characteristics as an officer."[21]

When addressing his father, a man who had never once adopted pejorative terms when speaking of African Americans, Charles Francis instead spoke of "the negro" and was generally positive in his assessments. "The negro makes a good soldier," he assured his father, and black infantrymen, "properly officered, would I believe be as effective as any in the world." But while the young officer toned down his rhetoric when writing to London, his comments nevertheless revealed a man who held decidedly upper-class views toward his social inferiors and betrayed a son of privilege who little pondered how bondage had shaped his men's lives and limited their minds. Blacks were especially suited, he supposed, for "those branches of the service where a high order of intelligence is less required." As African Americans lacked "mental vigor and energy," Adams presumed, the army was "the proper school for the race." Forgetting that the recruits who filled his regiment had devoted years to caring for their former masters' steeds, while other bondmen had labored as blacksmiths and carpenters, Adams believed the army could double as a "school for skilled labor and self reliance, as well as an engine of war." Having witnessed his men in battle below Petersburg, he had no doubts as to their "courage in action," but as to their "mental and moral energy," he warned his father, he "entertain[ed] grave doubts."[22]

As the fall came on, Adams's health grew as grim as his morale. "Poisoned by incessant feeding on hard-tack and meat freshly killed and fried in pork-fat," he later wrote, together with camping amid "decaying animal matter," left him feeling broken. "Very uncomfortable with my diarrhea & towards night resorted again to my opium," Adams told his diary. "The inordinate drinking of black coffee—quarts of it, each day"—were followed by copious amounts of whiskey each evening. "My present ambition is to see the war over, so that I may see my way out of the army," he sighed to Henry. "I am tired of the Carnival of Death."[23]

THE BOREDOM AND WORSENING HEALTH OF CHARLES FRANCIS JR. were shared by other members of the far-flung Adams family. In London, the patriarch increasingly found life "monotonous and eventless." Were his family "contented," the senior Adams reflected, he "would cheerfully remain, at least during the warm weather." But "in the family there is more of ailing and discomfort than has been experienced during all the other portion of our residence, put together." Mary's health continued precarious, and more alarming still, Louisa reluctantly wrote of her "third severe illness within six months." Charles Francis Jr. had witnessed her distress during his last visit to Newport while courting Minnie, and Henry now guessed that "the silence about her in your letters and John's [suggested] that she must have been very seriously ill." Charles Francis Sr. feared that her problems were "not understood by her physicians" and suspected that Louisa's ailments were psychological, an "organic disease beyond their skill." Her pointless existence in Newport allowed for no "change for the better," so Charles Francis and Abby begged her to join them in London. "At this distance the suspense and the idea of her loneliness are extremely trying," Adams told his diary.[24]

The Kuhns set sail in mid-July 1864. "Lou had the finest passage ever known and was *not sick a moment*," John Quincy reported to Charles Francis after receiving word from Henry, "passing all her time on deck, eating like a pig." Having expected to see a thin, tired Louisa, the family was more than a bit surprised by her recent weight gain. "Loo is fatter than a porpoise," Henry confirmed to Charles Francis. While many upper-class Victorian wives starved themselves and cinched their bodies into painful corsets, the thirty-three-year-old Louisa adopted the reverse tactic, rebelling against a patriarchal demand that women be submissive, deferential, and attenuated: to exist only to serve others. Although "generally jolly" while aboard the steamer, Louisa immediately came to loathe London, trying Henry's patience by condemning "England from morning till night." While Henry found enough to criticize among Britain's ruling classes, he had "led here a not unhappy life," characteristically employing a double negative as he described his fortunate existence far from the front. But Louisa bored Henry "extremely with her perseverance of vituperation." Henry never had "the energy to hate any country or person as she does," he protested to Charles Francis Jr.[25]

Charles Francis Sr. and Abby labored to distract their unhappy daughter by touring the countryside and taking in Kew Gardens, but to little avail. "Poor Loo will bore herself to death," Henry fretted, adding that she appeared to "blame" the family for her unhappiness. "Poor girl! she is too clever to occupy herself permanently, and also too clever not to be martyred by want of occupation." Whether Henry or her parents ever suggested to Louisa that she pursue the wartime work typical of women of her age and class is unclear, and their diaries are silent on the question. In Manhattan, Dr. Elizabeth Blackwell had founded the Women's Central Relief Association to coordinate volunteer activities and train female nurses. Other elite women donated their time to the United States Sanitary Commission, which acted as an advisory board to the Medical Bureau in the War Department. Even John Quincy, as an aide to Governor Andrew, played a minor role in the Union war effort. But of all the adult Adams children, only the brilliant, miserable Louisa preferred genteel boredom and complaining to national service.[26]

Equally worrisome for the family was Mary's asthma, which worsened as the fall wore on. After Mary suffered a violent series of "paroxysms," Charles Francis Sr. called in two specialists, who recommended that she leave the dank, smoky air of London for Cheltenham, a spa town in the west country. Adams packed Abby and Mary off, together with the Kuhns, hoping that Mary's "late attack of congestion of the lungs" would improve and that Louisa's concerns for her younger sister might take her mind off her own woes. "I am afraid we have all of us stayed in this ungenial climate a little too long," Adams wrote to John Gorham Palfrey. "My wish is to be relieved."[27]

The trip did Mary much good but did little to improve Louisa's mood. "Mary has been steadily recovering and is now apparently quite well," Henry reported to his brother. But just as Mary began to improve, her father observed, "Louisa seemed to be rather failing in her process of recovery." For his part, Henry suspected "that she will always be ailing." After her illness of the previous spring, Louisa had begun to treat herself with mercury, a common ingredient in patent medicines sold to women to cure "any private Distemper." The alleged cure left Louisa "shaken" and her health further damaged. "She is evidently very much bored by our life," Henry warned Charles Francis Jr., "and she would like to go on to the Continent."[28]

After a stay of five months, Louisa and her husband quit London for the Continent. "Loo and Kuhn have left us," Henry notified Charles Francis, "chattering and fighting and scolding according to their wont." Her parents were distraught. "An unhealthy sort of existence at Newport terminating in a dreadful illness which has shattered her body and nerves to an extraordinary degree, now presents her only as the wreck of her former self," Charles Francis Sr. wrote. All Adams men, dating back scores of years, were unusually single-minded, often at the cost of friendships and relationships. But both Charles Francis Sr. and Henry were correct in believing that Louisa had responded to that tradition by adopting the opposite habits. "In the absence of occupations both of her and her husband," her father thought, they embraced a "fleeting and unsatisfactory" existence. "She feels herself capable of doing more and better than she is or will be, which makes her restless and disappointed." Henry agreed. "Loo has missed her mark in life," he worried, "and she is destined to be an unhappy little woman."[29]

Either because Henry was anxious about his sister and considered joining her in Europe or because he also was as yet unsure about the future course of his life, when Henry Wilson, the Legation's senior secretary, opted to return to the states, Henry declined Seward's offer to move into a paid position. Despite the ongoing personal friction between undersecretary Benjamin Moran and the Adams family, Charles Francis Sr. recognized Moran's abilities and urged Seward to elevate him into

Wilson's post and promote Henry into Moran's. Having desired a paid position with the Legation in 1861, if only for the prestige, Henry now declined the offer. Charles Francis Sr. was forced to pen an "apology for my son Henry" to the State Department. "My term however is drawing so near to its close that the matter has little intrinsic importance," Charles Francis assumed, quite incorrectly.[30]

ALTHOUGH ADAMS WAS DESTINED TO REMAIN IN LONDON FOR JUST over another three years, his hopes of returning home were founded on the belief that the presidential contest appeared to be turning in Lincoln's favor. News of Sherman's capture of Atlanta reached London in mid-September, and Adams was politically savvy enough to understand that the victory was a spectacular boon to northern morale. "This success will do much to change the tone of the public sentiment," Adams knew, just as it would damage Democratic hopes, as the party's platform had adopted a peace-at-any-price statement. One month later, on October 12, eighty-seven-year-old Supreme Court Chief Justice Roger Taney died after nearly three decades on the bench. Never one to forgive a deceased opponent, Charles Francis judged Taney's demise "as fortunate": it eliminated a defender "of a dangerous policy" regarding slavery's expansion, and the opening energized Republican voters, who guessed—as did Adams—that Lincoln would replace him with either Seward or his old Free Soil ally Salmon Chase. At Point Lookout, Charles Francis Jr. was equally delighted, knowing that as Republicans were already poised to retain Congress and the White House, Taney's death "gives us control of the Judiciary" as well. His black troopers, like the president himself, had worried that Taney might attempt to strike down the Emancipation Proclamation. But now, he declared, "the darling wish of Taney's last days is doomed and not to be realized." As did his father, the lieutenant colonel assumed that the president would select Chase, and Charles Francis Jr. thought there was no "better man" for the chair.[31]

Charles Francis Jr. was sick enough by early November to request, and receive, a one-month medical leave, which would also allow him to be in Boston on Election Day. He reached Quincy by November 6 but "felt sick & tired & didn't go out with John but slept." The next day was "the great election day," and although still far from rested, he and John cast their ballots and then spent the dining and drinking before paying a call on Governor Andrew. "I never saw a more orderly election," he wrote Henry. "All seemed to breathe more freely when the result was known, but there was a sober serious time in the general feeling not usually noticed." By the evening's end, the crowd had grown celebratory, and the inebriated brothers "crowed lustily over our clean sweep in Quincy and Boston."[32]

Word of Lincoln's victory reached London on November 21. "This is a result in which we may be permitted humbly to rejoice," Charles Francis Sr. reflected. In a series of letters to his brother-in-law Edward Everett, the minister took heart in the fact that the "Constitution has come through the great strain put upon it with ease, and the Government is for the moment stronger than ever it was." Resolutions from English antislavery groups poured in at the Legation, and as the enormous significance of the Republican victory became clear—Lincoln captured 55 percent of the popular vote and 91 percent of the electoral vote—Adams was filled "with pride." As an Adams, Charles Francis Sr. rarely exhibited much faith in popular democracy, but he now "confess[ed] to a much stronger conviction of the value of our popular institutions than I ever dared before."[33]

Both the minister and his officer son believed that the war effort had been hindered by critics of the president, foreign and domestic. "This election has relieved us of the [political] fire in the rear" from northern Democrats, Charles Francis Jr. assured Henry, "and now we can devote an undivided attention to the remnants of the Confederacy." His father agreed, writing that a solid majority of northern voters, in "the face of intrigues of every kind carried on for months both within and without the lines," had expressed their confidence in Republican policies and indicated a desire to see them carried through. Confederate hopes had rested with a McClellan victory over Lincoln and a negotiated peace, but with black armies in the field and Republicans discussing the need for a constitutional amendment to replace the wartime Emancipation Proclamation, the "slave question must before long be removed from the path," the elder Adams believed. Southern dreams "of independence as the instrument to protect slavery" had perished with the election. "What is there left to fight about?"[34]

Either because of the election news or the fact that he was away from hardtack and the unsanitary camp in Maryland, Charles Francis soon "woke up & felt well." With a few days remaining on his furlough, he hurried to Newport to visit the grieving Minnie before returning south. "You may tell Fanny that I this morning called on the Ogden woman-kind and am in a bad way," he laughed to his elder brother. "Oh John! I never loved before! Our charming friend of last winter is more charming in mourning and I left the house maundering." Charles Francis dreaded returning to his regiment, but his "ebony spouse awaits," and the army required him to "sternly sink the vision of pleasant possibilities in the stern realities of my niggers." New Year's Eve found him back at Point Lookout, celebrating the conclusion of 1864 "with flip, punch & tobacco." Just after midnight, his "legs & stomach gave out" from the potent combination of alcohols, and he retired to his bed and diary. "So I finished the year," he scribbled into his journal, "which was a good year to me."[35]

John Quincy fell easily into his younger brother's racist humor, smirking that both he and Fanny were struck by the way Charles Francis was torn "between love and duty" to Minnie and his obligation to "the legion of dusky warriors which under the bold image of an Ethiopian bride you picture awaiting your embrace." The way that the eldest son of the fourth generation modeled his discourse on that of Charles Francis surely reminded the latter that his brother was content to follow his lead, unlike Henry, whose brilliance and independence of mind kept their brotherly rivalry alive. Yet as the only married male of his generation, John Quincy thought it necessary to dispense some advice of the heart, reminding his brother that it "would have been a clever thing to send [Minnie] a box of bon-bons at New Years."[36]

Across the ocean, Charles Francis Sr. began to wonder how Lincoln's reelection affected his own duties. Charles Mackay, the Manhattan-based correspondent for the *London Times*, reported rumors that Seward wished to retire from the State Department and either return to the Senate or replace Adams at the Court of St. James. Should that happen, Mackay speculated, Adams would "take the Secretary's place." Henry judged the potential exchange an "annoying idea," and having little faith in the veracity of the *Times*, he assured Charles Francis Jr. that "it can't be true, or else Mackay wouldn't write it." But the American press picked up the rumors too. "Should Mr. Seward decide to go abroad," the *Cleveland Morning Leader* reported, "Charles Francis Adams is the most probable—indeed, the only talked of successor to the Premiership." And the State Department, every Adams knew, was the traditional prelude to the presidency.[37]

The senior Adams was uncharacteristically silent on the rumors, perhaps not wishing to reveal his ambitions even to the privacy of his diary. But as he predicted, events in the states had a dramatic impact in London. In early January of 1865, Foreign Secretary John Russell ordered the handful of Confederate naval officers in Britain to return home. Several weeks later, Fort Fisher, which protected the vital trading route into Wilmington, North Carolina, fell into Union hands, and with it the last major southern port used by blockade runners. The election "at once put an end to the chief reliance of the conspirators," Adams informed Everett. "Foreign assistance is less likely than ever." Even the habitually anti-American *London Times* promptly dropped "its contemptuous and flippant style of criticism." Although Adams was disinclined to forgive "the governing class for the very gross manner in which they have betrayed their partiality to our disadvantage," he adopted a kindlier view toward the British factory workers who had stood by the Union. Not that he sympathized with the economic demands of workers on either side of the Atlantic, but Adams shared their insistence on voting rights. "Our victory will be equally their triumph," he assured Seward.[38]

News as yet traveled slowly. Adams posted his latest missive to Everett on January 27, but his brother-in-law had died fifteen days before at the age of seventy. Seward wrote with the sad news, observing that "his earnest and well directed labors" in behalf of the administration, mostly as a fund-raiser and speaker, had "won for him the confidence and affection of the American people." For much of their lives, the two men had not been close, and Adams bluntly admitted to his journal that until the past few years, he would hardly have looked "upon this event with much regret." In the antebellum years, Everett was too quick "to subject himself to the influence of Mr. Webster, a man whom in all the moral aspects of his life" had never been worthy of emulation. But after the attack upon Fort Sumter, Adams reflected, Everett finally "began to emancipate himself [from] his moral timidity." Adams, in fact, had hoped that Everett would take his place in London. As he expected, Abby took the death hard, as "in her youth [she] was much under his care."[39]

Although Adams was more than a decade younger than Everett and would not turn fifty-eight until the following August, his brother-in-law's death made him feel old and increased his yearning to sail for America. Rather than formally request leave, Adams penned a private note to Seward, expressing his "wish to return as soon" as he could "without injury to the public interest." Aware of rumors about a cabinet position, Adams hoped to make it abundantly clear that he had no intentions of supplanting Seward. His only desire was "of returning to private life." Henry feared that if Seward urged his father to stay, he would do so, or that Lincoln might beg him to accept the State Department. "This is the only alternative I can see," Henry complained to Charles Francis Jr. Weary of his own official duties, Henry "dread[ed] either almost equally." Aware of his family's opinions, the elder Adams suggested that Henry take Abby, Mary, and Brooks to Italy to rendezvous with the Kuhns, while he remained in London "as a temporary occupant till a successor is appointed."[40]

Henry accepted the task, but not happily. Rarely patient with his mother and dismissive of his younger sister, Henry found them intolerable to travel with. Charles Francis Sr. hoped that springtime in Italy might improve Mary's health, but she refused to "take care of herself," Henry grumbled to Charles Francis Jr. "Mary is the most perverse and obstinate girl I ever saw in my life." As for his mother, after a "lovely day's journey, and an excellent dinner," Henry reported, Abby routinely complained that she had "seen nothing yet on this journey that any one could call pleasure." Suspecting that his brother, who had always preferred Abby to their father, might think him too harsh, Henry insisted that his characterization was "far from exaggerated." His mother's "unvarying practice of dwelling on the dark points of a picture" led him to regard the remainder of their trip "with alarm and complete it with relief." Worse yet, when Louisa and her husband arrived, they neither got along with each other nor with the rest of the family. "Another three months together would probably widen the distance between Loo and us into a regular breach," he warned his father. In return, Louisa and Mary bestowed the nickname of "Mausoleum" on their dour brother. "And well they may," Henry admitted to Charles Francis Jr., "for temper and nerve have been worn to a point that leaves little hope for me except in a tomb."[41]

"UNSOUGHT BY ME AND UNDESIRED, CAME OFFERS OF PROMOTION," Charles Francis Jr. informed his father, and for an Adams, the appearance of indifference was of paramount importance. As 1865 began, and with it the expectation of spring campaigns, it became increasingly clear that Colonel Henry Russell had not recovered sufficiently from his wounds of the previous June. Although the War Department would not sign off on the paperwork until February 15, Russell informed Governor Andrew of his need to step aside and, as he promised Adams, "spoke of Charley Adams as a good person" for the colonelcy. "The events of the coming year I, for one, seek not to foresee," Charles Francis Jr. reflected, yet he prayed "that all blessings were not yet expended in the past" and that providence "will supply its cakes and ales in due quantity also in the future."[42]

While the Fifth awaited orders, the new colonel devoted the days to drilling his regiments on both their mounts and their carbines. "But when dusk comes," he wrote to Henry, "then comes my pleasure." At five each evening, Adams lit his lamps and a fire in his quarters, rolled a cigarette and poured himself a whiskey, and then spent the next six hours writing letters and studying tactics. As had many an Adams before him, Charles Francis took pride in his friendless, solitary existence. "I never go out, and people rarely drop in on me," he bragged to Henry, "so that a long evening is given me," and those moments he "enjoy[ed] intensely."[43]

In early March, Adams received instructions to bring his regiment south and join Grant's forces near Petersburg. The news that his son and the black troopers were to serve in the final operations around Richmond "sobered" the elder Adams and prompted the hope that Lee might finally grasp "that no benefit can be expected from the slaughter of more men." Yet even as the minister worried about his son, the old Free Soiler took heart in newspaper accounts that told of Sherman's advance through South Carolina. "At last the armed hand has reached that nurse of seditions, and is dealing out evenhanded justice in the midst of the slave population," Adams marveled after reading of the mid-February capture of Charleston. To South Carolina's white minority, "emancipation is most emphatically revolution, for a large majority [of the population] are blacks."[44]

At about the same time, word also reached London that during the previous December, Minnie had accepted Charles Francis's proposal of marriage. Charles Francis Sr. and Abby were hardly surprised. "We have been under some suspicion of this for a good while," Adams reflected, and during her fall trip to Britain, Louisa had spoken "very highly of her." The idea of his second son—and the one in whom he placed the most confidence—"landing the young lady brought tears to my eyes," Adams admitted. "There is much sterling merit in him, and a share of abilities which ought to establish him honorably in life." The minister hurried off a letter to Edward Ogden, Minnie's father, explaining his "natural enthusiasm" for the happy news but also his sympathies with the Ogden family "on the severe affliction brought upon you by the devotion of your son to his duty in this painful war." Similar if uncommonly thoughtful reflections inspired Charles Francis Jr. to worry about his fiancée. "I'm only sorry on Minnie's account," he wrote John Quincy. "Her brother's death will weigh on her now and destroy all her confidence in my safety." He urged his brother and Fanny to "run down" to Newport "and pass a Sunday with her." Habitually proud of his brusque, discourteous manner, Charles Francis's love for Minnie brought out a different side of his character, yet it was also one, unfortunately, that he chose to cultivate only with his future bride.[45]

Other letters and newspapers arriving at the Legation told of Lincoln's second inaugural address, one already hailed by journalists as among the greatest orations of the age. The elder Adams, while impressed, was hardly effusive in his praise. "Though not as polished as a rhetorician would have made it," he thought, "this production is the first of [Lincoln's] official declarations which in loftiness of tone approaches to the grandeur of the situation." But Adams attributed its heights to the moment rather than to the man: "No one not excepting Washington himself, has occupied one more sublime." However, Charles Francis Jr. instinctively grasped its greatness. "That rail splitter is one of the wonders of the day," he lectured his father. "Once at Gettysburg and now again on a greater occasion he has shown a capacity for rising to the demands of the hour." Having spent the last years venturing his life in the cause of union and emancipation, the young colonel thrilled to see Lincoln bluntly state that the desire to "strengthen, perpetuate, and extend" slavery "was the object for which the insurgents" fought. "What will Europe think of this utterance of the rude ruler, of whom they have nourished so lofty a contempt? Not a prince or minister in all Europe could have risen to such an equality with the occasion."[46]

The father and son were united, however, on the absurdity of reports coming out of Richmond that President Davis intended to liberate and arm a regiment of African Americans. "The rebels are so fruitful of schemes of all sorts," the minister remarked, "notwithstanding all preceding it have failed." If the Confederate government "put arms in their hands," Charles Francis Jr. agreed, "those devils would paddle over to us so quick they couldn't catch them." Lee's Army of Northern Virginia was down to 22,000 men, rumor had it, and if Richmond even tried a minor experiment in black soldiers, the colonel guessed, those few whites left would desert, "for those are the remains of the men who fought for slavery."[47]

As the Adamses correctly predicted, Davis's last-ditch attempt to save his country was too late by scores of years. About half a dozen free blacks enlisted, and Virginia governor William Smith donated two slaves who had been sentenced to hang for burglary. By then, Grant had determined to punch through Lee's defenses, and Colonel Adams agreed that "Lee's army should be held [and] engaged at any cost and sacrifice." On Sunday, April 2, Adams, as he later recalled, "was ordered to hurry my regiment out as though Hell kicked me," and in the confusion, he found himself in charge of his regiment and another thousand white cavalrymen. "I have seen more wear and tear of horse-flesh than I ever saw on a march before," he wrote John Quincy that evening. The makeshift brigade was nearly impossible to handle, "being made up of all sorts of detachments and being without any staff or organization." Weary and anxious, Adams curled up by the side of the road and slept.[48]

The previous evening, however, Lee had abandoned Petersburg and fled west, leaving the twenty-five-mile road north into Richmond open to American armies. Confederate General Richard Ewell was ordered to destroy all bridges, military stores, and warehouses that might be of use to Grant's forces. Rising at dawn, Adams and his men mounted and then waited, impatiently. At seven o'clock, "after fretting, fuming, and chafing for an order," one arrived for the Fifth to advance up the Darbytown Road. To their front, they could hear "heavy explosions" and see the flames of boats, bridges, wharfs, and even one blasted ironclad. The Fifth rode past broken breastworks, some of them topped with heavy guns; others were "Quaker guns," thick logs painted black. At about nine o'clock, the troopers entered the city's suburbs, Charles Francis proudly wrote John Quincy. "What a piece of luck it was," Adams thought, as he led the first troops into Richmond. "That I, after all these years of fighting and toil and danger, of doubt, discouragement and almost despair, should as an emblem of the results of this war, lead into Richmond a regiment of black cavalry."[49]

As the troopers reached the Capitol Square, black Virginians flooded the streets and, as one officer recorded, "danced and shouted and prayed and blessed the Lord and thanked him that the Yankees had come." The cavalrymen, already tall upon their mounts, stood up in their stirrups and waved their swords above their heads, sparking "the wildest demonstrations of joy on the part of the colored people." The smoke from still-burning buildings darkened the morning sun, and cinders rained down on the triumphal march. Even so, the "whole day and scene was one never to be forgotten," Charles Francis marveled. "It was the event of my life hitherto."[50]

From second-floor windows, a few war-weary residents of both races unfurled American flags. Major A. H. Stevens climbed the steps to the roof of the capitol building to pull down the Virginia state flag and raise the regiment's colors. So taken was he by the victorious moment that Adams dropped his usual racial epithets. "Black faces seemed to spring out of the ground," he reported to John Quincy, "and, rushing into the ranks, some of the blacks even embraced the knees of the officers." General Godfrey Weitzel set up a command post in the abandoned House of Delegates, and amid the "smoke, cinders, and confusion," Adams dismounted and reported to the general, who offered the colonel a "hasty drink" before tasking him with setting up a mounted picket line around the city. That night, Adams rode through the city and was surprised to find that "perfect order and quiet prevailed everywhere." Parts of Richmond continued to smolder, but Adams witnessed "no fighting, no drunkenness, no pillage, [and] no noise." Had he not been there himself to see Richmond fall, he "should not have known that the city had been captured."[51]

Adams spent most of the next day patrolling the fallen capital. White residents were "panic-stricken" that the black troopers had come to sack the city, and as Adams dismounted near one woman's elegant home, she "went into hysterics and insisted on having a scene" until he was able to convince her otherwise. Most whites were indignant over the retreating Confederates torching the city, "and curses on Jeff Davis are heard loud and frequent." The Union high command had relocated into Davis's executive mansion, and Adams lunched there, meeting Admiral David Farragut. "The whole thing seems like a dream," Adams assured John Quincy. "I can't realize that after all, *I* have been reserved to see all this and to be even a part of it, that today I am 'picketing' Richmond."[52]

Ten days later, a telegram landed on Charles Francis Sr.'s table telling of the fall of Petersburg and Richmond but saying nothing about the whereabouts of his son, which gave "rise to anxiety" about the next set of letters. Finally, on April 24, Fanny wrote with the news that Charles Francis Jr. had "led his regiment" into the Confederate capital. "So my mind was again at ease," the minister told his diary, "and I felt light-hearted and gay." Adams immediately wrote to the son he had so tried to dissuade from enlisting. "It was a singular circumstance that you, in the fourth generation of our family," he wrote, "should have been the first to put your foot in the capital of the Ancient Dominion, and that too, at the head of a corps which prefigured the downfall" of slavery. Although the elder Adams at long last understood the point his son had made four years earlier about the responsibilities of their family, he declined to admit that he had been wrong. Rather, he took his grandfather to task, but with some justice. It was "the third and fourth generation which is paying the bitter penalty for what must now be admitted were the short-comings of the original founders of the Union" in not eradicating slavery during their lifetimes.[53]

Yet if Adams appeared to finally understand his son, and to grasp the importance of black troopers liberating Richmond, he failed to comprehend the larger political visions of former slaves. Those troopers in the Fifth who had been born into slavery knew that equality, and not merely freedom, was the opposite of bondage. Just days after the Fifth had ridden into the Confederate capital, Lincoln visited the city, and as word of the president's arrival spread, Lincoln found himself surrounded by blacks shouting "Bless the Lord, Father Abrahams Come." Upon returning to the White House, an equally large throng poured onto the grounds below the north portico. In answer to shouts and calls to say a few words, Lincoln appeared at a second-floor window and read a prepared text. He promised "no persecution, no bloody work" for the defeated Confederates, but he insisted also that "the more intelligent" blacks, and certainly those who had served in the military, deserved the right to vote. Black Americans and progressive Republicans cheered, but Adams thought otherwise. "The President is still flickering about Richmond, utterly unconscious of the nature of his position and innocent of dignity," he groused. As for Lincoln's carefully worded speech, Adams saw only a president utterly incapable of grasping the solemnity and dignity of "his own position," a leader delivering a "speech to a chance crowd at his door." "How constantly my misgivings about him recur," Adams sighed.[54]

WITH THE END OF THE WAR IN SIGHT, SEWARD URGED ADAMS TO contact John Russell and request that Britain formally withdraw its 1861 recognition of belligerent rights for the collapsing Confederacy. Even for the small handful of southern sympathizers left in Parliament, the fall of Charleston and Richmond, Adams took pleasure in observing, "made a profound impression." Russell consented, and Adams sat in the balcony as the House of Commons debated the proposal. Adams judged the "arguments feeble enough" on both sides. But it little mattered now, he understood, and his only regret was that the American government had to press the Palmerston ministry on the issue. Russell, Adams thought, should instead have offered a "manly and frank retraction of an originally hasty step" in the name of "conciliating good feelings for the future."[55]

That done, Adams decided the time had come to renew what previously had been an unofficial entreaty to be relieved of his post. Despite their long friendship, Seward had chosen to respond to his feelers by not responding. Then came word that Adams's predecessor in London, George Mifflin Dallas, had passed away, and as with Everett's death, Adams again felt very old. "I stand in need of all my patience to put up with this rude treatment," he fumed. Adams was little surprised that Lincoln, who lacked "that highest kind of Christian training which constitutes the true definition of a gentleman," had not replied. "But Mr. Seward has both education and nature to fit him for it." On March 29, Adams renewed his request, complaining to Seward that he had unfairly been kept "in a state of suspense for more than four months." Had Seward bothered to explain why Adams was needed in London, he "should have acquiesced in the necessity with what philosophy I might." But after four years of service, Adams bluntly confided to his diary, he was disinclined to "disguise the degree of annoyance" he felt "at what appears to have been a great want of courtesy, to say the least of it."[56]

All his anger melted away on April 21, when Adams received two letters from Washington, one from Secretary of War Stanton and the other from Seward's assistant William Hunter. Both told of the Good Friday assassination of Lincoln and the "painful and severe wounds" inflicted on Seward, who had been stabbed five times on the face and neck by former Confederate soldier Lewis Powell. In a moment, Adams felt his life "completely overturned," and having posted an angry missive to his old friend, Adams feared that both Seward and his son Frederick had only a "slight prospect of recovery." In a terrible way, Adams mused, it was "fitting that what began with perjury, fraud, and treachery should end in private assassination." Such was "the fruit of the seed that was sown in the slavery of the African race." Although ever one to doubt the president's capacity for greatness, he had been impressed by Lincoln's talk of national healing, and he judged his death an irreparable blow to the country. "There was a grandeur about the national movement under his direction," Adams thought. Several Union supporters called at his house, but Adams was in no mood to receive visitors. Still pondering the meaning of these events, Adams concluded his daily journal entry with an insensitive if prophetic thought: "For his own fame the President could not have selected a more happy close."[57]

Although he suspected that his letters would arrive too late, Adams promptly mailed off a series of missives to Seward. Still believing that the secretary of state had been "the balance wheel of the machine of government," Adams told Seward he prayed that the secretary's absence "will be short," as his "aid was likely to be much needed in the impending effort to recement the divided portions of our Union." Adams assured Seward that well-wishers continued to knock at the Legation's door, and he sent along a number of clippings from sympathetic newspapers. At long last, Adams observed, the London press grasped "the noble qualities of the President." The tragedy, Adams understood, meant that he had to "abandon the long cherished hope of a return" home, for his steady hand was yet required in Britain. But in late June, by which time it was clear that Seward would survive his wounds, Adams "respectfully" entreated that Seward and Andrew Johnson, the new president, allow him to return home in the spring of 1866. "I shall then have been five years" in London, he reminded them, a "period longer than that of any of my predecessors." By then, he hoped, "the relations between the two countries will have so fallen back into their old channels."[58]

Lincoln's fate was well-known in London, but even so, on May 1 Adams thought it his duty to inform Russell of the calamity: "In communicating this melancholy event I feel persuaded that your Lordship and the British nation will not fail to participate in the general grief" shared by most Americans. Curiously, as assassin John Wilkes Booth remained at large until his death in a Virginia barn on April 26, official Washington suspected that the fugitive actor had caught a ship for Britain. Just in case, Adams penned a second note to Russell on May 6, asking that a "warrant be issued for his apprehension" under the Anglo-American extradition treaty of 1822. Several days after, word reached the Legation of Booth's death.[59]

Adams's first note to the foreign secretary carried the barbed hint that the Palmerston ministry had been slow to support the Union cause. But with Queen Victoria already having survived five assassination attempts, the British public did not require Adams's pointed reminder to demonstrate proper sympathy. Both houses of Parliament appealed to Victoria to "take suitable notice" of the occasion, and across the island, antislavery societies forwarded addresses and resolutions to the Legation. The wives and daughters of cabinet secretaries signed a collective letter of condolence for Mary Lincoln, which Adams mailed to the distraught First Lady. "I think I hazard nothing in affirming that the sentiments expressed in the note are felt universally in this Kingdom," Adams wrote, adding that "all loyal Americans" in London "sympathized with the greatest sufferer."[60]

Britain's compassionate response prompted Adams to reconsider his customarily uncharitable opinion of the martyred president. Thinking back to the spring of 1861, when he had journeyed to Washington to accept his London posting, Adams compared the "untried and almost grotesque-looking figure" and the wretched condition of the nation with the successful state of "public affairs at the moment of his death." It was, Adams conceded, "one of the most marvelous transformations recorded in history." In Boston, John Quincy agreed, writing of the city's plunge into "the lowest depths of despair and mourning." Unlike his father, John Quincy had been impressed by Lincoln's final speech, thinking it "foreshadowed a plan of action so wise and so conciliatory." Writing to his elder brother from Virginia, Charles Francis Jr. shared the family's concern that Andrew Johnson was not the right man for that dark hour, but for all the wrong reasons. Misjudging the Tennessean's complicated relationship with his region's planter class, Charles Francis feared that "Johnson will just hang every Southern leader he can lay his hands on." In reality, Johnson planned no such thing, but the fact that the Adams family would soon support the accidental president's policy of conciliating the white South revealed the gulf between their disdain for slavery and their lack of support for the aspirations of recently liberated black Americans.[61]

"By the first of June you will not be able in these parts to find any Confederates," Charles Francis Jr. assured his father. "The war is really over." Jefferson Davis was captured on May 10 while fleeing south through Georgia, and the elder Adams enjoyed a laugh over the false rumors that the former Confederate president was captured disguised in "his wife's petticoats. Alas! What an ignominious fate!" If the federal government "could punish him only by condemning him to wear them for the rest of his natural life." But as ever bemused by upper-class British opinion, Adams found it curious that even while grieving for the fallen Lincoln, the public expressed "intense interest" in Davis's fate. Adams too hoped Davis would not be hanged, but he thought English solicitude for the Mississippi planter "one of the [strange] phenomena of this remarkable era."[62]

With nobody to fight, Charles Francis Jr. settled into camp life when not patrolling the streets of Richmond. Female camp followers became a persistent problem, as food was scarce and freedwomen searched for potential husbands among the black cavalrymen. Adams "stirred the females in camp up with the longest sort of pole just as if I wasn't an engaged man," he laughed, adopting a dubious sexual reference. "Lord! You should have heard the cackling and seen the dust and feathers fly." Having just recently assured John Quincy that his regiment would do nothing to "discredit the State," he now characterized his bored troopers as "curious cattle," impervious to "threat or punishment." As he had early in the war, Adams suspected that black soldiers lacked basic morality, and he complained that at least one-third of his troopers were "the damnedest thieves and rascals alive."[63]

Unhappily, white Virginians shared his doubts, and Richmond's elites found the troopers' lack of deference an affront to traditional racial mores. On April 16, just two weeks after marching into the city, Adams received orders to report to General Edward Ord, a Maryland-born officer, at Fort Monroe and answer charges that he had permitted his regiment to "straggle and maraud." Few of the former bondmen in the Fifth cared to step into the streets as white women passed them by, as antebellum custom had required, and although Adams thought the charges were not "likely to prove serious," he agreed that his "sweet Africans [had] been cutting up rough," at least in southern eyes. Adams reached the fort by five o'clock that evening "and remained there apparently utterly forgotten and unnoticed" for the next eleven days.[64]

Adams finally decided to press the issue, writing to Ord that he demanded to be either charged or released and allowed to return to Richmond. The general evidently concluded that holding the son of the minister to Britain would not suit his own career plans, for he intended to remain in the postwar army. Adams was not only released that evening, but Ord also invited him to join his family as they sailed for Richmond. Charles Francis Jr. promptly wrote to John Quincy, explaining his side of the story should it "creep into the papers" and urging him to "keep quiet about it" if not, especially with their father. Rather than support his men against the empty claims of former Confederates, Adams instead chose to believe that black cavalrymen could not be responsible for themselves "in unfamiliar positions." The fault was his, he decided, for briefly believing otherwise. John Quincy agreed, assuring his brother that he too regretted "the delightful mess your damned niggers had put you in." As had Charles Francis Jr., John Quincy compared the troopers to animals, writing that they were "damned mean cattle compared with a good average white man." For a man named for his antislavery grandfather, John Quincy II's rhetoric was not a good omen for the future.[65]

As Charles Francis Jr.'s weight dropped to 130 pounds because of a debilitating bout of malaria, John Quincy urged him to resign his commission. After his brief arrest, however, Charles Francis Jr. rejected his brother's entreaties, insisting that his regiment required a firm hand and that he had little confidence in Horace Weld, his lieutenant-colonel. "Simply, my dear fellow," he replied, "because I cannot without losing credit," and Weld was "not fit to command." Even so, Adams worried about rumors that the Fifth would next be posted to Texas, where Confederate General Edmund Kirby Smith had yet to surrender: "Way down Texas! I swear to man!!" In London, Charles Francis Sr. also thought it likely that his son would lead his regiment into Texas as a "point of honor." Then, on May 26, Smith negotiated the surrender of his Trans-Mississippi Department. As the War Department was prepared to transfer Colonel Samuel Chamberlain from the First Cavalry to the Fifth, Adams saw "no reason for a man remaining in the service at any sacrifice to himself." In late May, he "dragged" himself onto his horse and rode north on medical furlough.[66]

On June 28, Doctor Ebenezer Woodward examined Adams at John Quincy's home and reported him "suffering from chronic diarrhea, and general disability" caused by "attacks of dysentery and malarial fever, the gradual result of long military service." Another doctor confirmed that diagnosis, declaring Adams an "invalid." Several days later, on July 21, Adams formally tendered his resignation to the secretary of war, providing documentation that his condition "utterly precluded my doing any further service for an indefinite period." Stanton agreed and signed his discharge papers on August 1. And so, Adams concluded, "After an active service of three years, seven months and twelve days, I turned to civilian occupations." Or, as his father, at long last finally satisfied with his son, put it: "This act of the drama is over."[67]

THE MINISTER FOUND HIS JOB INCREASINGLY MUNDANE. "MANY persons are now applying at this Legation for passports to return home, who belong to the disaffected States," Adams informed the State Department in late May, "and some of them perhaps have been more or less disaffected themselves." Adams had not anticipated this problem and requested advice on procedures and policies from Washington. None of the applicants had been important combatants. Typical was Arthur Sinclair, a twenty-two-year-old son of a onetime US Navy officer who had sided with the Confederacy. The father's sin was treason, Adams suspected, but the son had spent the war in Liverpool "in some superintending capacity" as Jefferson Davis sought to purchase a navy. Until he heard back from the still-recovering Seward, Adams thought it best to require applicants to take "the oath of allegiance" and suggest they prepare to sail for America unless told otherwise.[68]

The previous March, Congress had established the Bureau of Refugees, Freedmen, and Abandoned Lands, commonly known simply as the Freedmen's Bureau, to provide provisions and clothing and assist slaves and destitute whites in settling upon uninhabited estates, and British antislavery societies flooded the Legation with gifts and goods. Many older societies, such as the Union and Emancipation Society of Glasgow, changed their names to "Freedmen's Associations," and groups in Birmingham, the Midlands, and Edinburgh shipped crates of goods to London "for the use of colored freedmen." Adams dutifully signed the invoices and arranged for shipment, yet he believed that such commonplace tasks were hardly worthy of his time.[69]

Adams was particularly annoyed by his everyday responsibilities when momentous questions were being debated back home. "Reconstruction is looming rapidly up here and public opinion in New England stands in great need of guidance," Charles Francis Jr. hinted to his father. Many Republicans, he claimed, "don't want peace, unless with it comes the hangman." Charles Francis Jr. and John Quincy believed that the next step for their father, as had been the destiny of both their grandfather and great-grandfather, was to quit London for the White House, or at least for the governor's chair or the State Department, should Seward be elevated to the presidency in 1868. Seward, Charles Francis Jr. counseled his father, could be "depended upon to be moderate," but New England Republicans such as Sumner were "all against him." The beleaguered secretary "needs you in Massachusetts more than in London," he added, knowing that the bored, frustrated minister felt precisely the same way.[70]

Henry shared his brother's view that Republican demands for political reconstruction across the South—reforms also desired by the former troopers of the Fifth Cavalry—were as yet unnecessary. He expected to find Sumner in the vanguard of progressive legislation, but Henry was dismayed to find that family friend Dana was also voicing his concerns about President Johnson's determination to appease the white South. Why were Republicans "in such an amusing provincial hurry to get into opposition?" he asked his brother Charles Francis. As did his father, Henry believed that as the again-united country was "done with slavery," fighting about land reforms and voting rights for liberated bondmen was wholly unnecessary. "Let us give [the South] time," he argued. "I doubt about black states," he observed to Charles Francis Jr. in terms he knew his brother would understand. "I fancy white is better breeding stock." As yet, Charles Francis Jr. was uncommitted on the franchise, and while John Quincy favored "universal negro suffrage," he did so for purely practical reasons. "To be sure they are not fit for it," he mused, obviously thinking about former slaves, as free black men had long been able to vote in Massachusetts. But "without it I should doubt if they could maintain themselves, still less make any advance to fitness." The idea of natural rights, so critical to his great-grandfather's political thought, evidently played no role in John Quincy's calculations.[71]

While Henry merely complained about Dana, the minister fired off a series of letters to his old friend. In June, Dana had delivered a lecture at Faneuil Hall that quickly came to be known as the "grasp of war" speech. In it, Dana argued that a war was not over until all of its objectives had been achieved. "The conquering party may hold the other in the grasp of war until it has secured whatever it has a right to require," he insisted to thunderous applause. Where Lincoln, in his final speech, had advocated extending the franchise to black soldiers and educated African

Americans, Johnson was increasingly hostile to civil rights for African Americans and, for their readmission to the Union, proposed requiring only that the southern states ratify the Thirteenth Amendment, abolishing slavery. To Dana's theory, the elder Adams could never consent: "I cannot give my assent to your idea of the possibility of an indefinite extension of a system of tutelage in the States under the war power." The planter class "committed a most grievous mistake" in secession, he believed, but it had paid the price. "The political influence which they threw away can never be recovered." But once the rebellion was "put down, the States resume their ancient status of perfect equality" with those in the North. To dictate "terms and conditions as have never been required of any other state," such as black voting rights, which in fact were then denied to black veterans in the midwestern states, "introduces an inequality among the whole number which changes the entire form of Government." If Adams was correct in thinking it hypocritical for the victorious North to impose requirements on the defeated Confederacy that it did not desire for itself, he was nonetheless silent regarding the so-called "Black Codes" that southern legislatures had begun to impose on freedpeople in hopes of denying them property and political rights. For Adams, political theory trumped human rights. "I have not half done—perhaps I may not resume" the debate, Adams angrily signed off. "At any rate you see how radically we disagree."[72]

Instead of further fighting with old friends, Adams chose to devote himself to what he prayed would be his final duty before returning home: preparing the legal ground for claims of damages against "Her Majesty's Government" for recognizing "insurgents as belligerents before they had a single vessel afloat," as well as for depredations committed by British-built southern privateers after the surrender of the Army of Northern Virginia. James Iredell Waddell, commander of the *CSS Shenandoah*, plundered ten northern whaling ships in the Arctic as late as June 1865. In response, Adams crafted a long dispatch to Russell on what he called "damages arising from the British pirates" that even the normally underwhelmed Benjamin Moran applauded as "the best he ever wrote." Republican newspapers demanded that Waddell, who had surrendered his ship in Liverpool, be extradited to the United States. Even the *London Times* approved of such demands, but "does the Times suppose that the hanging of Captain Waddell would satisfy the American claims for the Alabama and Shenandoah damages?"[73]

American demands stalled that fall when Lord Palmerston unexpect-edly died on October 18, two days before his eighty-first birthday. Henry, for one, felt no sadness. The elder Adams, he observed, had become "almost a historical monument in London," while "his old opponents disappeared." The late prime minister possessed only "one really active antipathy, and that antipathy was America," he observed. His passing, Henry guessed, "will weaken England and strengthen us." John Russell, a decade younger at seventy-three, was again to serve as prime minister—a position he had previously held from 1846 to 1852—while George Villiers, the Earl of Clarendon, took over the foreign office. "Lord Russell is no match for us, as has long been evident," Henry assured Charles Francis Jr., "and Lord Clarendon would certainly not be an advance on Lord Russell." The obvious problem for the Adams family, Henry immediately recognized, was that the shake-up in London meant that Seward would resist changing "our representation abroad or would be wise to do so." That meant that his father's dream of returning home that spring, "as papa still pretends to expect," was not likely to become reality. The fact that the secretary of state had "given us not even the ghost of a sign" was surely bad news, Henry suspected.[74]

Charles Francis Sr. took a different view. He had postponed his plans once, following the death of Lincoln and the attempt on Seward's life, but the reshuffling of the British ministry was an altogether different matter. Adams picked up his pen to congratulate Russell on his elevation and to express his "sincere regret at the termination" of the many exchanges it had been his "fortune to enjoy with yourself." Adams then waited only days before reminding Seward of his request of the previous spring. Having planned to quit London, Adams observed, he had not renewed his lease at his Portland Place home. "Hence I shall be out in the street in March next." Having now served abroad longer than any diplomat chosen by Lincoln and Seward in early 1861, he was "anxious

Mary "Minnie" Ogden Adams was thirty-three when painted by Francis Millet in 1876. From their first meeting during the Civil War, Charles Francis Adams Jr. was smitten. Part of the attraction was that Minnie was not just rich but pleasant and kind, and Adams admitted that he saw in her a natural contrast to his own prickly personality. "I thought I had never met so charming and attractive a person as she," he admitted. *Courtesy National Park Service.*

to return" to Massachusetts. "I do trust that this time I may not be kept in the suspense I was last year," Adams concluded. Once again, however, Adams was to be disappointed. After a silence of many weeks, Seward replied that Adams was indispensable for the expected claims negotiations and begged him to remain at the Legation for at least another year. Adams agreed and apologized to his old friend for seeming "rather too earnest in soliciting some answer."[75]

Henry was resigned to the delay, but Abby was disconsolate, as it meant that they would miss Charles Francis's marriage to Minnie, which he refused to postpone. The couple wed in Newport on November 8, just three months after his return home, with only John Quincy and Fanny representing the Adams family. Charles Francis did promise to stop in London on the way to the Continent for their honeymoon so that his parents and siblings could meet his new wife. Henry wrote to send his love to Minnie and assure her that he would be "on the gay and sunny Mersey, to see her arrival." But congenitally unable to draft a simple note of congratulations to his older brother, Henry also felt it necessary to expound on his "own objections to marriage, [which] were not radical, though deep." Henry insisted that his married friends—although he had few enough of either status in London—appeared briefly happy upon becoming wed: "But it doesn't last." One should be passionate about one's spouse, and Henry doubted he "could ever feel it." If only, he mused, he could find a "woman who will take care of me, and keep me out of mischief, a good, masculine female, to make me work." As most of the Adamses had learned to do years before upon the receipt of strange missives from one another, the new groom wisely opted not to reply.[76]

Despite a four-year absence from American shores, the Adams patriarch had hardly been forgotten at home. This was largely because the press continued to sing his praises for his exceptional labors abroad on behalf of the American cause, but also because his sons kept the Adams name before the public, especially in Massachusetts. With Seward's career increasingly chained to the unpopular Andrew Johnson, Adams emerged as one of the most admired men in the North, particularly because his discontent with his party's stand on Reconstruction reforms was known only to a handful of correspondents. But modern America required candidates who wished to be candidates. For an Adams, such unseemly grasping for political preference would never do.

9

"NO POLITICAL ASSOCIATIONS WHATEVER"

The Independents

For the Legation, the year 1866 began in silence. "There is little to note in the events of the past week," the minister notified Secretary Seward on January 4. With the business of the war behind him, Charles Francis Adams Sr. looked forward to completing a small number of mundane tasks before sailing home with his family the next fall. "The tone of the press toward the United States" continued to improve, and the ruling classes approved of President Andrew Johnson's policy of conciliating the defeated South, so much so that the reputation "of the country never has been so high before." Having resolved a series of crises over the past five years, Adams was confident that his labors were complete. "I foresee little further danger of difficulty here," he assured Seward, "no matter who may be called to direct affairs" in London.[1]

Events were to prove Adams unduly optimistic. British refusals to concede that they had been far from neutral during the early months of the war would provide one final challenge for Adams. In the end, his successful negotiation of America's demands elevated him higher yet in the nation's esteem and kept his name before the press. In the process, hints or offers of political rewards came his way, from seats in the cabinet to congressional or gubernatorial chairs in his home state, and from a possible elevation into the Senate to a chance at the presidency. But Adams's refusal to accept any position without the sort of national, bipartisan acclaim that had placed George Washington in the executive office or, at the very least, without being beseeched to accept the top cabinet spot by men he regarded as his intellectual inferiors, doomed his hopes to become the third President Adams. At the same time, his sons' growing alienation from a modern, egalitarian America peopled by black voters and congressmen drove the entire family into an opposition that left them men without a party, and a dynasty without a country.

BEFORE RETURNING TO HIS DIPLOMATIC CHORES, ADAMS WAS ABLE to spend two months with Charles Francis Jr. and his new bride, Minnie. Quite possibly, the elder Adams relished the visit more than did his son, writing John Palfrey that his "son the Colonel"—referring to him by an army rank he had once disdained—enjoyed a "pleasant stay." By comparison, Charles Francis Jr. later admitted that had he "possessed the happy, ingratiating, social faculty" even in a "moderate degree," he might have met any number of famous statesmen and writers while in London.[2]

Charles Francis Jr. and Minnie left for the Continent in early February, and for the next seven months, he promised John Quincy, he "violently eschewed all things American," refusing to read newspapers or even "think or talk [of] American affairs." The couple spent most of their honeymoon in Rome, which Adams described as "medieval and unique." Adams declined to keep a diary while traveling, and he neglected to mention Minnie in his letters to John Quincy, but most likely she appreciated their travels more than did her husband. "I did enjoy Europe—after a fashion," the new husband insisted. "That I failed, and failed woefully, to avail myself of my opportunities, goes without saying," he wrote with brutal self-knowledge, "for it was I!"[3]

After packing his son off for Europe, Charles Francis Sr. returned to the question of claims growing out of losses stemming from Confederate ships built in British shipyards. But as he assured Seward, Adams believed that the new Russell ministry would make quick work of the matter. As early as October 1863, in the wake of the Union victories at Gettysburg and Vicksburg, Adams had proposed to Russell that his nation consider paying for the damages inflicted on American shipping, which Adams had hinted would be modest. Three years later, as Adams well knew, his own countrymen were weary of fighting, and with French adventurism in Mexico an ongoing problem, Seward was willing to accept a formal apology and a promise of payment for provable injuries. Even Senator Charles Sumner, who rarely sided with Seward on any question, agreed that in the name of international good feelings, the Johnson administration "would have accepted very little." One unnamed British cabinet minister approached Adams, asking whether his country might consent to "some plan of commission" based on what both countries agreed were "the great principles of international law." Adams thought that likely, but in responding to George Villiers, the Earl of Clarendon and the new foreign secretary, he was so firm in insisting that Palmerston's administration had been negligent in not employing *"all the means in the power of the Government"* to halt Confederate shipbuilding that he underlined that passage."[4]

Although Prime Minister Russell grumbled to the press that American demands were "most burdensome," Adams continued to hope for an early resolution. He peppered Clarendon with affidavits from traders and consuls in British ports and bluntly reminded the foreign minister that Britain, with its vast shipping empire, was the nation most at risk from future foreign belligerents. When Clarendon raised a new issue in February, audaciously claiming that US law was vague when it came to enemy ships constructed in foreign ports, Adams fired back that Clarendon's predecessor had "never initiated any proposition to the United States to improve [its] legislation against abuses of neutrality in this Kingdom" during the war years. If the Russell ministry appeared unbending on the question of damages, Adams observed to Seward, he gathered from the formerly hostile London press that the public hoped to find some common ground for settlement.[5]

Adams's methodical groundwork was thrown into turmoil, however, when on March 1 the ailing John Russell notified the queen of his inability to continue in his post. The Liberal prime minister did promise to serve for several more months, until the end of June, but as Clarendon served at Russell's pleasure, Adams correctly guessed that the incoming prime minister, rumored to be Conservative leader Edward Smith-Stanley, the fourteenth Earl of Derby, would choose somebody from his own party. (That June, in fact, Smith-Stanley handed the post to his own son, Edward Henry Stanley, the fifteenth Earl.) For months, as Charles Francis and Abby hoped to return home, all governmental business remained, in a word, "suspended." Having already survived one parliamentary shake-up, Adams was in no mood to patiently wait out a second. "But the President and the Secretary have, unluckily for me, failed to see the matter in the same light," Adams complained to John Gorham Palfrey. Both Johnson and Seward informed the Washington press of their desire that Adams remain in London for another year, which, Adams griped, "effectively shuts up my mouth from any farther note of remonstrance." And so that August, Adams began a "fifth volume of [his] Diary in London." Adams at least took solace in that his "share of public life" mirrored that of his "father and grandfather" and that the next fall would finally bring "the restoration of peace and quiet."[6]

In the meantime, the minister and his family entertained Americans traveling in Britain. Among those on the grand tour was Robert Hooper, a prominent Boston physician whose son Edward was studying at Cambridge. On May 16, Hooper and his two daughters—Ellen and Marian, known to her family as Clover—joined a large dinner party at the Legation. Henry recorded only that a "Dr. & Miss Hooper" were among the thirty-one guests, but what, if anything, he thought of Clover he failed to record.[7]

That July, Adams had a final meeting with the outgoing foreign secretary before being introduced to Edward Henry Stanley. Although Adams himself knew something of the expectations imposed on sons by famous fathers, the minister was prepared to be unimpressed by the new secretary, nineteen years his junior. Rather to his surprise, Stanley opened the interview by graciously promising that he had "always favored the cultivation of friendly relations" with the United States. Stanley regretted that their countries had grown estranged "during the late struggle," which he adroitly blamed not on Palmerston or Russell but on unidentified speeches made in Parliament and "the ill temper of the newspapers." Adams thought it likely that the two could reach a quick accommodation on damages and that within the year he would finally be living in Quincy.[8]

With both Congress and Parliament out of session, in September Adams opted for a grand tour himself, at least with Abby, Henry, and Mary, while Brooks, who had turned eighteen the previous June, was shipped back to Massachusetts to begin his studies at Harvard. Having several times persuaded Adams to remain in Britain, Seward had no inclination to deny his request, and the minister informed Stanley that the State Department had granted him permission "to be absent for a few weeks on an excursion to the Continent." In fact, Adams stretched his tour to nearly two months, as the family wandered through France—tarrying in Paris for days longer than planned, Charles Francis complained, "mainly for the benefit of Mrs. Adams"—Prussia, Belgium, and Holland. Although he had his father there to guide the group, Henry sourly pronounced the vacation to be "far from agreeable," when compared to his previous trip to the Continent, complaining of the "horribly expensive" Paris hotel and the fact that the city was "over-run with Americans."[9]

Upon returning to London as winter approached, Adams prepared to enter final negotiations and pack up his household. During their next interview, Stanley agreed to mediation on American claims, although he insisted that his predecessor's 1861 proclamation of neutrality not be subject to the decisions of a third party. Even the *London Times* urged the new ministry to approve a "settlement of some kind." Some conservative Britons, Adams suspected, little cared for the United States, but with the war won, "the tendency of public opinion will be to overbear all those obstacles." Unfortunately, just as British opinion turned in America's favor, Seward complicated matters by adopting an uncompromising position and demanding that no prior restrictions be placed upon the yet unnamed arbiter. Adams had chided Russell for years over what he regarded as a precipitate statement by Palmerston's government, but he also believed that sovereign nations had a right under international law to decide when to issue declarations of neutrality. Worse yet, Seward followed up that directive by privately suggesting to Adams that the United States might accept the Bahamas in exchange for the *Alabama* claims, a humiliating trade that he knew Stanley would never agree to. As the spring of 1867 arrived, and with it the anniversary of his arrival in Britain, Adams quietly admitted to having "lost all confidence in the judgment of Mr. Seward."[10]

On June 24, one week before pouring his fears into his diary, Adams remembered it was the birthday of his son Brooks, "nineteen years old and my youngest." The day "marked the passage of time," he sighed. Adding to his woes, the elder Adams was concerned about his son's progress at Harvard. Although Brooks was slightly older than most of his 149 classmates, the pressure to perform at the level of his three elder brothers at the family's ancestral college was immense. Back from his honeymoon travels in Europe, Charles Francis rode over to Cambridge to check on his brother. Brooks "looks decidedly fat and sleepy, and seems to have a decided inclination to be lazy," he reported to his disappointed father. In spite of his professors' best efforts, Brooks "shirk[ed] the thorough comprehension of the studies prescribed to him by his alma mater." Luckily for what remained of his peace of mind, the minister evidently never discovered that at a June 1867 meeting, the faculty voted to privately admonish Brooks and another student for copying each other's work at the final Latin examinations.[11]

IN THE SAME MONTH OF 1866 THAT BROOKS BEGAN HIS STUDIES AT Harvard, Charles Francis and Minnie returned to America. As a wedding gift, the senior Adams had granted his son an allowance of $3,000 a year, and the couple settled into a "little house on the Neponset Road" in Quincy. Although the months abroad had restored his health, Adams had grown increasingly morose as the time came to sail for Boston, for he had no clear idea how he might "work out [his] destiny" in civilian life. "I was far from an amiable or considerate husband" during this period, he confessed. Adams had just turned thirty-one, and having been accustomed as a colonel to a "constant atmosphere of deference and subordination," he now feared becoming little more than an "office boy." Adams was hardly shy about sharing his gloom, so several family friends approached his father with job offers. Aware of John Quincy's fondness for the life of a country gentleman, railroad magnate John Murray Forbes offered to sell Charles Francis Jr. land at an inexpensive price, and Richard Henry Dana promised a position in his Boston law firm. But Charles Francis Sr. assured Forbes that should his son wish to pursue a rural life, he himself already owned more than enough to "to break [his] back in these days of hard taxation." The senior Adams was also aware of his son's "prejudices against the law," a bias he refused to countenance. Although well-intentioned, Dana's offer struck Charles Francis Jr. as "far more than merely discouraging—it was humiliating." However, his father was confident that there was a "great deal of energy" in his son, who would surely "succeed in hitting the right mode of application" once he settled upon a vocation.[12]

To his father's surprise, however, Charles Francis grudgingly returned to the law, although not in Dana's office. "I had no choice," Adams admitted. "I had to do something; but I did it with a sinking heart. I felt I had no aptitude that way." But accepting the occasional property case was hardly necessary for the young couple's finances; Adams merely desired to placate his father and his father-in-law while establishing himself in business: "I fixed on the railroad system as the most developing force and largest field of the day, and determined to attach myself to it." The decision, he later remarked, was audacious, given his utter lack of background in commerce or transportation. Moreover, as an Adams, Charles Francis refused the usual career path of an apprenticeship with an already-established company, believing that to be unnecessary given his intellectual gifts. Instead, he picked up his pen and began work on what he hoped would become a series of articles suitable for the venerable

North American Review. Adams hammered out his first essays during a frosty winter in Newport. His father-in-law's extensive library was close at hand, yet Charles Francis "hardly consulted a book," although, as he later conceded, he "knew nothing of my subject."[13]

Publishing two pieces in the April 1867 editions of the *North American Review* and the *American Law Review*, Adams insisted that the "application of steam to locomotion [was the] most far-reaching engine of social revolution which has ever blessed or cursed the earth." Previous generations of Boston businessmen had imported southern cotton for New England's mills or taken to the seas in search of "distant lands." But Massachusetts had fallen behind "the great, commercial, cosmopolitan New York." The solution was "fresh channels" of track into the territories so that the "wealth of the newly-developed West could be poured into [Boston's] lap." Had he substituted the word "canals" for "railroads," the essays might have read like any Whig pamphlet from the 1830s. That was particularly true for his complaints that what held Massachusetts back was "the ebbs and floods of a democratic form of government." Too many postwar politicians failed to grasp the scientific forces that drove economic change, he observed. Fittingly, the grandson of John Quincy Adams, a political theorist who had never shown any use for limited federal power, called for business-minded leaders who were willing to cultivate "the forces of modern development." With a flourish that his great-grandfather would have admired, Adams recommended that state assemblies, where politicians were mired in "flounder and spasm," defer to their intellectual betters, a "body of trained thinkers—men capable of directing public sentiment." Men such as himself.[14]

Proud of his maiden efforts, Charles Francis promptly mailed off copies of his essays to London. Perhaps annoyed that his son was neglecting his legal career in exchange for an $80 royalty from the *North American Review*, the minister simply declined to reply. And if Charles Francis expected enthusiastic praise from his younger brother, he had forgotten the fourth generation's fiercely competitive nature. Ignoring the content of the pieces, Henry instead remarked only that Charles Francis's prose style was "too flabby in places and wants squeezing to take the fat out." When a wounded Charles Francis complained that Henry had ignored the thrust of his essays, Henry raised the stakes by conceding that he harbored "much more decisive objection[s]" to his brother's theories, bluntly asking, "Do your facts justify your arguments?" Then, returning to matters of style, Henry was brutal. When it came to explaining theory, Charles Francis was "dreadfully bad; so bad" that Henry was "ashamed" of him. "You wrote better than this at College," Henry added, warming to his subject. "Your affectations are intolerable. You flounder like an ill-trained actor in your efforts to amuse and to be vivacious." Having scolded his older brother, Henry then turned on his younger brother and concluded his letter by reporting that Brooks, looking a bit too "stout," had just arrived in London after his first year at Harvard.[15]

Henry had little more regard for Charles Francis Jr.'s skills as a family negotiator. For the past seven months, John Quincy's wife, Fanny, had ceased to answer Abby's letters, and Henry urged his brother to discern the cause of the family rift. "Have you sufficient discretion and delicacy of touch" to talk quietly to John Quincy, Henry wondered, aware of Charles Francis's irascible nature. "Don't blunder about it, for God's sake." As Henry feared, Charles Francis Jr. proved a maladroit envoy. When his brother's explanation arrived in London, Henry received it "very like an earthquake" and burned the letter without discussing its contents with his mother. Either John Quincy or Fanny then wrote to Henry, furious that he and Charles Francis Jr. had "stir[red] up strife." Fanny had given birth to a third child, Charles Francis III, a year before in August 1866, and perhaps she resented her mother-in-law's child-rearing advice from afar. Whatever the reason for the quarrel, Henry judged it wise for him and Charles Francis Jr. "to get out of the way when the inevitable explosion comes." Cryptically, Henry feared the issue to be more of a problem "for the next generation than for ours."[16]

Henry was at least gracious enough to send his "love to Minnie" after word reached London of the July 27 birth of her first child, Mary Ogden Adams. But the young bachelor could not resist adding that his brother's thoughts "on the subject of her confinement [were] rubbish." Given such exchanges, Charles Francis wisely decided against sending Henry his latest essay in the *North American Review*, published in April 1868. Building on his previous articles, Adams recommended that the state assembly establish a railroad commission comprising experts able to "knowingly and systematically [and] in obedience to some natural law" stem Boston's decline into "decadence" and insignificance. As Adams anticipated, his criticisms of Boston as a second-rate "large town" irritated the city's established business class, and one newspaper, curiously, chided him for failing to suggest a "remedy for the evil he complains of." His blunt critique suggested that Adams harbored few hopes of ever seeking elective office, but as a member of the state's first family and the essayist advancing the idea, he judged it likely that should the legislature decide to "organize its intelligence" into a commission, a gubernatorial appointment would be his without the asking.[17]

It took two more essays to prod the legislature into action. In yet another series of articles for the *American Law Review* and the *North American Review*, Adams exposed Cornelius "Commodore" Vanderbilt's attempts to buy the controlling shares of the Erie Railroad, an effort that prompted his rivals, Jay Gould and Jim Fisk, to flood the market with newly manufactured capital stock, "dumped, as it were, by the cartload" on Wall Street. Expanded into a short book, *Chapters of Erie and Other Essays* advanced Adams's premise that without governmental oversight by disinterested elites, the nation's economy was easy prey for the corrupt and vulgar. Although Adams judged his volume a "careful piece of literary work," the publisher advanced him only $150, and, insulted, he sent the check back. But the essays fulfilled their intended purpose. That spring, the Grand Army of the Republic post in Quincy invited Adams to deliver its Fourth of July address, a tradition cherished by several generations of the family. Just days later, Governor William Clafin nominated Adams to serve on the state's new railroad commission. "Careful preparation told," Adams mused. "At last I had worked myself into my proper position and an environment natural to me."[18]

WHILE CHARLES FRANCIS JR. WAS CHARTING HIS COURSE, THE REST of the family was busy watching the state of politics in America and the escalating battle between congressional Republicans and Andrew Johnson "with the most profound regret." Although the accidental president had at length required the defeated Confederate states to ratify the Thirteenth Amendment as the price of readmission, southern planters had responded to the president's leniency by passing a series of restrictive state laws in late 1865 and early 1866, collectively dubbed the Black Codes. Typical was Mississippi's code, which allowed freedmen to "sue and be sued," but its authors wished it understood that none of the law's provisions "shall be so construed as to allow any freeman, free negro, or mulatto to rent or lease any lands." In response, Congress began to draft the first-ever civil rights act, which became law in April 1866 after Republicans overrode the president's veto. Never once mentioning the southern statutes that forced even moderate Republicans to act, Charles Francis Sr. instead confessed to Dana "that the President appears to me right, and Congress wrong." Placing new restrictions upon southern states, Adams fretted, defied the will of the nation's founders and placed too much power in Washington. When Dana countered that if allowed to stand, the Black Codes would "lead to certain evil results to the negroes," Adams refused to concede that the laws were designed to deny freed people access to land. "Admitting even this to be the case, which I yet hold not to be proved," Adams replied, "still the effects upon the whole people of so vital a change in the organic law may be far more fearful."[19]

Adams's growing estrangement with the party he had helped to forge revealed a deeply conservative strain when it came to his views on African Americans. Although he assured Dana that his only concerns were constitutional, his ruminations on black abilities were simply more refined than those of his sons John Quincy and Charles Francis; they differed only in tone. Even as a young assemblyman, his crusades against his state's racially restrictive laws had not been waged in behalf of black Bostonians but rather against New England's last vestiges of slavery. As recently as 1864, when reading Englishman John Hanning Speke's account of exploring the headwaters of the Nile, Adams remarked that it was "almost impossible to resist the conviction that there is a decided natural inferiority of race." As an antislavery man and a free-soiler, Adams welcomed the ratification of the Thirteenth Amendment. But that, he lectured Dana, was the "single" change he wished to see in the Constitution. Otherwise, his "dearest wish" was to "see the Union confirmed and the Constitution restored with as little jar as possible to its provisions."[20]

After Confederate veterans fought back against the Civil Rights Act by massacring forty-six blacks in a May 1866 Memphis race riot and murdering another forty-four in New Orleans, Republicans passed a flurry of legislation in the early spring of 1867 designed to nullify the Black Codes and enfranchise southern blacks. In what were to become four interlocking laws collectively known as the Military Reconstruction Act, Congress divided the former Confederacy into five military districts, each under the command of a general responsible for seeing federal laws enforced. Before final readmission to the Union, southern states were obliged to ratify the Fourteenth Amendment—which overturned Roger Taney's 1857 denial of black citizenship—and to allow "all loyal male citizens twenty-one years of age" to vote "without distinction of race." Reading of this, Adams read himself out of his party, if only in his diary. "The attempt to rally the negro vote of the South" to assist Republicans in the next year's presidential contest "will only breed a storm," Adams fumed. "After all, it may be, as a choice between evils, better that the democratic party shall carry the country." Like the president, Adams did not even care to embrace the term "Reconstruction." Nothing was "more clear" to Adams "than that the work of reestablishment must be done by the other side" of the aisle.[21]

If anything, Henry was even more adamant in denouncing Reconstruction as "monstrous." In part, Henry's disdain for postwar reforms grew out of his loyalty to his father. When Dana passed through London that August, the two old friends had a "tremendous battle" over the topic after dinner. Although Henry did not place Dana "in the same class" as Senators Sumner and Henry Wilson, both former allies turned foes, he thought it a pity that his father was "again in a miserable minority in Massachusetts, without a friend to work with." As Henry clearly desired to see his father elevated to higher office, the fact that the elder Adams had lost any base of support in his home state was enough to convince him that the Republican majority in Congress had "botched every single measure demanded for the public good." However, loyalty to family blinded Henry to the realities of the postwar South. In a statement that would try irony's patience, Henry complained that Republicans were "violating the rights of minorities more persistently than the worst pro-slavery Congress ever could do." In using the term "minorities," Henry did not mean the four million recently liberated black Americans but rather what remained of the antebellum planter class, his grandfather's old adversaries.[22]

Having never journeyed south of Washington, Henry, unlike Charles Francis Jr., had no experience with plantation societies, nor had he much contact with freed slaves. Black men had long voted in his home state without drawing his ire, and undoubtedly much of his contempt for the Military Reconstruction Act was based on class rather than racial considerations. Even so, for a young man who cheered the news of each Union victory, that Henry accepted every southern grievance as fact was as curious as it was tragic. As did defeated Confederates, Henry feared that the enfranchisement of freedmen would result in a "society dissolved, and brigandage universal." Assuming that the advancement of black political rights somehow meant the diminution of white rights, Henry groused that "it is now law that the negro is better than the white man." However, Henry was particularly annoyed to discover that Charles Francis Jr., despite his overt racism toward his troopers, did not share his views and in fact thought Johnson guilty of an impeachable offence. "Your position and mine are different," Henry huffed. "On the whole I am glad that you have made your bed with Congress." But when Charles Francis explained his views at length, Henry replied only that he declined to read his letter to their father, as "your argument would be rubbish."[23]

DESPITE HIS RELUCTANT ENDORSEMENT OF BLACK VOTING RIGHTS as a method of racial advancement, John Quincy shared his father's grave doubts about Reconstruction and, with his father's and Henry's blessing, abandoned his life of a country gentleman and announced his candidacy for the state assembly. For all his growing doubts about the increasingly reform-minded course of his party, Adams remained a Republican, and that, together with what he called his "loud-sounding name" and wartime service as aide to Governor Andrew, earned him a seat in the House for the session set to begin in January 1866. As a freshman legislator, Adams perhaps intended to ease into his new role, but his strong opinions and famous name promptly forced him to weigh his loyalties. In late February, President Johnson vetoed the extension of the Freedmen's Bureau, and in the process accused a number of leading Republicans, including Sumner and Wilson, of treason and plots of assassination. Republicans in the assembly introduced resolutions condemning the president's attack, but minority Democrats held up the vote. At length, Adams rose to chide the Democrats, insisting that it was "more manly" to vote down the resolutions "than to postpone them." But just as Republicans began to applaud, Adams added that the Democrats required more time to clarify their positions. House Speaker James Stone angrily cut Adams off, but not before several members loudly whispered that his real motivation was his family's long-standing feud with the state's two senators. He had been "hit with great savagery," John Quincy complained to Charles Francis Jr. He understood that his career as a Bay State Republican was at an end.[24]

Six months later, organizers of the National Union Conference, which was designed to build centrist support for the policies of the beleaguered Johnson on the eve of the 1866 off-year elections, invited John Quincy to serve as a delegate to their Philadelphia meeting. As it became clear that the August conference would be dominated by such conservative Democrats as South Carolina Governor (and former Confederate Senator) James Lawrence Orr, Adams lost heart. After the Columbia, South Carolina, *Daily Phoenix* hinted that John Quincy spoke for his father, "the Minister to England," Adams claimed illness and never boarded the train for Philadelphia. However, that October he served as the presiding officer of the Massachusetts Union Convention in Boston. Despite his involvement, Adams could not persuade the conference to engage important national issues or constitutional matters. Instead, the meeting merely endorsed increased veterans' pensions and a statewide eight-hour factory day for laboring men. John's political allies, Henry sighed, were "worse than none." Henry admired his brother for "fighting for the weaker side" in his Republican-dominated state, but the "pressure of a united public opinion against one man, is an awful thing."[25]

By election eve, it was clear that any attempt to craft a new, centrist party had failed. Following Johnson's disastrous eighteen-day speaking tour across the North—known as his "Swing Around the Circle"—in which the president often appeared drunk and berated his audiences, even the most moderate Republicans declined to endorse Johnson's course. In Massachusetts, Republicans increased their already-impressive majority, and John Quincy, running as a National Unionist, lost his bid for reelection by a sizable margin. (As it involved an Adams, his loss to Republican G. L. Gill made the news even in distant Idaho Territory.) "Politics are too dirty for me," he griped to Charles Francis Jr. "I am striving for a preposterous preeminence when I dream of a pure" system of statesmanship "without concession to popular fantasy or prejudice." Hearing of the defeat in London, Charles Francis Sr. was not surprised, but he hoped that his eldest son would not quit the field. "The moment is not arrived for John to commit himself irrevocably with any party," he predicted, incorrectly. So confident was the senior Adams that the Republicans' policies were wrongheaded, and failing to grasp that Johnson's stubborn determination to veto the mildest reform measures glued together the Republican opposition, the senior Adams yet hoped that the Republicans might "divide in opinion" to the point that his son could "cooperate with one section of them to some useful end."[26]

Shortly after the election, the Republican *Boston Advertiser* branded John Quincy an apostate and, just as the pro-Whig *Boston Atlas* had done to his father forty years before, drummed him out of the party. Either out of gratitude for Adams's support during the previous campaign or in hopes of eliciting a public endorsement from his famous father, in March 1867 President Johnson nominated John Quincy for the position of naval officer for Boston, a cushy port collector's post that required Senate confirmation. Not having been told of the appointment in advance, Adams immediately telegraphed the president, asking that his name be withdrawn. Before Johnson could do so, however, Sumner and Wilson invoked their privilege as the state's senators and moved that action on the nomination be tabled. The rejection made national news, even more so than the loss of Adams's seat in the legislature. Southern and Democratic editors, the grandsons of men who had despised his grandfather, rushed to defend John Quincy. "Radical gratitude is remarkable," huffed the Memphis *Public Ledger*, while the *Charleston Daily News* denounced Sumner and Wilson as "two comparatively little men who learned the anti-slavery alphabet at the school of the Adamses." A "mean, contemptible act," added an Illinois journalist loyal to Johnson.[27]

Several old friends of the elder Adams wrote to London, hoping to alert the minister to the political realities of the home front and to warn that John Quincy would destroy any further hopes of political advancement if he continued to side with Johnson. The fact that the southern press had become the family's defenders should itself have served as a cautionary note, but the elder Adams refused to see that hard truth. When Dana made the mistake of suggesting it would have been "folly" for John Quincy to accept the port authority posting, Adams bristled. Far from being foolish, he snapped, the fact that the president "voluntarily selected him for a position of responsibility" harkened back to "the purer days of the Republic, when men were selected without agency of their own or consultation with them." His son and Johnson happened "to agree in opinion on certain great public questions now before the country," and because of that, two former allies had engaged in an act of "purely partisan malignity." Henry thought so too, assuring Charles Francis Jr. that "John alone has acted the part of a man." For Henry, the fact that his contrarian positions had now cost John Quincy two political positions was a badge of honor: "I admire John all the more for what he has done." Rarely charitable toward one another, the Adamses instinctively grew protective when criticized by outsiders.[28]

As had been typical of his family for generations when faced with adversity, John Quincy simply plunged ahead, never stopping to consider why the congressional majority believed protections for freedmen to be increasingly necessary. Despite Republican demands for ratification of the Fourteenth Amendment, both Carolinas and Louisiana voted against approval, and shortly after his rejection by the Senate, Adams delivered a fiery speech in Boston, praising southern recalcitrance. "I am glad the Southern States rejected it and refused to dishonor their leaders, dead and alive," he shouted. "I would have despised them had they acted differently." Abandoning his earlier, if grudging, support for black voting rights, Adams now characterized the Republican position as "the South must be governed by negroes." Largely ignored by the New England press, the speech was widely hailed across the South. A Columbia editor praised it as a "glorious speech," claiming South Carolina's white minority "would rather have the good opinion of Mr. Adams and men of his stamp, than the snarky patronage of the radical host."[29]

Despite the sudden fondness for Adamses among former Confederates, Bay State Democrats decided to adopt John Quincy as one of their own. In part, they had no choice but to throw caution to the wind, as in 1866 Republican gubernatorial candidate Alexander Bullock had defeated Democratic nominee Theodore Sweetzer by a three-to-one margin. As did state legislators, Massachusetts governors served one-year terms, and when Democrats met in their October 1867 convention, the idea of advancing a famous surname was much discussed. More-traditional Democrats were primarily interested in repealing the state's prohibitory liquor laws, and according to critical newspapers, whiskey flowed freely at the convention. In the end, a coalition of liquor wholesalers, who had previously formed a lobbying group called the Personal Liberty League, banded together with what one journalist dubbed "fanatical Adams men" to secure him the nomination. With unintentional irony, the convention adopted the anti-prohibitionist slogan "Adams and Liberty," a phrase first used in 1848 by Free-Soilers but in a very different context. Once again, the southern press cheered the move, with one South Carolina newspaper proclaiming the one-term assemblyman to be "one of the ablest men of New England." Only one Nashville paper dissented, warning that his was a "family that has done more than any other in America, to inculcate

High Federal principles, and construct a doctrinal basis for the present Radical schemes."[30]

As with Johnson's submission of his name for the naval post, John Quincy was unaware of the nomination until notified after the convention dissolved. Perhaps conscious of the family's long-standing determination not to campaign for position, the Democrats assumed that if told while the convention was still meeting, Adams might have declined the honor. For several days, Adams mulled over the question, uncertain about whether he should accept. Despite the events and speeches of the past months, John Quincy had not yet "come out flat" as a Democrat. Finally, he decided that his "pressing duty [was] to check the republicans before it is too late." No matter the outcome, he promised Charles Francis Jr., a "man who embarks on such a voyage as mine must make up his mind to take his fate with fortitude or his fortune with an equal mind." In his letter of acceptance, Adams observed that while the governor's chair was a state position, he planned to stand on national issues. Democrats expected no less, but in a concluding statement that pleased his new party and perhaps looked ahead toward appeasing the handful of yet-dubious southern editors, Adams broke with his family, past and present, in promising "to see the doctrine of states rights rescued from unmerited obloquy."[31]

In the end, the Democrats' gambit failed, but just barely. The incumbent increased his previous year's tally by 6,000 votes, but Adams ran far ahead of the Democrats statewide, swept the Boston precincts, and captured nearly 44,000 votes more than Sweetzer had in 1866. Adams was also delighted that the voters in Quincy wished to return him to the assembly. "I am good for a 20,000 [vote] licking and must bear it as well as I can," he assured Charles Francis. (In point of fact, Bullock bested Adams by 27,946 votes out of 168,666 cast.) In London, his father mused that the promising returns served "as a commentary on the act of the two Senators" in denying his son the collector's post. All Adamses, well aware of both their family's and their nation's past, understood that temporary setbacks often opened new political paths. "This will do better for him than to be successful just now," the elder Adams supposed. The editor of the *Boston Pilot* thought so too, remarking that by returning to his old seat in the General Court, Adams could keep his name before the public and "advance the principles he so ably advocated."[32]

John Quincy's rising fame reminded his father that he had been too long away from American shores. On November 26 he again posted a private letter to Seward, apprising the secretary of his "determination to resign" his position on April 1. But what might happen after that was an open question. As a habitual reader of Washington and Manhattan newspapers, Adams was hardly unaware of speculation that Johnson was considering a cabinet shake-up in hopes of salvaging his presidency and staving off impeachment. Should the president do so, the *New York Herald* editorialized, he required a cabinet "of new men, identified with the war for Union." For State, the editor insisted, Adams would "be universally accepted." The Philadelphia *Evening Telegraph* concurred, observing that as he remained popular among moderate Republicans and northern "war Democrats," Adams could also serve as Johnson's "protector and leader against the Northern Radicals." The rumors were far from fanciful. Weary of politics and unpopular with his party for standing by Johnson, Seward routinely contemplated retirement. Should he resign, Seward hinted to one reporter, he wished "Charles Francis Adams to be his successor." Johnson was aware of Adams's estrangement from Sumner and Wilson, so his possible promotion made enormous sense.[33]

Other editors thought Adams worthy of even higher office. Although one Philadelphia newspaper conceded that many Republicans hoped to nominate Grant in 1868, it praised Adams as "the ablest and best man for President that the United States can produce." A Wheeling journalist agreed that the party might select Grant but judged him a far lesser potential president than "first class statesmen" Adams or Chief Justice Salmon Chase. John Quincy greeted the editorials with enthusiasm, but his father was less sanguine. Given the angry tenor in Washington as House Republicans prepared their list of impeachable offenses against the sitting president, Adams claimed to feel "nausea" at the prospect of "getting mixed up" in the divisive political scene. Having recently informed Seward of his plans to sail for home, the gossip prompted Adams to reconsider and "wait on this side [of the Atlantic] until that storm blows over."[34]

On February 24, 1868, the House voted 128 to 47 to impeach the president for violating the Tenure of Office Act and attempting to replace Secretary of War Edwin Stanton with General Lorenzo Thomas. "Moderation does not seem to be the quality the most in vogue" in Washington, the senior Adams sighed. The American papers mailed to the Legation told of nothing "but strife and confusion." With the Republican and Democratic parties prepared to meet in their conventions in May and July, respectively, Adams thought it wisest to return to Boston that spring but immediately announce his resolution "to retirement to private life." He felt himself thoroughly out of step with his old party on Reconstruction reforms, yet unlike his son John Quincy, he could not reconcile himself to becoming a Democrat. Having helped to build two antislavery parties in 1848 and 1854, Adams now claimed "no political associations whatever."[35]

The impeachment struggle so absorbed the embattled administration that virtually all activity was suspended at the Legation. As the Senate moved toward a final vote on acquittal or removal, Adams believed his party "all mad" and mourned that his "fine country" had fallen "prey to such miserable squabbling." The old attorney condemned the eleven-count indictment as "flimsy," although he reserved some of his censure for Johnson. The president lacked "discretion and entirely ignored consultation" with powerful men on Capitol Hill, Adams observed. That was an understatement about a Tennessee Democrat who had freed his domestic slaves only toward the end of the war and whose disdain for black voting rights was infamous among black activists such as Frederick Douglass. Rather to Adams's "surprise," on May 16 the Senate voted 35 to 19 against Johnson—a majority but not the requisite two-thirds for removal—with seven moderate Republicans siding with the president. "I rejoice at this as an indication that there is still some principle left as well as good sense," a satisfied Adams observed. The fact that Johnson would remain in office until the following March, however, only renewed rumors in the press that Seward wished to retire and that "Adams will be assigned to the State Department." But the fact that Johnson was not guilty of an impeachable offense, the minister concluded, did not mean that he was a fit president to serve above a member of the Adams family.[36]

To force Seward's hand, in the previous December Adams had drafted a "formal letter of resignation" that followed his earlier private missive. This time, his determination to retire from Britain would become common knowledge, and whether the press took that to mean Adams was considering a run at the White House was not something he could control. Shortly after Lincoln's assassination, Adams reminded Seward in his letter, he had asked to be relieved of his duties but had stayed on at the new president's request. Two years later, relations between the two countries had "become so far simplified" that he was no longer required in London. As he anticipated, the rumors began to circulate around Washington in early February. In search of details, several journalists contacted Seward, who neither denied nor affirmed the reports. "On the theory that 'silence gives consent,'" one reported, the rumors appeared to be "well-founded." When Seward still refused to go on the record, other newspapers guessed that Adams's request was a matter of "personal honor" in that he could no longer serve Johnson or that Britain had pushed him out in hopes of placating "the clamors of the Fenians," Irish republicans who regarded Adams as hostile to their hopes of independence.[37]

Later that month, a reluctant Seward announced the resignation. Since Adams's 1861 appointment had been approved by the Senate, the Tenure of Office Act required that the Senate take action on Adams's request. Pennsylvania Senator Simon Cameron, whose son Donald was to play a complicated role in Henry's future romantic life, introduced the required legislation, which passed by a voice vote. To replace Adams, Johnson tapped Maryland's Reverdy Johnson, a Whig turned Democrat whose prewar legal experiences included defending prospective slaveholder John Sanford in the Dred Scott case. Nominee Johnson was seventy-two and nearly blind, but with an incoming administration less than a year away, the Senate regarded him as a placeholder, his tenure in Britain "little more than an office visit."[38]

With that, Adams began a round of farewell banquets and honorific dinners. The British League of Peace and Liberty invited him to a celebration of Anglo-American amity featuring an address by John Bright, a Quaker abolitionist who had always supported the Union cause. Archibald Tate, the bishop of London, invited the family to a private repast, prompting Adams to reflect that "one of the penalties of diplomatic life" was having to say farewell to new but dear friends. "We shall not soon forget the uniform curtesy shown to us," Adams assured Tate. Even the *London Times*, which had devoted endless pages to reproving Adams and his cause, praised the retiring minister as "always fair and courteous" before concluding with one parting shot: "There have been times, no doubt, when we should have liked him better if he could have put before us the views of his government in a less rigid and inflexible form."[39]

On May 12, Adams took his leave of Queen Victoria. To honor his years of service, the queen requested a "special audience" of favored guests. Adams presented his official letter of departure, and rather to his surprise, the normally reserved minister, as he wrote that evening, found himself "much more agitated than I expected." He had prepared a short statement pledging his nation's friendship, but several times Adams had to pause "from forgetting what I was to tell her." Victoria, twelve years his junior but still in mourning black, "replied in very few words and in a very natural and sympathetic tone." Upon returning to his rented home, Adams reflected that he now "was a stranger to 54 Portland Place." His seven years in London, he thought with considerable satisfaction, had "been the culminating ones of my prosperous life." Promising his diary that he desired no higher office, Adams instead chose to regard "the difficulties and trials of the period" the peak of his career, "neither hoping nor seeking to enjoy so much again."[40]

Having assured his journal of his indifference regarding any political future, a claim that he possibly believed at that moment, Adams worried that the *China*, the steamer his family had booked for their return, was due to arrive in Manhattan on June 20, just weeks before the Democrats planned to meet in Tammany Hall to nominate a candidate. The timing, he feared, might be taken by the Democrats as a sign he wished to be considered an aspirant. "This is so very contrary to all my desires," he fretted, and with good reason. On May 25 a self-described group of "Conservative politicians" gathered at a Manhattan hotel, where a series of speakers "were most enthusiastic in their laudations of Mr. Adams." Not knowing their man, however, the conferees proposed a ticket of Chase and Adams, with the chief justice in the top spot, as if Adams could be enticed to accept a secondary position that his grandfather had famously loathed.[41]

If Adams expected to slip quietly through New York City, he was mistaken. Journalists tracked his progress across the Atlantic, and even before the *China* docked on June 27, plans were under way for a public reception in his honor. Adams endured this "ovation" before sailing on to Boston, where several more receptions awaited him. One public affair at the Horticultural Hall was attended by an "immense audience of business and professional men." Following a lengthy oration in his honor, Adams rose and delivered the expected self-deprecatory response. He had tried only to do his "duty," Adams insisted. Had he served his country well, it was only because of a "degree of good fortune that has seldom fallen to the lot of one similarly attached." Then, foolishly, Adams announced that he would rather greet his admirers "informally and individually and shake them cordially by the hand." As one editor observed, several hours of a "protracted and fatiguing hand-shaking followed." Finally, on July 10, Charles Francis and Abby reached the old house in Quincy. Adams promptly "set to work to reestablish my home as it was," a task "not perfectly easy, especially as my sons John and Charles had successively occupied the mansion." But he was home.[42]

HAVING RETURNED WITH HIS PARENTS, HENRY, NOW THIRTY AND, by his own admission, "very—very bald," had to decide quickly on the next stage of his life. Although, as Charles Francis Sr. assured Seward, Henry had "been of the highest service" to the Legation during their long years in London, he had drawn no salary, and his only official title had been private secretary to his father. By his age, Henry's celebrated grandfather had already served as minister to the Netherlands and had married. His last American occupation, such as it was, had been to write anonymous essays for the *Boston Daily Advertiser*. Journalism, Henry conceded to his brother Charles Francis, was "the last resource of the educated poor who could not be artists and would not be tutors," but given his disdain for the practice of law—together with his poor training in Germany—that appeared his only respectable option. Manhattan was too crowded with competitors, and Boston, for a young man who suddenly wished to chart his own course, too close. Newspaper positions beckoned elsewhere in New England, but only if he wished to trade upon his famous surname. In October 1868, three months after his return, Henry became the first Adams to relocate to Washington without holding elective or appointive position, or even without firm prospects. Until he secured a position, Henry accepted a room from Attorney General William Evarts, a Johnson loyalist the Adamses had first met several years before in London. His brother Charles Francis worried that Henry was "taking a direction which will separate us from him gradually forever." His parents blessed his decision, but perhaps remembering his long-ago mistress, Charles Francis Sr. cautioned his son against the capital's "silly young women."[43]

Secluded in Quincy, Henry's father insisted that he was "not sorry to be out of the field of domestic politics during this season." Harvard College came calling with offers of the campus presidency, but Adams declined the honor, graciously neglecting to mention that decades before it had required him to sit twice for his Latin exams. The offer was wholly unsolicited, which normally pleased an Adams, but Harvard's was not the presidency he preferred. Instead, Adams announced that he planned to devote the coming years to editing his father's diaries, a project that eventually required twelve volumes.[44]

While the elder Adams retired into his study, John Quincy prepared to broaden his political horizons. In early September, Massachusetts Democrats again nominated Adams for governor, although neither he nor his father expected him to receive a larger vote than he had in the previous contest. Instead, the prospect that intrigued him was an invitation from Wade Hampton, a former Confederate general and the new chairman of

South Carolina's state Democratic Party, to speak in both Columbia and Charleston. Hampton was aware of the family's criticisms of Reconstruction, and he hoped Adams might both address "the misrepresentation of the Radicals" and the potential "fraternal relations" between white southerners and New England Democrats. Despite having made his loyalties clear for some years, Adams sought the advice of his father, aware that some moderate Republicans still hoped to elevate Charles Francis Sr. into higher office. John Quincy's father admitted that it was a strange turn of fate that the region "which always opposed our family on purely sectional grounds, and [had] defeated the reelection of both the Presidents should now design to beg the interposition of the fourth generation." But the elder Adams harbored ambitions for his son and advised him to accept. Although Hampton, John Quincy replied, "greatly exaggerate[d] any influence" he might wield as the leader of a "small and very unpopular minority" in Massachusetts, he was pleased to accept.[45]

John Quincy and Fanny sailed south on October 3. Despite the fact that Hampton was a bitter opponent of enfranchising his state's majority population, Charles Francis Sr. marveled that his son's trip represented "one of the noble moments in our otherwise guilty politics." Adams prayed his son's speech might mark an important step in sectional reconciliation, but even if it did not, he guessed without irony, John Quincy's overture was an "event in the political record of our name which will be worth remembering." Charles Francis Sr. was even more delighted when one of his friends assured him that John Quincy was "the most rising man in America, and likely to be the head of the democratic party"—not as a result of any accomplishments but rather because of his illustrious surname. His own career, he supposed, had ended the previous summer when he returned home at age sixty. But John Quincy, at thirty-five, had "the aptitude" to excel in future years. Such, Adams thought, were the "vicissitudes of life."[46]

John Quincy's Columbia oration took place on October 12. A crowd, including Zebulon Vance, the former Confederate governor of North Carolina, had grown too large to fit into the capitol building, and the organizers shifted the event outside. Adams began by confessing to his family's antislavery history and admitted himself a "humble supporter of Mr. Lincoln." But he quickly turned to the concept of shared blame. If South Carolina was wrong in secession, his own section was equally guilty of "madness" and "political intemperance." As had his father, Adams excoriated the Civil Rights and Reconstruction Acts on constitutional grounds only, as laws "based on conquest and the right[s] of the victor" while barely hinting at the Black Codes, "vagrant laws," and race riots that had forced reluctant Republicans to act. But black voting rights, he added, "will seriously aggravate the difficulties which beset your way back to a cheerful and peaceful" place in the Union. Although Adams had been in the state only a few days, he reported to his audience that he had not witnessed any local "ill-will to the negro." Then, in an absurd claim that his brother the colonel would have scoffed at, Adams reminded his listeners that Columbia's slaves were "faithful to you in your years of struggle" and that while southern soldiers "were at the front he did not free himself." Until calmer voices resumed power in the North, Adams beseeched white Carolinians to be charitable to "this vast, ignorant, and frequently thriftless" freed population. "Extreme, and very impatient" men such as Sumner could not live forever.[47]

Four days later, on Friday evening, Adams delivered a second address at the Charleston Hotel. His oration was similar to the earlier Columbia speech, but this time Adams thought to say a few charitable words about the former commander of the Army of Northern Virginia. The spirit of Robert E. Lee, he shouted, would one day prevail across the entire republic. The Charleston *Mercury*, the longtime fiery voice of southern reaction, groused that it was easy for a New Englander to counsel patience on the matter of universal suffrage: the Bay State was home to but a miniscule black population. But other southern journalists praised Adams as "one of the hardest working and ablest" men in Massachusetts and claimed that his two speeches had a "striking effect" on his audiences. However, Adams may not have been aware that earlier that day, in a brutal rejection of his pleas for calm, three white South Carolinians had assassinated State Senator Benjamin Franklin Randolph, a former chaplain with the US Colored Troops, as he boarded a train in Hodges' Depot.[48]

After spending several days at former Governor James Lawrence Orr's estate, Adams accompanied the South Carolinian to Washington, where they enjoyed a lengthy interview with President Johnson and visited with Charles Francis Jr., who was in the capitol on business. While there, Adams received several more offers to speak; Richmond businessman Asa Snyder hoped that while John Quincy was close by, he might deliver speeches across Virginia. Despite the consistent reports of election-year murders of black southerner activists, Charles Francis Sr. pronounced the trip a triumph. The Columbia speech, the proud father wrote, was "full of thought and broad views of statesmanship, such as are not common in these days of littleness among our politicians." But even allowing for parental pride, the fact that Adams thought his son, a two-term state assemblyman with no significant legislation to his name, had "no equal among the men of his age in America, and not many of any age," suggested that he had transferred his hopes of family acclaim for the coming generation from businessman Charles Francis Jr. to his eldest son and political aspirant.[49]

By then, the political season was well under way. Despite his efforts to disappear into his study in Quincy, Adams read dozens of editorials that advanced his name for the presidency, either as a conservative Republican or a liberal Democrat. Given his well-known criticisms of Reconstruction, it was hardly surprising that South Carolina editors, from the Columbia *Daily Phoenix* to the *Yorkville Enquirer*, urged his nomination by the Democrats. But so too did publishers in Boston and Manhattan. Knowing that Adams favored an earlier political culture, in which gentlemen did not seek political office, Democratic operatives instead wrote to John Quincy, urging him to intercede with his father. In March 1868, even before the elder Adams returned home, August Belmont, a German-born banker who had chaired the Democratic National Committee since 1860, queried John Quincy over whether his father would accept the nomination. "To me this is alarming, as it dissipates all of my plans of comfort if I entertain the proposition," Charles Francis Sr. fretted. Yet if he refused to serve, that smacked of "sheer cowardice or selfish indulgence." It was his duty to do what he could "to aid the country in its difficulties." Adams slept on the matter, and the next morning he felt "less cause of uneasiness in the enquiry than" previously imagined. Because of his "utter isolation" in Quincy, nobody could accuse him of any corrupt bargain—an 1825 charge made by Andrew Jackson's partisans that haunted his father for years—so his affirmative reply was, to his mind, a "thoroughly independent one," as he was confident that John Quincy would "not commit [him] to accept any platform excepting such as" he could "fully approve."[50]

That vague promise satisfied Belmont but few other party leaders, who preferred a less equivocal candidate. When the Democrats converged on Tammany Hall in early July, the only vote cast for an Adams was bestowed on delegate John Quincy by a South Carolina admirer. Finally, on the twenty-second ballot, the convention tapped former New York Governor Horatio Seymour and Francis Preston Blair Jr. of Missouri, a former Republican congressman and member of the powerful Blair dynasty. The ticket was an unintended gift for Republicans. Seymour had once referred to the 1863 draft rioters as "my friends," while Blair had recently published an open letter calling for the next president to simply "declare the reconstruction acts null and void; compel the army to undo its usurpations at the South; [and] allow the white people to reorganize their [state] governments." Hoping for a centrist statement on constitutional principles rather than the bitter denunciation of black voting rights that the conclave adopted, John Quincy quit the convention before it adjourned, telling journalists he was "disgusted with the platform."[51]

Renegade Republicans and pragmatic conservatives were not finished with the elder Adams, however. Just five weeks after the Manhattan convention, Democrats in Massachusetts approached John Quincy about the possibility of his father running for his old congressional seat in the Third District. This meant challenging sitting Congressman Ginery Twichell, a Republican in a Republican district, to again become one of 243 members of the House. "Nothing could take me back but an absolute call from the people," Adams groaned, "the nature of which I could not mistake." Such a mandate envisioned by Adams required Twichell to step aside, something that he had no intention of doing, so this inquiry went nowhere. However, rather more serious was a move by moderate Republicans to replace Sumner in the Senate, a scheme reported from Kansas to Virginia and publicly supported in Washington by Henry. Senators were selected by state legislatures, which the Republicans controlled in Massachusetts, but centrists believed that with John Quincy on the Democratic ballot for governor, a coalition of Democrats and Republican moderates could unite behind the elder Adams. The prospect was realistic enough to give Sumner pause. "If the people of Mass. turn from me, I shall not complain," he promised poet Henry Longfellow. "I have done my duty." Ironically, so many Democratic editors—and especially those outside the state—endorsed Adams and prematurely rejoiced about their victory that his handful of Republican supporters grew nervous and instead voted to give Sumner a fourth term.[52]

Never having seriously expected the Republicans to nominate anybody but Grant for the presidency, Adams was not much surprised to hear that the general was chosen by acclamation on the first ballot. However, the Adams name still meant enough to party stalwarts that the Republican chairman sought a public endorsement for their ticket. Republicans in Quincy and Boston invited Adams to speak; he pled "rest and retirement" and instead mailed a lukewarm endorsement to the Philadelphia *Enquirer*. "You are perfectly right in presuming I have in no respect varied from my attachment to the principles I held before my departure from the United States," he admitted in his public statement. But rather than endorse the platform or even mention Grant by name, Adams instead swore loyalty to "the Constitution as our protection against assaults from without as well as within." The brief, vague statement appeased almost nobody. One Nashville editor observed that "this was not what the Grant" supporters desired, adding, "It is plain enough [Adams] is no Radical." But Democrats who wished to run Adams in the future were equally disappointed. The letter, one Virginia journalist groused, proclaimed "his continued adhesion to the Radical party." In the privacy of his journal, Adams poured out his doubts about the general. "Grant is not the Titan to work out the salvation of the land," he worried. As Election Day neared, Adams was confident that Grant would carry the day but less sure of the consequences. "We shall now see pretty soon, what the fate of the constitution is to be," he wrote in mid-October. "I have my little hope of saving it."[53]

At least initially, the Adams brothers were far more enthusiastic. Charles Francis Jr. had yet to lose his wartime admiration for Grant's battlefield calm and resolute decision making. The fact that Sumner had opposed Grant's nomination was recommendation enough for the fourth generation. Much to the dismay of New England Democrats, gubernatorial candidate John Quincy announced that he planned to cast his ballot for Grant. The successful general had "finished the war, and that is enough to entitle him to my respect and admiration," John Quincy informed one stunned editor. "I do believe he is an upright, honorable man, who will try to do his best, not for a party only, but for the whole people of the country." With his two older brothers on board, Henry joined the crusade. "Grant represented order," he insisted. Henry hoped that as a Washington outsider who had never held political office, Grant would ignore partisan politicians in favor of men of merit. A Grant administration, in short, might do for politics what Charles Francis Jr. thought the rule of the best sort could do for the railroad business.[54]

On November 3, Charles Francis Sr. walked to the town hall to cast his vote. Paper ballots listing all the candidates' names did not yet exist; instead, voters obtained lengthy tickets that featured only one party's aspirants, which were then deposited into boxes or jars according to party affiliation. Having determined to vote for Grant on the national ticket but his son on the state form, he acquired both. But such was his "great distrust" of Grant, "more than I ever had before in my life," that the normally unflappable Adams grew muddled, and he inserted the tickets into the wrong boxes. A few minutes later, Adams realized his mistake and returned. The charitable poll watchers allowed him to correct his error, but southern editors angry with Adams for his reluctant endorsement of Grant publicized the "ludicrous incident," hinting that Adams was no longer the formidable intellect he once was. Worse yet, John Quincy lost both his race for governor and seat in the legislature. The defeat, the elder Adams assured himself, would do his son "no harm," for he had "made a great reputation to compensate for it."[55]

Just days later, Adams was in Boston when he spied a "large company" moving toward him, with Sumner taking the lead. Adams had dreaded the moment as "one that might be very embarrassing on both sides." Having just achieved reelection, however, Sumner was in no mood to hold old grudges. "He saluted me with more cordiality than I manifested in return," Adams admitted. Adams quickly tried to retreat from the "awkward" encounter, but Sumner adroitly turned the conversation to mutual friends in Britain, pleasantly chatting of old associates. If Adams was embarrassed to discover that their feud of seven years largely existed on his side only, he promised himself that he had been "perfectly courteous and civil," just as he might have greeted any "general acquaintance."[56]

Several weeks after, Adams encountered another prominent Republican when Grant conducted a postelection tour of the Northeast. Compounding Adams's unease with the president-elect was the fact that Manhattan and Philadelphia editors had begun to discuss his logical post in the cabinet. The *New York Herald* recommended General William T. Sherman for the War Department and judged Adams a perfect fit for State. Although his father's old cabinet position was the only spot that Adams might accept, his concerns about Grant's abilities made him reluctant to even consider the prospect. "My future has been so distinctly laid out for myself that even the possibility of a change comes to my mind like a disturbing and annoying element," he insisted. Yet if Grant offered him the post, especially in person, Adams knew he would have to accept.[57]

The two met at a public dinner in Boston on December 5. New York papers continued to suggest that the real purpose of Grant's visit was to discuss the cabinet, but when the evening finally arrived, as Charles Francis Jr. later put it, the old soldier and the old diplomat "scrutinized the other with curiosity." If the taciturn general expected any hint from Adams that he coveted the post or even wished to discuss foreign affairs informally over the meal, he went away disappointed. Later that evening, Adams admitted that Grant had "maintained his reserve with perfect success." Whether that was because Grant preferred not to tip his hand or because of an "inability to converse with any font of resources to sustain himself" was a question that Adams could not yet answer. Despite the inability of each man to judge the character of the other, the newspapers, both North and South, persisted in reporting that the Grant visit constituted a "search for Cabinet material," with one editor concocting a scenario in which Grant considered Adams "his confidential communicant."[58]

Although one Memphis editor confidently reported that Grant had tapped Adams for the top position as late as February 21, 1869, others began to pick up leaks that despite earlier rumors, Adams would not "be included in the selection." One reporter suggested that Grant needed to win over Sumner, who chaired the Senate Foreign Relations Committee, and that the "jealous" Sumner would "never forgive the selection" of Adams. Another thought it a tragic error if Grant made "the mistake of passing over Charles Francis Adams, by all odds the fittest, ablest, and best equipped statesman in the country."[59]

When Grant finally announced his choice of Hamilton Fish, a former governor of New York who had last held elective office in 1857, Henry was stunned. Having relocated to Washington to cover and perhaps even serve in what he expected to be a reform-minded administration, Henry mourned that the selection of a nonentity who had spent the war years raising money to equip New York troops "changed his intended future into an absurdity so laughable as to make him ashamed of it." Although Fish was a wealthy descendant of New Amsterdam's Dutch founders and a moderate Republican who frowned on black voting rights, and so was precisely the sort of centrist that Henry claimed to support, the Adamses believed him a mediocrity whose undistinguished political career could hardly match that of Charles Francis Sr. "My instincts seem to repel me so much from" Grant, the elder Adams huffed, that he was "relieved" at not having been tempted "by any offer" from the president-elect. Upon reading the text of Grant's inaugural address, Adams gave it average marks. It was a "clear, business like declaration of his views on specific measures," he mused, but it contained "no breadth or loftiness of view, no comprehensive policy, nothing above commonplace." But then, Adams had never cared much for Lincoln's orations either, and perhaps his central complaint was that he was not delivering the address himself.[60]

The entire Adams family quickly went into opposition. Although Charles Francis Jr. largely devoted his hours to crafting articles advocating federal control—although not ownership—of the nation's railroads and chairing the Massachusetts Board of Railroad Commissioners, an appointive position he held until July 1879, he let it be known that he thought Grant's cabinet a collection of second-raters. Crusading journalist Henry took Grant to task in the pages of the *North American Review* and the *Edinburgh Review* for failing to endorse civil service reform adequately and took heart in the fact that the Democratic National Committee reprinted his two essays in pamphlet form with the intention of circulating 250,000 copies. Always happiest when unhappy, Henry took pride in the fact that his father's old foes sought to wield his name as a weapon against a Republican administration. "My family is buried politically beyond recovery for years," he assured a friend with curious satisfaction. "I am becoming more and more isolated as far as allies go." The elder Adams did not even wait for the inauguration before writing a widely reprinted editorial in which he called for the abolition of the Electoral College. Noting that Grant's popular vote victory of 5 percent was far smaller than his electoral margin of 44 percent, Adams groused that "such a system led both parties to look upon fraud as a political necessity." Some months later, Adams complained to an old friend that he had prayed that Grant, "like his predecessor Lincoln," would rise to the office. "I have been so far utterly disappointed."[61]

With the family relegated to the political wilderness, Henry decided that he had seen enough of Washington. "There are few of my political friends left in power now," he observed, "and those few will soon go out." Salvation arrived in early 1870 in a letter from Cambridge. Charles William Eliot, who had accepted the presidency of Harvard after it was declined by Charles Francis Sr., wrote to offer Henry the position of assistant professor of history. The position carried a salary of $400 per year, but one condition was that Henry also had to take over the editorship of the *North American Review* from Ephraim Gurney, who had shifted into the role of dean. Together with his private investments and family allowances, Henry could count on roughly $6,000 of total annual income. The one flaw was that Eliot required Henry to teach medieval history, a subject, he laughed, of which he was "utterly and grossly ignorant."[62]

To prepare for the fall's classes, Henry sailed for London on a research trip in June, with plans to visit his sister Louisa, who had settled in Florence, before returning home in August. Henry had just reached Britain when a telegram arrived reporting that while Louisa was on a holiday near Bagni di Lucca, her carriage had overturned, crushing her foot. On June 30, after racing across the continent, Henry arrived at her hotel, which had been "turned into a sort of camp, and a dozen of [his] sister's friends regularly keeping guard." A disconsolate Charles Kuhn sat beside her bed. A deadly tetanus infection had already set in, and for the next eight days, Henry reported, Louisa "swum in chloroform, morphine, opium, and every kind of most violent counter-agent and poison like nicotine and Calabar beans." Although she could barely speak between locked teeth, the brilliant Louisa remained the imperious older sister of Henry's boyhood. "She never loses courage nor head," Henry marveled. In "the middle of her most awful convulsions," Louisa gave "orders and [came] out with sallies of fun and humorous comments which set us all laughing in spite of our terror." When another week passed and Louisa was neither better nor worse, Henry began to hope that "after swallowing more deadly poison that would have killed all of us," she might pull through. But Louisa died on the morning of Wednesday, July 13, having just passed her thirty-ninth birthday.[63]

In accordance with her "dying orders," Louisa was buried in Florence's Protestant Cemetery, final home to poet Elizabeth Barrett Browning and abolitionist minister Theodore Parker. Wisely, Henry cabled his brother Charles Francis rather than his parents; evidently, however, his elder brother, who was on business in Binghamton, proved difficult to locate. Fearing that his parents might somehow hear of the accident from a mutual friend, Henry also cabled his sisters-in-law Minnie and Mary, urging them to see to his parents. Charles Francis Jr. arrived in Quincy on July 16 and found the old house "as quiet as could be expected." The precise details of "poor Lou's death" had not yet arrived, and he "dread[ed] their

While Louisa was on an 1870 holiday near Bagni di Lucca, Italy, her carriage overturned, crushing her foot. Henry arrived in time to be with his sister when she died of tetanus on July 13, having just passed her thirty-ninth birthday. In accordance with her "dying orders," Louisa was buried in Florence's Protestant Cemetery, also the final home of poet Elizabeth Barrett Browning. For decades, her grave was lost after her marker toppled over; it remains leaning against a stone wall, the inscription facing inward. *Photos courtesy Leigh Fought.*

coming." But Charles Francis Jr. was also annoyed that Henry had failed to send a lengthy missive. "Why was it telegraphed!"[64]

For the next several days, Charles Francis Jr. rode out to Quincy each morning to check on his parents, and just two days later he "found them much more composed than I had expected." But although he shuttered his emotions to the world, the elder Adams retreated into his study and his sorrows, leaving Abby to grieve with Mary, her sons, and her daughters-in-law. For more than a week, Charles Francis Sr. refused to pick up a pen. Finally, on July 26, he waded into his backlog of correspondence and letters of condolence. "Our late severe domestic affliction has so absorbed my attention, that the outer world and its events seemed of little account in the comparison," Adams apologized to one old friend. "This is the prerogative of grief."[65]

Seventeen months later, on Thursday, December 28, 1871, after a labor of only thirty minutes, Minnie gave birth to her second child. After already producing one healthy girl four years before, "Minnie was greatly disappointed in the sex," Charles Francis Jr. confided to his diary. Or perhaps he simply read her emotions in such a way, as the dissatisfied father added "& so was I, but better luck next time." John Quincy's second child, George Caspar, was thriving, and Charles Francis was anxious to have a son to carry on the family name. After assuring himself that Minnie was doing well, Charles Francis stopped by his office "as usual" before opting to "walk home, to walk off a sense of unfounded disappointment." But the fact that the child was a girl allowed her parents to name her Louisa Catherine, after both her late aunt and her great-grandmother.[66]

"A good night's sleep made me feel better," Charles Francis Jr. wrote the next morning. Minnie was "doing nicely and picking up fast." Even the dour Charles Francis had reason to be optimistic, and not merely because he was father to two healthy daughters. Minnie was yet young, and Henry was in the process of falling in love, or at least finding a mate whom he imagined to be his mirror image. The Adams brothers were not the only Americans to be dismayed by the casual ethics on display in the Grant administration, leading to one final opportunity to place Charles Francis Sr. in the Executive Mansion, but not before he performed one more diplomatic miracle for his country.[67]

10

"I SHALL NEVER UNDERSTAND WHY HE WENT NO FARTHER"

A Singular, Unsolved Family

As Charles Francis Sr. puttered about in his library, organizing his father's papers, mourning the death of his eldest child, and cataloguing his ancient-world coin collection, he could hardly have been insensible of events abroad or of how affairs in London might vanquish his plans to quietly sit out Grant's first term. Having once hoped to finalize any claims for reparations caused by Britain's willingness to allow Confederate ships to be constructed along its docks before his departure for home, Adams had left the matter in the hands of his successor, Reverdy Johnson. The Maryland Democrat had been understood to be a placeholder until the next election, yet he dutifully began negotiations with George Villiers, the Earl of Clarendon and foreign secretary under Prime Minister William Gladstone. The resulting Johnson-Clarendon treaty had arrived in Washington with a month remaining in Andrew Johnson's term. When asked by journalists, Adams had pronounced it a "good treaty" and urged ratification "with some slight changes." But the Senate regarded the minister as a disreputable envoy of an impeached president and refused to take it up until April 13, 1869, at which point it was soundly rejected by a vote of 54 to 1.[1]

Disappointed over not being offered the State Department portfolio, Sumner chose to use his perch as chairman of the Foreign Relations Committee to sabotage all further negotiations. Johnson had agreed to "direct damages" inflicted on American vessels—that is, precise figures of lost cargoes and ships that could be documented by American companies. Hamilton Fish estimated that during its two years in existence, the CSS *Alabama* had captured sixty-five prizes valued at six million dollars. Having earlier signaled his support for that figure, Sumner wrote to the new secretary of state, indicating that he now believed that sum was "inadequate & does injustice" to the case. He could not "be a party" to any solution that "enfeebles any of the just grounds" of restitution, Sumner observed, claiming his position had "already [been] expounded by Seward, Adams & myself." In a speech published in pamphlet form, Sumner then introduced the notion of "indirect claims" to cover losses based on the presumed prolongation of the war because of Confederate privateers. That figure, Sumner admitted, could stretch into the billions of dollars. To his diary, Adams worried that Sumner's demands were so extravagant that there was "no chance of negotiation left, unless the English have lost all their spirit and character." To a reporter, Adams sourly added that Sumner's speech "did more harm than good." Adams always attributed Sumner's behavior to the darkest of motives, but in this case he was right. As a longtime Anglophile, Sumner had no intention of provoking war with Britain; he sought only to embarrass the new president.[2]

When in May 1869 Grant packed off John Motley to London as the new minister, Adams breathed a sigh of relief. A former minister to Russia and a Massachusetts Republican, Motley was an old friend and one of the few Grant supporters in whom Adams placed any confidence. Sumner's speech infuriated official London and inspired Benjamin Moran, still the Legation's secretary, to warn his superiors that "John Bull is getting into a bad temper with us." But after feelings cooled in Parliament, Gladstone realized the time was propitious for an Anglo-American understanding. The escalating tensions between France and Prussia, together with aggressive Russian advances into the Black Sea, alerted the prime minister to the need to settle all remaining questions with the United States. The result was the May 1871 Treaty of Washington, which called for teams of commissioners to plead their nation's cases regarding war claims to a board of negotiators chosen by Britain, the United States, Italy, the Swiss confederation, and Brazil. The arbitration would take place in Geneva, Switzerland. This time, on May 24, 1871, the Senate consented to ratification by a vote of 50 to 12. Journalists promptly pounced. Who better to lead the American team than Adams? "He is comparatively a young man yet," a New Orleans editor observed, "and is capable of doing much good service" in the cause of his country.[3]

The same New Orleans newspaper that advocated for Adams did so despite his son John Quincy, whom it described as an aspiring politician "tinctured with the impure Democracy that still pervades the country." Perhaps, the editor guessed, John Quincy's recent speeches in the South were a "bid for the presidency." Grant had the same concerns. When Fish urged the president to appoint the senior Adams as lead commissioner, Grant demurred, remarking that Adams was too independent. The placid old soldier spent little time worrying about potential 1872 opponents, but given his narrow popular-vote victory, neither did he care to give any rival an early advantage, especially if either of his possible challengers bore the surname of America's first family.[4]

But the press, from Oregon to Vermont and from Knoxville to Nashville, kept the possible appointment alive, insisting that the naming of Adams would "be received with general favor." Fish also continued to press for Adams, believing that a president with no foreign policy experience required an envoy with an intimate knowledge of British affairs. Finally, at a cabinet meeting on August 1, the entire body urged Grant to give way, and the next morning the president announced his intentions to tender the appointment to Adams. Given the frostiness between the two men, however, one editor "doubted whether he would accept."[5]

Adams had no intention of declining, either because, like Fish, he believed himself the most qualified man for the task or because, for all his protestations of coveting anonymity, part of him still hoped to follow his ancestors into the presidency. The following afternoon, Adams invited Brooks, who was home after finishing his first semester at Harvard Law, to walk with him around their grounds in Quincy. Adams proposed that Brooks accompany him to Geneva as his private secretary. Although that would require Brooks to miss the fall semester, Adams desired a companion and confidant—the still-grieving Abby announced that she planned to remain in Massachusetts with Mary—and with Henry ensconced in the classroom and the married Charles Francis pursuing a career in railroads, the twenty-three-year-old Brooks was the obvious candidate. Brooks was reluctant to set aside his legal studies, but "after some conversation" he consented. Rather than look as if he had campaigned for the appointment, Adams waited five more days before cabling Grant his acceptance. As Grant perhaps feared, journalists hailed the move. "A better man could scarcely have been selected," one Washington journalist insisted, and Adams's willingness to serve was a "cause of general satisfaction." In several cases, newspapers carried brief biographies of the minister, marveling that while a boy in St. Petersburg, he had "learned to speak Russian, German, and French, as well as English."[6]

As he had a decade before, Adams traveled to Washington to accept the position in person and to confer with Grant and Fish about the negotiations. The meeting went almost as badly as did Adams's 1861 discussion with Lincoln. As yet, the Geneva conference had no starting date, and when Adams inquired about when the administration wished him to be in Europe, Grant appeared a bit surprised and "answered in a hesitating tone" that he expected the negotiations to begin in December. Several days later, Adams received a note from Fish assuring him that because the president had "perfect confidence" in his judgment, the matter did "not admit of instructions." Adams and Brooks departed Boston on November 12. Abby was too distressed to see them off, but when they reached the docks, Adams was pleased to see Henry, Charles Francis Jr., John Quincy and his wife and sons, and several old friends. After farewells, Adams and Brooks located their quarters and prepared themselves as best they could for their "imprisonment."[7]

Just before he sailed, Adams discovered that Prime Minister Gladstone had selected Sir Alexander Cockburn, the lord chief justice, as the British commissioner, to be assisted by Lord Tenterden and a professor of foreign affairs, Montagne Bernard. The group, including the board of arbitrators, first rendezvoused in London for two days of organizational talks before moving on to the neutral venue of Geneva. Adams was not much impressed by the Brazilian arbiter, the Baron d'Itajuba, who had resided with his German wife in Europe for the past three decades and neither spoke nor understood English, which Adams judged "to be rather an obstacle." But Cockburn, Adams instinctively grasped, was every bit his equal. The son of a former minister to Colombia and the German state of Württemberg, Cockburn had been born in Romania and educated in the law at Cambridge. Fluent in French, Cockburn was familiar with German, Italian, and Spanish. Even before they left for Switzerland, however, it "became plain" to Adams that the British strategy was to drag out negotiations for so long, perhaps even through the following fall, that Adams might abandon the talks and be replaced by a less formidable adversary.[8]

Adams and Brooks had just arrived in Geneva in January 1872, where they were joined by Charles Kuhn, when they found a letter from Henry. Abby had suffered a nervous breakdown. "Just at present mamma appears to be buoying herself up entirely with the idea that you will come back to take her out," Henry cautioned. Not wishing to "disturb her quiet," Henry avoided either discouraging or encouraging "her in this notion." But Charles Francis Sr.'s letters from Switzerland would soon "begin to arrive," removing any fantasies of an early arrival, and at that point "the strain will be a sharp one." Henry consulted doctors about his mother's "nervous prostration," but even so he traveled to Quincy each day to check her condition. "If this goes on," Henry confided to a friend, "I might as well give up pretending to teach, for I shall disgrace myself to my scholars." Mary chimed in as well: "Her worries have now got quite her control." Without awaiting official leave, Adams left Brooks in Europe and sailed for Manhattan aboard the steamer *Algeria*, telling journalists only that his wife was unwell.[9]

Not knowing the extent or nature of Abby's illness, Fish cabled Adams on February 21, 1872, the day he docked in New York City, requesting that he first journey to Washington to confer about the negotiations. Gladstone had been delivering ever-more-incendiary speeches in Parliament, and Fish was concerned that the Geneva conference was being set up for failure. For an Adams, duty was paramount, and he complied. Adams thought his discussion with Fish most productive. "A man of clear judgment and plain sense," Adams concluded. Not so the president. The fastidious Adams was annoyed that Grant appeared for the meeting "rather shabbily dressed," a complaint he had once made of Lincoln. Grant was also worried about "the uncompromising position taken by Mr. Gladstone," but having endured years of similar vitriol by Parliament, Adams assured the two that he "did not consider things desperate." Thinking that negotiations were similar to battle, Grant suggested that if Cockburn declined arbitration, Adams should address the arbitrators "just the same as if [Britain had] made an appearance." The idea struck Adams as "so preposterous," he told his diary, that "I had some difficulty to keep my countenance fixed as if I was studying the wall." After a silence of some moments, Fish observed that the judges would surely refuse to hear the case unless both parties were present. After that, Grant "confined himself to puffing his cigar and complaining of a cold he had caught." Adams promised Fish that he still had faith in the process and boarded the train for home.[10]

"The governor has come home," Henry assured a worried Brooks, "and we are all right again. Mamma is as well as ever." In part, Abby's recovery was the result of press speculation that the negotiations had collapsed, but the elder Adams promised her that even if he had to return to Geneva, he would never allow the task to grow into the endless ordeal of their time at the Legation. Hints also arrived from London that Gladstone's ire was a "protest [only] against the admission of indirect damages," which Adams found a "great relief." Dining one evening with Henry and Richard Henry Dana, the three discussed the chances of Senate ratification of a treaty that did not adhere to Sumner's demands. For Adams, Sumner's objections posed a welcome challenge. Let Sumner and his allies "protest against it as much as they liked," Adams remarked, "and even prepare themselves to refuse to abide by any decision" handed down by the judges. As Fish was now more confident of success, and Abby improved enough to travel, Adams booked passage for Britain for April 24.[11]

Adams stopped first in London so that Moran could update him on the mood in Parliament. Moran was pessimistic, estimating the chances of a successful negotiation to be "by no means favorable." Adams was inclined to believe him, if only because his arrival was met with an editorial in the London *Morning Post* charging that the former minister was incapable of serving as an "impartial" negotiator in Geneva. Understanding that his job was to defend his country's interests, Adams read the curious editorial as an attempt "to prejudice unfavorably" any Parliamentary desire to compromise. On May 13 he reached Paris, where Brooks met him at the station. As a man who respected precision and patterns, Adams could not help noticing that he had sailed away from London "on the same day when I first entered it in 1861 and again when I quitted it in 1868." Unlike the sour Henry, Adams always enjoyed Paris and looked forward to a few "pleasant" days with Brooks before returning to Switzerland. But he also reflected that the "high life as it is called has become burdensome," and he wished only to finish the task assigned him and return to Quincy.[12]

NEGOTIATIONS SOON BEGAN IN GENEVA, BUT IN AMERICA, FATE had other plans for the Adams family. The 1872 presidential election season was under way, and while Henry found time again to advance his father's name, he had also fallen in love. The object of his affections was Marian Hooper, the twenty-eight-year-old daughter of Boston physician Robert Hooper. Marian's mother, transcendentalist poet Ellen Sturgis Hooper, had died when her daughter was only five, and the grieving doctor grew very close to his youngest child. Clover, as her mother had nicknamed her, had volunteered for the US Sanitary Commission during the war, taking on the sort of service that Louisa had disdained, and then in 1866 traveled with her father and sisters to Britain, where she had met Henry briefly when they dined at the Legation. This time, they crossed paths in early 1872 at the home of Clover's sister, Ellen, who was married to Ephraim Gurney, Henry's predecessor at the *North American Review*. Henry had yet to buy or rent his own home in Cambridge, preferring instead to take a few rooms in the home of his deceased uncle Edward Everett. Almost from the moment he met Clover again, Henry later confided to Brooks, he decided to pursue her and had "driven [at] it very steadily."[13]

If Clover was slightly above the normal age for Boston socialites to marry, Henry, at thirty-four, had come to believe himself a confirmed bachelor. During his years in London, he had sought no attachments. "The young American was not worth the young Englishwoman's notice," Henry later admitted, "and never received it." As recently as 1869, Henry had been a groomsman in a friend's wedding but refused to take an interest in even "the prettiest and most fashionable girls" there. He could "flirt" with a young woman, he joked, only if she was "in a deep consumption and will die of it." Both his parents and grandparents lacked the deep, personal attachment exhibited by John and Abigail, and perhaps lacking better models of affection, Henry had suspected he would never marry. "My heart is now as immoveable as a stone," he thought, "and I sometimes doubt whether marriage is possible except as a matter of convenience."[14]

Henry never explained to his parents or brothers what drew him to Clover. Perhaps he saw more than a bit of himself in the sophisticated, wealthy, but often unhappy loner. Where Charles Francis Jr. wanted a foil, a caring partner to balance out his contrariness, Henry desired a mirror reflection. Within the month, they had an understanding. With the brutal honesty typical of his family, Henry described his "young female" to his friend Charles Gaskell—but not to his family, who as yet knew nothing of his "fiancée"—in a pair of letters. Henry ran down the list of debits and benefits. "She is certainly not handsome; nor would she be quite called plain," he began. "Her manners are quiet," but she was "fond of society and amusement" and had a good sense of humor. Her conversations "on the whole [went] pretty sensibly." Nor would she

Marian "Clover" Hooper was always sensitive about her looks, and although she was an avid and skillful photographer herself, few images of her face exist. Unlike others in the Adams family, she never wished to have her portrait painted. When describing his fiancée to an old friend, Henry wrote that "she is certainly not handsome; nor would she be quite called plain." *Courtesy Massachusetts Historical Society.*

attempt to isolate Henry from his friends. "She knows her own mind uncommon well." Her accent was not "*very* American," and she could read German and Latin. On the other side of the ledger, "she really knows nothing well," and her Greek was poor. She tended to speak too "garrulously," and her spelling was imperfect. Her features, about which Clover was overly sensitive, "are much too prominent." "She dresses badly," but at least she was "open to instruction" on that score, and "*We*," Henry assured Gaskell, "shall improve her." Henry was sure that his friends, if not his family, would like her for her "intelligence and sympathy," but just in case Gaskell had missed the remark in the first letter, Henry concluded the second by emphasizing that they would not be attracted to her for her "beauty, for she is certainly not beautiful." Even for an Adams, Henry made a pathetic lover.[15]

Clover's family was pleased by the engagement. Gurney had spent many an evening with Henry during the past months, and Dr. Hooper thought the match a good one. Dr. Oliver Wendell Holmes, who had known both

Clover and Henry for years, wrote a note of congratulations to Charles Francis Sr. "I am sure you cannot but be happy by the prospect of receiving Miss Hooper, whom we have found and you will find so worthy of love and esteem into your family." But the Adamses were less confident. Charles Francis Sr., who was then in Quincy caring for Abby, was "surprised" by the news. The fact that Abby was about to lose her favorite son to another woman perhaps played a role in her breakdown. The fact that Henry first offered up the news to younger brother Brooks rather than to Charles Francis Jr., now the eldest living sibling, suggested that he was anxious about his brother's response, and with good reason. When told of the engagement, Charles Francis Jr., worried about rumors of mental illness in Clover's mother's family, blurted out "Heavens!—no! they're all as crazy as coots. She'll kill herself, just like her aunt!"[16]

The Adamses' diffidence toward Clover helped drive Henry away from their influence, and although the presidential season was under way, he announced himself uninterested in politics. Not so John Quincy, who believed that 1872 provided his father with his best opportunity yet to capture the executive prize. Although the worst would not be known until after the election, Grant's administration was already becoming synonymous with corruption and scandal. Some Republicans demanded civil service reform, while others believed that the time had come to reduce sectional tensions by withdrawing the remaining federal troops from the South. Feminists had recently formed the National Woman Suffrage Association and the American Woman Suffrage Association, placing demands for female suffrage on the national agenda. Among those believing Grant "unfit for the Presidential office" was Charles Sumner, although like his African American Republican allies, he was not one who wished for an end to Reconstruction reforms. Calling themselves the Liberal Republicans, the dissidents had held a small, one-day conference in Jefferson City, Missouri, on January 24, where they announced their set of political principles. As a final act, they issued a call for a national convention for May 1 in Cincinnati, hoping to get the jump on the mainstream Republican and Democratic conventions, set for June and July, respectively. Because of their advocacy for an end to Reconstruction, the Liberal Republicans hoped to attract some Democrats, or at least voters who felt adrift from either party. Unsurprisingly, the disaffected, independent-minded Charles Francis Sr. promptly sprang to mind. "Try Charles Francis Adams," the Cincinnati *Commercial Republican* suggested. "There is no better material than Adams." As an indication of how broad Adams's support was, Wendell Phillips Garrison, the son of the abolitionist, wrote an editorial for the *Nation* in which he observed that "Chas. Francis Adams's name is most prominent, & seems to me most available. I think the Democratic party would accept him, & if they did, Grant's chances would not be worth a rush."[17]

The political chatter was nothing new to Adams, who had faced seemingly endless rumors about his intentions ever since returning from Britain. Back in July 1869, Manhattan newspapers had reported that Democrats were interested in nominating him for the governor's race, "which is a hint," one editor suspected, "for Young John to stand out of the way." By 1871, journalists as far west as Carson City, Nevada, had announced that both Charles Francis Sr. and John Quincy were in "open alliance" with the Democrats, making the party stronger than it had "been at any time since 1856." Only one office, however, could entice the elder Adams out of retirement, and that July he gave an interview claiming he no longer had "any interest in politics." Yet when asked about the possibility of a third-party movement, Adams had vacillated. "Well, I can't, of course, say what it will amount to," he acknowledged. "The Democrats have made a great many mistakes," so any move toward moderation was "no doubt a step in the right direction if they wish to become the party of the country." One reform-minded editor took that not to be a firm refusal. "When our party becomes strong enough to hold the balance of power," he predicted, "then such men as Adams will begin to recognize it."[18]

The journalistic drumbeat of speculation only increased in late February 1872, when Adams briefly returned to home to care for his wife. A number of Washington insiders evidently believed that Abby's illness was merely a ruse and that Adams had left Geneva so he could better coordinate a campaign. August Belmont, the longtime chairman of the Democratic National Committee who had tried to recruit Adams in 1868, again told Manhattan journalists that he favored Adams as either the Liberal Republican or Democratic nominee. Several South Carolina newspapers flatly announced that Adams was a "moderate Democrat," while others argued that if nominated by the Cincinnati convention, Adams could "fight an independent battle." Should Adams receive the Liberal nod in May and then also capture the Democratic endorsement, a Chicago journalist suggested, there would be only "two candidates in the field," and Adams might represent a "majority of the American people." There was, in fact, considerable evidence for the logic of that hope. General William Bartlett of Massachusetts, who had been elected a delegate to the June Republican convention, promised the *New-York Tribune* that "if the Cincinnati Convention shall have the wisdom to nominate [Adams], the people will have the independence to elect [him]." Attracted by the Adams's public break with the so-called Radical Republicans, a Tennessee editor agreed that Adams was not merely the best candidate but also "the only man capable of rescuing the country from the corruptionists, and calming the contending waves of faction."[19]

On April 16, just as Adams was preparing to again depart for Geneva, Charles Francis Jr. arrived with several letters from prominent Liberal Republicans, urging Adams to dispatch John Quincy and Charles Francis to Cincinnati "as a council to respond for me in my absence," Adams noted in his diary. The writers also hoped for a clear statement of Adams's positions on the issues of the day and a pledge that his sons were empowered to "advance my nomination." That sort of politicking was anathema to Adams's patrician sensibilities, and he refused both to respond and to permit his sons to attend the convention. "Thus far the whole business has been very flattering to my vanity," Adams admitted, "as it displays the public estimation in which I am held by both parties." But only if the Cincinnati gathering resulted in an "unequivocal popular demand for an elevated line of policy" that might "check all the downward tendencies of the times," Adams told his son, could he "justify my consideration of the question." Two days later another letter arrived, this one from David Wells, the former editor of the Illinois *Springfield Republican* and a Johnson supporter. Wells begged Adams to appoint some "authority to act for" him at the convention and bluntly inquired of his "disposition to accept if nominated." Adams replied that he refused to allow anyone to "trade for me"—a phrase that dripped with contempt for party deal makers—and that he could "not accept a nomination if it was not unequivocally the sense of the assembly."[20]

As if tone-deaf to Adams's extraordinary demand that he be unanimously chosen by a grateful convention, Democratic journalists continued to advocate fusion, with one Connecticut editor going so far as to recommend the constitutionally impermissible ticket of Charles Francis Sr. and John Quincy Adams. A more realistic Charleston editor urged a ticket of Adams and outgoing Illinois senator Lyman Trumbull, who had angered Republican voters by voting to acquit Johnson. Hoping to goad Adams into a more pragmatic position, Thurlow Weed, the Albany political handler who had orchestrated the nominations of Zachary Taylor and John C. Frémont and had tried to secure Seward the top spot in 1860, journeyed to Quincy from Albany and joined the chorus of voices wishing for one of the younger Adams to be present in Ohio. Adams again refused to countenance "the management which usually carried the day in such assemblages," an insult, whether intended or not, of Seward's onetime handler. In any case, Weed was seventy-five and, as Adams put it, "past the age of management for which he used to be so famous." And past the age to be of any service to Adams.[21]

Later that day, April 24, Adams left Boston for Manhattan and, soon after, the Continent. Fearing that Abby might relapse if left behind, this time they sailed together. Just before Charles Francis Sr.'s ship left the docks, Wells released Adams's letter to the Washington press. Newspapers from Ohio to Delaware quickly reprinted the missive. Insisting that although he did not desire the nomination, he would, Adams wrote, accept an "unequivocal one, based upon considerations of my character earned in public life." Should he turn his back on his country during its present "emergency," Adams said he could not call himself a patriot. But the prize could not "be negotiated for," and nobody, from Weed to his sons, was empowered to bargain on his behalf. Adams then observed that he was familiar with the Jefferson City declaration of principles, which any "honest republican or democrat" could readily accept. "If the good people who meet in Cincinnati really believe that they need such an anomalous being as I am," Adams concluded, "they must express it in a manner to convince me of it."[22]

Politicians and editors were unsure of what to make of Adams's statement. One Missouri Democratic newspaper, bluntly named the *Weekly Caucasian*, read it as an acceptance, emphasizing the sentence in which Adams agreed he could run on the new party's principles. Others took it to mean that Adams "virtually declines the nomination." At least one Washington editor understood it precisely as Adams had meant it. The letter demonstrated "manly independence" of either major party and provided a "very high opinion of his character." In a time of growing corruption and partisan bickering, Adams had proved himself a "very able man, and no demagogue." The *Cincinnati Enquirer*, a newspaper situated to exert enormous influence over the convention, not only insisted that Adams would accept the nomination but also that plans were under way to use an "identical chair in which John Adams sat when he placed his signature on the immortal Declaration" for the president of the assemblage.[23]

The Liberal Republican convention opened on May 1. As a new party, the Liberals had engaged in no delegate selection process. The planners who booked Cincinnati's Exhibition Hall expected as many as 7,000 spectators and 400 self-appointed delegates. The reformers present hailed from all corners of the republic and included dissidents of both parties, but as always, regional delegates tended to support favorite sons. New Yorkers, for the most part, supported *Tribune* editor Horace Greeley, although thanks to Belmont, a "small portion" of their numbers endorsed Adams. New Englanders stood fast behind Adams, whom the Democratic *Boston Courier* endorsed, but because of Wells's influence in the Midwest, so too did "Ohio folks." Illinois men pulled for Trumbull or Justice David Davis, once Lincoln's campaign manager. The *Sacramento Union* endorsed Adams, but the few Californians present were the exception. Most western representatives, the Washington *Daily National Republican* observed, were "violently opposed" to his candidacy. "The polished gentleman of a distinguished family does not suit the taste of the rough Democracy of the West," the editor suspected. Republicans in attendance insisted that regular party members previously cool to the reform movement had quietly promised to break with Grant if the nominee were Adams, while, despite earlier talk of fusion, Fernando Wood, the powerful chairman of the Joint Caucus of Democratic senators and representatives, threatened to support a separate Democratic ticket if Cincinnati went for Adams.[24]

Far out at sea, Adams fended off questions about the convention from his fellow passengers. "I feel a degree of indifference which is surprising even to myself," he reflected. "I suppose this springs mainly from the strong conviction of the impracticability of such an event on the only condition to which I would give it my assent." But, in fact, as the first day's convention proceedings closed, journalists judged Adams's prospects to be "brightening." Delegates from Louisiana, Texas, and Alabama announced themselves "unanimous for him," perhaps because of John Quincy's growing fame in the former Confederacy. Despite Wood's warning, Belmont bragged that if Adams received the nod, Democrats would "support him without waiting for a formal endorsement of their assembled delegates." References to Adams in the first day's speeches were met with "prolonged cheers," and when the first ballot was counted on May 2, Adams, with 203 votes, was far out in front of the other candidates. Greeley was second with 147, and Trumbull was third with 110. Because delegates scattered their ballots among four others, including Chief Justice Chase, who earned an embarrassing two votes, nobody received the simple majority necessary for nomination. However, most attendees assumed that the next morning's ballot would propel Adams over the top, and the Committee on Resolutions prepared "to report Charles Francis Adams as the nominee." The "Grant men are trembling in their boots," a Pennsylvania reporter wrote, "lest Adams should be the nominee."[25]

Events took a curious turn on the second ballot after New York's Democratic delegates rejected Belmont's advice, arguing that their state's Irish voters, typically a reliably Democratic bloc, regarded the former minister as "the bitter and malignant enemy of their brothers in British bastilles." At the same moment, former Confederate vice president Alexander Stephens published a lengthy editorial denouncing efforts to "hitch the democratic car to the radical engine by working up Charles Francis Adams as a candidate." In reality, Adams had devoted endless hours to getting Irish-born but naturalized American citizens out of Dublin's infamous Kilmainham Gaol, while Sumner and black Republicans loyal to Grant rejected the idea that Adams had ever been a radical. But the gambit worked enough to push Greeley ahead on the second ballot, 245 to 243. Adams then pulled into the lead for the next three ballots, but on the sixth and last ballot, as the official secretary put it, a "scene of great confusion and noise followed." Pennsylvania shifted its fifty votes to Greeley, and a "stampede of changes" to the New Yorker followed. With 482 to 187, Greeley emerged as the nominee, with Missouri Governor Benjamin Gratz Brown as his running mate.[26]

When informed of the news by disappointed supporters after docking in Britain, Adams took the blow with the stoicism typical of earlier generations of his family. He found it "highly gratifying" that "the intelligence and character of the body was for me." As the voting had gone through numerous ballots, however, Adams thought it just as "well that it did not carry the day." Had he, rather than the eccentric New York editor, received the endorsement of such a divided convention, he would have had "the ungracious duty of maintaining" the conditions he laid out to Wells "by refusing the offer and mortifying my friends." Writing to the unwell Seward, Adams hoped that his old friend might acknowledge that he had "never cherished any dreams of the Presidency." Lesser men would have resorted to "intrigue for the nomination," but Adams swore that he had witnessed too "much of that kind of thing done" not to regard it with "thorough contempt." Having come very close to a presidential nomination himself in 1860, Seward understood the art of self-deprecatory denial well enough to feel no need to reply.[27]

Reformers regarded the failure to nominate Adams as a lost opportunity. Few practical politicians could imagine Greeley as presidential material. Having served in Congress for only three months following a special election, Greeley was a tireless supporter of temperance and vegetarianism, and he had famously advocated phrenological tests for train conductors. Although an antislavery Republican, Greeley had made news by posting the bail for jailed Confederate President Jefferson Davis. Mainstream Republicans thought the nomination a gift. "He will certainly not detract a solitary vote from the Republican party," one Republican editor rejoiced. "Adams was the only man among the candidates who might have done us any harm." Southern whites were particularly distressed, believing Adams their best chance of placing a moderate in the White House. His defeat, a Tennessee reporter complained, demonstrated the ugly truth that "in American politics, only that man has a chance of success who will descend to trading and trafficking." One annoyed Chicago editor placed the blame squarely on Adams and his quaint notions of acclamation, however, which the journalist thought belonged to an earlier day. Unlike the other candidates, Adams refused to allow "any organization in his service." Having read his letter to Wells listing his conditions, delegates worried that at the last minute Adams might reject the nomination, a move that would prove deadly to the infant party. All Adams had to do was to indicate that he stood with the reform movement, the editor griped. "It has been said of him that he is an iceberg." The charge stung. "I perceive some of the newspapers with us are pleased to describe me as a cold man," Adams hastily wrote one supporter. He wished his friends to know how much he prized their "generous and unsolicited" support in Cincinnati, adding that he "should indeed have a heart of ice" if he failed to thank them for their efforts.[28]

Preparing for his wedding and briefly liberated from politics, Henry had taken "pleasure" in seeing his father off again to Geneva, insisting that he was "comparatively little disturbed by the infernal row which is going on." But his brother Charles Francis was incensed: "Greeley nominated!!! Words fail to do justice to my disgust & surprise." The senior Adams himself did not quickly forget his close brush with the presidency; as late as January 1875 he was still reflecting on the convention in his diary. His earliest supporters continued to regret his letter to Wells, believing it a fatal "provocation and an obstacle." However, Adams persisted in thinking it saved him "from an unpleasant trial and mortification, whilst it increased my permanent reputation." The one "safe rule" to follow in life was "to aim at what is right and true, and let the consequences take care of themselves."[29]

CHARLES FRANCIS SR., ABBY, AND BROOKS WERE IN EUROPE ON June 27, 1872, when a small party of thirteen, counting the bride and groom, gathered at Robert Hooper's summer estate in Beverly Farms, Massachusetts. "For once I am to carry out the idea of my most cherished prejudice," Henry told his friend Charles Gaskell, "and have a wedding which is absolutely private." Henry and Clover had known each other for less than five months, but the bride was joyful, assuring her sister that "I love you more because I love Henry Adams very much." Apart from Dr. Hooper, only siblings and their spouses were invited; the clergyman, Henry promised the uninvited Gaskell, was a "very jolly young flow of our set." John Quincy and Charles Francis Jr. attended, as did their wives. The noon ceremony "lasted in the neighborhood of two minutes, after which we all trundled into luncheon and sat down anywhere," a displeased Charles Francis Jr. informed his father. Clover "proceeded to calm her agitation by carving a pair of cold roast chickens." Charles Francis insisted that he and John Quincy "labored hard [to] stimulate an aspect of gaiety," but that was never his strong suit; moreover, "the champagne wasn't cool and made its appearance only in very inadequate quantities." In the early afternoon, Clover and Henry left for a seaside cottage provided by her uncle. Charles Francis was home by four. "It was no wedding at all," he scribbled into his diary that evening.[30]

On July 9 the newlyweds boarded the steamer *Siberia* for Britain, with plans then to cross the channel and slowly make their way toward Geneva. For Clover, being so far removed from the only parent she had known since age five was challenging. From Antwerp, she wrote her father to report that she was "always homesick for you," and from Dresden she added "I miss you all the time, and miss you very much." From Venice: "I miss you very, very much, and think so often of your love." Making actual contact with the Adamses only made matters worse. Clover probably did not know that Brooks had also attempted to dissuade his brother from marrying into a family that he regarded as unstable, but Abby let her displeasure be known at a party one evening, Clover observed, when she and Henry "played the role of an old married couple and only talked." When the couple refused to dance, Abby grew "quite disgusted" with her daughter-in-law, who replied simply that the waltz was "not in my line." Especially by comparison to one gregarious Italian acquaintance, Clover felt like an "undemonstrative New Englander."[31]

Clover's distress only worsened in late November, when they reached Alexandria and prepared to sail up the Nile on the *Isis*, a private *dahabeah* of three single cabins, a stateroom, and a small dining room. The budding historian Henry enjoyed the Great Pyramids and the Sphinx, pronouncing himself an "enthusiastic Egyptologist." But Clover felt as if she "were blind and deaf and dumb too," and was so depressed that for more than a week she was unable to write her father. When at last she did, Clover admitted that she had "tried to write in the past ten days but gave it up in despair." More, of course, than the slow pace of travel fueled Clover's unhappiness. Having turned twenty-nine in Europe, she was accustomed to her independence, and she was far and away her father's favorite. Now she was merely a part of the famous and famously cold Adams family and the wife of a rising intellectual who, while attentive and patient, was dour and unromantic. "Life is such a jumble of impressions just now," she confided to her father. In Geneva, Henry's parents were displeased but not much surprised. The couple's reports from Egypt, Charles Francis Sr. told his diary, were "much less enthusiastic than that of most travelers."[32]

The two fed on each other's unhappiness. After several months in Egypt, Henry and Clover moved on for Rome, where a doctor prescribed "rest, broth, quinine and wine" for them both. They remained in Italy for a fortnight before booking a hotel suite on Paris's Rue de Rivoli. Contact with the rest of the Adamses never helped Clover's mood, but the couple were surprised one morning by an unexpected visit from Charles Francis Jr., on his way to Vienna and an international trade fair. Charles Francis found his brother "very depressed" and "in a state of cold and general debility," nursing a "bowl of gruel" while Clover lay in bed "with 'grippe' and fever." Attempting to be good hosts, they offered Charles Francis a cup of Turkish coffee, which somehow only infuriated him all the more. "Damn their Turkish coffee!" Already in a foul humor because of the inability of most Parisians to converse in English, Charles Francis was angry that Henry offered him a bedroom "about the size of a kennel." Charles Francis declined the room and poured his fury and disappointment into a letter home. "My brother has grown to be a damned, solemn, pompous little ass, and his wife is an infernal bore," he exploded to Minnie. "Oh, Lord, how I hate her!—she talks in a low voice, and prances along like a palfrey [horse]—bah!" In August 1873 they sailed for Massachusetts, with Henry stopping in Quincy to see his parents, who were back from Geneva, and Clover heading straight for Beverly Farms. Henry expected that Clover would join him for a quick visit in Quincy, but she begged off, instead setting up their new household in Boston at 91 Marlborough Street, just two blocks from the Beacon Street home of Robert Hooper.[33]

By then, the elder Adams had returned home "in Triumphe," as he bragged to his journal. Upon arriving again in Geneva, both Adams and Alexander Cockburn, the head British negotiator, began to prepare their cases for the Board of Arbitration. Comprising Jacob Stampfli of Switzerland, Count Sclopis of Italy, and the Baron d'Itajuba of Brazil, the board, one American editor worried, consisted of noblemen who "were not at all inclined to give the United States an advantage." Having resided in Britain long enough to guess that Gladstone's escalating tone in Parliament was largely designed to appease his party, Adams decided to ignore both Sumner's demands and rumors in London that the Geneva talks would be abandoned. On June 19, 1872, he persuaded the tribunal to rule out indirect claims, although that question was not technically before them for adjudication. Cockburn indicated that such a step might satisfy his government, and Adams promptly notified Secretary Fish; first Washington and then London agreed to exclude indirect claims and move toward a final settlement. By late August, the board unanimously ruled against Britain in the individual cases of the *Sumter, Nashville, Georgia,* and *Al-*

abama. A split decision upheld British liability regarding the *Florida* and the *Shenandoah.* Then still in Europe, Henry was impressed by his father's handiwork but guessed that the total damages "will not much exceed three millions sterling."[34]

Much to Henry's surprise and Gladstone's dismay, the board settled upon an award of $15,500,000 in gold. "The victory was complete," Charles Francis Jr. marveled. Brooks was undecided about whether to move to Berlin to study German or return to Boston and practice law, but the senior Adamses, Charles Francis Sr. remarked, "bid Goodbye to Europe with not a single regret." Abby had never cared for travel, and at sixty-five Adams found the "perpetual transition from place to place more and more painful." He realized that he had reached the precise age when his grandfather had left the presidency, but also the same age when his father, "rebelling at the idea" of retirement, sought election to Congress. His Geneva negotiations and his final chance at the presidency behind him, Adams believed he "had a right to rest," if perhaps somewhat uneasily. A career of public service, he mused, "was a very fascinating occupation, but like drinking brandy. The more you indulge in it, the more uncomfortable it leaves you when you stop."[35]

Just prior to Adams's return, the Democrats met in their national convention and, as expected, endorsed the nomination of Greeley and Gratz Brown. Former Missouri senator Carl Schurz waged a final effort to replace Gratz Brown in the second spot with Adams, but the attempt failed miserably, in large part because nobody at the Baltimore conference imagined that Adams might accept the lower position. In a time of fierce party loyalty, there simply was no place for independents. Few knew whether Adams actually remained a Republican, one Democratic editor observed, but if so, "nobody in that party trusts him." His son John Quincy, the editor noted, "has since been twice the Democratic candidate for Governor of Massachusetts." In an era of partisan heat, Adams remained cool and reserved, and so a man without a party.[36]

The Democrats' embrace of Greeley left the Adams sons, as Henry observed, "in a very curious position." Like most Republicans, Greeley was a high-tariff man, yet Democrats and Liberals tended toward free trade.

John Quincy, despite his consistent electoral defeats in Massachusetts, yet hoped for a future with the Democrats, and despite family loyalties, the party expected him to endorse their candidate. "I don't see how he is to occupy such a position," Henry wrote to his father from Italy, "except as a personal matter of opposition to Greeley." As Charles Francis Sr. did not dock in Manhattan until November 13, he was spared the ordeal of actually having to cast a ballot. At length, John Quincy announced himself for Greeley, but Charles Francis Jr. was having none of it. Speaking in Boston on the eve of the election, Charles Francis Jr. explained his reasons for "withdrawing from the Cincinnati movement and for supporting Grant." Greeley had a "peculiar unfitness" for the presidency, and in Baltimore, he charged, his Democratic supporters had engaged in the sort of "trading, truckling spirit" no Adams should countenance.[37]

The inevitable result of such confusion and political mismanagement was a Grant landslide. The general carried 31 states and captured 55.6 percent of the popular vote. Sadder yet for Greeley, his wife, Molly, had died of consumption on October 30. Greeley himself soon lost his reason, uttering "wild words about business and about the election." He died in a sanatorium in Pleasantville, New York, on November 29, just days after the election. Electors bound to Greeley threw their votes to other candidates, mostly Gratz Brown, so in the end, Greeley technically earned zero electoral votes. "This is the penalty which the poor man paid for his nomination," the elder Adams thought. "What might have been my own condition at this moment, if I had been defeated as he was. Instead of which I am my own man."[38]

Adams, probably correctly, guessed that he too would have lost to Grant, if not nearly as decisively. African American Republican voters, and especially Frederick Douglass, who edited a pamphlet supporting Grant, remained loyal to the Republicans. But the staid Adams, unlike Greeley, enjoyed wide support across the country. As an irritated Secretary Fish put it, his admirers engaged in the "annually returning periodic demand" that Adams be made "Governor, President—Town Clerk or something." Fish's sarcasm, however, was lost on many serious political activists. Shortly after the election, Thurlow Weed journeyed to Boston, hoping to discover whether Adams might be interested in replacing Fish at State. Of course, Adams replied that he "had no confidence in the President, which would justify me in taking the post." Significantly, however, Adams later carefully trimmed and retained an 1880 editorial speculating that had Adams won the Liberal nomination in 1872, even in defeat a "formidable opposition party would have been formed around Mr. Adams, and that gentleman probably would have become President in 1877." That guess might have been accurate enough, but the editor was not privy to a secret that Adams had begun to regularly fret about: "I am constantly brought to the conviction that my faculties are gradually yielding to the progress of time, for which due allowance must also be made."[39]

Other grim reminders of time passing came with the death of Seward in October 1872. Adams traveled to Albany the following April to deliver the funeral oration, a fitting tribute, he decided, as in 1848 Seward had eulogized his father, John Quincy, in the same church. "Charles Francis Adams is not merely the son of Mr. Seward's friend, but is himself the friend of Mr. Seward's later years," the *Albany Evening Journal* reminded. Somewhat thornier for Adams was the March 1874 death of Charles Sumner. Hoping that Adams might be inclined to pardon his sometimes critic and remember their earlier years as antislavery allies, Richard Henry Dana urged Adams to join a roster of speakers at Faneuil Hall. "My day for Faneuil Hall speeches was over," Adams snapped. But when invited to serve at the funeral as a pallbearer, Adams felt that he could hardly refuse. The oration by writer George Winston Curtis left him unmoved, however. Hearing it, Adams groused, "it might be inferred that [Sumner] was the Luther or Calvin of the reformation of Slavery." That evening, Adams enumerated a long list of grievances into his journal, from Sumner's failure to pass "any measure whatsoever" to "his violent declamations" that helped to hasten the coming of war. "At no moment of his career did he show any proof of high practical wisdom as a Statesman. He could never cooperate to gain an end because he never admitted of difference of opinion." Even Massachusetts Democrats praised Sumner, whose Senate career spanned twenty-three years, in speeches and editorials, but forgiveness, to an Adams, was no virtue.[40]

Adams anticipated the next move. The Massachusetts legislature would not wish to leave Sumner's Senate seat open for long. One year before, in early 1873, when Henry Wilson left the Senate to become Grant's second vice president, an editorial in the *Nation* advanced Adams's name for the vacancy. "To me the thing is not desirable," Adams remarked at the time, thinking ahead toward 1876. "My situation in the Country cannot be improved by the possession of any office whatever." In April 1874, however, Adams was more interested, in part, perhaps, as a final victory over Sumner. But although Adams received twelve votes in the assembly, a curious coalition elevated William Washburn, a moderate Republican and a placeholder, into the seat. Vice President Wilson, once Adams's coeditor on the *Daily Whig*, personally intervened in the process, warning Republican legislators that Adams would only cause further Republican division. But as he stubbornly refused to clearly identify himself as a Democrat, few of that party, including John Quincy, once again in the House, supported his cause. "My son and many others who I know well are on the record as voting against me," Adams groaned. "My country has exhibited even less gratitude to me than it did to Mr. Seward. Why should I expect even a compliment?"[41]

One final chance, Adams guessed, occurred that fall of 1874 after a "revolution in our politics." Thanks to the depression of the previous year and "the shambling incompetence of Grant," in Adams's estimation, the Republican candidate for governor lost his bid and the Democrats increased their numbers in the assembly. "There has been much straggling effort to elect me" to the Senate, Adams was pleased to observe, "which issues in a coalition of democrats and dissatisfied republicans." Considering his "independent attitude," Adams regarded "this as a very high compliment." But despite his garnering ninety-eight votes, the legislature finally selected Republican Henry Dawes to replace Washburn. The endless series of near misses for the Adamses was met with mirth from the editor of the hostile Boston *Journal*, who mockingly recommended a "family ticket" for state offices: "For Governor, Chas. Francis Adams (Ind.); for Secretary of State, John Quincy Adams (Dem.); for Treasurer, Chas. Francis Adams, Jr. (Rep.); for Auditor, Henry Adams (Ind.); for

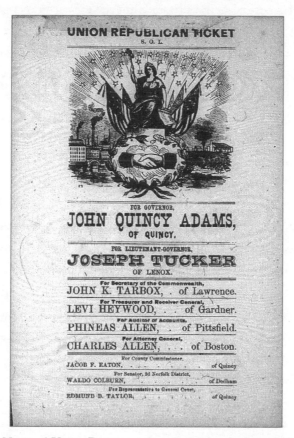

The short-lived National Union Party served as the bridge for John Quincy Adams II's transition from Republican to Democrat in the years just after the Civil War. Until 1918, Massachusetts governors served one-year terms, providing Adams with ample opportunities to run—and to lose. His running mate, former Republican Joseph Tucker, had lost a leg at the Battle of Plains Store, Louisiana, and was then serving in the statehouse. *Courtesy National Park Service.*

Attorney General, Brooks Adams (Rep.). It is all in the family, and yet well distributed among the parties."[42]

The family's scattered political loyalties did not survive the next twelve months. By early 1876, the front-runner for the Republican presidential nomination was Maine Senator James G. Blaine, a former House speaker suspected of accepting bribes from the Union Pacific Railroad. Henry regarded that possibility as a "stroke of luck," as Blaine, a Grant loyalist, would drive all reformers into the opposition. As ever, Carl Schurz believed

Charles Francis Sr. to be the proper candidate for a grand party of independent crusaders, and Schurz even indulged in the fantasy that Adams might receive the nomination of both major parties. Henry was not so naive, but he and his brother Charles Francis called for a conference of like-minded men to meet in Manhattan in February, prior to the national conventions. In mid-February, about 170 "men of intelligence and sobriety," one journalist counted, met in the Fifth Avenue Hotel. Most were Republicans horrified by the prospect of Blaine. Yale president Theodore Woolsey gaveled the meeting to order, but Charles Francis Jr. delivered a rousing speech that brought the attendees to their feet. "It hit the mark square and hard so that for a few hours I enjoyed the intoxication of oratory," Charles Francis reveled. The conclave was widely covered by the press, especially in the South, and Henry publicly hoped that southern Democrats, furious over the passage of the 1875 Civil Rights Act, might support their movement. "Just now I am engaged single-handedly in the slight task of organizing a new party to contest the next Presidential election," Henry informed a friend. "I propose to do no less than decide the election of 1876."[43]

Although standing once again for reelection to the assembly, John Quincy remained out of the fray. His daughter Fannie contracted diphtheria and died on April 11 at the age of two; her eldest brother, John Quincy III, followed the next morning, having just reached his fourteenth birthday. The stunned parents could barely cope with the loss. John Quincy had always been an atypical Adams, "the only one of the family," Henry once admitted, "who can make one laugh when one's ship is sinking." Remembering the loss of his son Arthur so many years before, Charles Francis Sr. was moved to "tears," as he knew his eldest son "had set all of his happiness" on his children. The brothers rallied for the funerals, serving as pallbearers for the small coffins. At the service, a grieving Charles Francis Sr. "prayed to be taken away" in their place. "Why was it not I to be taken before the clouds came down over me," he mourned. Abby spent days sitting beside the couple at the graves near the Mount Wollaston farm. "John looks like an old man, the lines so deep and the expression so unhappy," Abby wrote. Fanny suffered too, "but differently, so sad and quiet."[44]

While Fanny and John Quincy mourned, Henry and Charles Francis Jr. returned to their political labors. Rather to their surprise, when the Republicans gathered in Cincinnati in early June, they abandoned Blaine for Rutherford B. Hayes, the newly elected governor of Ohio and a former congressman and general. Just nine days later, the Democrats met in St. Louis and nominated New York Governor Samuel Tilden. After Hayes promised to support civil service reform and serve but a single term if elected, any thoughts of a third party vanished. "Unless I am very much mistaken," Schurz wrote to a dubious Charles Francis Jr., "Cincinnati has nominated our man without knowing it." Henry disagreed, dismissing the Ohioan as a "third-rate nonentity, whose only recommendation is that he is obnoxious to no one." The brothers worried—incorrectly, as it turned out—that as a former Union officer, Hayes would attempt to protect the rights of black southerners, whereas Tilden, who had compiled an admirable reputation as an anticorruption politician and also endorsed civil service reform, promised to end "the rapacity of carpetbag tyrannies." Henry was disappointed for his father, grumbling that the "tendency to blackguard the Adamses generally is irresistible to the average American politician." Yet when it came to Tilden, Henry supposed he could "give the democratic party again some principles and some brains, and so force the republicans to a higher level." Although he still hoped "to increase the independent power," if forced to choose between the two, he "inclined" towards Tilden.[45]

By September, the entire family publicly stood with Tilden. The *New York World* proudly printed a roster of onetime "Lincoln Republicans" who now supported the Democratic ticket. Charles Francis Adams Sr.'s name topped the list; toward the bottom, below other, more famous dissidents such as Trumbull, Gratz Brown, and David Wells, appeared Charles Francis Jr. and Henry. At twenty-eight, Brooks was as yet too little known to matter, and as a longtime Democrat, John Quincy had not been a "Lincoln Republican" in years. To appease his new party, Charles Francis Sr. reluctantly allowed the Democrats to name him their gubernatorial candidate. Only one unforgiving Ohio editor declined to welcome the Adamses into the Democratic fold, charging that Schurz and Charles Francis Sr. had "originated the negro party," which although "pretending to be conservators of the peace [had] promulgated the vilest Communistic doctrines throughout the Southern states" by liberating black "capital and labor."[46]

"Great was my surprise to find that the election of Mr. Tilden was conceded beyond a doubt," Adams assured his journal on November 8. Tilden's 254,235-ballot margin of victory marked the first time since 1856 that a Democrat had captured the popular vote. The story was quite different in Massachusetts, however, as incumbent Republican Alexander Rice bested Adams by 21,000 votes, a 13 percent margin. "I dreaded the possibility of an election for Governor, and of that burden I am fully relieved," Adams added, undoubtedly this time with sincerity. John Quincy, running for the state senate, also lost his bid. But as ever, family friends and editors jumped to the conclusion that Tilden's first task would be to appoint "renegade Republican" Adams to the State Department, an "impression," Adams huffed, "which has no justification whatever in any thing that has happened yet." Even so, Adams concluded his journal entry that evening by gazing ahead: "I am again my own master, ready to judge the future as I have done the past. My account with the Republican party has been settled in full."[47]

Within days, Tilden's victory became less clear, as Republicans uncovered evidence of rampant intimidation of black voters by white vigilantes in Louisiana, Florida, and South Carolina. In South Carolina, former Confederate General Martin Gary had published a thirty-nine-point agenda on how Democrats might capture the state, in which he suggested that the "necessities of the times require" that some South Carolina Republicans "should die." Although northern papers contained endless stories of southern atrocities, Adams thought only of the institutional problems that the confused election posed, worrying that the Constitution created "no arbiter to decide the doubt." Three days after the election, however, Adams found himself pressed into service as just such an arbiter. As the most famous northern Democrat aside from Tilden, Adams received a cable from New Orleans Democrats begging him to travel to Louisiana "to help witness" the state's recount. In response, Adams promised only that he would take the train to Manhattan to confer with party leaders. Brooks agreed to accompany him, but during the journey he spoke with several determined Democratic activists who made it clear that their agenda was to craft a "purely partisan report." That gave the elder Adams pause, and even when Tilden himself urged Adams to go, he begged off for reasons "partly personal and partly political." As they walked back to their hotel, Brooks encouraged his father to "take an active part in the political struggle," but Adams demurred. "Another year like this would kill me," he decided.[48]

Despite that, Adams was persuaded to return to Manhattan just before Christmas for a "sort of Council," as Charles Francis Sr. dubbed it, with Tilden and other northern Democrats. Congress was preparing legislation to create a fifteen-member electoral commission comprising equal numbers of senators, congressmen, and Supreme Court justices to settle the dispute. Once again, Adams failed to mention the rising tide of southern violence, complaining only of "the determination of republican leaders to force the election of Hayes." For Hayes himself, Adams insisted, he had "not a particle of ill will," for the alleged "fraud and bribery was in the election, not by him." Once again, however, Adams declined to travel south. Abby was again unwell, this time with sciatica, for which Manhattan doctors prescribed electrical treatments. A guilty Adams blamed their past "vagabond life" for her "growing illness."[49]

In mid-February 1877 the commission, by an 8 to 7 vote, awarded all three disputed states to Hayes, handing him a 185 to 184 electoral victory. Adams denounced the decision as a "victory of fraud and corruption," and he sat down to write a note of condolence to Tilden. "It is a source of gratification to me to think that I made the right choice in the late election," Adams promised, remarking that Hayes "must forever carry upon his brow the stamp of fraud." The letter earned Adams one final invitation to Manhattan to confer with Tilden. The defeated candidate, Adams noted, "said not a word derogatory" about Hayes, but Tilden was bitter in his belief that some of the commission members "had been paid" for their votes. Neither man, evidently, thought it curious that Mississippi, with its black majority population, had fallen to Democratic control, or that South Carolina, which was also predominantly black, should have ever been in dispute. Instead, Adams returned to Quincy praising Tilden as a "Statesman on a higher plane than I had given him credit for."[50]

With his father refusing to fight on, Brooks decided the time had come to enter the fray. That July, Brooks was asked by the state's Democratic leadership to stand for the legislature. Having just been badly beaten himself, and having watched as John Quincy lost yet again, Charles Francis Sr. counseled his son that "his chance of success [was] not strong, but I encouraged him to assent." The November 1877 tally was one of the closest in state history. Brooks lost by just two votes, and to deepen the wound, he discovered that two of his maternal uncles, Peter Chardon Brooks and Shepherd Brooks, had voted for his Republican opponent. A "good deal excited," Brooks stormed into his father's home, shouting about Abby's brothers and forcing a regretful Charles Francis Sr. to apologize to his election-night visitors.[51]

When Adams had warned Tilden the previous November that personal matters would keep him in the Northeast, he was alluding not only to Abby's sciatica but also to her worsening mood. The pain in her legs and back left her, as Henry concluded, "more depressed than she always was by the various exigencies of life." Abby also blamed their endless travels for her condition, and she let her husband know it. "We feel things so utterly unlike," she wrote her husband from New York City while receiving treatments. "Things that kill me you never think of twice." Unable to deal with Abby's discontent, Charles Francis Sr. typically remained in Quincy when she saw her Manhattan doctors, leaving it to Mary to accompany her mother. "Three times you have written you was coming and three times given it up," Abby complained. "Why write so if you do not intend it? It is nothing to you but the disappointment is more than I can bear." When her sons stayed away, that too earned her wrath. "It serves John and Charles right to suffer as they do," she

As the most contented Adams of her generation, the placid Mary Gardiner was expected to remain single and care for her parents in their old age. In early 1877, however, Mary, then thirty-two, informed her father that she had accepted an offer of marriage made by thirty-nine-year-old Dr. Henry Quincy. Charles Francis Sr. was as pleased as Abby was devastated. *Courtesy Massachusetts Historical Society.*

once remarked. On a later occasion, her two youngest sons joined her list: "What are Henry and Brooks to me?" When Clover's father, Robert Hooper, neglected to invite them to his house for Thanksgiving, he also suffered her fury.[52]

Abby evidently believed that Mary, at thirty-two long past the age of marriage, would remain her devoted caregiver. But in early 1877, Mary informed her parents that she had accepted an offer of marriage made by thirty-nine-year-old Dr. Henry Quincy, the son of family friend Edmund. Charles Francis Sr. was as pleased as Abby was devastated. "My daughter is no longer what she has been for so many years the joy of the household," he acknowledged. "It is well for her that it is so." The wedding took place in the old house on June 20. "At a little after one o'clock I brought my dear daughter into the long room where Henry Quincy the groom met her," Adams wrote in his diary that night. After the couple departed, Charles Francis Jr. and Minnie, understanding how upset Abby was, remained behind to "cheer us up." Evidently, Charles Francis

Jr. regarded his efforts as a failure, as that evening he described the wedding in a single line: "Marriage at 1 o'cl & not at all gay."[53]

FOLLOWING THEIR ILL-FATED HONEYMOON, HENRY AND CLOVER returned to Massachusetts, Clover to dote on her father and Henry to return to his classroom at Harvard. In addition to his labors as editor of the *North American Review*, Adams created a new course on American colonial history, inspiring him to consider writing a series of early American biographies and even a grand narrative of the nation's first years. Henry's Harvard salary made up only a small portion of the couple's income, and by 1877, Adams determined to resign his position and move back to Washington so that he might research and write full-time. The move meant Clover would see her father less, but Henry promised that each summer they would escape Washington's swampy weather for the cooler climes of Beverly Farms. The couple leased a "charming old ranch" from art dealer William Corcoran at 1501 H Street, one block from President's Square (renamed Lafayette Square the following year). After two winters there, they moved to a different Corcoran property, a yellow house at 1607 H Street, which allowed Henry to gaze across the square at the Executive Mansion. Suspecting that Henry intended to return to politics, Massachusetts journalist William Robinson, a longtime Sumner loyalist, fired a parting shot: "Mr. Henry Adams had too much of the English, and diplomatic and supercilious character which belongs to the New York *Nation* to allow him to become a useful public man."[54]

Relocating four hundred miles to the south failed to extricate Clover and Henry from Adams family dynamics. After Clover wrote her father that Henry felt "like a gentleman" for the first time in his life, the quip somehow reached Abby, who responded with rage. In a scathing letter to her daughter-in-law, Abby called Clover a "fool" and let her know that the family had never cared for her. "If we are fools we are," Clover sighed, but they were "too old to reform." Several months later, hoping to mend the breach, Charles Francis Sr. made plans to rendezvous with the two,

Henry's parents never much cared for their son's choice in a wife, and Charles Francis Sr. was already suffering from dementia when Clover photographed the pair as they sat on the porch of the Old House in Quincy. Although the front door is open, the image is hardly welcoming, and by shooting the Adamses just below eye level, Clover caught her in-laws, as always, gazing down at her with open disdain. *Courtesy Massachusetts Historical Society.*

only to miss them because of a miscommunication. "I have no feelings but affection and love" for Henry, the unhappy father confided to his journal. "I pity rather than dislike his wife. But henceforth I must regard her as a marplot," a meddler who ruins everything.[55]

The fourth generation also maintained its competitive quarrels. In 1879 Henry published his first major effort, *The Life of Albert Gallatin*, a biography of the Swiss-born treasury secretary and diplomat. A two-part, anonymous review in the *Nation* was brutal: "In its superficial make-up this volume falls a little short on being an outrage both on Albert Gallatin and on every one who wishes to know anything about him." The reviewer listed the numerous problems with the biography, which were in fact substantial. The "clumsy volume" of 697 pages failed to integrate lengthy letters and quotations into the text, and entire pages appeared in French with no translations. "Mr. Adams has sinned knowingly, and is accordingly entitled to no mercy," the reviewer insisted, especially as the author appeared to believe "that vivacity is trickery, and that there is some positive merit in dullness." Henry recognized the prose style immediately and wisely chose not to respond. Clover was less forgiving. She had already developed a profound dislike of Charles Francis Jr., and the cruel attack by one brother upon another only intensified her aversion.[56]

Despite the biography's poor sales, Henry moved ahead with his plans to write a grand narrative of the Jefferson and Madison administrations. Summering at Beverly Farms, Adams decided to peruse Harvard's vast collection of early American newspapers. "My request is that you would kindly allow me to consult the files *here*," Adams imperiously informed the college's archivist. The summers in Massachusetts also allowed Henry to watch over his parents, whom he feared were "older than they have a right to be." Henry was right to be concerned. Although only seventy-three, Charles Francis had fretted about his diminished capacity for most of the past decade. As early as 1873, Adams noted "the decided decline of my memory." One year later, he remarked that the "decay of my physical powers is not so decided as those of memory and calculation." When journalists speculated in 1877 that Tilden might offer him the State Department, Adams admitted that the "rapid decline of my memory" was good reason to "retire from all places of responsibility." Finally, on November 2, 1880, Adams caught the train into Boston to vote and then returned home to draft his final journal entry: "a proper place to terminate a Diary that has continued from the fourth of May in the year 1824 to this date fifty six years and six months."[57]

While researching what he intended to be a multivolume history of the early republic, Henry found time to write his first novel, a political satire called *Democracy*. Published anonymously by Henry Holt in 1880, the slim novel chronicled the political education of Madeleine Lee, a bored socialite courted by Senator Silas Ratcliffe of Peonia, Illinois. The novel allowed Adams to settle old scores, as his villain—the "Rat" and "Peon" were too heavy-handed to ignore—was clearly based on Blaine, while Lee was a combination of Adams's intelligence and Clover's sensitivity. Initially fascinated by Ratcliffe, Lee eventually retreats after discovering that he had taken part in election fraud during the Civil War, which he justifies on the grounds of preserving the Union. In an early hint of his rising anti-Semitism, Henry gave a Jewish financier the surname of Schneidekoupon—literally, "coupon clipper"—or one who lives on his investments. Although the authorship would not become known until after his death, the novel burned bridges for Henry, at least to his private satisfaction. "I bade politics good-bye when I published *Democracy*," he later told Brooks.[58]

Only a few close friends knew the author's identity, and the book's publication initiated a frenzy of speculation among Washington insiders. Blaine suspected the culprit to be Clarence King, an author and geologist and one of the few of Henry's friends to know the truth. When the senator encountered King at a party, he brusquely stomped away. Charles Francis Jr., not privy to the secret, published a lukewarm review in the *Nation*, saying: "The work is crude, with a half-educated touch which is always provokingly near being very good." Because its protagonist was a bright woman, some speculation settled on Mary Loring, the daughter of a retired Boston judge, and even on Clover. When one of Clover's aunts suggested that her niece was the author, Henry was furious. "My wife never wrote for publication in her life and could not write if she tried," he snapped. Aware of her husband's views that women were "utterly unconscious of the pathetic impossibility of improving those poor little hard, thin, wiry, one-stringed instruments which they call their minds," Clover dutifully agreed that her aunt was being foolish.[59]

Henry's low estimation of women's intellectual abilities began to change in 1882, however, after he met Elizabeth Sherman Cameron, known to her friends as Lizzie. The daughter of bankrupt judge Charles Sherman, Lizzie had fallen in love with a young New York attorney. But her uncles, Senator John Sherman and General William T. Sherman, were so concerned about their brother's finances that they arranged for her to marry Pennsylvania Senator and widower J. Donald Cameron, twenty-four years her senior. Lizzie was never happy with the match and until the eve of her wedding begged her uncles to release her from the arrangement. Henry always had an eye for female beauty, once remarking to Charles Gaskell that he made "it a rule to be friends with all the

The second wife of Pennsylvania Senator J. Donald Cameron, twenty-four years her senior, Elizabeth "Lizzie" Sherman Cameron dazzled Henry Adams from the moment they met in 1882. After Clover's death, Lizzie hinted that she was leaving her hard-drinking husband and boarding a steamer for France. But their 1897 rendezvous proved a disappointment to them both. "Above all," Lizzie wrote, "I cannot say anything of all that I feel to you." *Courtesy Library of Congress.*

prettiest girls." Washington society praised Lizzie as a celebrated beauty, with one relative insisting that she made "most women look like 35 cents" by comparison. Both Clover and Henry promptly took a fancy to Lizzie, although Clover, more than a decade older, was painfully aware of their differences in appearance, as well as with Henry's infatuation with her. However, none in their circle cared for the senator, and when the couple sailed to Europe in 1883, Henry refused to provide them with letters of introduction, telling his old friend John Hay that he could not "saddle" his friends with Cameron, whom he thought a "lump of clay."[60]

Not surprisingly, Lizzie appears as a character in Henry's second novel, *Esther*, published in 1884 under the name of Frances Compton Snow. This time, Adams demanded of a dubious Henry Holt that it be published without fanfare or advertisement so that it might fail or succeed on its own merits. Predictably, the novel sank like a stone. Its single review, in the little-read *Athenaeum*, was dismissive. "Like many another American novels," the reviewer observed, it was both "clever and inconclusive." Snow's "chief object," the unsuspicious critic noted, was "to show that she is up to the mark in art, science, religion, agnosticism, and society." The "study (for it can hardly be called a story) is wanting in human interest."[61]

Both Clover and Lizzie knew that Henry was the author, and both recognized themselves in the novel. Esther, named after the Esther Dudley who appeared in Nathaniel Hawthorne's *Twice Told Tales*, was clearly modeled on Clover. Here Clover, an aspiring photographer, became Esther, an untalented painter and a "second-rate amateur." Her father was drawn as a Mr. Dudley, an unwell widower who "amused the rest of his life by spoiling" his only child, a daughter. The young, desirable Catherine Brooke was clearly Lizzie, whose "innocent eagerness to submit was charming." But when describing Esther, Henry fell back on the description of Clover he had once provided for Gaskell. "In the first place she has a bad figure," one character explains. "She is too slight, too thin; she looks fragile, willowy, as the cheap novels call it, as though you could break her in halves like a switch." Lizzie was undoubtedly flattered by her fictional portrait, but for a woman as sensitive as Clover, and one already so displeased about her long "Hooper nose" that she refused to have her portrait painted, the novel surely stung. Married into a family with generations of Harvard degrees, Clover could scarcely miss references to Esther's lack of brilliance. "She picks up all she knows without an effort and knows nothing well," an older painter remarks of Esther. "Her mind is as irregular as her face."[62]

Otherwise, Henry continued to pore over yellowing newspapers and visit foreign archives in search of critical documents. In early 1885, interested in a panel on "Materials for American History in Foreign Archives," Henry traveled to Saratoga Springs, New York, to attend the second annual meeting of the American Historical Association. Rather to his dismay, as Henry fancied himself the historian in the family, he discovered his brother Charles Francis in attendance, with Brooks promising to appear at the next year's conference. Worse yet, the organization permitted Lucy Maynard Salmon, a professor at Vassar College, to appear on the program, prompting Henry to grouse that the presence of "C. F. Adams was rather disastrous to history" and that Salmon's talk veered into "cemetery theory & female story-telling."[63]

However, Henry was kind enough to take Brooks into his home in 1881, when the thirty-three-year-old attorney suffered a mental breakdown. Having lost his election to the legislature and then failing to persuade a young woman of his acquaintance to accept his proposals of marriage, Brooks fell into despair. Like his brothers, Brooks noticed the decline of his father's intellectual powers, and as he remained in Boston while Charles Francis Jr. traveled on business and John Quincy mourned the death of his children, it fell to Brooks to act as caretaker. Once nearly as affable as John Quincy, Brooks quickly turned combative and melancholy, repeatedly telling the family that he simply wished to die. Together with the understanding Clover, Henry begged his brother to come to Washington for an extended visit. Henry admitted that he and Clover felt "surrounded by a hospital of broken-down family and friends," but they patiently nursed Brooks back to emotional and physical health. Initially unable to walk half a mile or even focus on a single page in a book, Brooks took long walks with his brother and listened in the evenings as Clover read aloud. Stockier than his brother, if not much taller, Brooks was pleased to discover that the diminutive Clover had removed several inches from the legs of her chairs. After several months, Henry took Brooks aside and urged him to find a purpose in life: "Get well—you will get well—and then I shall expect great things of you, for you have broken down through idleness."[64]

Upon returning north, Brooks marched into the offices of the floundering *Boston Daily Globe* and volunteered his services as an essayist. The editor agreed, and Brooks began to churn out essays on the Supreme Court, currency issues, and "Oppressive Taxation of the Poor." Longer essays appeared in the *Atlantic Monthly*, one of which grew into his first book, *The Emancipation of Massachusetts*. Brooks's blunt debunking of the Puritan myths that most Massachusetts Protestants held dear was met with mixed reviews. One journalist praised the five-hundred-page volume, which stretched through the Revolution, as evidence that the "Adams family seems to be holding its own, if not improving somewhat, in the way of intellectual ability." Another was pleased by Adams's efforts to redress old scholarly imbalances, applauding his depiction of ancestor Samuel Adams as "severely just." More critical reviewers observed that Brooks was a "lawyer by profession" who failed to "have learnt the difference between drawing an indictment and writing a history." As always, the harshest detractor of an Adams was another Adams. Charles Francis Jr. derided the book, writing in his diary that it was "poor stuff" produced by a "writer not to the manor born."[65]

Despite finding his calling, Brooks remained abrasive and argumentative, and his conversation grew ever more profane, even in polite society. Increasingly, Brooks's essays suggested that humans were mere pawns driven by larger scientific and economic forces, a theory rejected by his businessman brother. As Charles Francis Jr. complained to his diary in 1886, "Brooks here, parading more Brooks than would seem possible." Even so, in August of 1889, Brooks fell in love. The object of his affection was thirty-six-year-old Evelyn Davis, the daughter of an admiral and the sister of the wife of State Assemblyman Henry Cabot Lodge, one of Henry's former Harvard students. Brooks, now forty-one, proposed an immediate marriage, and much to his family's surprise, Evelyn, known to her friends as Daisy, agreed. The wedding took place in three weeks' time, so quickly that Henry, who was in Canada on a research trip, was unable to attend. As the brother whom Brooks most admired, Henry apologized for his absence but assured a friend that he "strongly approved the rapidity" of the wedding. "I want to secure my new sister before she has time to get tired of me."[66]

THE PLACID DAISY PROVED TO BE ONE OF THE FEW PEOPLE WHO could tolerate Brooks's moods, but the union produced no children. However, his brother Charles Francis remained determined to father a son to carry on the family name. In 1873, following the birth of daughters Mary Ogden and Louisa Catherine, Minnie had again become pregnant. "Another daughter was born to me at 6:50 this morning," a dismayed Charles

Francis told his diary on December 3. "I didn't swear and shan't, but my disappointment is bitter." Minnie was "comfortable," so Adams left for his office to "drown [his] disappointment in work." Finally, in July 1875 a very pregnant Minnie sent Charles Francis racing for the doctor and "cleared the house for action." Adams "did not dare go home for fear of hearing of 'another' daughter," so he "set my teeth" and went for a long walk, "feeling sick." As he returned, Adams was met by Minnie's sister, who announced the birth of "twins—boys! Oh! the relief—it completely swamped my surprise." The proud father and relieved mother named the boys John and Henry II.[67]

Adams was often on the road, however, especially in the West. He continued to serve on the state railway commission, a post he had held since 1869, but in 1876 he became president of the Kansas City Stock Yards Company, a site chosen for the "reception, care, sale, and delivery" of livestock to New England. Under his guidance, the company purchased forty-two additional acres of land for loading docks, exchange buildings, company offices, and even a billiard hall and barbershop. Having already achieved considerable affluence, in 1879, at the age of forty-four, Adams resigned from the railroad commission to better devote his time to increasing his wealth. Without giving up his presidency of the stockyards, he took on the chairmanship of the Board of Arbitration of the Trunk Line Railroads, a position that required considerable tact and skills as a negotiator. As Adams himself later admitted, "I was not the man to do it."[68]

Three years later, in 1882, Charles Francis was invited to serve on the board of the Union Pacific Railroad. Then arrived the opportunity of a lifetime. Congress was unhappy with the management of company president Sidney Dillon, for the Union Pacific had set up the Crédit Mobilier of America, a holding company that resulted in a scandal of false invoices and insider trading. After Congress requested that Adams visit the company office in Omaha to audit its books, which were, he discovered, "in a shocking bad way," Dillon announced his retirement in the spring of 1884. Congress threatened to place the railroad in receivership unless Adams consented to replace Dillon. Stockholders cheered the move, with a Los Angeles newspaper reporting that Adams was "noted

Painted by portraitist Francis Millet in 1876, the same year that he captured Minnie on canvas, this image depicts a rising robber baron and public intellectual: Charles Francis Adams Jr. Two years before, Adams had been tapped to serve as president of the Massachusetts Historical Society, and within the decade he would rise to take control of the Union Pacific Railroad. *Courtesy National Park Service.*

for the skill and ability with which he acquits himself." But despite the vast boost in income, Adams regretted being away so often from his boys. Remembering the impact that parental absences had wrought on earlier generations of his family, Adams admitted that he was "sacrificing things worth incomparably more." He was also aware that in a family of reformers, he had become a robber baron, if an ethical one, not dissimilar to the wealthy business-minded Whigs his father had railed against in his younger days.[69]

Certainly, Adams's rise to wealth and influence only served to reinforce his views that only the best men should govern. In a series of speeches and essays, Adams condemned the 1887 Interstate Commerce Act, which required railroad rates to be "reasonable and just," on the grounds that most voters lacked any knowledge "on which railroad discussion can be based." The working class, he suspected, could never be improved: "The essence of a proletariat is to seek the political control of a community through a close combination of vice, ignorance, and brute force, wholly inaccessible to reason." Although his railroad employed Chinese laborers, he hoped that they would never be allowed to vote, as they were neither Christian "nor in any way akin to us [or] intellectually approachable by us." Universal male suffrage, in short, meant a "European, and especially a Celtic proletariat on the Atlantic coast, an African proletariat on the shores of the Gulf, and a Chinese proletariat on the Pacific."[70]

IN 1884, THE SAME YEAR THAT CHARLES FRANCIS TOOK CONTROL of the Union Pacific, two momentous events took place in the lives of Henry and Clover, although the former did not much notice the first at the time. Clover had become an accomplished photographer, taking images of herself, Henry, her father, and, rather against their will, her in-laws. One that proved especially good was that of historian George Bancroft. John Hay was so impressed by it that he recommended it to his friend Richard Gilder, the editor of *Century* magazine, to accompany a possible feature on the aged scholar. Clover assured her father that she "was amused" by Gilder's offer, and Gilder also suggested that Henry might write the piece on Bancroft. In fact, Clover was flattered to be asked by the respected editor. However, Henry chose to speak for his wife when he explained to Hay that "we have declined Mr. Gilder's pleasing offer." Adams rarely received compensation for his scholarship, and in fact he was publishing his history of the early republic at a loss. Accepting recompense for one's work was simply not something Brahmins did. Photography was fine for his wife as a hobby, but not as a profession that would attract a popular audience.[71]

The second event occurred several months later, when in March 1885 seventy-five-year-old Robert Hooper was stricken with angina pectoris. Henry had predicted this crisis in *Esther*, but not enough to be prepared for Clover's response. Clover raced to her father's winter home in Cambridge, but over the next months Henry visited only twice, in part because his own parents' health distressed him so. "My poor father is a complete wreck, and my mother almost a cripple," he wrote to a friend from his Washington home, "while, only within a few weeks my wife's father has broken down" and was in "his last moments." Hooper lost consciousness and died on April 13, never having lost his "humor and courage," Clover remarked. The family buried him in the Mount Auburn Cemetery in Cambridge beside his wife, Ellen, who had died thirty-seven years before.[72]

Clover returned to Henry and Washington, where they were building a much larger house adjacent to one being constructed by Hay. But Clover confided to Henry that she was "no longer alive" and doubted she would recover. She even asked Henry his opinions on the morality of suicide, and having considered it himself years before, Henry clumsily responded that her right to do so was probably as good as his. On Sunday morning, December 6, Henry left the house to see his dentist about a painful toothache. Sundays were always Clover's opportunity to write to her father, so instead she addressed her missive to her sister Ellen. "If I had only one single point of character or goodness," she confessed, "I would stand on that and grow back to life." When Henry returned home, he found Clover's body sprawled on a rug near an upstairs fireplace. She had swallowed potassium cyanide, which she used to develop her photographs; most likely, the poison, which cut off her ability to process oxygen, took thirty minutes to perform its task.[73]

Although the two brothers had grown distant in recent years, Henry's first thought was to cable Charles Francis, and then Edward Hooper and Ellen Gurney. Charles Francis was in Boston on business, but the telegram found him at six that evening, and he caught the eleven o'clock train for Washington. John Quincy and his son George reached Washington that Tuesday. Henry appeared "as steady and sweet and thoughtful of us as possible," Ellen thought, and for once, Charles Francis appeared contrite over his treatment of his sister-in-law. "Me," he confessed to his diary, "she never liked; nor can I blame her much for that—I trod all over her, offending her in every way." Clover was buried on Wednesday in Rock Creek Cemetery below St. Paul's Church. Because a churchyard was hallowed ground and suicide considered a sin, Henry was pleased that Unitarian minister Edward Hull accepted his story of heart failure. Charles Francis, however, ever a stickler for proper ritual, thought it inappropriate that Clover was buried in a wicker basket, a Hooper family tradition. In later years, as he approached his own mortality, Charles Francis impressed upon his daughters the necessity of a solid wood coffin.[74]

Henry sent a "little trinket" that had belonged to Clover to Lizzie Cameron, asking her to "sometimes wear it." Otherwise, he went into seclusion, begging old friends to respect his grief and privacy. The Washington press mourned her loss, memorializing the forty-two-year-old Clover as a "woman of most cordial and charming manners, a brilliant and original conversationalist." Initial stories reported that she "had been an invalid for some time" and that the "cause of death was paralysis of the heart." On December 9, however, the *Washington Critic* ran a bold-faced head: "Was It a Case of Suicide?" One day later, the Washington *National Republican* chimed in, wondering whether the death was a "sad case of accident or mental aberration." Clover "intended to take her own life," another journalist reported. "She came to her death through an overdose of potassium, administered by herself." Tragically, only one year later, Clover's brother-in-law Ephraim Gurney unexpectedly passed away. Her sister Ellen, unable to accept the death of three beloved family members within twelve months, lost her reason. Institutionalized for her health, Ellen escaped her sickroom one evening and stepped in front of a freight train.[75]

Although he yet survived, Charles Francis Sr. was unaware of his son's pain. Since 1882, an attendant had resided with him, taking the seventy-nine-year-old diplomat for "gentle outdoor exercise," one editor reported, or a "drive in the city or [in] Quincy." Journalists emphasized that while Adams remained vigorous, his "gradual intellectual decay" was such that since 1884, the only member of his family he recognized was "his estimable wife." The end came at 1:57 in the morning of Sunday, November 21, 1886. Henry, who had fled to the far ends of the globe in hopes of escaping his sadness, was in Japan when warned by his brothers to hasten home. Charles Francis, John Quincy, Mary, and Brooks were all present. "On the whole everything was as little painful as could be expected," Henry remarked. Abby, "though old and broken, has got through the

Following Clover's suicide, Henry commissioned sculptor Augustus Saint-Gaudens and architect Stanford White to create a memorial to mark her grave in Washington's Rock Creek Cemetery. Together with Saint-Gaudens's Robert Gould Shaw Memorial on the Boston Common, this haunting tribute to Clover is regarded as one of his most famous sculptures. After Henry's death in 1918, he was also interred beneath this monument, which bears no names. *Photo by author.*

shock of my father's death as well as was rationally possible," he told a friend. "The death was of course not a surprise." Journalists lamented not only his passing but also the fact that he never held the presidency. "How fast are we being robbed of our shining lights by the hand of time," one editor mourned.[76]

Charles Francis was buried in Mount Wollaston Cemetery in Quincy, near the graves of his son John Quincy's children. His estate of $1,250,000 was dispersed among the family, except for $10,000 bequeathed to the Adams Temple and School Fund, a trust for educational purposes created by his grandfather John Adams. But John Quincy, responsible for his parents' finances, was reluctant to execute the will, as it marked a final farewell he was not yet prepared to make. A still-grieving Henry was less sympathetic. "For God's sake let it be paid," Henry snapped.[77]

After that, Abby, Charles Francis's often-unhappy companion of fifty-eight years, declined rapidly. Her "infirmities" became "so great as to require the constant presence" of one of her children, Henry explained, and because he was the only one unburdened by career or family—his sister Mary had given birth to two daughters in 1885 and 1888, Dorothy Quincy and Elinor Quincy—it fell to him to "be the one in residence." On June 2, 1889, Henry found his mother comatose and rallied his brothers. "At about 10 o'cl in the evening of to-day my mother ceased breathing," Charles Francis wrote late that night. "She had not been conscious since Sunday." As was typical, journalists described the eighty-one-year-old Abby as either the surviving widow of the celebrated diplomat or the "mother of Hon. Charles Francis Adams, president of the Union Pacific." Fanny, John Quincy's wife, used the occasion to demand his final retirement from public life, as he too had aged dramatically since the death of his children. For the past twenty years, John Quincy had moderated the Quincy town meeting, but to please Fanny he abandoned his farm for the Glades, a beach resort property in Minot, Massachusetts, that he had purchased with Charles Francis in 1880. "Apparently I am to be the last of the family to occupy this house [in Quincy] which has been our retreat in all times of trouble for just one hundred years," Henry told Lizzie Cameron. "I suppose if two presidents could come back here to eat out their hearts in disappointment and disgust, one of their unknown descendants can bore himself for a single season to close up the family den."[78]

The death of his parents, perhaps even more so than the suicide of his wife, left Henry unusually introspective. "My mother's death severs, I think, the last tie that binds me to my old life," he confessed to a friend. Although he had been Abby's favorite son, she had rarely been happy, and in old age her "life became excessively burdensome to her, and enjoyment of what she had was impossible." Regrettably, Henry suspected that he had "inherited her disposition, for I could not see anything in life worth having." But for Henry, and perhaps for his brothers as well, Charles Francis Sr. remained an "unsolved problem." Their father, Henry observed to Charles Francis Jr., was a most "singular man," one who never appeared conscious "of the world being different from what he wanted it to be." Both his grandfather's and his own generation, he believed, were marked by the "trait of restlessness," while their father "never much cared for change." But like all Adamses, Henry concluded, Charles Francis Sr. could never truly decide whether he coveted national fame and office or simply to be left alone at home, "polishing his coins." Usually so astute at discerning the strengths and weaknesses in others, Henry thought his father "so complete, as far as he went, that I shall never understand why he went no farther." In being baffled by that, Henry was hardly alone.[79]

EPILOGUE:
"NOT ONE FIGURE THAT WILL BE REMEMBERED"

The Fall of the House of Adams

C HARLES FRANCIS SR. REJECTED THE GILDED AGE AND THE PO-
litical modernity it represented, not merely because of its scandals
and corruption but also because he remained wedded to the political culture of his grandfather's day. If Adams could never come to terms with—
even in the privacy of his journal—whether he wished to serve his country
as the third President Adams or, as a bemused Henry remarked, live quietly as a private man with his coins and books, it was because he could
not understand a political system that did not automatically rally behind
its best men. As an intellectual who had helped to forge two antislavery
parties; earned election to his state's House and Senate; was then sent to
Washington, where as a young congressman he took a hand in trying
to achieve a compromise to heal his nation's divisions; and then almost
single-handedly kept Britain from intervening in the Civil War, Adams
was correct in thinking himself uniquely prepared to hold the republic's

highest office—as qualified as, if not perhaps more than, his illustrious ancestors. But Adams confused crass deal making and politicking with a simple, honest expression of a willingness to serve, and that misperception likely cost him the prize.

By comparison, his children were lost in modern America not so much because they rejected its political values—certainly Charles Francis Jr. embraced the pursuit of wealth and influence—but because they so disliked many of the men and the assertive women who peopled the postwar nation. Although the family had long exhibited patrician attitudes toward the less-educated, the foreign-born (those who were not Protestants), and the less-fortunate, earlier generations had usually set those biases aside as they crusaded to make their country live up to its finest ideals. Even as a young reformer, Charles Francis Sr. had been keenly aware of race and never indicated the smallest desire to get to know the black men with whom he often shared the Boston or Buffalo stage. Yet neither did he reveal the sort of contempt for those he regarded as his social inferiors that became so tragically common among his sons.

Clover, for instance, understood her husband's dim views of her intellectual gifts and those of most women, but those opinions were not unique to Henry. In many families, the sons and grandsons of brilliant, determined women grew up to be feminists. As a congressman, John Quincy, raised by a Revolutionary mother, regarded the right of petition—which implied citizenship—a constitutional prerogative of all Americans regardless of gender. Yet John Quincy II, the grandson of a woman who had braved the Russian frontier in wartime, was so appalled by the notion of women's suffrage that he thought it necessary to draft a letter to the *New York Times* explaining why women should remain in their separate, domestic sphere. The desire of women to vote contravened the "division of activities and functions," he lectured, that lay "at the foundations of society." Brooks agreed, arguing that "the family system [was] the woman rather than that of the man." But with their demands for political rights, "the woman has renounced her job, she is ashamed of her sex."[1]

John Quincy's disdain for women's abilities took a personal turn with the Panic of 1893, the worst depression yet in US history. Brooks, who had moved into the old house in Quincy, had invested heavily in western land, and Charles Francis Jr.'s business losses were so great that he had to borrow $900,000 from a wealthy friend he wrongly thought solvent. (The friend, Frederick Ames, died of apoplexy the following year.) The Crowninshields still possessed a vast fortune, and Fanny offered to assist her husband, who remained in charge of the family's trust, but John Quincy refused. Charles Francis was infuriated over his brother's stubbornness, complaining to his wife, Minnie, that had John Quincy accepted his wife's money, "we should have gone through the ordeal in excellent shape—but as it was I had to carry him, lug him along by sheer force."[2]

John Quincy had never ceased to mourn the death of his children, and the financial blow crushed his remaining will to survive. Charles Francis admitted that his eldest brother's "helplessness of condition alarms me more and more," and although John Quincy wished to be left alone, the family urged Fanny to take him abroad, hoping that foreign sights might somehow heal his mind and spirit. In April 1894, while in Britain on business, Charles Francis checked in on Fanny and John Quincy and found him a "hopeless wreck." Several months later, the travelers returned to Quincy, but in early August John Quincy suffered a mild stroke. One week later, at 5:30 A.M. on August 14, John Quincy died after a second and more serious stroke. Only sixty, he had outlived his mother by just five years. "It was a thunderbolt," Charles Francis wrote when word of his brother's passing reached London. "I never knew life without John." Given John Quincy's condition, however, it surely came as no shock. More candid was Charles Francis's assessment of their relationship: "Early in life he dominated me, later, I dominated him."[3]

"The deceased leaves a widow and three sons," one newspaper reported. "There is also a daughter, Abigail, who is about fifteen years of age." George Casper, the eldest son, was to die in 1900 at the age of thirty-seven. The coach of Harvard's football team, George inherited the family disease that carried off his alcoholic great-uncle George. John Quincy's widow, Fanny, died in May 1911, by which time most editors had forgotten about her husband and instead eulogized her as the daughter-in-law of Charles Francis Sr., "minister to Great Britain." However, Charles Francis III enjoyed a long life and a distinguished career. His father had been dead only two years when he was elected Quincy's mayor, and after years of banking and running the New Haven and Hartford Railroad, Adams, a Republican, served as secretary of the navy under Herbert Hoover. He died in 1954 at the age of eighty-seven; his younger brother, Arthur, died in 1949, while his sister Abigail lived on until 1974, dying at the age of ninety-four.[4]

The Panic of 1893 had a different impact on Henry, if an equally unfortunate one. For many New England patricians, one of the common complaints about the Gilded Age was that crude "new-money" financiers had supplanted respected "old-money" families such as the Adamses, whose incomes often originated in land. After Henry also lost money in the shares he held with the Baring Brothers, a British merchant bank, he developed a profound distaste for unbridled wealth. That was common enough with those hurt by the depression, but in his case, it brought Henry's simmering anti-Semitism to the fore, as he came to regard "bankers" and "Jews" as synonymous terms. As early as 1880, when British Prime Minister Benjamin Disraeli, who was born Jewish but raised Anglican, fell from power, Henry was delighted: "That Jew bagman with his quack medicines has been ordered off the premises." Anti-Semitism also ran in Clover's family. One night, as her brother Edward tucked his daughters into bed, one of the girls thought to pray that "everybody will sleep well, *except the Jews*." Edward considered that charming, as his daughter undoubtedly reflected his sentiments. But Henry's irrational hatred rapidly escalated after the panic. British banks, he warned former Assistant Secretary of State John Hay in 1895, were "almost wholly in Jew hands, and a new set of rich Jews has inundated" the affluent Mayfair district of London. With complete sincerity, Henry believed that "the Jew question is really the most serious of our problems," as it was "Capitalist Methods run to their logical extreme." One year later, when discussing the ongoing debate over the gold standard, Adams insisted that America's foreign debt was "all practically Jew money." In the wake of the 1893 crash, he feared, any "investment is sheer gambling. We are all in the hands of the Jews. They can do whatever they please with our [traditional cultural] values."[5]

Charles Francis Jr.'s intolerance followed a more predictable if no less tragic path. Although long critical of Reconstruction and ever given to the use of racial slurs, Adams had kept his theories of African American abilities private, sharing them only with his brothers. But in the last decade of the century, as Jim Crow segregation swept across much of the nation, Adams's racialist views became public. In part, Adams was "emancipated," as he put it, from his business responsibilities when in 1890 financier Jay Gould engineered a hostile takeover of the Union Pacific, forcing him into retirement at the age of fifty-five. Adams later claimed that the position had "become a prison house," and while he "loathed it," his desire for wealth had overruled other considerations. Now he had leisure to return to writing, his "proper vocation." He began a two-volume biography of family friend Richard Henry Dana, who had died eight years before, and agreed to write a brief biography of his father for Houghton Mifflin's American Statesmen series. His reflections on the past, unfortunately, drew him back to the issues of race and slavery that had propelled Dana and his own father into prominence.[6]

After completing the Dana manuscript, Adams decided to escape the Boston winter and take a quick vacation in Cuba with Edwin Atkins, an old business associate who owned land there. Slavery had been abolished in Cuba only in 1886, just four years earlier. The slave quarters reminded Adams of his wartime service in the South, but as most of the liberated bondpersons he encountered in Cuba had been born in Africa, he instinctively disliked them even more than he had his African American troopers. "They had pure negro features," he assured Minnie, and were "most unnaturally ugly." He conceded that "many of them were old, rheumatic and broken" by years of labor, but that was his sole empathetic moment. The remainder of his comments home to his wife spoke of meeting a "hideous old African woman" who was "squatting about all the while like a deformed monkey." His ruminations on race grew into an address to the American Historical Association, published in 1902 in its prestigious *Review*. Southern and Caribbean poverty, he lectured, was not simply the inevitable result of unfree labor but was also caused by the inherent inferiority of laborers of African descent. No "so-called inferior race or community has been elevated in its character, or made self-sustaining and self-governing, or even put on the way to that result through a condition of dependency or tutelage." In short, governmental efforts to assist people of color or bring them into political society were biologically untenable.[7]

Adams shared the concerns of other anti-imperialist racists that the nation's expansionism might result in voting rights for people even less qualified, in his estimation, than blacks in Alabama and Mississippi. In a 1906 essay for *Century* magazine, Adams built on his earlier lecture to suggest that African Americans could not elevate themselves and had to be lifted by others. Should they prove incapable of even that, then they had to be led by their superior white neighbors, and having lived in the South, Adams added, none were yet prepared for the ballot. "The work done by those who were in political control at the close of our Civil War was done in utter ignorance of ethnological law and total disregard of unalterable fact," he insisted. Not surprisingly, Adams's essays were as welcomed by white Southerners as John Quincy II's lectures had been years before. As William Copeland, publisher of the Richmond *Times-Dispatch*, editorialized, "I do not know of a man in the United States who is doing so much good as he." Charles Dodd, a historian at Virginia's Randolph-Macon College, peppered Adams with letters praising his good sense and scientific understanding of race.[8]

As bad as this was, so far Adams had only said aloud what most northern Democrats had long believed. But the contrarian in Charles Francis soon prompted him to move beyond condemning black southerners to praising white ones, including the Confederates he had once faced in the field. In 1902 Adams published a collection of essays, including his *American Historical Review* piece, under the title *Lee at Appomattox and Other Papers*. First delivered in Worcester, Massachusetts, Adams's essay on Lee was long on quotations if short on documentation and fell into the emerging Lost Cause mythology that Lee was a reluctant secessionist and an antislavery Virginian who wished only to heal the nation's wounds after 1865. The essay attracted considerable attention, and not just in the South. The University of Chicago invited Adams to speak on Lee, and he was pleased to accept, not only assuring his audience that the late Confederate general was "the highest type of man" but also advocating the "erection of a statue to him at Washington."[9]

That caught the attention of influential Virginians. In late 1906, President George Denny of Washington and Lee University invited Adams to come south as the keynote speaker in the next January's celebrations of Lee's centennial. The trip marked Charles Francis's first tour of Virginia since 1865, and he was displeased to see that it still bore the scars of war. It was, he sighed, "the same, old nigger-ridden Virginia, with its tumbled-down houses, its ragged rail fences, and red dirt roads." But upon reaching the university, his reception was "in every way satisfactory," and he flattered himself that the finished oration, published later that year, was "in the forefront of anything I may have done." In his lengthy speech, Adams claimed that Lee's Army of Northern Virginia succumbed only "to exhaustion, [and] to the end they were not overthrown in fight." That was a curious enough comment for a veteran of Gettysburg, but Adams only added to his historically dubious argument by turning on his father's generation and insisting that white southerners were essentially the victims of a "missile from a woman's hand," Harriet Beecher Stowe's "female and sentimental" depiction of slavery in her novel *Uncle Tom's Cabin*. The foolish "African-and-brother doctrines" of the "Uncle Tom period," he shouted, promoted the "sheerest of delusions" during the Reconstruction era. As he concluded, the all-white audience rose in applause, with many standing in line to shake his hand. It was gratifying, Adams thought, to have pleased "so many good people—so simple, straightforward, and genuine."[10]

The publication of *Lee's Centennial* in pamphlet form later that year brought Adams increased fame in some quarters, infamy in others. Mary Custis Lee, the general's aged, unmarried daughter, wrote that people were praising Charles Francis as one of the "greatest men" in America. Lyon Tyler, the president of the College of William and Mary and one of President John Tyler's fifteen white children, wrote to Adams that were the matter "left to the South, the Adams family would have the honor of having another representative in the President's Chair." As usual, Henry dissented, insisting that "poor dear old [General] Winfield Scott," who had remained loyal to the Union, was to his mind "the only respectable Virginian." Black journalists, together with enough northern Republicans to remind Adams that not all northern whites shared his prejudices, were far more critical. The *Cleveland Gazette* thought it especially sad that a "Massachusetts man" and a "descendant of the noted family of Adams" should seek the adulation of those whites who "undervalue and degrade the Afro-Americans." Veterans' organizations took umbrage with Adams's theory "that Jeff Davis was not whipped." The speeches also cast renewed attention on Adams's earlier essays on black inferiority. The Chicago *Broad Axe* invited Adams to observe the economic and social successes of the thousands of black Canadians "whose ancestors settled there over a century ago" and prospered, free of American antipathy. Yet another newspaper compared Adams to the race-baiting Senator Benjamin Tillman of South Carolina, while the aptly named Indianapolis *Freeman* wondered if Adams truly wished to "allow his name to rest in history where the Negro press has placed it" following the publication of his "witless theories that the Negro is incapable of progress."[11]

Charles Francis was far from contrite, of course. "Nothing really tells like being contemptuous," he advised Henry. But if Henry was unimpressed by his brother's newfound fondness for all things Confederate, he was even more appalled by Charles Francis's 1900 biography of their father. Henry disliked what he regarded as the brevity of the volume, insisting that such brief volumes "belittle the victim and the assassin equally," although at 426 pages, it was one of the longer books in publisher Houghton Mifflin's American Statesmen series. His central grievance, however, was he believed that his brother's general aversion to their father's personality hampered his assessment of his career. In reality, Charles Francis crafted a traditional public man study that said almost nothing about the elder Adams's private life or character, but Henry desired something more laudatory. "I've been trying to read my brother Charles' Life of our father, and it makes me sick," he confessed to Lizzie Cameron. He attempted to read the biography as if the subject was not his father. "I cannot, and should not do so," he concluded. The characters described in the book were "like bad photographs and distorted perspectives." At least Henry took some solace in the fact that he himself had not attempted the biography. "I did not assassinate my father."[12]

Knowing that Charles Francis little cared about his opinions, Henry never told his brother of his low estimation of the work. But younger brother Brooks idolized Henry, whose deeply researched and elegantly crafted studies of the administrations of Jefferson and Madison began to appear in 1899 and grew to encompass nine volumes. When Brooks ventured to follow Charles Francis's lead and write a biography of their grandfather, he foolishly sent the manuscript to Henry for his judgment. Upon its receipt, Henry assured Brooks that given his knowledge of the subject, "your vigorous thought, and your energetic style, you cannot fail to make a great book." Two weeks later, however, Henry returned eighty-one legal-size pages of suggestions for revision. If Henry judged Charles Francis's depiction of their father as too harsh, he regarded Brooks's interpretation as far too kind. "He had a nasty temper," and his entire public career, Henry had come to suspect, "shows that he loathed and hated America." Henry even faulted his grandfather for not sufficiently appreciating art. "I do not remember that he ever mentions interest in architecture, sculpture or painting." Henry urged his brother to reframe the biography and "put it all into some harmonious shape." Most of all, Henry thought their grandfather's life story should have a purpose: "No one with the intelligence of an average monkey will try to tell a story without leading up to its point." In sum, Brooks's "picture of our wonderful grandpapa is a psychological nightmare to his degenerate and decadent grandson." Brooks was badly wounded by Henry's remarks, especially as he had come to identify his own character with that of their grandfather. Rather than revise, Brooks simply boxed up the manuscript, never to be published.[13]

Instead, Brooks retreated into the distant past with *The Law of Civilization and Decay: An Essay on History*. Beginning with the Romans, Brooks attempted to prove that according to "scientific principles," every society passed through a cycle in which centralization ended with political degeneration. Drawing exclusively from secondary studies, Adams made no effort to play the objective historian; his data and evidence existed to support preexisting conclusions, not to inform his analysis. In writing about the English Reformation, for example, Brooks suggested that foreign dispatches best explained events in London because "the opinions of Englishmen are of no great value." *America's Economic Supremacy* and *The New Empire* quickly followed. As with his first effort, the volumes spanned vast periods of time and enormous portions of the globe. In some ways, while based on the model proposed in his first book, *The New Empire* broke important new ground by demonstrating how shifting trade routes had led to the rise and fall of ancient cities. But where Henry, the professional historian, carefully evaluated the primary sources he uncovered in foreign archives, Brooks allowed his philosophical prejudices to drive his analysis, and evidence that contradicted his theories was simply discarded. Consequently, academic reviewers were rarely kind. "Mr. Adams generally leaves the reader in the dark as regards the sources of his information," historian Clive Day observed in the *Yale Review*. "He quotes occasionally some good authorities in economic history," Day added, but clearly Adams could not be bothered to master basic facts, such as having the Huns invade Western Europe hundreds of years after they actually did. Brooks defended his scholarship, if only to Henry, insisting that his books were "not history or literature." His purpose, he explained, was "to present a method, not an historical study." After Brooks claimed that "any one can gather facts," Henry concluded that Brooks's scholarship was as odd as his support for imperialism, describing him to Lizzie as "my idiot-brother Brooks."[14]

Estranged from his brothers, Henry felt himself adrift. "Brooks is morbid," Henry concluded. As his own nerves were not what they once were, Henry doubted "whether contact with my brothers and sister is likely to sooth our mutual repose." As for Charles Francis, Henry mused, the two brothers had "never followed the same trail, and are long since out of sight of each other." Hoping to give Henry's life purpose, his old friend John Hay, now President William McKinley's secretary of state, floated the idea of an appointment as ambassador to Britain, a prospect that delighted official Washington as Adams would be the fourth of his name to hold the position. Uninterested, Henry instead fled to the South Pacific. In May 1897, with her marriage to now-former Senator Cam-

As the youngest surviving male of his generation, Brooks, photographed here in 1910, idolized his older brother Henry, ten years his senior. A diligent researcher, historian Henry believed his brother substituted theory and philosophy for evidence. After Brooks indignantly informed Henry that "any one can gather facts," Henry described his younger brother to a friend as "my idiot-brother Brooks." *Courtesy National Park Service.*

eron in tatters, Lizzie wrote to say that she was leaving her hard-drinking husband at home and boarding a steamer for France. What she hoped for, "I have often wanted to tell you, but cannot," Lizzie wrote elliptically. "Above all, I cannot say anything of all that I feel to you." Henry was in Tahiti when her letters finally reached him, but following a "wild, tearing jaunt" of 17,000 miles, he arrived in Paris. The reunion was a bitter disappointment for them both. Although her husband remained "on a [drinking] jag" in Pennsylvania, Lizzie was yet married. As ever, the sunburned, disheveled Adams—he had lost several teeth during the previous year—remained a poor suitor. Disappointed in the sad reality of the moment, Lizzie made sure that over the next few weeks the two were never alone. "Mrs. Cameron is no good," he groaned. "She has too much to do and lets everybody make use of her, which pleases no one." Most especially, Henry neglected to admit, himself.[15]

As had Brooks, Henry escaped into the mists of a distant past. Ever since his days abroad as his father's secretary, Adams had been fascinated by cathedrals, and as his fictional *Esther* indicated, the boy once dragged to Congregationalist services had begun to wrestle with matters of faith.

In 1904 Henry distributed to favored friends and a few university libraries *Mont-Saint Michel and Chartres*, in which he told the stories of the medieval abbey on the Norman coast and the nearby cathedral as a lengthy meditation on religion and the modern age. The book, he confided to an English correspondent, was his "declaration of principles as head of the Conservative Christian Anarchists; a party numbering one member." Psychologist William James was charmed by the "frolic power" of Henry's prose, and his brother, novelist Henry James, told Henry that he read the volume with "wonder, sympathy, and applause." For all its beauty, the book also revealed Henry's profound disquiet with modern society and its egalitarian impulses. The French peasant, Henry insisted in terms that he and his brothers often used when describing freedmen, immigrants, or Jews, was "suspicious of everybody and all things, whether material, social, or divine; he was far from civil, he was commonly gross." When encouraged by friends to allow the book a larger audience, Henry replied that the Virgin Mary was not a "commercial commodity." He would leave that to "Jew dealers in works of art." Alienated and alone, Henry described himself as "old, ugly, and idiotic." His father, he fretted, "lost his mind at seventy, and lived ten years" beyond that, and he feared that was his fate "in a few years more." The simple faith of the twelfth century was far pleasanter to contemplate.[16]

Three years later, in 1907, Henry again circulated a book for friends and family. Part autobiography and part philosophical commentary, *The Education of Henry Adams* delighted critics—it was, after Henry's death, awarded the Pulitzer Prize—and baffled his family. Relatives expecting a more traditional autobiography thought it curious that it was told in the third person and saddened that it erased the years of his marriage and never once mentioned Clover's name. Brooks later admitted that he had "warned [Henry] to weariness, that he had attempted too much," while Charles Francis dismissed the book as "simply silly." However, Henry's brothers at least enjoyed parts of the book, if not the same sections. Never having liked the Beacon Hill house, Charles Francis thought the early chapters beautifully depicted their childhood. "Lord! How you do bring it all back!" he marveled. "How we did hate Boston! How we loved Quincy!"

Brooks preferred the later chapters after Henry abandoned his "apparent effort to write fragments of biography" and instead focused on the "huge and awful tragedy" that was man's struggle with nature.[17]

Whatever his public utterances, the competitive Charles Francis was motivated to finish his own autobiography, a project he had started in 1900 but set aside to focus on *Lee's Centennial*. Of all people, only Henry was qualified to write his biography, Charles Francis admitted, but "of late years" his younger brother had neither "been in touch" nor was "in any particular degree sympathetic." So Charles proceeded to tell his own story, using a far more traditional style than that of *Education*. Despite his many accomplishments, from his wartime service to his railroad presidency, Adams judged that his life was not "the success it ought to have been." What, precisely, Adams was sorry he had not achieved he never stated, but who exactly was responsible for his failures was a topic he explored in great and brutal detail. If Adams had been hindered in his career by his "utter lack of a nice, ingratiating tact in my dealings with other men," the fault was not his. Rather, it was an "inherited deficiency, a family trait" bestowed upon him by his father. In the autobiography, Brooks received only a single mention and Henry but six references. But again and again, Charles Francis described "the coldness of temperament [so] natural" to his father and his "wholly wrong views" of important personal matters. Ironically, one of the few favorable things Charles Francis had to say about his father spoke to his own unhappiness with modern America. The elder Adams had taught his sons to believe only "in the equality of men before the law." But "social equality" was altogether another thing. "My father, at least, didn't force that on us." Rather than publish the work himself, Adams mailed the manuscript to the Massachusetts Historical Society in a sealed package in 1913, granting the society members permission to publish the "autobiographical sketch" if they wished. Eventually, family friend and Massachusetts Senator Henry Cabot Lodge did so, together with the memorial address that Lodge delivered after Charles Francis's death.[18]

Despite their differences, Charles Francis and Henry saw each other on occasion, especially during the winters when Charles Francis exchanged the Boston cold for Washington. On March 14, 1915, Charles Francis confided to his diary that he "was not well," feeling "very tired and out of breath." Even so, he dined that evening with Henry, "he and I alone and very dull." Pneumonia had set in, and Charles Francis died six days later at the age of seventy-nine. "A dismal week!" Henry reported to Lizzie. "My brother Charles and I had a race for our graves, and he won. An attack of grippe fell suddenly on his heart, and carried him off in a moment." Minnie was not with her husband when he died; she lived two more decades, dying on almost the same March day in 1935. Their twin sons, Henry and John, passed away in 1951 and 1964, respectively.[19]

Three years before, in early April 1912, Henry announced to Lizzie that he intended to make one final voyage to Britain. He finally decided that he was too infirm to make the trip, but not before booking passage on a new ship he planned to return home on: the *Titanic*. When it went down with great loss of life, Henry, whose one nod to the modern world was his fascination with technology, was badly shaken. Later that month, on April 24, his manservant, William Gray, noticed that the right-handed Henry was eating with his left hand. No sooner had Gray left the room than he heard a crash and returned to find Henry lying on the floor. With the help of the cook, Gray got Henry into bed and then rushed next door to the late John Hay's residence, for Henry refused to allow a telephone in his house. Gray first called Henry's doctors and then phoned Minnie. The next day, Henry was able to move his right leg and arm, but the left side of his body was paralyzed. On occasion, Henry was coherent, but at other times he appeared confused and agitated. A "complete recovery was not to be looked for," his doctor warned. The family rented a private railroad car to carry him north to one of Charles Francis's estates, Birnamwood, in South Lincoln, Massachusetts.[20]

Henry's sister, Mary, took charge of his care, hiring a staff to conduct physical therapy while trying to keep Lizzie Cameron at bay. Mary cabled Lizzie, who was in London, that there was nothing to be done and that in any case Henry would not recognize her, which was surely untrue. "I won't have her," Mary insisted. "There has been disagreeable scandal enough about that affair," she thought, "and we certainly cannot permit people to say that in his last illness she came from Europe to look after him." After visiting Henry and finding him "more changed and gone than had been reported," Henry James sent Lizzie a kinder note of warning: "To speak crudely and familiarly they clearly—by all their gestures—don't want you." When Lizzie announced that she nonetheless intended to visit Henry one final time, James was deeply moved. Her determination was "heroic," he marveled, and she was "magnificent." By 1918, Henry had improved enough to allow for his return to Washington, enabling him to see Lizzie as he pleased. On March 26, just after his eightieth birthday, Henry suffered another stroke after settling in for the night. "There was no look of pain on his face," his doctor observed, "only the strangest expression of consciousness and will and intellect." He was buried at Rock Creek Cemetery, beside Clover and beneath the statue he had commissioned for his wife from sculptor Augustus Saint-Gaudens.[21]

Brooks lived for another nine years, but not well or happily. He suffered from gout as early as 1896, and in 1922 he endured surgery for prostate cancer. In July 1925 he fainted, falling to the floor and rupturing an artery in his left leg. His wife, Daisy, herself frail, hired a staff of nurses, but as Brooks repeatedly cursed at them and kept loaded pistols on his night table, few remained for long. "I am not afraid of death, I care nothing for that," Brooks told one old friend. "But the boredom and pain of dying appall me." Daisy suffered a stroke and died in December 1926, and after that, Brooks sank rapidly. He died two months later, on February 14, 1927. By comparison to his more famous brothers, his death received little notice in the press. The few cursory obituaries commented not on his scholarship but simply noted that he was a "grandson of President John Quincy Adams." His sister, Mary, having already buried her husband, Henry Quincy, died in August 1928 at the age of eighty-two.[22]

ONE YEAR AFTER HENRY'S DEATH, BROOKS PUBLISHED A LENGTHY piece, "The Heritage of Henry Adams," together with three of Henry's dour, unpublished essays, as *The Degradation of the Democratic Dogma.*

Brooks began the essay by discussing their grandfather John Quincy, whose legacy to the family, he decided, was to impart upon his descendants the futility of progress and the ultimate decline of democracy. The first John Quincy "considered his life a failure," Brooks observed, "and from his point of view it was a failure." In the same fashion, Brooks thought, Henry "considered his life a failure, because he had not accomplished what at the outset he hoped to accomplish." The fact that Henry's volumes on the Jefferson and Madison years were so diligently researched and elegantly written that they would remain in print a century after their initial publication might suggest that his professional life was anything but a "failure." Yet Henry himself thought so.[23]

As did Charles Francis Jr. of his own life. Toward the end of his railroad career he also reflected on his and on his family's conflicted definitions of glory. Earlier generations of Adamses always equated greatness with political success, which explained why John Adams thought himself a disappointment in 1801 and John Quincy felt the same in 1829. Of the fourth generation, only John Quincy II sought political office, but he was rejected by voters more often than not for his reactionary response to progressive reforms. "The experience of my family for a hundred years ought to be a warning to me there," Charles Francis told himself. "They had all that political preferment could give. Were they happy or contented by it?" The question answered itself, yet by then Charles Francis was sadly aware that his chosen career had provided him with wealth but not with happiness: "I am tired; and the prizes I am after, well, if I gained them all, are not worth having."[24]

If Charles Francis's and Henry's contemporaries judged them failures, however, perhaps it was neither because they declined to seek political office nor because they died sour, discontented men, but because they turned their backs on the broad-minded agenda pursued by their grandfather during his congressional years. In his last, valiant years in the House, John Quincy had come to understand that race (and even class) was less important than character, yet his grandson John Quincy II instead preferred the political culture of an earlier age, in which every man knew his place and women remained silent. Imagining one's life to be wasted was a painful realization, yet in a strange, circular fashion Charles Francis, Henry, and Brooks all came to fear that their life choices provided evidence of their collective belief that progress was a fantasy and that egalitarian hopes of a more democratic republic were wrongheaded.

The Adams family, Brooks suggested, demonstrated the scientific reality of his theories that all societies endured cycles of success and decay. What was true for nations, Brooks insisted, was equally true of America's first political dynasty. One year before his stroke, the aging historian Henry made much the same point to his retired railroad magnate brother. "Since the Civil War, I think we have produced not one figure that will be remembered [in] a life-time," Henry wrote Charles Francis from Paris. "What is more curious, I think the figures have not existed. The men have not been born." However, the decision not to seek elective office was a conscious one, just as it was, in Charles Francis Jr.'s case, to exchange national service for the pursuit of profit. Charles Francis Sr.'s failure to capture the prize of the presidency removed an enormous burden of pressure from the shoulders of his children, yet their decision to try *not* to be remembered by subsequent generations also failed to make them happy. Perhaps it was simply not in an Adams ever to be content, but they always knew whom to blame. "Of this growth [in pessimism] my grandfather is the main figure," Brooks observed, "not Henry or me. We are appendages only."[25]

ACKNOWLEDGMENTS

HEIRS OF AN HONORED NAME TURNED OUT TO BE A FAR MORE DIF-
ficult book to write than I had anticipated. For the first time, I discovered
the problem of too many documents. In the past I always dreamed of
uncovering more sources. A cache of letters from a veteran of the Massachusetts Fifty-Fourth, for instance, or an aged freedman's reminiscences
about the enslaved artisan Gabriel. By comparison, from their letters and
diaries to their essays, pamphlets, novels, and works of history, the Adams
family left behind a small mountain of highly quotable documentation.
I'm not sure when they slept.

But what ultimately made the project so difficult was finding the
right balance in writing about people who were both admirable and disagreeable. The Adamses were uniformly brilliant. They opposed slavery's
expansion into the West, fought for free speech, served their country in
the diplomatic corps and on the battlefield, and struggled to remove
racially based laws on the state level. They were also troubled, unlikable,
competitive, and often racist and anti-Semitic. The fourth generation of
Adams men rarely got along with one another or with their parents, endured unhappy marriages, and even criticized each other in print. They
died largely estranged from one another. Few of them appeared to have
many people they could truly count as friends.

Acknowledgments

As great good fortune would have it, however, I am blessed with a large number of clever friends and wonderful family members who supported me in this project and vastly helped to improve the manuscript. Longtime pals Andrew Burstein and Nancy Isenberg read my early chapters and permitted me an advance peek at *The Problem of Democracy*, their insightful new book on John and John Quincy Adams. Gary Kornblith and Manisha Sinha, the nation's leading authorities on abolitionism and political reform, took a look at the chapters that covered Charles Francis Sr.'s career as a youthful reformer and then sent back pages of comments and corrections.

I first met Andy, Nancy, Gary, and Manisha some years ago at the annual meeting of SHEAR (the Society for Historians of the Early Republic), which remains my favorite conference. At SHEAR's 1988 conclave, one of the first I attended, I was invited to share a pint with John Belohlavek, who continues to read and improve my chapters; our Saturday martinis remain the highlight of the conference. SHEAR also introduced me to Mike Crane and Brother John Quist, who much enhanced the antebellum sections of the book. Matt Mason, the skillful biographer of Adams in-law Edward Everett—a relation that Charles Francis Sr. never much warmed to—provided me with wise suggestions on how to improve those sections of the manuscript, as did Jeff Forret, who generously took time off from his own writing to read mine. I'm deeply grateful to you all for your brilliant scholarship, kind assistance, and companionship.

For the chapters on the war years, I turned to a group of talented historians who are far more than just colleagues. Lesley Gordon and Diane Sommerville saved me from several blunders, as did Jenny Lloyd and Susan Goodier, while Richard Follett provided sound advice on my transatlantic pages. Jonathan Lande was properly horrified by Charles Francis Jr.'s casual racism, while John David Smith sent me scampering back to my bookshelves to double-check several references. Stan Harrold, the enemy of the unnecessary adjective, forced me to write more clearly and succinctly. As I've said before, Stan's edits are not for the faint of heart.

At the Massachusetts Historical Society, home of the Adams papers, Sara Martin was always quick to answer my many questions about the collection. At Le Moyne College, Wayne Stevens, the Sherlock Holmes of research librarians, tracked down obscure pamphlets and monographs and imported microfilm for me by the box load. As always, I am grateful to the college's Committee on Research and Development for its generous support for image rights and reproductions. At Basic Books, Dan Gerstle helped launch this project and, as with *Thunder at the Gates*, peppered me with astute thoughts on where to trim, where to add, and how to shape the overall project. Roger Labrie and Donald Pharr performed terrific editorial work on the manuscript, and Lara Heimert kept the project chugging along and was patient with my missed deadlines. And as always, I cannot say enough about Dan Green, my wonderful agent. Every great project, it seems, begins with a phone call from Dan, who has as keen a sense of history as any scholar I've ever met.

My pal Donald Wright now reads and fixes my chapters on his laptop, which is a pity as this means that I no longer get to enjoy his hilarious doodles in the margins. But his bracketed jokes always make me laugh. It takes a true friend to read and mark up an entire manuscript, and I've lost track of how many times Don has done that for me. Other longtime pals were buried beneath their own projects and deadlines, but Alan Gallay, Graham Hodges, and Clarence Taylor all allowed me to bounce ideas off them and made smart suggestions on how to deal with problems that I encountered along the path. It's also good to have Clarence and Marsha Bratt back in Central New York, at least for part of the year.

While I was researching and writing this book, those closest to me witnessed sadness and loss, but also great joy. My brilliant wife, historian Leigh Fought, when not raking in awards for her own scholarship, greatly improved my manuscript and surely heard far more anecdotes about the Adams family than she cared to. But more than that, Leigh just puts up with me, which is no easy task. My two daughters, Kearney and Hannah, were too busy with their own amazing adventures to read any of these pages (yet). But they are dazzling and industrious and perfect in every way, and they make my life a joy. Best of all, in the last year, my honored family grew with the addition of Marc Hughes; one could not hope for a finer young man as a son-in-law. To quote the great rock philosopher David Gilmour: "I need no blessings but I'm counting mine."

NOTES

Abbreviations Used in the Notes

ABA	Abigail Brown Brooks Adams
AL	Abraham Lincoln
BA	Peter Chardon Brooks Adams
CFA	Charles Francis Adams Sr.
CFA2	Charles Francis Adams Jr.
CS	Charles Sumner
GWA	George Washington Adams
HA	Henry Brooks Adams
JGP	John Gorham Palfrey
JQA	John Quincy Adams
JQA2	John Quincy Adams II
LC	Library of Congress
LCA	Louisa Catherine Johnson Adams
LCA2	Louisa Catherine Adams Kuhn
MA	Mary Gardiner Adams Quincy
OR	*The War of the Rebellion: A Compilation of the Official Records of the Union and Confederate Armies*
RHD	Richard Henry Dana
WHS	William Henry Seward

PROLOGUE

1. *Congressional Globe*, 30th Cong., 1st Sess., 381; *Barre (MA) Patriot*, February 25, 1848; Pittsfield *Berkshire County Whig*, March 2, 1848; Brattleboro *Semi-Weekly Eagle*, February 25, 1848; Concord *New Hampshire Patriot and State Gazette*, February 24, 1848.

2. New London *Morning News*, February 23, 1848, February 28, 1848; Brattleboro *Semi-Weekly Eagle*, February 25, 1848; Amherst *Farmer's Cabinet*, February 24, 1848, March 2, 1848; *Pittsfield (MA) Sun*, February 24, 1848.

3. Samuel Flagg Bemis, *John Quincy Adams and the Union* (New York, 1956), 536–537; Paul Nagel, *The Adams Women: Abigail and Louisa Adams, Their Sisters and Daughters* (New York, 1987), 289.

4. Brattleboro *Semi-Weekly Eagle*, February 29, 1848; Amherst *Farmer's Cabinet*, March 9, 1848; New London *Morning News*, March 4, 1848.

5. CFA Diary, February 22, 1848, Adams Papers. See Amherst *Farmer's Cabinet*, November 11, 1846. See also CFA Diary, November 24, 1846, and CFA's letter to LCA, November 22, 1846, both in Adams Papers, on JQA's earlier stroke. All citations to Adams Papers refer to the collections of the Massachusetts Historical Society.

6. Louisa Thomas, *Louisa: The Extraordinary Life of Mrs. Adams* (New York, 2016), 452; Nancy Isenberg and Andrew Burstein, *The Problem of Democracy: The Presidents Adams Confront the Cult of Personality* (New York, 2019), 429; *Barre (MA) Gazette*, February 25, 1848; New London *Morning News*, February 24, 1848, February 25, 1848, February 26, 1848, February 29, 1848; *Pittsfield (MA) Sun*, February 24, 1848.

7. CFA Diary, February 24, 1848, Adams Papers.

8. CFA Diary, February 25, 1848, Adams Papers.

9. Chris DeRose, *Congressman Lincoln: The Making of America's Greatest President* (New York, 2013), 160; Pittsfield *Berkshire County Whig*, March 2, 1848; *Barre (MA) Patriot*, March 3, 1848; Brattleboro *Semi-Weekly Eagle*, March 3, 1848; Amherst *Farmer's Cabinet*, March 2, 1848; Ossining *Hudson River Chronicle*, February 29, 1848.

10. James Traub, *John Quincy Adams, Militant Spirit* (New York, 2016), 531; Brattleboro *Semi-Weekly Eagle*, February 29, 1848, March 3, 1848; Amherst *Farmer's Cabinet*, March 9, 1848; Barre *Wachusett Star*, February 29, 1848; *Barre (MA) Gazette*, March 10, 1848; New London *Morning News*, February 29, 1848.

11. Brattleboro *Semi-Weekly Eagle*, February 29, 1848, March 7, 1848, March 24, 1848; Amherst *Farmer's Cabinet*, March 2, 1848; Pittsfield *Berkshire County*

Whig, March 2, 1848; New London *Morning News*, February 25, 1848; Strouds-burg *Jeffersonian Republican*, March 3, 1848; *North Star*, March 3, 1848; Walter Stahr, *Seward: Lincoln's Indispensable Man* (New York, 2012), 108; Concord *New Hampshire Patriot and State Gazette*, April 20, 1848; *Barre (MA) Patriot*, March 10, 1848.

12. *Barre (MA) Patriot*, March 17, 1848; Pittsfield *Berkshire County Whig*, March 2, 1848, April 6, 1848; Brattleboro *Semi-Weekly Eagle*, February 25, 1848; New London *Morning News*, March 17, 1848; *North Star*, March 31, 1848, April 21, 1848.

13. *North Star*, March 10, 1848.

14. New London *Morning News*, March 10, 1848; Pittsfield *Berkshire County Whig*, March 16, 1848; *Barre (MA) Patriot*, March 10, 1848.

15. Robert Remini, *Henry Clay: Statesman for the Union* (New York, 1991), 699–700; CFA to Henry Clay, May 24, 1848, Adams Papers.

16. Amherst *Farmer's Cabinet*, March 16, 1848; Barre *Wachusett Star*, February 29, 1848.

17. CFA to C. H. Dillaway, July 14, 1857, Adams Papers.

18. Lynn Hudson Parsons, *John Quincy Adams* (Madison, 1998), 206–207.

19. Robert Remini, *John Quincy Adams* (New York, 2002), 137–138; James Oakes, *Freedom National: The Destruction of Slavery in the United States, 1861–1865* (New York, 2013), 36–37.

20. Manisha Sinha, *The Slave's Cause: A History of Abolition* (New Haven, 2016), 251; Leonard Richards, *The Life and Times of Congressman John Quincy Adams* (New York, 1986), 118; *Rutland (VT) Herald*, June 11, 1839.

21. Remini, *Adams*, 140; Joanne Freeman, *The Field of Blood: Violence in Congress and the Road to Civil War* (New York, 2018), 115.

22. Fred Kaplan, *John Quincy Adams* (New York, 2014), 491; William Lee Miller, *Arguing about Slavery: The Great Battle in the United States Congress* (New York, 1996), 306.

23. Benjamin Lundy, *The War in Texas* (Philadelphia, 1836); *Rutland (Vermont) Herald*, June 21, 1836.

24. *North Star*, March 10, 1848; Traub, *Adams*, 462–463.

25. Sinha, *Slave's Cause*, 409; CFA Diary, February 27, 1841, Adams Papers; Marcus Rediker, *The* Amistad *Rebellion: An Atlantic Odyssey of Slavery and Freedom* (New York, 2012), 181–182.

26. Rediker, Amistad *Rebellion*, 190; Howard Jones, *Mutiny on the* Amistad (New York, 1987), 180; CFA to JQA, March 18, 1841, Adams Papers; Parsons, *Adams*, 239–240.

27. CFA to Edward Everett, March 9, 1848, Adams Papers.

28. Paul Nagel, *Descent from Glory: Four Generations of the John Adams Family* (New York, 1983), 3; John Ferling, *John Adams: A Life* (Knoxville, 1992), 170–171.

29. Nagel, *Adams Women*, 162; Paul Nagel, *John Quincy Adams: A Public Life, a Private Life* (New York, 1998), 60; CFA, May 24, 1848, Adams Papers.

30. CFA2, *An Autobiography* (Cambridge, 1916), 11.

31. J. C. Levenson, "The Etiology of Israel Adams: The Onset, Waning, and Relevance of Henry Adams's Anti-Semitism," *New Literary History* 25 (1994): 583–584.

32. Edward Kirkland, *Charles Francis Adams, Jr., 1835–1915: The Patrician at Bay* (Cambridge, 1965), 221.

33. BA and HA, *The Degradation of Democratic Dogma* (New York, 1919), vii.

CHAPTER 1: GENERATIONS

1. Richard Brookhiser, *America's First Dynasty: The Adamses, 1735–1918* (New York, 2002), 113; Margery Heffron, *Louisa Catherine: The Other Mrs. Adams* (New Haven, 2014), 189–190.

2. Traub, *Adams*, 105–106.

3. Parsons, *Adams*, 94–95; Thomas, *Louisa*, 157–158; Boston *Columbian Centinel*, November 3, 1802; Salem *Essex Register*, May 11, 1808; CFA2, *Charles Francis Adams* (Boston, 1900), 3–4.

4. Lynne Withey, *Dearest Friend: A Life of Abigail Adams* (New York, 1981), 296–297; CFA2, *Charles Francis Adams*, 4.

5. Martin Duberman, *Charles Francis Adams, 1807–1886* (Stanford, 1960), 7; Nagel, *Descent from Glory*, 112.

6. Duberman, *Adams*, 7; LCA Diary, December 14, 1809, in *Diary and Autobiographical Writings of Louisa Catherine Adams*, ed. Judith Graham (Cambridge, 2013), 1: 303; Nagel, *Descent from Glory*, 137.

7. Jane Cook, *American Phoenix: John Quincy and Louisa Adams* (Nashville, 2013), 414; Thomas, *Louisa*, 19–20.

8. Curtis Cate, *The War of the Two Emperors: The Duel between Napoleon and Alexander* (New York, 1985), 5; CFA2, *Adams*, 5; Traub, *Adams*, 192.

9. CFA2, *Adams*, 7; "Narrative of a Journey from Russia to France," in *A Traveled First Lady: Writings of Louisa Catherine Adams*, ed. Margaret Hogan (Cambridge, 2014), 210–211.

10. CFA2, *Adams*, 7; CFA to C. H. Dillaway, July 14, 1857, Adams Papers.

11. Heffron, *Louisa Catherine*, 272–273.

12. CFA2, *Adams*, 8–9; Thomas, *Louisa*, 242; CFA to C. H. Dillaway, July 14, 1857, CFA to Robert White, May 14, 1852, both in Adams Papers.

13. Parsons, *Adams*, 130–131; CFA to C. H. Dillaway, July 14, 1857, Adams Papers; CFA Jr., *Adams*, 10.

14. Duberman, *Adams*, 14; GWA, "Review of 1825," Adams Papers; CFA2, *Adams*, 11; Brookhiser, *America's First Dynasty*, 114.

15. GWA, Autobiographical Essay, 1825, Adams Papers.

16. CFA to C. H. Dillaway, July 14, 1857, CFA to Charles Sumner, September 15, 1848, both in Adams Papers; Duberman, *Adams*, 18–19.

17. Traub, *Adams*, 227, 252; William Cooper, *The Lost Founding Father: John Quincy Adams and the Transformation of American Politics* (New York, 2017), 200.

18. GWA Diary, August 23, 1825, CFA Diary, May 10, 1822, both in Adams Papers; Nagel, *Descent from Glory*, 142; Brookhiser, *America's First Dynasty*, 114.

19. Jack Shepherd, *Cannibals of the Heart: A Personal Biography of Louisa Catherine and John Quincy Adams* (New York, 1980), 283; CFA to C. H. Dillaway, July 14, 1857, Adams Papers.

20. Catherine Allgor, *Parlor Politics: In Which the Ladies of Washington Help Build a City and a Government* (Charlottesville, 2000), 170–172.

21. Shepherd, *Cannibals*, 272; Nagel, *Descent from Glory*, 142; CFA Diary, April 24, 1827, Adams Papers.

22. Duberman, *Adams*, 27; Nagel, *Adams Women*, 249; Traub, *Adams*, 338. Curiously, Charles Francis first raised the subject of marriage with his brother George in August 1825, several months before he first met Abby. Presumably, he was not considering proposing to his mistress. See GWA Diary, August 19, 1825, Adams Papers.

23. Nagel, *Adams Women*, 249; Shepherd, *Cannibals of the Heart*, 278, 287.

24. Duberman, *Adams*, 28; CFA to C. H. Dillaway, July 14, 1857, CFA Diary, April 24, 1827, both in Adams Papers.

25. CFA to Peter Brooks, May 24, 1827, Adams Papers.

26. CFA to JQA, January 22, 1828, April 28, 1828, CFA to Peter Brooks, October 26, 1828, all in Adams Papers.

27. Shepherd, *Cannibals of the Heart*, 299; CFA2, *Adams*, 13; Nagel, *Adams Women*, 263; New London *Morning News*, April 3, 1848; New Orleans *Weekly Louisianan*, August 24, 1871; Washington *Evening Star*, June 20, 1889.

28. Traub, *Adams*, 337–338; Parsons, *Adams*, 188.

29. GWA Diary, August 4, 1825, August 5, 1825, GWA, "Review of 1825," all in Adams Papers.

30. GWA Diary, December 31, 1825, Adams Papers.

31. *Report of a Trial: Miles Farmer versus Dr. David Humphreys Storer* (Boston, 1831), 7–12.

32. Parsons, *Adams*, 204; Shepherd, *Cannibals of the Heart*, 316–317.

33. Shepherd, *Cannibals of the Heart*, 318; Isenberg and Burstein, *The Problem of Democracy*, 384; Doug Wead, *All the Presidents' Children* (New York, 2003), 16.

34. *Report of a Trial*, 13–16.

35. Wilmington *Register*, May 30, 1829.

36. Nagel, *Descent from Glory*, 151.

37. Wilmington *Delaware Journal*, April 22, 1828, May 23, 1828.

38. Thomas, *Louisa*, 387; Traub, *Adams*, 386.

39. Thomas, *Louisa*, 406–407; Parsons, *Adams*, 220.

40. Traub, *Adams*, 420; Duberman, *Adams*, 52.

41. On this ideal, see E. Anthony Rotundo, "Learning about Manhood: Gender Ideals and the Middle-Class Family in Nineteenth Century America," in *Manliness and Morality: Middle-Class Masculinity in Britain and America, 1800–1940*, James Anthony Mangan and James Walvin, eds. (Manchester, 1987), 35–51.

CHAPTER 2: THE ASSEMBLYMAN

1. Nagel, *Descent from Glory*, 182–183. On naming, see Gloria Main, "Naming Children in Early New England," *Journal of Interdisciplinary History* 27 (Summer, 1996): 13; C. Dallett Hemphill, *Siblings: Brothers and Sisters in American History* (New York, 2011), 62.

2. Nagel, *Descent from Glory*, 185, 189; CFA Diary, February 16, 1838, Adams Papers; CFA2, *Autobiography*, 5.

3. Brooks Simpson, *The Political Education of Henry Adams* (Columbia, 1996), 2; HA, *The Education of Henry Adams* (New York, 1983 ed.), 752; ABA to CFA, December 3, 1851, Adams Papers; CFA2, *Autobiography*, 13.

4. Nagel, *Descent from Glory*, 190; Nagel, *Adams Women*, 269; CFA2, *Autobiography*, 13–14.

5. HA, *Education*, 752; CFA Diary, February 16, 1841, Adams Papers; Nancy Cott, *The Bonds of Womanhood: "Women's Sphere" in New England, 1780–1835* (New Haven, 1977), 101–105; Nagel, *Descent from Glory*, 204–205.

6. Edward Chalfant, *Both Sides of the Ocean: A Biography of Henry Adams, His First Life, 1838–1862* (New York, 1982), 26; HA, *Education*, 752; CFA2, *Autobiography*, 22, 29–30.

7. HA, *Education*, 753; William Dusinberre, *Henry Adams: The Myth of Failure* (Charlottesville, 1980), 14. On the ideal of domesticity, see Natasha Kraus,

A New Type of Womanhood: Discursive Politics and Social Change in Antebellum America (Durham, 2008), 30–31.

8. HA, *Education*, 744–745.

9. Nagel, *Adams Women*, 270–271; CFA Diary, February 9, 1846, Adams Papers.

10. CFA2, *Adams*, 29–30; CFA to JQA, March 27, 1837, Adams Papers.

11. CFA2, *Adams*, 33; Boston *Morning Post*, December 3, 1837; CFA to Alexander Everett, March 3, 1837, CFA Diary, December 2, 1837, both in Adams Papers.

12. CFA2, *Adams*, 38–42; CFA to JQA, January 15, 1831, CFA to (no first name given) Andrews, October 30, 1839, CFA to C. H. Dillaway, July 14, 1857, all in Adams Papers.

13. CFA to C. H. Dillaway, July 14, 1857, CFA Diary, September 10, 1846, CFA to CS, September 15, 1848, CFA to M. Hale, October 28, 1840, all in Adams Papers.

14. CFA2, *Adams*, 44; CFA Diary, November 10, 1840, Adams Papers; Indiana *Richmond Palladium*, December 3, 1840.

15. CFA2, *Adams*, 44; CFA Diary, November 9, 1840, Adams Papers.

16. CFA Diary, October 14, 1840, January 6, 1841, February 24, 1841, April 4, 1841, April 6, 1841, all in Adams Papers.

17. CFA Diary, November 9, 1840, November 8, 1841, both in Adams Papers.

18. Albert Von Frank, *The Trials of Anthony Burns: Freedom and Slavery in Emerson's Boston* (Cambridge, 1998), 35; Leslie Goldstein, "A 'Triumph of Freedom' after All? *Prigg v. Pennsylvania* Re-examined," *Law and History Review* 29 (2011): 763–796; Joseph Nogee, "The Prigg Case and Fugitive Slavery, 1842–1850," *Journal of Negro History* 39 (1954): 185–205.

19. Gary Collison, *Shadrach Minkins: From Slave to Citizen* (Cambridge, 1997), 87; James and Lois Horton, *In Hope of Liberty: Culture, Community and Protest among Northern Free Blacks, 1770–1860* (New York, 1997), 99; *Commonwealth of Massachusetts, House [Report] No. 9* (Boston, 1843).

20. *Commonwealth of Massachusetts, House [Report] No. 41* (Boston, 1843); CFA to Francis Bird, February 16, 1861, CFA to James Congdon, March 30, 1843, CFA to JQA, January 14, 1844, CFA Diary, January 30, 1843, February 1, 1843, March 4, 1843, all in Adams Papers.

21. On the 1786 law, see Douglas Egerton, *Death or Liberty: African Americans and Revolutionary America* (New York, 2009), 121; Amber Moulton, *The Fight for Interracial Marriage Rights in Antebellum Massachusetts* (Cambridge, 2015), 129–131; Nicholas Gayatt, *Bind Us Apart: How Enlightened Americans*

Invented Racial Segregation (New York, 2016), 174; CFA Diary, January 27, 1841, February 2, 1842, February 16, 1842, March 1, 1842, January 24, 1843, February 4, 1843, February 22, 1843, all in Adams Papers.

22. Peggy Pascoe, *What Comes Naturally: Miscegenation Law and the Making of Race in America* (New York, 2009), 21; David Gerber, *Black Ohio and the Color Line, 1860–1915* (Champaign, 1976), 27; CFA Diary, February 24, 1843, Adams Papers.

23. Miller, *Arguing about Slavery*, 260; Brookhiser, *America's First Dynasty*, 117; Stephen and Paul Kendrick, *Sarah's Long Walk: How the Free Blacks of Boston and Their Struggle for Equality Changed America* (Boston, 2004), 61; *Richmond Enquirer*, October 14, 1845; CFA Diary, February 10, 1842, February 6, 1843, March 5, 1843, March 20, 1843, March 23, 1843, all in Adams Papers.

24. Amherst *Farmers' Cabinet*, July 14, 1843; CFA to Caleb Swan, June 15, 1843, Adams Papers; *New York Herald*, May 19, 1843; *New York Tribune*, May 18, 1843, July 6, 1843; *Hudson River Chronicle*, May 23, 1843; HA, *Education*, 742.

25. Montpelier *Green-Mountain Freeman*, September 27, 1844; Pittsfield *Berkshire County Whig*, September 26, 1844.

26. Remini, *Clay*, 660; unidentified newspaper clipping, November 1844, CFA Diary, February 16, 1844, February 18, 1844, February 20, 1844, February 21, 1844, May 1, 1844, November 8, 1844, November 12, 1844, all in Adams Papers.

27. Edward Crapol, *John Tyler: The Accidental President* (Chapel Hill, 2006), 221; *New York Herald*, January 31, 1845; CFA Diary, January 13, 1845, February 22, 1845, March 15, 1845, all in Adams Papers.

28. Unidentified newspaper clipping, May 1845, CFA Diary, March 25, 1848, both in Adams Papers.

29. Sinha, *Slave's Cause*, 480; Washington *Daily Union*, October 25, 1845; Fayetteville *North Carolinian*, November 1, 1845.

30. CFA2, *Adams*, 50–51; *Richmond Enquirer*, September 1, 1846; CFA to C. H. Dillaway, July 14, 1857, CFA Diary, November 6, 1843, February 21, 1845, March 26, 1845, October 2, 1845, October 8, 1845, CFA to J. T. Stevenson, October 2, 1845, all in Adams Papers.

31. CFA2, *Adams*, 68; CFA Diary, March 4, 1845, March 6, 1845, October 10, 1845, May 28, 1846, June 16, 1846, CFA to Linus Lowell, October 30, 1845, all in Adams Papers.

32. Maurice Baxter, *One and Inseparable: Daniel Webster and the Union* (Cambridge, 1984), 386; David Donald, *Charles Sumner and the Coming of the Civil War* (New York, 1960), 147; Anne-Marie Taylor, *Young Charles Sumner and the*

Legacy of the American Enlightenment (Amherst, 2001), 175; CFA Diary, May 16, 1846, Adams Papers; Keene *New Hampshire Sentinel*, September 30, 1846; *Pittsfield (MA) Sun*, October 1, 1846; *Rutland (VT) Herald*, October 1, 1846; Montpelier *Green Mountain Freeman*, July 2, 1846.

33. CFA2, *Adams*, 70; Donald, *Sumner*, 148; Frederick Blue, *The Free Soilers: Third Party Politics 1848–54* (Urbana, 1974), 36; Frederick Douglass to CFA, June 27, 1847, in *The Frederick Douglass Papers: Series 3*, ed. John McKivigan (New Haven, 2009), 220–221; CFA to Joshua Giddings, February 22, 1847, October 19, 1847, November 28, 1847, CFA to Samuel Sewall, October 10, 1845, CFA Diary, July 22, 1845, all in Adams Papers.

34. *Pittsfield (MA) Sun*, October 21, 1847, November 5, 1846; *Boston Atlas*, October 31, 1846; CFA Diary, October 31, 1846, Adams Papers.

35. New London *Morning News*, March 7, 1848; Brattleboro *Semi-Weekly Eagle*, March 17, 1848, March 24, 1848; Elkton *Cecil Whig*, March 4, 1848.

36. Brattleboro *Semi-Weekly Eagle*, February 29, 1848, May 8, 1848; Barre *Wachusett Star*, March 28, 1848; New London *Morning News*, April 3, 1848.

CHAPTER 3: THE FREE-SOILER

1. CFA Diary, March 4, 1848, Adams Papers.

2. William W. Freehling, *The Road to Disunion: Secessionists at Bay* (New York, 1990), 458; Parsons, *Adams*, 467.

3. David Potter, *The Impending Crisis, 1848–1861* (New York, 1977), 71; Willard Klunder, *Lewis Cass and the Politics of Moderation* (Kent, 1996), 163, 243.

4. Robert Remini, *Daniel Webster: The Man and His Time* (New York, 1997), 391; Michael Holt, *The Rise and Fall of the American Whig Party* (New York, 1999), 282; K. Jack Bauer, *Zachary Taylor: Soldier, Planter, Statesman of the Old Southwest* (Baton Rouge, 1985), 236–237.

5. Montpelier *Green-Mountain Freeman*, April 22, 1847.

6. Holt, *American Whig Party*, 333; CFA Diary, October 31, 1847, June 4, 1848, both in Adam Papers.

7. Concord *New Hampshire Patriot*, June 22, 1848, June 29, 1848; *Pittsfield (MA) Sun*, June 22, 1848; CFA speech, June 24, 1849, Adams Papers.

8. Eric Foner, *Free Soil, Free Labor, Free Men: The Ideology of the Republican Party before the Civil War* (New York, 1970), 124; Reinhard Johnson, *The Liberty Party, 1840–1848: Antislavery Third-Party Politics in the United States* (Baton Rouge, 2009); CFA to Harvey Smith, June 13, 1848, Adams Papers.

9. Concord *New Hampshire Patriot*, July 6, 1848; New Lisbon *Anti-Slavery Bugle*, July 21, 1848.

10. CFA to Thomas Wentworth Higginson, June 16, 1848, Adams Papers; Concord *New Hampshire Patriot*, July 6, 1848; *Pittsfield (MA) Sun*, July 6, 1848.

11. CFA to Henry Stanton, June 8, 1848, Adams Papers; Blue, *Free Soilers*, 68; Remini, *Webster*, 653; Pittsfield *Berkshire County Whig*, July 6, 1848; Brattleboro *Semi-Weekly Eagle*, July 3, 1848; *Barre (MA) Patriot*, June 30, 1848.

12. Potter, *Impending Crisis*, 80; New Lisbon *Anti-Slavery Bugle*, July 21, 1848; CFA Diary, June 24, 1848, CFA to JGP, June 23, 1848, both in Adams Papers.

13. Johnson, *Liberty Party*, 84; CS to CFA, July 30, 1848, in *Selected Letters of Charles Sumner*, ed. Beverly Palmer (Boston, 1990), 1: 239; CFA to Seth Gates, July 30, 1848, CFA to JGP, July 9, 1848, CFA Diary, August 6, 1848, all in Adams Papers.

14. CFA2, *Autobiography*, 32; CFA to Henry Stanton, July 21, 1848, CFA Diary, August 8, 1848, both in Adams Papers.

15. CFA Diary, August 9, 1848, Adams Papers; Duberman, *Adams*, 147; John Niven, *Salmon P. Chase: A Biography* (New York, 1995), 110; *North Star*, August 11, 1848. The *Richmond Enquirer* (August 15, 1848) placed the delegate total at "thirty thousand." The Second Universalist Church stood on the corner of Washington and Clinton, now the site of the Hotel Lafayette, and Courtyard Square is now Lafayette Square.

16. Pittsfield *Berkshire County Whig*, August 17, 1848; *North Star*, August 11, 1848; *Pittsfield (MA) Sun*, August 17, 1848; Washington *Weekly National Intelligencer*, August 12, 1848; CFA Diary, August 8, 1848, August 10, 1848, both in Adams Papers; Crisfield Johnson, *Centennial History of Erie County* (Buffalo, 1876), 437; *Oliver Dyer's Phonographic Report of the Proceedings of the National Free Soil Convention* (Buffalo, 1848), 5; Salt Lake City *Broad Axe*, May 21, 1898. This Butler was not the future General Benjamin F. Butler.

17. *Report of the Proceedings*, 7–8; *North Star*, August 11, 1848.

18. *Report of the Proceedings*, 8; CFA Diary, August 9, 1848, Adams Papers.

19. Amherst *Farmer's Cabinet*, August 17, 1848; Johnson, *Centennial History*, 439; *Report of the Proceedings*, 32; CFA Diary, August 10, 1848, Adams Papers.

20. *New York Herald*, August 11, 1848; Pittsfield *Berkshire Country Whig*, August 24, 1848; *Barre (MA) Gazette*, August 18, 1848; CFA Diary, August 10, 1848, Adams Papers.

21. Holt, *American Whig Party*, 339; New Orleans *Daily Crescent*, August 21, 1848; Blue, *Free Soilers*, 100; Johnson, *Liberty Party*, 86; *Report of the Proceedings*, 19–20.

22. Donald, *Sumner*, 167; CFA Diary, August 11, 1848, Adams Papers.

23. Montpelier *Green-Mountain Freeman*, September 7, 1848; Pittsfield *Berkshire County Whig*, September 7, 1848; *North Star*, September 8, 1848.

24. Brattleboro *Semi-Weekly Eagle*, August 14, 1848, August 21, 1848; *Boston Atlas*, September 15, 1848; *Barre (MA) Patriot*, September 8, 1848.

25. Montpelier *Vermont Watchman and State Journal*, November 9, 1848; Brattleboro *Semi-Weekly Eagle*, August 31, 1848.

26. Brattleboro *Semi-Weekly Eagle*, August 24, 1848, September 25, 1848; Ravenna *Portage Sentinel*, October 4, 1854; Duberman, *Adams*, 154.

27. CFA Diary, September 14, 1848, October 13, 1848, both in Adams Papers; Concord *New Hampshire Patriot*, November 2, 1848; *North Star*, September 15, 1848; Brattleboro *Semi-Weekly Eagle*, September 14, 1848.

28. *Pittsfield (MA) Sun*, October 18, 1849; Amherst *Farmer's Cabinet*, November 2, 1848; *New York Herald*, September 16, 1848; *North Star*, September 15, 1848.

29. *North Star*, September 15, 1848; Montpelier *Green-Mountain Freeman*, August 31, 1848, September 7, 1848; Pittsfield *Berkshire County Whig*, October 26, 1848.

30. Upper Sandusky *Democratic Pioneer*, August 18, 1848; *North Star*, September 29, 1848, October 6, 1848; *Pittsfield (MA) Sun*, August 31, 1848, October 26, 1848; Blue, *Free Soilers*, 114; CFA to Joshua Giddings, November 24, 1848, Adams Papers.

31. Holt, *American Whig Party*, 381; *Pittsfield (MA) Sun*, September 21, 1848; Brattleboro *Semi-Weekly Eagle*, October 2, 1848; CFA Diary, September 22, 1848, October 4, 1848, both in Adams Papers.

32. *North Star*, September 15, 1848, September 29, 1848; CFA Diary, October 13, 1848, Adams Papers.

33. *Pittsfield (MA) Sun*, October 26, 1848; Washington *Daily Union*, August 18, 1848; Concord *New Hampshire Patriot*, November 2, 1848, November 16, 1848.

34. Holman Hamilton, *Zachary Taylor: Soldier in the White House* (Boston, 1951), 125; Bauer, *Taylor*, 245; Johnson, *Liberty Party*, 90; Donald, *Sumner*, 177; George Julian, "Some Ante-Bellum Politics," *North American Review* (1896): 201; Brattleboro *Semi-Weekly Eagle*, August 28, 1848; *Barre (MA) Patriot*, September 1, 1848; CFA Diary, November 8, 1848, Adams Papers.

35. *North Star*, November 17, 1848; CFA Diary, November 9, 1848, Adams Papers; CFA2, *Adams*, 93; Amherst *Farmer's Cabinet*, February 1, 1849; *Barre (MA) Patriot*, February 16, 1849.

36. Washington *Republic*, January 1, 1850; Duberman, *Adams*, 154; Bauer, *Taylor*, 110; CFA to JGP, December 10, 1849, Adams Papers.

37. Fergus Bordewich, *America's Great Debate: Henry Clay, Stephen A. Douglas, and the Compromise That Preserved the Union* (New York, 2012), 5; CFA to John Hale, February 18, 1850, CFA Diary, February 4, 1850, both in Adams Papers.

38. Duberman, *Adams*, 165; CFA to JQA2, June 5, 1850, CFA to JGP, June 9, 1850, both in Adams Papers.

39. Irving Bartlett, *John C. Calhoun: A Biography* (New York, 1993), 372; Baxter, *One and Inseparable*, 410–415.

40. CFA to JGP, June 9, 1850, CFA to Ira Gardner, June 12, 1851, both in Adams Papers; HA, *Education*, 764; New Lisbon *Anti-Slavery Bugle*, January 25, 1851.

41. Charles Wiltse, *John C. Calhoun, Sectionalist* (Boston, 1951), 408–409; CFA Diary, March 6, 1850, April 2, 1850, CFA to JGP, June 9, 1850, December 9, 1850, all in Adams Papers.

42. Robert Rayback, *Millard Fillmore: Biography of a President* (Buffalo, 1972), 242; Holman Hamilton, *Prologue to Conflict: The Crisis and Compromise of 1850* (Lexington, 1964), 144–145; CFA Diary, July 10, 1850, September 16, 1850, both in Adams Papers.

43. Sinha, *Slave's Cause*, 490; Freehling, *Road to Disunion*, 510; CFA Diary, September 9, 1850, September 29, 1850, both in Adams Papers.

44. CFA Diary, October 12, 1850, Adams Papers; *Pittsfield (MA) Sun*, October 28, 1850; New Lisbon *Anti-Slavery Bugle*, November 2, 1850; New Orleans *Daily Crescent*, October 24, 1850.

45. *Richmond Enquirer*, October 18, 1850; New Lisbon *Anti-Slavery Bugle*, November 2, 1850; *Washington Union*, reprinted in *Washington National Era*, October 24, 1850; *Athens (TN) Post*, December 20, 1850.

46. New Orleans *Daily Crescent*, October 24, 1850; New Lisbon *Anti-Slavery Bugle*, November 2, 1850; Samuel Sewell to CFA, June 19, 1851, CFA to C. A. Phelps, March 7, 1855, CFA to Francis Bird, February 16, 1861, CFA Diary, October 12, 1850, October 14, 1850, all in Adams Papers.

47. CFA Diary, November 8, 1850, November 12, 1850, both in Adams Papers.

48. Washington *National Era*, February 20, 1851, July 27, 1854; Washington *Republic*, February 25, 1851; Montpelier *Vermont Watchman*, July 28, 1854.

49. Amherst *Farmer's Cabinet*, April 17, 1851; *Boston Commonwealth*, February 24, 1851; John Jarrett to CFA, June 20, 1851, CFA to J. H. Allen, December 18, 1852, CFA Diary, February 27, 1851, all in Adams Papers.

50. Angela Murphy, *The Jerry Rescue: The Fugitive Slave Law, Northern Rights, and the American Sectional Crisis* (New York, 2016), 16–18; Von Frank, *Anthony Burns*, 212; CFA Diary, October 2, 1850, October 26, 1850, May 25,

1854, May 29, 1854, June 2, 1854, CFA to Samuel May, September 30, 1852, CFA to John Thomas, September 24, 1856, all in Adams Papers.

51. HA, *Education*, 748; Taylor, *Young Charles Sumner*, 327; CFA Diary, January 8, 1851, Adams Papers.

52. CFA Diary, August 24, 1850, November 16, 1850, CFA to CS, December 10, 1850, CFA to George White, October 5, 1850, all in Adams Papers.

53. Washington *Daily Union*, January 16, 1851; CS to CFA, December 16, 1850, January 2, 1851, January 7, 1851, in *Letters of Sumner*, ed. Palmer, 1: 317–319; CFA Diary, August 24, 1850, Adams Papers.

54. Taylor, *Young Charles Sumner*, 332; Donald, *Sumner*, 202; *Boston Post* in Washington *Daily Union*, May 8, 1851; CFA Diary, April 24, 1851, Adams Papers.

55. Washington *National Era*, September 25, 1851, January 1, 1852; New Lisbon *Anti-Slavery Bugle*, July 5, 1851; *Barre (MA) Gazette*, September 19, 1851; *New York Herald*, September 17, 1851; Washington *Southern Press*, May 10, 1851; CFA2, *Adams*, 100.

56. *New York Herald*, March 11, 1852, March 30, 1852; Washington *Southern Press*, March 11, 1852; Stroudsburg *Jeffersonian Republican*, March 18, 1852; Montpelier *Green-Mountain Freeman*, April 29, 1852; James Stone to CFA, January 1, 1852, Adams Papers.

57. *New York Tribune*, May 24, 1852; Thomas, *Louisa*, 454–455; Nagel, *Adams Women*, 291; Mary Adams telegram to ABA, May 15, 1852, ABA to CFA, May 16, 1852, both in Adams Papers.

58. CFA Diary, August 26, 1852, November 14, 1852, both in Adams Papers. Mary continued to make bad investments, and her brother-in-law gave her more money in October 1860. See Mary Adams (widow of John Adams II) to CFA, October 11, 1860, Adams Papers.

59. Roy Nichols, *Franklin Pierce: Young Hickory of the Granite Hills* (Philadelphia, 1931), 202; Jackson *Flag of the Union*, January 14, 1853; CFA to CS, January 1, 1852, February 9, 1852, April 7, 1852, June 23, 1852, CFA to E. Hopkins, June 23, 1852, CFA Diary, June 23, 1852, all in Adams Papers.

60. Blue, *Free Soilers*, 241; Washington *National Era*, September 23, 1852; *Richmond Enquirer*, August 10, 1852; Washington *Southern Press*, July 19, 1852; *New York Herald*, July 3, 1852; Montpelier *Green-Mountain Freeman*, August 19, 1852; CFA to E. J. Hamlin, July 12, 1852, CFA to CS, August 15, 1852, CFA to E. A. Stansbury, August 24, 1852, CFA Diary, August 10, 1852, August 11, 1852, August 13, 1852, all in Adams Papers.

61. CFA Diary, September 5, 1852, September 21, 1852, November 12, 1852, all in Adams Papers; Wheeling *Daily Intelligencer*, October 22, 1852;

Washington *National Era*, October 28, 1852; *Norfolk (MA) Democrat*, October 26, 1852.

62. John Eisenhower, *Agent of Destiny: The Life and Times of General Winfield Scott* (New York, 1997), 329; Potter, *Impending Crisis*, 228; CFA Diary, September 16, 1852, November 3, 1852, November 10, 1862, all in Adams Papers.

63. *New York Herald*, August 21, 1852, December 24, 1852; Washington *National Era*, January 13, 1853; undated newspaper clipping (with election results), CFA Diary, October 28, 1852, CFA to Theodore Parker, March 24, 1853, all in Adams Papers.

64. CFA2 to CFA, May 14, 1851, May 19, 1851, May 21, 1851, all in Adams Papers.

65. HA, *Education*, 772–774; Ernest Samuels, *Young Henry Adams* (Cambridge, 1967), 9; CFA2 to CFA, May 21, 1851, CFA Diary, June 30, 1854, August 30, 1854, September 3, 1854, September 22, 1854, October 14, 1854, all in Adams Papers.

66. Nagel, *Descent from Glory*, 207; Edward Everett to ABA, April 8, 1854, CFA Diary, October 1, 1856, both in Adams Papers.

67. CFA Diary, June 26, 1854, September 3, 1854, both in Adams Papers.

68. LCA2 to CFA, November 15, 1854, December 20, 1854, March 15, 1855, ABA to CFA, March 19, 1855, LCA2 to ABA, March 7, 1855, all in Adams Papers. Louisa's handwriting, by comparison to the rest of the family's, was atrocious and earned a rebuke from her father. She wrote to him on July 20, 1851, promising that she had "tried to render it legible."

69. On neurasthenia, see Barbara Ehrenreich and Deirdre English, *For Her Own Good: 150 Years of the Experts' Advice to Women* (New York, 1978), 103–107; Chalfant, *Both Sides of the Ocean*, 69, uncharitably remarks that while Henry Adams "turned his life into a succession of complex plans and multiple efforts," Louisa "had no apparent ambition expect to enjoy being well-to-do," as if as an Adams woman she had any other option.

70. CFA to New York Convention, January 25, 1854, CFA to S. M. Gates, September 9, 1856, CFA to Samuel Whitecourt, March 23, 1856, Julia Griffiths to CFA, May 14, 1855, CFA to Julia Griffiths, May 18, 1855, all in Adams Papers.

71. *New York Herald*, January 31, 1855; *Pittsfield (MA) Sun*, February 23, 1854; Washington *National Era*, February 22, 1855; John Allen to CFA, February 4, 1854, CFA to Samuel May, November 24, 1854, CFA to J. Rockwell, November 9, 1855, all in Adams Papers.

72. Stanley Harrold, *Gamaliel Bailey and Antislavery Union* (Kent, 1986), 170; Washington *National Era*, August 23, 1855; Blue, *Free Soilers*, 284; *Pittsfield*

(MA) Sun, August 23, 1855, August 30, 1855; CFA to Gamaliel Bailey, January 20, 1855, CFA to J. Orton, February 20, 1855, CFA to George Bradburn, April 20, 1855, all in Adams Papers.

73. CFA Diary, February 14, 1856, May 23, 1856, May 24, 1856, CFA to JGP, July 18, 1856, all in Adams Papers.

74. John Bicknell, *Lincoln's Pathfinder: John C. Frémont and the Violent Election of 1856* (Chicago, 2017), 177–178; *New York Daily Tribune*, June 7, 1856; Washington *National Era*, June 12, 1856, June 26, 1856; CFA Diary, January 24, 1856, June 17–June 19, 1856, CFA to JGP, July 18, 1856, all in Adams Papers.

75. *Evansville Daily Journal*, July 16, 1856; New Lisbon *Anti-Slavery Bugle*, May 16, 1857; Washington *Evening Star*, July 2, 1856; Honolulu *Pacific Commercial Advertiser*, July 23, 1857; *Lewisburg Chronicle*, June 5, 1857.

76. *New York Herald*, October 10, 1856; *New York Tribune*, September 17, 1856; CFA Diary, October 9, 1856, Adams Papers.

77. Washington *Evening Star*, September 5, 1856; CFA to Francis Bird, October 16, 1854, CFA Diary, June 19, 1856, both in Adams Papers. Despite Adams's protestations, both Brookhiser, *America's First Dynasty*, 128, and Duberman, *Adams*, 208, agree that he badly wanted the nomination that year.

78. Jean Baker, *James Buchanan* (New York, 2004), 72; Kirkland, *Adams*, 13; CFA2, *Autobiography*, 32; CFA to Gamaliel Bailey, December 17, 1856, CFA to S. M. Gates, September 9, 1856, both in Adams Papers.

79. CFA Diary, October 17, 1856, November 6, 1856, both in Adams Papers.

CHAPTER 4: THE CONGRESSMAN

1. *Pittsfield (MA) Sun*, December 30, 1858; Donald, *Sumner*, 342; CFA Diary, January 2, 1858, January 9, 1858, both in Adams Papers.

2. *Highland (OH) Weekly News*, July 1, 1858; *Cleveland Morning Leader*, June 24, 1858; *Alexandria Gazette*, June 23, 1858.

3. CFA Diary, December 3, 1857, Adams Papers; New Lisbon *Anti-Slavery Bugle*, February 28, 1857, March 21, 1857; *Pittsfield (MA) Sun*, July 2, 1857; *New York Daily Tribune*, June 25, 1857; *New York Herald*, June 25, 1857.

4. CFA Diary, January 26, 1858, August 18, 1858, CFA to E. Bradbury, August 25, 1858, all in Adams Papers.

5. Washington *National Era*, October 14, 1858; *Highland (OH) Weekly News*, October 28, 1858; *New York Daily Tribune*, October 21, 1858; *Randolph County (IN) Journal*, October 14, 1858; unidentified newspaper clipping, October 1858, CFA to CS, October 3, 1858, October 8, 1858, all in Adams Papers.

6. CFA to Velorous Taft, October 12, 1858, Adams Papers; Washington *National Era*, October 28, 1858; *New York Herald*, October 18, 1858; Boston *Daily Traveler*, October 28, 1858.

7. Ohio *Western Reserve Chronicle*, October 22, 1858; Washington *National Era*, October 28, 1858; CFA Diary, September 25, 1858, October 8, 1858, October 16, 1858, October 26, 1858, all in Adams Papers.

8. Washington *National Era*, November 11, 1858; Michigan *Cass County Republican*, November 11, 1858; CS to CFA, September 8, 1858, February 5, 1859, CS to ABA, November 7, 1858, in *Letters of Sumner*, ed. Palmer, 1: 511, 514, 520–521; unidentified newspaper clipping, November 1858, CFA to CS, November 21, 1858, CFA to Theodore Parker, November 12, 1858, CFA Diary, November 2, 1858, November 3, 1858, all in Adams Papers.

9. Duberman, *Adams*, 212; CFA2, *Adams*, 105.

10. *Pittsfield (MA) Sun*, November 11, 1858; *Nashville Union and American*, November 12, 1858.

11. Edward Chalfant, *Better in Darkness: A Biography of Henry Adams, His Second Life, 1862–1891* (New York, 1997), 80–81; Charles Kuhn to CFA, January 6, 1856, CFA Diary, October 12, 1857, January 30, 1858, March 12, 1858, all in Adams Papers; CS to CFA, September 8, 1858, in *Letters of Sumner*, ed. Palmer, 1: 511.

12. Nagel, *Descent from Glory*, 217–218; HA, *Education*, 785; CFA to CS, October 3, 1858, Adams Papers.

13. Michael De Gruccio, "Manhood, Race, Failure, and Reconciliation: Charles Francis Adams Jr. and the American Civil War," *New England Quarterly* 81 (2008): 640; CFA2, *Autobiography*, 42; CFA Diary, November 10, 1858, Adams Papers.

14. CFA to CS, November 21, 1858, Adams Papers; CS to CFA, September 8, 1858, in *Letters of Sumner*, ed. Palmer, 1: 511; HA to CFA2, November 3, 1858, in *The Letters of Henry Adams*, ed. J. C. Levenson (Cambridge, 1982), 1: 5; HA, *Education*, 789.

15. Chalfant, *Both Sides of the Ocean*, 103; Levenson, "Etiology of Israel Adams," 574; Arthur Beringause, *Brooks Adams: A Biography* (New York, 1955), 22; HA to CFA2, December 17, 1858, in *Letters*, ed. Levenson, 1: 9.

16. Beringause, *Brooks Adams*, 25–26. Today, Brooks would most likely be diagnosed with attention deficit disorder.

17. HA to CFA2, January 18, 1859, November 23, 1859, in *Letters*, ed. Levenson, 1: 14, 67.

18. HA to ABA, August 16, 1860, CFA Diary, April 20, 1860, both in Adams Papers; HA, *Education*, 797; HA to CS, January 28, 1859, HA to CFA2,

May 9, 1860, HA to ABA, October 26, 1859, April 19, 1860, in *Letters*, ed. Levenson, 1: 59, 127–128, 141.

19. Robert Robertson, "Louisa Catherine Adams Kuhn: Florentine Adventures," *MHR* 11 (2009): 126–128.

20. HA to ABA, January 6, 1860, July 1, 1860, in *Letters*, ed. Levenson, 1: 78, 181.

21. *Cincinnati Daily Press*, April 9, 1860; Washington *Evening Star*, January 8, 1859, April 5, 1860; *Pittsfield (MA) Sun*, June 16, 1859; *Washington Union*, January 8, 1859.

22. Matthew Mason, *Apostle of Union: A Political Biography of Edward Everett* (Chapel Hill, 2016), 220; Washington *National Era*, July 14, 1859; *Portage (OH) County Democrat*, July 20, 1859; CFA to HA, July 16, 1859, Adams Papers.

23. Amanda Foreman, *A World on Fire: Britain's Crucial Role in the American Civil War* (New York, 2010), 48; CFA Diary, November 4, 1859, November 7, 1859, November 24, 1859, all in Adams Papers.

24. CFA2, *Adams*, 105–107; CFA2, *Autobiography*, 49.

25. Wheeling *Daily Intelligencer*, January 31, 1860; *Cleveland Morning Leader*, February 3, 1860; HA, *Education*, 814; CFA Diary, April 6, 1860, Adams Papers.

26. *New York Herald*, May 23,1860; *Congressional Globe*, 36th Cong., 1st Sess., 911; *Liberator*, March 4, 1860; *Trenton (NJ) State Gazette*, March 13, 1860; CFA Diary, April 19, 1860, Adams Papers.

27. *Burlington Free Press*, June 15, 1860; *Lansing State Republican*, May 2, 1860; *Cleveland Morning Leader*, June 7, 1860; CFA to John Motley, February 4, 1860, Adams Papers.

28. *Congressional Globe*, 36th Cong., 1st Sess., 2513–2516.

29. *Burlington Free Press*, June 15, 1860; CFA2, *Autobiography*, 47; CFA to CS, November 21, 1858, CFA to Edward Pierce, February 8, 1860, CFA to Samuel Sewall, February 22, 1860, CFA Diary, February 10, 1860, May 3, 1860, all in Adams Papers; Douglas Egerton, *Year of Meteors: Stephen Douglas, Abraham Lincoln, and the Election That Brought on the Civil War* (New York, 2010), chapter 2, chronicles the Charleston convention.

30. CFA2, *Adams*, 114; CFA to Edward Pierce, May 3, 1860, Adams Papers; HA, *Education*, 813.

31. Egerton, *Year of Meteors*, 141–143; CFA to Edward Pierce, March 12, 1860, CFA to J. Ingersoll Borditch, June 4, 1860, CFA Diary, May 18, 1860, all in Adams Papers.

32. Stahr, *Seward*, 196; CFA to WHS, May 22, 1861, CFA Diary, May 30, 1860, both in Adams Papers.

33. CFA Diary, May 11, 1860, June 23, 1860, both in Adams Papers.

34. Stahr, *Seward*, 200; MA to HA, August 16, 1860, CFA Diary, August 14, 1860, both in Adams Papers; CFA2, *Autobiography*, 52.

35. CFA2, *Autobiography*, 61–62.

36. *Cincinnati Daily Press*, September 10, 1860; *Holmes County (OH) Republican*, September 13, 1860; CFA2, *Autobiography*, 63.

37. David Donald, *Lincoln* (New York, 1995), 254; CFA2, *Autobiography*, 64–65. The elder Adams's Philadelphia speech was reprinted in the *Philadelphia North American and United States Gazette*, August 29, 1860.

38. CFA2, *Autobiography*, 66.

39. CFA Diary, October 17, 1860, Adams Papers; HA, *Education*, 809–810.

40. Egerton, *Year of Meteors*, 209–210; telegram from A. Berry to CFA, November 6, 1860, unidentified newspaper clipping, November 1860, CFA Diary, November 7, 1860, November 9, 1860, all in Adams Papers.

41. AL to WHS, December 8, 1860, in Lincoln Papers, LC; CFA to WHS, November 11, 1860, CFA Diary, November 11, 1860, December 27, 1860, all in Adams Papers.

42. Indianapolis *Indiana State Sentinel*, January 9, 1861; JGP to AL, October 25, 1860, in Lincoln Papers, LC; CFA to JGP, January 5, 1861, CFA Diary, November 15, 1860, November 16, 1860, November 17, 1860, November 23, 1860, all in Adams Papers.

43. CFA Diary, November 11, 1860, November 14, 1860, both in Adams Papers.

44. James Buchanan, "Message to the Senate and House," December 3, 1860, in *Congressional Globe: Senate Journal*, 36th Cong., 2nd Sess., 7–32; CFA Diary, December 2, 1860, December 4, 1860, HA to CFA2, December 9, 1860, all in Adams Papers.

45. *Charleston Mercury Extra*, December 20, 1860; CFA Diary, December 15, 1860, December 20, 1860, CFA to N. Quincy, December 15, 1860, CFA to Linus Lowell, December 16, 1860, CFA to RHD, December 23, 1860, CFA to John Murray Forbes, December 31, 1860, all in Adams Papers.

46. HA to ABA, September 7, 1860, Adams Papers; Donald, *Sumner*, 368; Simpson, *Political Education*, 12–13; Mark Stegmaier, ed. *Henry Adams in the Secession Crisis: Dispatches to the* Boston Daily Advertiser, *December 1860–March 1861* (Baton Rouge, 2012), 38.

47. Potter, *Impending Crisis*, 562; CFA Diary, November 19, 1860, CFA to J. Francis Fisher, December 31, 1860, HA to CFA2, January 2, 1861, all in Adams Papers; CFA2, *Autobiography*, 74.

48. CFA2, *Adams*, 132; Duberman, *Adams*, 228; *Washington National Intelligencer*, December 14, 1861; *Bellows Falls (VT) Times*, December 14, 1860; *Congressional Globe*, 36th Cong., 2nd Sess., 62; CFA Diary, December 5, 1860, December 11, 1860, December 12, 1860, all in Adams Papers.

49. Potter, *Impending Crisis*, 522–523; CFA Diary, December 22, 1860, Adams Papers.

50. CFA to J. D. Baldwin, January 11, 1861, CFA to John A. Andrew, February 8, 1861, both in Adams Papers.

51. CFA to E. Bamfield, January 13, 1861, CFA to Alpheus Hardy, February 11, 1861, CFA to John Murray Forbes, February 5, 1861, CFA to RHD, December 23, 1860, CFA Diary, December 17, 1860, December 18, 1860, all in Adams Papers; HA to CFA2, January 8, 1861, in *Letters*, ed. Levenson, 1: 219. On the difficulties facing runaways from the Lower South, see John Hope Franklin and Loren Schweninger, *Runaway Slaves: Rebels on the Plantation* (New York, 1999), 116–120.

52. Michael Holt, *The Election of 1860* (Lawrence, 2017), 204; *Congressional Globe*, 36th Cong., 2nd Sess., 112; CFA Diary, December 29, 1860, Adams Papers.

53. CFA Diary, December 25, 1860, CFA to E. Bamfield, January 13, 1861, CFA to W. Robinson, January 5, 1861, CFA to T. Taft, February 16, 1861, all in Adams Papers. In fact, this author's paternal grandfather grew cotton in New Mexico, while a maternal grandfather planted cotton just outside of Phoenix.

54. Washington *National Republican*, February 12, 1861; CFA to A. Howard, February 7, 1861, CFA to Ira Steward, January 7, 1861, both in Adams Papers.

55. CFA Diary, February 28, 1861, CFA to Francis Fischer, December 31, 1860, CFA to John A. Dix, January 6, 1861, HA to CFA2, December 22, 1860, December 26, 1860, all in Adams Papers.

56. George Fogg to AL, January 1, 1861, in Lincoln Papers, LC; CFA Diary, December 27, 1860, January 8, 1861, CFA to Edward Pierce, January 1, 1861, all in Adams Papers.

57. Potter, *Impending Crisis*, 533; CFA Diary, December 29, 1860, CFA to T. Taft, February 16, 1861, CFA to B. Wood, January 8, 1861, CFA to CFA2, December 21, 1857, HA to CFA2, December 18, 1860, December 26, 1860, all in Adams Papers; *Adams in the Secession Crisis*, ed. Stegmaier, 78.

58. *Cincinnati Daily Press*, January 22, 1861; Donald, *Sumner*, 374; CFA2 to CFA, January 7, 1861, Adams Papers; CFA2, *Autobiography*, 88.

59. Chalfant, *Both Sides of the Ocean*, 209; Samuels, *Young Henry Adams*, 85.

60. Donald, *Sumner*, 375; HA to CFA2, January 17, 1861, in *Letters*, ed. Levenson, 1: 222; CFA Diary, January 13, 1861, January 29, 1861, CFA to Francis Bird, February 11, 1861, CFA to JGP, November 22, 1862, all in Adams Papers.

61. Thomas Corwin to AL, January 16, 1861, in Lincoln Papers, LC; *Washington National Intelligencer*, January 4, 1861; Joshua Giddings to CFA, December 10, 1860, CFA to CFA2, December 21, 1860, CFA to B. Wood, January 8, 1861, CFA to W. Robinson, January 5, 1861, all in Adams Papers.

62. Albany *Evening Journal*, January 12, 1861; *New York Times*, January 17, 1861; *Adams in the Secession Crisis*, ed. Stegmaier, 98; Amherst *Farmer's Cabinet*, January 25, 1861; CFA to CFA2, January 15, 1861, CFA to Francis Fisher, December 31, 1860, CFA Diary, January 15, 1861, all in Adams Papers.

63. *Adams in the Secession Crisis*, ed. Stegmaier, 64; CFA Diary, January 1, 1861, Adams Papers; Duberman, *Adams*, 241.

64. CFA2, *Adams*, 141; Washington *National Republican*, February 2, 1861; *Congressional Globe*, 36th Cong., 2nd Sess., Appendix, 124.

65. *Congressional Globe*, 36th Cong., 2nd Sess., Appendix, 125–126.

66. *Congressional Globe*, 36th Cong., 2nd Sess., Appendix, 127.

67. CFA2, *Adams*, 113; Washington *National Republican*, February 2, 1861; HA to CFA2, January 31, 1861, in *Letters*, ed. Levenson, 1: 227; CFA Diary, January 31, 1861, Adams Papers.

68. CFA to JGP, January 5, 1861, CFA to CFA2, December 15, 1860, both in Adams Papers; CFA2, *Autobiography*, 76–77; HA, *Education*, 816.

69. Harold Holzer, *Lincoln: President Elect: Abraham Lincoln and the Great Secession Winter* (New York, 2008), 407; CFA Diary, February 24, 1861, Adams Papers; HA, *Education*, 816.

70. CFA2, *Autobiography*, 96–97; CFA Diary, March 4, 1861, Adams Papers.

71. CFA Diary, March 4, 1861, Adams Papers.

72. HA, *Education*, 817; CFA Diary, March 4, 1861, Adams Papers.

73. CFA2, *Autobiography*, 90–91.

74. Stahr, *Seward*, 261; CFA2, *Autobiography*, 90; CFA to Charles Dewey, March 6, 1861, CFA Diary, March 31, 1861, April 12, 1861, all in Adams Papers.

75. CFA Diary, April 13, 1861, April 15, 1861, both in Adams Papers.

Chapter 5: The Minister

1. CFA Diary, March 19, 1861, Adams Papers; CS to the Duchess of Argyll, March 19, 1861, in *Letters of Sumner*, ed. Palmer, 2: 60–61; CFA2, *Autobiography*, 107.

2. Garry Wills, *Henry Adams and the Making of America* (New York, 2005), 14.

3. CFA Diary, March 20, 1861, Adams Papers; CFA2, *Autobiography*, 107.

4. CFA Diary, March 19, 1861, Adams Papers.

5. CFA Diary, March 19, 1861, Adams Papers.

6. CFA Diary, March 19, 1861, Adams Papers; Philip Van Doren Stern, *When the Guns Roared: World Aspects of the American Civil War* (Garden City, 1965), 75; "Our Diplomacy during the Rebellion," *North American Review* (April 1866): 449.

7. CFA Diary, February 23, 1861, Adams Papers; Elihu Washburn to AL, December 9, 1860, Hannibal Hamlin to AL, December 10, 1860, Hannibal Hamlin to AL, December 14, 1860, Peleg Chandler and J. H. Mitchell to AL, January 3, 1861, John A. Andrew to AL, January 20, 1861, Henry Wilson to AL, January 5, 1861, Simon Cameron to AL, January 2, 1861, John Alley to AL, January 4, 1861, Francis Blair Sr. to AL, January 14, 1861, Leonard Swett to AL, January 4, 1861, Leonard Swett to AL, January 5, 1860, Massachusetts Congressional Delegation to AL, January 4, 1861, all in AL Papers, LC; HA to CFA2, January 11, 1861, in *Letters*, ed. Levenson, 1: 220.

8. AL to WHS, March 11, 1861, WHS to AL, March 11, 1861, both in AL Papers, LC.

9. Foreman, *World on Fire*, 71; *Pomeroy (OH) Weekly Telegraph*, April 5, 1861; *Nashville Union and American*, March 19, 1861; Amherst *Farmer's Cabinet*, February 22, 1861; CFA Diary, March 28, 1861, Adams Papers; CFA2, *Adams*, 145.

10. CFA to WHS, April 13, 1861, CFA to RHD, June 11, 1862, both in Adams Papers.

11. Salt Lake City *Mountaineer*, April 27, 1861; *Cleveland Morning Leader*, March 20, 1861; *Evansville Daily Journal*, March 30, 1861; *Barre (MA) Gazette*, March 29, 1861; *Port Tobacco (MD) Times*, March 21, 1861; *New York Herald*, March 20, 1861; *Bradford (PA) Reporter*, April 4, 1861; Washington *Evening Star*, March 28, 1861.

12. Richmond *Daily Dispatch*, March 20, 1861; *Richmond Enquirer*, March 23, 1861; *New Orleans Daily Crescent*, March 29, 1861.

13. Hannibal Hamlin to AL, December 10, 1860, AL Papers, LC; Simpson, *Political Education*, 15; Chalfant, *Better in Darkness*, 26; HA, *Education*, 821.

14. Nagel, *Descent from Glory*, 211–213; Howard Jones, *Union in Peril: The Crisis over British Intervention in the Civil War* (Chapel Hill, 1992), 30; CFA2, *Autobiography*, 113.

15. CFA to Christopher Robinson, March 26, 1861, CFA to E. C. Banfield, March 22, 1861, CFA to E. A. Davis, April 5, 1861, all in Adams Papers; *Plymouth (IN) Weekly Democrat*, May 23, 1861; Brookhiser, *America's First Dynasty*, 132.

16. Amherst *Farmer's Cabinet*, May 3, 1861; CFA Diary, May 1, Adams Papers.

17. CFA Diary, May 13, 1861, CFA to WHS, May 17, 1861, CFA to Baring Brothers, April 16, 1861, all in Adams Papers.

18. *New York Herald*, May 31, 1861; CFA to Edward Everett, July 12, 1861, CFA Diary, May 16, 1861, both in Adams Papers.

19. Stern, *When the Guns Roared*, 50; CFA to JGP, July 12, 1861, Adams Papers.

20. HA to CFA2, May 16, 1861, in *Letters*, ed. Levenson, 1: 236; Samuels, *Young Henry Adams*, 101; Thornton Anderson, *Brooks Adams, Constructive Conservative* (Ithaca, 1951), 6–7.

21. CFA to WHS, May 21, 1861, Adams Papers; Jones, *Union in Peril*, 27–28; Mason, *Everett*, 297.

22. Stahr, *Seward*, 290; CFA to WHS, June 21, 1861, Adams Papers.

23. CFA2, *Adams*, 152–153; David Brown, *Palmerston: A Biography* (New Haven, 2011), 455; Jones, *Union in Peril*, 18–24; Don Doyle, *The Cause of All Nations: An International History of the American Civil War* (New York, 2014), 65–66.

24. Jones, *Union in Peril*, 44; Stern, *When the Guns Roared*, 51; CFA to WHS, May 21, 1861, Adams Papers.

25. Paul Scherer, *Lord John Russell: A Biography* (Philadelphia, 1999), 291; Robert May, *The Union, the Confederacy, and the Atlantic Rim* (West Lafayette, 1995), 4; WHS to AL, May 21, 1861, in AL Papers, LC; HA to CFA2, June 10, 1861, in *The Letters of Henry Adams, 1858–1891*, ed. Worthington Ford (Cambridge, 1930), 93; CFA to WHS, June 14, 1861, Adams Papers.

26. John Belohlavek, *George Mifflin Dallas, Jacksonian Patrician* (University Park, 1977), 180; Eric Walther, *William Lowndes Yancey and the Coming of the Civil War* (Chapel Hill, 2006), 308.

27. Stern, *When the Guns Roared*, 54; Theodore Lyman to CFA, November 7, 1861, CFA to WHS, May 17, 1861, CFA to WHS, June 14, 1861, CFA to William Dayton, July 2, 1861, all in Adams Papers.

28. CFA Diary, June 11, 1861, July 11, 1861, July 24, 1861, August 12, 1861, October 8, 1861, all in Adams Papers.

29. CFA to John Forbes, August 30, 1861, CFA to Edward Everett, October 25, 1861, CFA to JGP, July 12, 1861, CFA to RHD, June 11, 1862, CFA to WHS, June 6, 1861, all in Adams Papers.

30. *Memphis Daily Appeal*, December 24, 1862; CFA to RHD, June 14, 1861, CFA to WHS, June 21, 1861, CFA to JGP, October 18, 1861, CFA to Thomas Corwin, September 4, 1861, all in Adams Papers.

31. CFA to WHS, May 21, 1861, CFA to WHS, July 19, 1862, both in Adams Papers.

32. Chalfant, *Both Sides of the Ocean*, 291; James M. McPherson, *Battle Cry of Freedom: The Civil War Era* (New York, 1988), 344–347.

33. CFA to RHD, August 28, 1861, CFA to Thomas Corwin, September 4, 1861, both in Adams Papers; Amherst *Farmer's Cabinet*, August 30, 1861.

34. Jones, *Union in Peril*, 58–59; Brown, *Palmerston*, 452.

35. William Schouler, *A History of Massachusetts in the Civil War* (Cambridge, 1868), 91; Simpson, *Political Education*, 16; HA to CFA, August 5, 1861, CFA to HA, August 23, 1861, in *A Cycle of Adams Letters, 1861–1865*, ed. Worthington Ford (Boston, 1920), 1: 24–25, 30–31.

36. CFA Diary, August 18, 1861, September 3, 1861, both in Adams Papers.

37. CFA Diary, November 12, 1861, CFA to WHS, November 15, 1861, CFA to Theodore Lyman, November 7, 1861, all in Adams Papers; CFA2, "The Trent Affair," *Massachusetts Historical Society Proceedings* 37 (1911): 20.

38. CFA to WHS, November 29, 1861, Adams Papers; Robert Young, *Senator James Murray Mason: Defender of the Old South* (Knoxville, 1998), 114; CFA2, *Adams*, 547–548.

39. HA, *Education*, 828; CFA to WHS, November 29, 1861, Adams Papers; Benjamin Moran Diary, November 29, 1861, in *The Journal of Benjamin Moran, 1857–1865*, ed. Sarah Wallace (Chicago, 1948), 1: 915.

40. CFA2, *Adams*, 226; Moran Diary, November 29, 1861, in *Journal*, ed. Wallace, 1: 915; CFA to WHS, December 11, 1861, Adams Papers.

41. CFA to WHS, November 29, 1861 (two letters of this date), December 6, 1861, December 12, 1861, December 20, 1861, CFA Diary, November 30, 1861, all in Adams Papers.

42. CFA to WHS, December 3, 1861, CFA to RHD, December 13, 1861, CFA to Edward Everett, January 10, 1862, all in Adams Papers; HA to CFA2, December 13, 1861, in *Cycle of Letters*, ed. Ford, 1: 83.

43. Hermione Hobhouse, *Prince Albert: His Life and Work* (London, 1983), 154–155; *Wilmington (NC) Journal*, January 9, 1862; WHS to CFA, November 27, 1861, in *OR*, Series 2, Vol. 2, 1102; CFA2, *Adams*, 227; CFA Diary, December 15, 1861, December 19, 1861, both in Adams Papers.

44. WHS to CFA, December 27, 1861, December 28, 1861, both in *OR*, Series 2, Vol. 2, 1143, 1157; Wheeling *Daily Intelligencer*, November 22, 1861; CFA to WHS, December 12, 1861, January 17, 1862, CFA to WHS, December 20, 1861, December 27, 1861, CFA to J. L. Westley, December 26, 1861, all in Adams Papers.

45. CFA to CFA2, February 24, 1862, in *Cycle of Letters*, ed. Ford, 1: 114; CFA to Cassius Clay, January 14, 1862, CFA to Edward Everett, January 24, 1862, both in Adams Papers.

46. HA to Frederick Seward, April 4, 1862, in *Letters*, ed. Levenson, 1: 288; Moran Diary, May 6, 1862, in *Journal*, ed. Wallace, 1: 997; CFA to WHS, March 13, 1862, CFA Diary, February 10, 1862, both in Adams Papers; CFA to CFA2, May 20, 1862, in *Cycle of Letters*, ed. Ford, 1: 150.

47. James M. McPherson, *Crossroads of Freedom: Antietam* (New York, 2002), 39–40; CFA Diary, February 17, 1862, CFA to WHS, January 17, 1862, February 13, 1862, CFA to Edward Everett, February 21, 1862, CFA to John Forbes, March 14, 1862, all in Adams Papers.

48. CFA to Edward Everett, September 5, 1862, CFA to WHS, January 31, 1862, June 26, 1862, July 3, 1862, September 12, 1862, December 4, 1862, all in Adams Papers.

49. CFA to Edward Everett, May 2, 1862, CFA to WHS, January 3, 1862, CFA Diary, March 19, 1862, May 3, 1862, May 26, 1862, all in Adams Papers. On these laws, see Eric Foner, *The Fiery Trial: Abraham Lincoln and American Slavery* (New York, 2010), 198–202.

50. CFA Diary, March 24, 1862, Adams Papers.

51. Stephen Sears, *George B. McClellan: The Young Napoleon* (New York, 1988), 240–242; CFA to Edward Everett, March 7, 1862, CFA to WHS, June 26, 1862, both in Adams Papers.

52. CFA Diary, June 28, 1862, July 10, 1862, CFA to Edward Everett, July 18, 1862, all in Adams Papers.

53. CFA2, *Adams*, 349; HA to CFA2, July 19, 1862, in *Cycle of Letters*, ed. Ford, 1: 166–167; CFA to WHS, May 8, 1862, June 2, 1862, June 13, 1862, July 17, 1862, July 24, 1862, CFA to JGP, June 13, 1862, CFA to Thurlow Weed, July 18, 1862, all in Adams Papers.

54. Wesley Loy, "10 Rumford Place: Doing Confederate Business in Liverpool," *South Carolina Historical Magazine* 98 (1997): 352; CFA to WHS, January 10, 1862, April 25, 1862, both in Adams Papers; CFA to WHS, September 6, 1861, September 14, 1861, CFA to John Russell, August 15, 1861, all in *OR*, Series 1, Vol. 6: 176–177, 265–266, 330–331; Brattleboro *Vermont Phoenix*, September 4, 1862; Columbus *Daily Ohio Statesman*, September 2, 1862; *New Bern Weekly Progress*, September 13, 1862; *Weekly Lancaster Gazette*, September 4, 1862.

55. Doyle, *Cause of All Nations*, 220–221; CFA to John Russell, March 25, 1862, CFA Diary, September 21, 1862, both in Adams Papers.

56. John Prest, *Lord John Russell* (New York, 1972), 394; Stern, *When the Guns Roared*, 210–211; Jones, *Union in Peril*, 146–147; HA, *Education*, 856; CFA Diary, July 31, 1862, Adams Papers.

57. Scherer, *Russell*, 293; HA, *Education*, 858–859.

58. Stern, *When the Guns Roared*, 154–155; CFA to WHS, October 10, 1862, Adams Papers; HA, *Education*, 862–863.

59. McPherson, *Crossroads of Freedom*, 109; Stephen Sears, *Landscape Turned Red: The Battle of Antietam* (Boston, 1983), 306–307; CFA Diary, September 26, 1862, CFA to WHS, October 5, 1862, both in Adams Papers.

60. McPherson, *Crossroads of Freedom*, 142; HA to CFA2, October 17, 1862, in *Cycle of Letters*, ed. Ford, 1: 192; CFA Diary, October 19, 1862, October 22, 1862, CFA to WHS, October 5, 1862, CFA to JGP, November 22, 1862, all in Adams Papers.

61. Allen Guelzo, *Lincoln's Emancipation Proclamation: The End of Slavery in America* (New York, 2004), 153; CFA Diary, July 22, 1862, Adams Papers.

62. Scherer, *Russell*, 294; HA to CFA2, January 23, 1863, in *Cycle of Letters*, ed. Ford, 1: 243; CFA to John Gorrie, November 17, 1862, CFA to William Dayton, October 5, 1862, CFA to George Thompson, November 16, 1862, CFA Diary, October 4, 1862, all in Adams Papers.

63. HA to CFA2, January 23, 1863, in *Cycle of Letters*, ed. Ford, 1: 243; CFA Diary, October 22, 1861, December 6, 1861, CFA to Edward Everett, October 25, 1861, CFA to WHS, June 21, 1861, CFA to RHD, June 27, 1861, all in Adams Papers.

64. David Donald, *Charles Sumner and the Rights of Man* (New York, 1970), 71, 83; Moran Diary, January 5, 1863, in *Journal*, ed. Wallace, 1: 1103; *Alexandria Gazette*, October 28, 1862, December 20, 1862; *New York Herald*, September 25, 1862; Washington *National Republican*, October 29, 1862; Montpelier *Green-Mountain Freeman*, October 29, 1862, November 4, 1862; *Bellows (VT) Falls Times*, October 31, 1862; CFA Diary, September 21, 1862, September 23, 1862, CFA to RHD, November 22, 1862, all in Adams Papers.

65. CFA Diary, December 11, 1862, Adams Papers; *Chicago Tribune*, January 13, 1863; Amherst *Farmer's Cabinet*, January 15, 1863; Washington *Daily National Republican*, January 13, 1863.

CHAPTER 6: THE OFFICER

1. CFA2, *Autobiography*, 114–116.

2. CFA2, *Autobiography*, 115–117; HA, *Education*, 821; CFA2 to JQA2, May 11, 1861, Adams Papers; William Schouler, *A History of Massachusetts in the Civil War* (Boston, 1871), 658.

3. CFA2, *Autobiography*, 118–119.

4. CFA2 to CFA, June 10, 1861, in *Cycle of Letters*, ed. Ford, 1: 9–11.

5. HA to CFA2, July 2, 1861, in *Cycle of Letters*, ed. Ford, 1: 17.

6. CFA2 to ABA, July 9, 1861, in *Cycle of Letters*, ed. Ford, 1: 18–19; CFA2, *Autobiography*, 121.

7. CFA2 to HA, August 23, 1861, December 10, 1861, CFA2 to CFA, July 23, 1861, in *Cycle of Letters*, ed. Ford, 1: 22–23, 30, 79; CFA2, *Autobiography*, 123–124.

8. CFA Diary, November 10, 1861, Adams Papers; CFA2 to CFA, November 26, 1861, in *Cycle of Letters*, ed. Ford, 1: 72–73.

9. CFA Diary, December 9, 1861, January 2, 1862, both in Adams Papers; CFA to CFA2, December 12, 1861, in *Cycle of Letters*, ed. Ford, 1: 81.

10. CFA2 to HA, December 8, 1861, in *Cycle of Letters*, ed. Ford, 1: 78; CFA2, *Autobiography*, 124.

11. HA to CFA2, December 13, 1861, December 28, 1861, CFA2 to HA, January (no date) 1862, HA to CFA2, February 14, 1862, in *Cycle of Letters*, ed. Ford, 1: 82, 94, 102–103, 112.

12. CFA2 to JQA2, February 5, 1862, CFA Diary, February 14, 1862, both in Adams Papers; Nagel, *Descent from Glory*, 240.

13. Kirkland, *Adams*, 24–25; CFA2 to HA, December 10, 1861, December 19, 1861, in *Cycle of Letters*, ed. Ford, 1: 80, 86; CFA2, *Autobiography*, 126; Caspar Crowninshield, *A History of the First Regiment of Massachusetts Cavalry Volunteers* (Boston, 1891), 9–10; Francis Brown, *Harvard University in the War, 1861–1865* (Boston, 1886), 87.

14. CFA2, *Autobiography*, 137; Crowninshield, *First Regiment*, 6, 11.

15. Stephen Starr, "The First Massachusetts Volunteer Cavalry," *Proceedings of the Massachusetts Historical Society* 87 (1975): 99; CFA2 to JQA2, January 1, 1862, Adams Papers; CFA2 to HA, January 3, 1862, in *Cycle of Letters*, ed. Ford, 1: 97; CFA2, *Autobiography*, 138.

16. CFA2, *Autobiography*, 131–133, 139; Schouler, *Massachusetts in the Civil War*, 389, 645; CFA2 to JQA2, January 5, 1862, Adams Papers; CFA2 to HA, January 3, 1862, in *Cycle of Letters*, ed. Ford, 1: 98.

17. CFA2 to JQA2, February 2, 1862, Adams Papers.

18. CFA2 to JQA2, February 2, 1862, April 23, 1862, May 2, 1862, all in Adams Papers.

19. CFA2 to HA, January (no date) 1862, CFA2 to ABA, February 2, 1862, in *Cycle of Letters*, ed. Ford, 1: 103, 111; CFA Diary, January 22, 1862, Adams Papers.

20. CFA2 to ABA, February 2, 1862, in *Cycle of Letters*, ed. Ford, 1: 111–112.

21. CFA2 to CFA, March 11, 1862, CFA2 to HA, April 6, 1862, in *Cycle of Letters*, ed. Ford, 1: 111, 127, 130–131.

22. CFA2 to CFA, March 11, 1862, in *Cycle of Letters*, ed. Ford, 1: 118.

23. Crowninshield, *First Regiment*, 304–305.

24. Stephen V. Ash, *Firebrand of Liberty: The Story of Two Black Regiments That Changed the Course of the Civil War* (New York: 2008), 22; Joseph Glatthaar, *Forged in Battle: The Civil War Alliance of Black Soldiers and White Officers* (New York, 1990), 6–7; CFA2 to CFA, July 28, 1862, August 10, 1862, in *Cycle of Letters*, ed. Ford, 1: 169–170, 174.

25. Michael DeGruccio, "Manhood, Race, Failure, and Reconciliation: Charles Francis Adams Jr. and the American Civil War," *New England Quarterly* 81 (2008): 654; HA to CFA2, July 19, 1862, CFA2 to HA, July 28, 1862, in *Cycle of Letters*, ed. Ford, 1: 167, 171.

26. CFA Diary, April 16, 1862, Adams Papers.

27. CFA2 to JQA2, March 7, 1862, March 27, 1862, July 6, 1862, all in Adams Papers.

28. Starr, "First Massachusetts Volunteer Cavalry," 97; CFA2 to JQA2, March 7, 1862, March 27, 1862, April 18, 1862, June 13, 1862, July 6, 1862, all in Adams Papers.

29. CFA2 to CFA, June 18, 1862, in *Cycle of Letters*, ed. Ford, 1: 157; CFA2, *Autobiography*, 140; CFA2 to JQA2, May 24, 1862, June 4, 1862, both in Adams Papers; Stephen Wise, *Gate of Hell: Campaign for Charleston Harbor, 1863* (Columbia, 1994), 8–9.

30. CFA2 to JQA2, June 12, 1862, Adams Papers.

31. CFA2 to CFA, June 18, 1862, in *Cycle of Letters*, ed. Ford, 1: 157; CFA2, *Autobiography*, 141; CFA2 to JQA2, June 17, 1862, Adams Papers.

32. *Santa Fe Gazette*, July 26, 1862; Douglas Bostick, *Charleston under Siege* (Charleston, 2010), 17; CFA2, *Autobiography*, 141–142; CFA2 to JQA2, June 17, 1862, July 6, 1862, both in Adams Papers.

33. CFA2 to CFA, June 18, 1862, in *Cycle of Letters*, ed. Ford, 1: 156; CFA Diary, June 28, 1862, July 3, 1862, CFA2 to JQA2, June 26, 1862, June 17, 1862, all in Adams Papers.

34. CFA2 to CFA, June 28, 1862, August 27, 1862, in *Cycle of Letters*, ed. Ford, 1: 159–160, 176; Starr, "First Massachusetts Volunteer Cavalry," 93.

35. Port Royal *New South*, August 8, 1863; CFA2, *Autobiography*, 142; CFA2 to CFA, July 16, 1862, in *Cycle of Letters*, ed. Ford, 1: 164–165; CFA2 to JQA2, June 17, 1862, July 31, 1862, both in Adams Papers.

36. Crowninshield, *First Regiment*, 86; Brown, *Harvard University in the War*, 87; CFA2, *Autobiography*, 137; JQA2 to CFA2, July 5, 1862, Adams Papers.

37. Nagel, *Descent from Glory*, 209–210.

38. JQA2 to CFA2, July 28, 1862, CFA2 to JQA2, August 25, 1862, CFA Diary, September 10, 1862, all in Adams Papers; CFA2 to CFA, August 22, 1862, in *Cycle of Letters*, ed. Ford, 1: 175.

39. JQA2 to CFA2, July 28, 1862, Adams Papers.

40. CFA2 to JQA2, August 4, 1862, Adams Papers.

41. CFA2 to JQA2, August 4, 1862, August 28, 1862, August 31, 1862, JQA2 to CFA2, August 15, 1862, September 3, 1862, all in Adams Papers; CFA2, Regimental Descriptive Book, October 30, 1862, 1st Mass. Cavalry, National Archives; Brown, *Harvard University in the War*, 87. Bull Run casualties may be found in "Return of Casualties," in *OR*, Series 1, Vol. 12, 262, 561–562.

42. Starr, "First Massachusetts Volunteer Cavalry," 98; Crowninshield, *First Regiment*, 34; CFA2 to ABA, September 25, 1862, in *Cycle of Letters*, ed. Ford, 1: 185.

43. CFA2 to ABA, September 25, 1862, in *Cycle of Letters*, ed. Ford, 1: 186–187. Despite calling the Union forces "liberators," the women were presumably white, for CFA2 invariably commented on race when the person was of color.

44. CFA2 to ABA, September 25, 1862, in *Cycle of Letters*, ed. Ford, 1: 188; CFA2, *Autobiography*, 152–153.

45. Crowninshield, *First Regiment*, 15–16; CFA2 to JQA2, September 18, 1862, September 22, 1862, both in Adams Papers.

46. CFA2 to JQA2, September 18, 1862, September 25, 1862, October 12, 1862, all in Adams Papers.

47. Starr, "First Massachusetts Volunteer Cavalry," 98; Crowninshield, *First Regiment*, 16; CFA2 to JQA2, August 28, 1862, Adams Papers.

48. Starr, "First Massachusetts Volunteer Cavalry," 96; CFA2 to JQA2, October 17, 1862, November 28, 1862, December 8, 1862, all in Adams Papers.

49. Crowninshield, *First Regiment*, 87; JQA2 to CFA2, November 10, 1862, CFA2 to JQA2, November 13, 1862, November 19, 1862, all in Adams Papers.

50. CFA2 to CFA, December 21, 1862, in *Cycle of Letters*, ed. Ford, 1: 215; CFA2 to JQA2, December 8, 1862, JQA2 to CFA2, December 4, 1862, both in Adams Papers.

51. CFA Diary, December 11, 1862, December 22, 1862, December 25, 1862, December 27–28, 1862, all in Adams Papers.

52. CFA2 to CFA, December 21, 1862, in *Cycle of Letters*, ed. Ford, 1: 216–217; CFA2 to JQA2, December 24, 1862, Adams Papers.

53. CFA2 to CFA, December 21, 1862, in *Cycle of Letters*, ed. Ford, 1: 215–216.

CHAPTER 7: THE COMBATANTS

1. CFA Diary, January 13, 1863, Adams Papers.

2. "List of Persons Composing the Legation," January 1, 1868, CFA Diary, January 8, 1863, both in Adams Papers. The house that Adams rented is long gone and is now home to a Nationwide Insurance office.

3. CFA to WHS, January 15, 1863, January 22, 1863, CFA Diary, January 29, 1863, all in Adams Papers. On Davis's December 24, 1862, proclamation, see Douglas R. Egerton, *Thunder at the Gates: The Black Civil War Regiments That Redeemed America* (New York, 2016), 64. The theory that Lincoln issued the proclamation only to keep Britain out of the war was advanced by journalist Lerone Bennett Jr., *Forced into Glory: Abraham Lincoln's White Dream* (New York, 2000). But as Allen Guelzo, *Lincoln's Emancipation Proclamation: The End of Slavery in America* (New York, 2004), 247–248, observes in a thoughtful rejoinder, as a smart policy maker Lincoln understood that his proclamation would have numerous implications. Forcing British neutrality was merely one of them.

4. CFA to Edward Everett, January 23, 1863, February 13, 1863, February 27, 1863, CFA to Bayard Taylor, March 14, 1863, all in Adams Papers.

5. CFA to WHS, January 8, 1863, January 16, 1863, April 10, 1863, Thomas William to CFA, February 17, 1863, W. S. Nicholas to CFA, February 2, 1863, Thomas Porter to CFA, January 5, 1863, CFA to RHD, April 8, 1863, CFA Diary, January 2, 1863, all in Adams Papers; Washington *National Intelligencer*, March 5, 1863.

6. HA to CFA2, January 30, 1863, in *Cycle of Letters*, ed. Ford, 1: 251.

7. Doyle, *Cause of All Nations*, 248; CFA to John Bright, June 24, 1863, Adams Papers.

8. Moran Diary, February 27, 1863, in *Journal*, ed. Wallace, 1: 1125; CFA to Charles Loring, January 2, 1863, Adams Papers.

9. CFA2 to JQA2, January 31, 1863, Adams Papers.

10. CFA2 to JQA2, January 20, 1863, CFA Diary, April 20, 1863, both in Adams Papers.

11. JQA2 to CFA, February 9, 1863, CFA2 to JQA2, February 14, 1863, both in Adams Papers; Bliss Perry, *Life and Letters of Henry Lee Higginson* (Boston, 1921), 186.

12. CFA2 to JQA2, March 22, 1863, CFA Diary, May 17, 1863, both in Adams Papers; *Chicago Daily Tribune*, March 24, 1863.

13. HA to CFA2, May 1, 1863, in *Cycle of Letters*, ed. Ford, 1: 278–279.

14. CFA to Edward Everett, January 23, 1863, CFA to WHS, February 19, 1863, March 20, 1863, all in Adams Papers.

15. Moran Diary, March 2, 1863, in *Journal*, ed. Wallace, 1: 1125; CFA Diary, February 6, 1863, Adams Papers; HA to Frederick Seward, March 20, 1863, in *Letters*, ed. Levenson, 1: 337.

16. CFA Diary, March 14, 1863, CFA to John Russell, February 9, 1863, March 14, 1863, CFA to WHS, March 13, 1863, CFA to Edward Everett, March 20, 1863, all in Adams Papers.

17. CFA Diary, March 26, 1863, CFA to John Russell, April 18, 1863, October 23, 1863, all in Adams Papers.

18. CFA Diary, May 2, 1863, Adams Papers; Charles Sumner to Richard Cobden, April 21, 1863, in *Letters of Sumner*, ed. Palmer, 2: 159, n. 1; Moran Diary, April 21, 1863, May 22, 1863, in *Journal*, ed. Wallace, 1: 1148, 1166–1167.

19. HA to CFA2, June 18, 1863, in *Cycle of Letters*, ed. Ford, 2: 34; Moran Diary, May 22, June 5, 1863, June 17, 1863, in *Journal*, ed. Wallace, 1: 1166, 1171, 1175.

20. Loy, "10 Rumford Place," 368; Scherer, *Russell*, 296–297; CFA Diary, April 5, 1863, CFA to Edward Everett, April 29, 1863, both in Adams Papers; CFA to WHS, May 1, 1863, in *OR*, Series 3, Vol. 4, 213.

21. CFA Diary, May 11, 1863, CFA2 to JQA2, May 10, 1863, both in Adams Papers.

22. CFA to Edward Everett, February 27, 1863, May 15, 1863, CFA to RHD, April 8, 1863, all in Adams Papers.

23. McPherson, *Battle Cry*, 639–645; CFA Diary, May 14, 1863, May 23, 1863, May 26, 1863, CFA to C. A. Davis, May 21, 1863, all in Adams Papers.

24. CFA2 to JQA2, May 23, 1863, JQA2 to CFA2, May 28, 1863, both in Adams Papers; CFA2 to CFA, May 24, 1863, in *Cycle of Letters*, ed. Ford, 2: 14–15.

25. CFA2 to CFA, June 14, 1863, in *Cycle of Letters*, ed. Ford, 2: 26.

26. CFA2 to CFA, June 14, 1863, in *Cycle of Letters*, ed. Ford, 2: 26–28.

27. Crowninshield, *First Regiment*, 18; CFA2 to CFA, June 14, 1863, in *Cycle of Letters*, ed. Ford, 2: 30–32.

28. Perry, *Life of Higginson*, 194–195; Crowninshield, *First Regiment*, 103; CFA2 to JQA2, June 19, 1863, Adams Papers. Aldie sits at what is now the intersection of Routes 50 and 15, the latter leading north to Leesburg.

29. CFA2 to JQA2, June 19, 1863, CFA Diary, July 1, 1863, both in Adams Papers; *Cleveland Morning Leader*, June 25, 1863; Columbus *Daily Ohio Statesman*, June 25, 1863.

30. HA to CFA2, June 18, 1863, in *Cycle of Letters*, ed. Ford, 2: 34; CFA Diary, June 27, 1863, July 1, 1863, July 8, 1863, CFA to Edward Everett, July 3, 1863, all in Adams Papers.

31. CFA Diary, June 7, 1863, June 20, 1863, July 10, 1863, all in Adams Papers.

32. CFA2 Diary, June 26, 1863, June 27, 1863, June 28, 1863, July 2, 1863, all in Adams Papers; CFA2, *Autobiography*, 149–150; CFA2 to CFA, July 22, 1863, in *Cycle of Letters*, ed. Ford, 2: 56.

33. CFA2, *Autobiography*, 151; CFA2 to CFA, July 22, 1863, in *Cycle of Letters*, ed. Ford, 2: 56.

34. CFA2 Diary, July 6, 1863, July 8, 1863, CFA2 to JQA2, July 12, 1863, July 18, 1863, all in Adams Papers.

35. CFA Diary, July 16, 1863, July 19, 1863, CFA to Edward Everett, July 24, 1863, CFA to WHS, July 23, 1863, CFA to RHD, July 29, 1863, all in Adams Papers; CFA to CFA2, July 17, 1863, July 24, 1863, HA to CFA2, July 23, 1863, in *Cycle of Letters*, ed. Ford, 2: 45, 58–59, 63.

36. CFA Diary, July 18, 1863, July 20, 1863, July 23, 1863, July 30, 1863, all in Adams Papers; CFA to CFA2, July 31, 1863, in *Cycle of Letters*, ed. Ford, 2: 65–66.

37. CFA2 to CFA, July 22, 1863, in *Cycle of Letters*, ed. Ford, 2: 55; CFA to RHD, July 29, 1863, Adams Papers.

38. *New York Herald*, July 13, 1863; CFA to John Russell, July 7, 1863, CFA to WHS, July 10, 1863, both in Adams Papers. On Bold, see *London Times*, November 24, 1864. Curiously, Prioleau's first and middle names were Charles Kuhn, the same as Adams's son-in-law.

39. Coy Cross, *Lincoln's Man in Liverpool: Consul Dudley and the Legal Battle to Stop Confederate Warships* (DeKalb, 2007), 106; CFA to WHS, July 24, 1863, July 31, 1863, both in Adams Papers.

40. Thomas Ewing to AL, August 6, 1863, Gustavus Fox to AL, September 8, 1863, both in AL Papers, LC; CFA to WHS, September 3, 1863, Adams Papers; CFA2, *Adams*, 322–323.

41. CFA Diary, September 3, 1863, CFA to John Russell, September 3, 1863, both in Adams Papers; John Russell to CFA, September 4, 1863, in *Correspondence Concerning Claims against Great Britain Transmitted to the Senate of the United States* (Washington, 1870), 363.

42. CFA Diary, September 4, 1863, September 5, 1863, CFA to John Russell, September 5, 1863, all in Adams Papers; HA, *Education*, 878.

43. CFA to John Murray Forbes, September 7, 1863, CFA Diary, September 7, 1863, September 8, 1863, CFA to RHD, September 7, 1863, all in Adams Papers.

44. John Russell to CFA, September 8, 1863, CFA to John Russell, September 9, 1863, CFA to WHS, September 8, 1863, in *Correspondence Concerning Claims against Great Britain*, 364–366; CFA Diary, September 8, 1863, CFA to Edward Everett, September 9, 1863, CFA to WHS, September 10, 1863, all in Adams Papers.

45. Eli Evans, *Judah P. Benjamin: The Jewish Confederate* (New York, 1988), 236; HA, *Education*, 889; HA to CFA2, September 16, 1863, September 25, 1863, in *Letters*, ed. Levenson, 1: 392–393.

46. CFA to Edward Everett, October 1, 1863, Adams Papers; CFA to CFA2, October 2, 1863, in *Cycle of Letters*, ed. Ford, 2: 89; Moran Diary, October 5, 1863, in *Journal*, ed. Wallace, 1: 1218.

47. CFA to WHS, October 16, 1863, CFA to C. G. Loring, October 30, 1863, CFA to JGP, November 10, 1863, CFA to Edward Everett, November 17, 1863, all in Adams Papers; Stern, *When the Guns Roared*, 82–83.

48. CFA to WHS, October 29, 1863, November 6, 1863, December 17, 1863, CFA to John Russell, October 12, 1863, October 17, 1863, CFA Diary, December 5, 1863, all in Adams Papers; Loy, "10 Rumford Place," 371.

49. CFA to JGP, September 18, 1863, November 10, 1863, CFA to WHS, November 13, 1863, CFA to Edward Everett, December 17, 1863, all in Adams Papers.

50. CFA Diary, September 22, 1863, December 12, 1863, December 21, 1863, December 25, 1863, December 31, 1863, January 1, 1864, all in Adams Papers.

51. HA to CFA2, December 24, 1863, in *Letters*, ed. Levenson, 1: 419; CFA Diary, November 25, 1863, November 26, 1863, CFA to RHD, January 27, 1864, all in Adams Papers.

52. CFA2 Diary, October 22, 1863, October 23, 1863, CFA2 to JQA2, August 20, 1863, all in Adams Papers.

53. CFA2 Diary, October 22, 1863, October 23, 1863, CFA2 to JQA2, October 26, 1863, all in Adams Papers.

54. JQA2 to CFA2, August 9, 1863, October 5, 1863, CFA Diary, September 21, 1863, all in Adams Papers; Perry, *Life of Higginson*, 214.

55. CFA2 to CFA, October 31, 1863, in *Cycle of Letters*, ed. Ford, 2: 99–100.

56. CFA2 to CFA, December 25, 1863, in *Cycle of Letters*, ed. Ford, 2: 110; CFA2 Diary, December 25, 1863, Adams Papers.

57. Lorien Foote, *The Gentlemen and the Roughs: Violence, Honor, and Manhood in the Union Army* (New York, 2010), 122; CFA2 to CFA, January 16, 1864, in *Cycle of Letters*, ed. Ford, 2: 117–118; CFA2 to William Wardell, January 8, 1864, in Regimental Descriptive Book, First Cavalry, National Archives.

58. CFA Diary, January 19, 1864, January 24, 1864, February 1, 1864, February 3, 1864, all in Adams Papers.

59. CFA2, *Autobiography*, 149; Special Orders, No. 26, January 18, 1864, in Regimental Descriptive Book, First Cavalry, National Archives; CFA2 Diary, January 14, 1864, January 20, 1864, both in Adams Papers.

60. CFA2 Diary, January 24, 1864, Adams Papers.

61. CFA2 Diary, January 30, 1864, Adams Papers; CFA2, *Autobiography*, 164; Nagel, *Descent from Glory*, 246–247. Frederick Ogden's unit, originally the "First Regiment of Dragoons," was created by an act of Congress in 1833; in 1861 it was renamed the "First Cavalry Regiment."

62. CFA2 to JQA2, February 19, 1864, CFA Diary, February 15, 1864, February 16, 1864, all in Adams Papers.

63. CFA2 to JA2, February 19, 1864, Adams Papers.

64. CFA Diary, February 18, 1864, Adams Papers; Moran Diary, February 20, 1864, March 12, 1864, in *Journal*, ed. Wallace, 1: 1265, 1273.

65. Moran Diary, March 23, 1864, in *Journal*, ed. Wallace, 1: 1277.

66. CFA Diary, March 15, 1864, March 26, 1864, CFA2 Diary, March 26, 1864, all in Adams Papers.

67. CFA2 Diary, April 10, 1864, April 11, 1864, both in Adams Papers; Crowninshield, *First Regiment*, 200.

CHAPTER 8: THE COLONEL

1. Henry Pearson, *The Life of John A. Andrew* (Boston, 1904), 2: 91–92; New York *Weekly Anglo-African*, January 9, 1864.

2. JQA2 to CFA2, May 7, 1864, Adams Papers.

3. New York *Weekly Anglo-African*, December 19, 1863; JQA to CFA2, May 24, 1864, Adams Papers.

4. CFA2 Diary, April 19, 1864, April 28, 1864, Adams Papers; Perry, *Life of Higginson*, 215–216.

5. CFA2, *Autobiography*, 163; CFA2 to ABA, August 27, 1864, in *Cycle of Letters*, ed. Ford, 2: 188; CFA2 to JQA2, May 31, 1864, Adams Papers.

6. CFA2 Diary, May 14, 1864, May 15, 1864, CFA2 to JQA2, May 19, 1864, all in Adams Papers; CFA2 to ABA, August 12, 1864, CFA2 to CFA, May 29, 1864, in *Cycle of Letters*, ed. Ford, 2: 131, 175.

7. CFA to John Murray Forbes, September 7, 1863, CFA Diary, February 16, 1863, both in Adams Papers.

8. CFA Diary, May 16, 1864, CFA to RHD, April 8, 1863, both in Adams Papers.

9. CFA to RHD, January 27, 1864, CFA Diary, May 18, 1864, July 12, 1864, all in Adams Papers.

10. CFA Diary, June 6, 1864, June 14, 1864, June 26, 1864, all in Adams Papers.

11. CFA2 Diary, June 6, 1864, July 5, 1864, July 8, 1864, all in Adams Papers.

12. New York *Weekly Anglo-African*, June 4, 1864, July 30, 1864; *Liberator*, May 13, 1864; CFA2, *Autobiography*, 164; CFA2 to JQA2, September 29, 1864, Adams Papers; Noah Trudeau, "Proven Themselves in Every Respect to Be Men: Black Cavalry in the Civil War," in *Black Soldiers in Blue: African American Troops in the Civil War Era*, ed. John David Smith (Chapel Hill, 2002), 283, 287.

13. Nick Salvatore, *We All Got History: The Memory Books of Amos Webber* (New York, 1996), 132; Noah Trudeau, *Like Men of War: Black Troops in the Civil War, 1862–1865* (New York, 2002), 222; New York *Weekly Anglo-African*, June 25, 1864.

14. New York *Weekly Anglo-African*, June 25, 1864, July 9, 1864, July 23, 1864; *New York Times*, June 26, 1864.

15. John David Smith, "Let Us All Be Grateful That We Have Colored Troops That Will Fight," in *Black Soldiers in Blue*, ed. Smith, 56; CFA2 to JQA2, July 7, 1864, Adams Papers; *New York Herald*, July 27, 1865.

16. Joseph Stevens, *1863: The Rebirth of a Nation* (New York, 1999), 255; CFA2 to ABA, August 27, 1864, in *Cycle of Letters*, ed. Ford, 2: 186.

17. CFA2 to ABA, August 27, 1864, in *Cycle of Letters*, ed. Ford, 2: 186; CFA2 Diary, August 23, 1864, Adams Papers.

18. CFA2 to ABA, August 27, 1864, in *Cycle of Letters*, ed. Ford, 2: 186.

19. CFA2 to ABA, August 27, 1864, CFA2 to CFA, August 20, 1864, CFA to HA, September 18, 1864, in *Cycle of Letters*, ed. Ford, 2: 182, 188–189, 196; CFA2 to JQA2, August 24, 1864, Adams Papers.

20. CFA2 to JQA2, September 11, 1864, September 18, 1864, October 20, 1864, all in Adams Papers.

21. New York *Weekly Anglo-African*, May 7, 1864; CFA2 to HA, September 18, 1864, September 23, 1864, in *Cycle of Letters*, ed. Ford, 2: 194–195, 199.

22. CFA2 to CFA, November 2, 1864, in *Cycle of Letters*, ed. Ford, 2: 216–219.

23. CFA2, *Autobiography*, 156–157; CFA2 Diary, October 10, 1864, October 22, 1864, October 23, 1864, October 24, 1864, all in Adams Papers; CFA2 to HA, July 22, 1864, in *Cycle of Letters*, ed. Ford, 2: 167–168.

24. CFA Diary, May 12, 1864, August 2, 1864, September 23, 1864, all in Adams Papers; HA to CFA2, May 13, 1864, in *Letters*, ed. Levenson, 1: 430.

25. JQA2 to CFA2, July 23, 1864, CFA Diary, October 20, 1864, both in Adams Papers; HA to CFA2, October 21, 1864, in *Letters*, ed. Levenson, 1: 452. On the possible causes of Louisa's sudden weight gain, see Jennifer Maher, "Ripping the Bodice: Eating, Reading, and Revolt," *College Literature* 28 (2001): 64–83.

26. CFA Diary, September 4, 1864, Adams Papers; HA to CFA2, September 30, 1864, in *Letters*, ed. Levenson, 1: 447–448. On the activities of other elite women, see Kristie Ross, "Arranging a Doll's House: Refined Women as Union Nurses," in *Divided Houses: Gender and the Civil War* (New York, 1992), eds. Catherine Clinton and Nina Silber, 97–113.

27. CFA Diary, July 29, 1864, September 8, 1864, CFA to JGP, January 5, 1865, all in Adams Papers; Moran Diary, August 3, 1864, in *Journal*, ed. Wallace, 1: 1308.

28. Mary Carpenter, *Health, Medicine, and Society in Victorian England* (New York, 2009), 78; CFA Diary, September 13, 1864, Adams Papers; HA to CFA2, September 16, 1864, in *Letters*, ed. Levenson, 1: 445.

29. CFA Diary, December 10, 1865, Adams Papers; HA to CFA2, December 22, 1864, in *Letters*, ed. Levenson, 1: 462.

30. CFA Diary, July 14, 1864, August 18, 1864, August 25, 1864, all in Adams Papers.

31. CFA Diary, September 17, 1864, October 31, 1864, both in Adams Papers; CFA2 to HA, October 15, 1864, in *Cycle of Letters*, ed. Ford, 2: 206.

32. CFA2, Regimental Descriptive Book, November 3, 1864, 5th Mass. Cavalry, National Archives; CFA2 Diary, November 3, 1864, November 4, 1864, November 5, 1864, November 6, 1864, November 7, 1864, November 8, 1864, all in Adams Papers; CFA2 to HA, November 14, 1864, in *Cycle of Letters*, ed. Ford, 2: 223.

33. CFA Diary, November 23, 1864, CFA to WHS, November 3, 1864, CFA to Edward Everett, November 22, 1864, December 13, 1864, all in Adams Papers.

34. CFA2 to HA, November 14, 1864, CFA to CFA2, November 25, 1864, in *Cycle of Letters*, ed. Ford, 2: 223, 227–228.

35. CFA2 Diary, November 30, 1864, December 31, 1864, CFA2 to JQA2, December 13, 1864, all in Adams Papers.

36. JQA2 to CFA2, December 26, 1864, Adams Papers.

37. CFA Diary, November 21, 1864, Adams Papers; HA to CFA2, January 27, 1865, in *Letters*, ed. Levenson, 1: 466–467; *Cleveland Morning Leader*, November 26, 1864.

38. Stern, *When the Guns Roared*, 325; CFA to Edward Everett, January 27, 1865, CFA to WHS, February 2, 1865, February 10, 1865, all in Adams Papers.

39. Mason, *Everett*, 310–311; CFA Diary, January 30, 1865, Adams Papers.

40. CFA to WHS, November 24, 1864, March 20, 1865, both in Adams Papers; HA to CFA2, November 11, 1864, in *Cycle of Letters*, ed. Ford, 2: 220; HA to CFA2, November 25, 1864, in *Letters*, ed. Levenson, 1: 459.

41. Simpson, *Political Education*, 30; HA to CFA2, March 2, 1865, May 10, 1865, HA to CFA, March 6, 1865, in *Letters*, ed. Levenson, 1: 477–478, 483, 495.

42. *Liberator*, January 20, 1865; Brown, *Harvard University in the War*, 87; Perry, *Higginson*, 219; CFA2 to CFA, December 31, 1864, in *Cycle of Letters*, ed. Ford, 2: 240.

43. CFA2 to HA, January 1, 1865, in *Cycle of Letters*, ed. Ford, 2: 243. See also short biography of CFA2 in *Santa Fe New Mexican*, June 8, 1898.

44. CFA Diary, March 1, 1865, March 3, 1865, April 11, 1865, all in Adams Papers.

45. CFA Diary, March 4, 1865, March 14, 1865, CFA to Edward Ogden, March 8, 1865, CFA2 to JQA2, March 23, 1865, all in Adams Papers.

46. CFA Diary, March 17, 1865, Adams Papers; CFA2 to CFA, March 7, 1865, in *Cycle of Letters*, ed. Ford, 2: 257–258.

47. CFA to WHS, February 9, 1865, Adams Papers; CFA2 to CFA, December 18, 1864, in *Cycle of Letters*, ed. Ford, 2: 235–236.

48. Bruce Levine, *Confederate Emancipation: Southern Plans to Free and Arm Slaves during the Civil War* (New York, 2005), 126–127; CFA2 to JQA2, April 1, 1865, April 2, 1865, both in Adams Papers; CFA2 to CFA, April 10, 1865, in *Cycle of Letters*, ed. Ford, 2: 261.

49. Chandra Manning, *What This Cruel War Was Over: Soldiers, Slavery, and the Civil War* (New York, 2007), 213; Foner, *Fiery Trial*, 328; New York *Weekly Anglo-African*, April 22, 1865; CFA2 to CFA, April 10, 1865, in *Cycle of Letters*, ed. Ford, 2: 261; CFA2 to JQA2, April 4, 1865, Adams Papers.

50. Benjamin Quarles, *The Negro in the Civil War* (New York, 1953), 331; *Liberator*, April 14, 1865; CFA2 to JQA2, April 4, 1865, Adams Papers.

51. *Liberator*, April 14, 1865; CFA2 to JQA2, April 4, 1865, Adams Papers.

52. CFA2 to JQA2, April 4, 1865, Adams Papers.

53. CFA Diary, April 15, 1865, April 23, 1865, April 24, 1865, all in Adams Papers; CFA to CFA2, April 28, 1865, in *Cycle of Letters*, ed. Ford, 2: 265.

54. Donald, *Lincoln*, 576–582; CFA Diary, April 19, 1865, April 24, 1865, both in Adams Papers.

55. St. Albans *Vermont Transcript*, February 17, 1865; *New York Herald*, February 11, 1865; CFA to WHS, March 9, 1865, March 14, 1865, CFA to William Hunter, May 18, 1865, all in Adams Papers.

56. CFA Diary, January 16, 1865, March 18, 1865, March 22, 1865, CFA to WHS, March 29, 1865, all in Adams Papers.

57. Edwin Stanton to CFA, April 15, 1865, William Hunter to CFA, April 15, 1865, in OR, Series 1, Vol. 46, 784–786; CFA Diary, April 26, 1865, Adams Papers.

58. HA, *Education*, 912; CFA Diary, April 26, 1865, CFA to WHS, April 21, 1865, April 28, 1865, June 23, 1865, CFA to Charles Dillaway, June 2, 1865, all in Adams Papers.

59. CFA to John Russell, May 1, 1865, May 6, 1865, CFA to William Hunter, May 6, 1865, all in Adams Papers.

60. CFA to William Hunter, May 4, 1865, May 25, 1865, CFA to Mary Lincoln, May 19, 1865, all in Adams Papers.

61. CFA to Vernon Harcourt, May 3, 1865, JQA2 to CFA2, April 16, 1865, CFA2 to JQA2, April 17, 1865, all in Adams Papers.

62. CFA2 to CFA, April 10, 1865, in *Cycle of Letters*, ed. Ford, 2: 263; CFA to George Bancroft, May 26, 1865, CFA to William Hunter, June 15, 1865, both in Adams Papers.

63. CFA2 to JQA2, March 23, 1865, April 17, 1865, both in Adams Papers.

64. CFA2 to JQA2, April 17, 1865, May 2, 1865, both in Adams Papers.

65. CFA2, *Autobiography*, 166; CFA2 to JQA2, April 17, 1865, May 2, 1865, JQA2 to CFA2, April 25, 1865, all in Adams Papers.

66. CFA2, *Autobiography*, 166; CFA2 to JQA2, May 19, 1865, JQA2 to CFA2, May 23, 1865, CFA to JGP, June 15, 1865, all in Adams Papers.

67. Ebenezer Woodward to JQA2, June 28, 1865, Aaron Hooker, Report, July 30, 1865, CFA2 to Edwin Stanton, July 21, 1865, E. D. Townsend, Special Order No. 413, August 1, 1865, all in CFA2, Regimental Descriptive Book, 1865, 5th Massachusetts Cavalry, National Archives; CFA to CFA2, March 24, 1865, in *Cycle of Letters*, ed. Ford, 2: 259.

68. CFA to William Hunter, May 25, 1865, June 15, 1865, both in Adams Papers.

69. CFA to William Fessenden, March 2, 1865, March 17, 1865, CFA to WHS, March 23, 1865, CFA to Hugh McCulloch, April 13, 1865, all in Adams Papers.

70. CFA2 to CFA, February 7, 1865, in *Cycle of Letters*, ed. Ford, 2: 252–253.

71. HA to CFA2, July 14, 1865, in *Letters*, ed. Levenson, 1: 498; JQA2 to CFA2, May 23, 1865, Adams Papers.

72. *Chicago Tribune*, June 22, 1865; CFA to RHD, October 11, 1865, October 18, 1865, March 7, 1860, all in Adams Papers.

73. CFA to John Russell, September 18, 1865, Adams Papers; Moran Diary, May 20, 1865, in *Journal*, ed. Wallace, 1: 1430; *Rutland Weekly Herald*, October 26, 1865; Findlay *Hancock Jeffersonian*, June 30, 1865; *Norfolk Post*, November 30, 1865.

74. CFA to WHS, October 19, 1865, October 21, 1865, both in Adams Papers; Woodsfield *Spirit of Democracy*, July 5, 1865; HA, *Education*, 914; HA to CFA2, October 20, 1865, in *Letters*, ed. Levenson, 1: 500.

75. CFA to John Russell, November 6, 1865, CFA to WHS, November 21, 1865, January 5, 1866, all in Adams Papers.

76. *New York Herald*, November 15, 1865; HA to CFA2, October 20, 1865, in *Letters*, ed. Levenson, 1: 501.

Chapter 9: The Independents

1. CFA Diary, December 31, 1865, Adams Papers; CFA to WHS, January 4, 1866, in *Papers Relating to Foreign Affairs* (Washington, 1866), 1: 42.

2. CFA to JGP, February 8, 1866, Adams Papers; CFA2, *Autobiography*, 168.

3. CFA2 to JQA2, July 19, 1866, Adams Papers; CFA2, *Autobiography*, 168.

4. London *Morning Post*, October 11, 1865; Allan Nevin, *Hamilton Fish: The Inner Workings of the Grant Administration* (New York, 1957), 1: 147; CFA to WHS, December 21, 1865, CFA to George Villiers, November 18, 1865, both in Adams Papers.

5. CFA to George Villiers, December 28, 1865, in *Papers Relating to Foreign Affairs*, 1: 45–53; CFA to George Villiers, March 12, 1866, CFA to WHS, November 23, 1866, both in Adams Papers.

6. CFA to WHS, March 1, 1866, July 5, 1866, CFA to John Palfrey, February 8, 1866, CFA Diary, August 1, 1866, all in Adams Papers.

7. Chalfant, *Better in Darkness*, 117; Natalie Dykstra, *Clover Adams: A Gilded and Heartbreaking Life* (New York, 2012), 48.

8. CFA to WHS, July 7, 1866, July 12, 1866, both in Adams Papers.

9. Anderson, *Brooks Adams*, 20; CFA to WHS, June 23, 1866, CFA to Edward Henry Stanley, September 24, 1866, CFA Diary, November 10, 1866, CFA to JGP, December 6, 1866, all in Adams Papers; HA to Charles Gaskell, August 25, 1867, in *Letters*, ed. Levenson, 1: 547.

10. Duberman, *Adams*, 329–330; CFA to WHS, January 25, 1867, CFA Diary, July 3, 1867, July 13, 1867, all in Adams Papers.

11. CFA Diary, June 24, 1867; Arthur Beringause, *Brooks Adams: A Biography* (New York, 1955), 41.

12. CFA to RHD, December 5, 1866, CFA to John Murray Forbes, March 7, 1866, both in Adams Papers; CFA2, *Autobiography*, 169–170. Writing in 1912, Charles Francis Jr. was notoriously careless with dates, claiming on one page that they returned to Boston in October and then on the following page claiming September. He also remarked that he was thirty upon returning home, when in fact he had turned thirty-one the previous May.

13. CFA2, *Autobiography*, 171–172.

14. CFA2, *Autobiography*, 172; Samuel DeCanio, *Democracy and the Origins of the American Regulatory State* (New Haven, 2015), 185; Noam Maggor, *Brahmin Capitalism: Frontiers of Wealth and Populism in America's First Gilded Age* (Cambridge, 2017), 55–56; CFA2, "The Railroad System," *North American Review* 104 (1867): 479–480; CFA2, "Legislative Control over Railway Charters," *American Law Review* 1 (1867): 25–46.

15. HA to CFA2, April 30, 1867, July 30, 1867, in *Letters*, ed. Levenson, 1: 530, 542–546.

16. HA to CFA2, May 18, 1867, June 22, 1867, in *Letters*, ed. Levenson, 1: 534, 537.

17. HA to CFA2, September 4, 1867, in *Letters*, ed. Levenson, 1: 549; Kirkland, *Adams*, 39; *Bedford Inquirer*, February 11, 1870; Montpelier *Green-Mountain Freeman*, April 29, 1868.

18. CFA2, *Autobiography*, 172–173; CFA2, *Chapters of Erie and Other Essays* (Boston, 1871), 6; Montpelier *Green-Mountain Freeman*, July 28, 1869; CFA2 Diary, January 14, 1869, January 19, 1869, both in Adams Papers.

19. Christopher Waldrep, *Roots of Disorder: Race and Criminal Justice in the American South* (Urbana, 1998), 106; CFA to JGP, August 28, 1866, CFA to RHD, March 7, 1866, both in Adams Papers.

20. Brookhiser, *America's First Dynasty*, 137–138; CFA to RHD, December 5, 1866, Adams Papers.

21. Hans Trefousse, *Andrew Johnson: A Biography* (New York, 1989), 278; *Cincinnati Gazette*, February 11, 1867; CFA Diary, April 8, 1867, December 4, 1867, both in Adams Papers.

22. HA to JGP, August 23, 1866, in *Letters*, ed. Levenson, 1: 509–510. Simpson makes this point in *Political Education*, 25–26.

23. Simpson, *Political Education*, 25; HA to CFA2, March 1, 1867, April 21, 1868, in *Letters*, ed. Levenson, 1: 524, 570.

24. Robert Mirak, "John Quincy Adams, Jr., and the Reconstruction Crisis," *New England Quarterly* 35 (1962): 190–193.

25. Mirak, "Adams and Reconstruction," 195; Columbia *Daily Phoenix*, August 8, 1866; HA to JGP, August 23, 1866, in *Letters*, ed. Levenson, 1: 510.

26. Mirak, "Adams and Reconstruction," 196; CFA Diary, November 21, 1866, Adams Papers; Idaho City *Idaho World*, January 26, 1867. Out of roughly one thousand votes cast in the Quincy district, Adams lost by more than one hundred ballots.

27. Simpson, *Political Education*, 27; *Nashville Union and Dispatch*, March 12, 1867; *Alexandria Gazette*, March 11, 1867; *New-York Tribune*, March 11, 1867; *Rutland (Vermont) Weekly Herald*, March 14, 1867; Columbus *Daily Ohio Statesman*, March 12, 1867, March 20, 1867; Rock Island *Evening Argus*, March 19, 1867; *Alexandria Gazette*, March 15, 1867; Memphis *Public Ledger*, March 15, 1867; *Charleston Daily News*, March 15, 1867, April 6, 1867.

28. CFA to RHD, May 23, 1867, Adams Papers; HA to CFA2, April 3, 1867, in *Letters*, ed. Levenson, 1: 528.

29. *Newberry Herald*, July 17, 1867; Columbia *Daily Phoenix*, February 2, 1867.

30. Mirak, "Adams and Reconstruction," 197–198; *Wilmington Journal*, October 18, 1867; *Yorkville (SC) Enquirer*, October 10, 1867; *Nashville Union and Dispatch*, October 6, 1867.

31. Mirak, "Adams and Reconstruction," 198; JQA2 to CFA2, November 27, 1867, Adams Papers.

32. Mirak, "Adams and Reconstruction," 200; JQA2 to CFA2, November 3, 1867, CFA Diary, November 16, 1867, November 26, 1867, all in Adams Papers.

33. CFA Diary, November 26, 1867, Adams Papers; Washington *Evening Star*, September 12, 1867; *New York Herald*, September 24, 1866; Philadelphia *Evening Telegraph*, September 23, 1866, February 23, 1867.

34. *Anderson (SC) Intelligencer*, July 17, 1867; *Wheeling Daily Intelligencer*, July 12, 1867; Philadelphia *Evening Telegraph*, October 24, 1867; *Sunbury (PA) American*, October 13, 1866; CFA Diary, November 29, 1867, Adams Papers.

35. CFA Diary, January 5, 1868, January 8, 1868, both in Adams Papers.

36. CFA Diary, March 2, 1868, March 9, 1868, March 16, 1868, May 19, 1868, all in Adams Papers; Hagerstown *Maryland Free Press*, June 18, 1868.

37. CFA Diary, December 21, 1867, CFA to WHS, December 21, 1867, both in Adams Papers; Washington *Evening Star*, February 3, 1868; Montpelier *Green-Mountain Freeman*, February 12, 1868; *Bedford Inquirer*, February 14, 1868.

38. CFA Diary, January 25, 1868, Adams Papers; *Staunton Spectator*, February 11, 1868; Columbia *Daily Phoenix*, February 4, 1868; *New Orleans Republican*, February 4, 1868; Donald, *Sumner*, 2: 364.

39. *Evansville Journal*, March 13, 1868; CFA to Bishop of London, February 10, 1868, Adams Papers; *London Times*, February 29, 1868.

40. Washington *Evening Star*, May 14, 1868; CFA Diary, April 30, 1868, May 18, 1868, both in Adams Papers.

41. CFA Diary, March 9, 1868, Adams Papers; St. Albans *Vermont Daily Transcript*, May 25, 1868.

42. Philadelphia *Evening Telegraph*, July 2, 1868, July 23, 1868; Washington *National Republican*, July 8, 1868; *Alexandria Gazette*, July 24, 1868; Columbus *Daily Ohio Statesman*, July 22, 1868; St. Albans *Vermont Daily Transcript*, July 25, 1868; *New York Herald*, July 22, 1868; CFA Diary, July 10, 1868, Adams Papers.

43. CFA to WHS, September 25, 1868, Adams Papers; Ernest Samuels, *Henry Adams: The Middle Years* (Cambridge, 1958), 4; Brookhiser, *America's First Dynasty*, 152; Wills, *Henry Adams*, 74; Patricia O'Toole, *The Five of Hearts: An Intimate Portrait of Henry Adams and His Friends* (New York, 1990), 6–7.

44. CFA Diary, November 11, 1868, CFA to WHS, September 25, 1868, both in Adams Papers; Brookhiser, *America's First Dynasty*, 141.

45. CFA Diary, September 2, 1868, September 27, 1868, both in Adams Papers; Wade Hampton to JQA2, September 22, 1868, JQA2 to Wade Hampton, September 28, 1868, both in *Massachusetts and South Carolina: Correspondence*, ed. JQA2 (Boston, 1868), 1–3.

46. CFA Diary, October 4, 1868, October 10, 1868, both in Adams Papers.

47. *Massachusetts and South Carolina*, ed. JQA2, 12–23.

48. Paul Nagel, "Reconstruction, Adams Style," *Journal of Southern History* 52 (1982): 6–7; Raleigh *Weekly North-Carolina Standard*, October 28, 1868.

49. *Yorkville (SC) Enquirer*, October 29, 1868; JQA2 to Asa Snyder, November 21, 1868, CFA Diary, October 16, 1868, both in Adams Papers.

50. *Yorkville (SC) Enquirer*, May 21, 1868; Boston *Post*, May 20, 1868; Columbia *Daily Phoenix*, July 2, 1868; *New York Herald*, July 5, 1868; CFA Diary, March 23, 1868, March 24, 1868, both in Adams Papers.

51. Washington *National Republican*, July 8, 1868; William Parish, *Frank Blair: Lincoln's Conservative* (Columbia, MO, 1998), 254–260; Washington *National Intelligencer*, July 4, 1868; San Francisco *Elevator*, October 30, 1868; *New Orleans Republican*, July 23, 1868.

52. CFA Diary, August 16, 1868, Adams Papers; *Emporia (KS) News*, August 7, 1868; *Alexandria Gazette*, July 30, 1868; Charles Sumner to Henry Longfellow, August 4, 1868, in *Letters of Sumner*, ed. Palmer, 2: 438; Donald, *Sumner*, 2: 345; *New York Herald*, August 6, 1868.

53. Columbus *Daily Ohio Statesman*, August 10, 1868; *Alexandria Gazette*, August 10, 1868; *Nashville Union and Dispatch*, August 16, 1868; CFA Diary, July 18, 1868, October 14, 1868, both in Adams Papers.

54. Brooks Simpson, *Let Us Have Peace: Ulysses S. Grant and the Politics of War and Reconstruction, 1861–1868* (Chapel Hill, 1991), 249; Simpson, *Political Education*, 38.

55. *New Orleans Republican*, November 13, 1868; *Nashville Union and American*, November 12, 1868; CFA Diary, November 3, 1868, November 4, 1868, both in Adams Papers.

56. CFA Diary, November 18, 1868, Adams Papers.

57. *New York Herald*, November 5, 1868; Philadelphia *Evening Telegraph*, November 6, 1868; CFA Diary, November 11, 1868, Adams Papers.

58. CFA2, *Adams*, 379; Philadelphia *Evening Telegraph*, December 21, 1868; *Charleston Daily News*, January 16, 1869; CFA Diary, December 5, 1868, December 8, 1868, both in Adams Papers; *New York Herald*, December 3, 1868, December 28, 1868.

59. *Memphis Daily Appeal*, February 21, 1869; Philadelphia *Evening Telegraph*, January 6, 1869; *New Orleans Crescent*, January 10, 1869; *Evansville Journal*, February 22, 1869; Richmond *Daily Dispatch*, February 18, 1869.

60. B. H. Gilley, "*Democracy*: Henry Adams and the Role of a Political Leader," *Biography* 14 (1991): 351; CFA Diary, December 19, 1868, March 4, 1869, both in Adams Papers.

61. CFA2, *Autobiography*, 176; Alexandria *Daily State Journal*, January 11, 1871; Gilley, "Adams and the Role," 359; Ari Hoogenboom, *Outlawing the Spoils: A History of the Civil Service Reform Movement* (Urbana, 1961), 62, 65–66; HA to Charles Gaskell, September 29, 1870, in *Letters*, ed. Levenson, 2: 81; *New York Tribune*, February 19, 1869; CFA to John Motley, July 26, 1870, Adams Papers.

62. John Taliaferro, *All the Great Prizes: The Life of John Hay* (New York, 2013), 177; Simpson, *Political Education*, 72; Samuels, *Young Henry Adams*, 204.

63. Robertson, "Louisa Kuhn," 144; HA to Charles Gaskell, July 8, 1870, July 13, 1870, in *Letters*, ed. Levenson, 2: 73–74.

64. CFA2 Diary, July 15, 1870, July 16, 1870, July 17, 1870, all in Adams Papers.

65. CFA2 Diary, July 18, 1870, CFA to John Motley, July 26, 1870, both in Adams Papers.

66. CFA2 Diary, December 28, 1871, Adams Papers.

67. CFA2 Diary, December 29, 1871, Adams Papers.

CHAPTER 10: A SINGULAR, UNSOLVED FAMILY

1. William S. McFeely, *Grant: A Biography* (New York, 1981), 335; *Charleston Daily News*, April 24, 1869; Richmond *Daily Dispatch*, April 22, 1869; CFA2, *Adams*, 380.

2. Charles Sumner to Hamilton Fish, May 17, 1869, in *Letters of Sumner*, ed. Palmer: 2; CFA2, *Adams*, 380, 458–459; Richmond *Daily Dispatch*, April 22, 1869.

3. McFeely, *Grant*, 336; *Alexandria Gazette*, May 25, 1871; Washington *Evening Star*, May 25, 1871; Washington *New National Era*, May 25, 1871; *Philadelphia Evening Telegraph*, May 30, 1871; *New Orleans Republican*, May 28, 1871.

4. *New Orleans Republican*, May 28, 1871; Chalfant, *Better in Darkness*, 246.

5. Alexandria *Daily State Journal*, July 5, 1871; *Nashville Union and American*, August 2, 1871; *Bellows (VT) Times*, August 4, 1871; *Knoxville Daily Chronicle*, August 2, 1871; *New York Herald*, August 2, 1871; Dallas *Oregon Republican*, August 5, 1871.

6. Anderson, *Brooks Adams*, 20; Beringause, *Brooks Adams*, 50; HA to Charles Gaskell, October 2, 1871, in *Letters*, ed. Levenson, 2: 118; *Alexandria Gazette*, August 9, 1871; Washington *New National Era*, August 17, 1871; *Charleston Daily News*, August 9, 1871; New Orleans *Weekly Louisianan*, August 24, 1872.

7. CFA Diary, October 16, 1871, October 27, 1871, November 12, 1871, all in Adams Papers; *Rutland (VT) Weekly Herald*, November 23, 1871.

8. *New York Herald*, August 15, 1871, December 21, 1871; New Orleans *Weekly Louisianan*, August 20, 1871; *Alexandria Gazette*, December 20, 1871; CFA Diary, December 2, 1871, December 10, 1871, both in Adams Papers.

9. HA to CFA, January 21, 1872, HA to Charles Gaskell, January 22, 1872, in *Letters*, ed. Levenson, 2: 127–128; Eugenia Kaledin, *The Education of Mrs. Henry Adams* (Amherst, 1981), 64; *Alexandria Gazette*, February 23, 1872; Washington *Evening Star*, February 22, 1872; *New York Herald*, February 22, 1872.

10. CFA2, *Adams*, 389; Washington *Evening Star*, February 22, 1872; CFA Diary, February 22, 1872, February 23, 1872, both in Adams Papers.

11. HA to BA, March 3, 1872, in *Letters*, ed. Levenson, 2: 131; *Memphis Daily Appeal*, February 15, 1872; CFA Diary, February 7, 1872, March 2, 1872, April 13, 1872, CFA to Hamilton Fish, March 25, 1872, all in Adams Papers.

12. *New York Herald*, February 16, 1872; *Rutland (VT) Weekly Herald*, March 21, 1872; CFA Diary, May 6, 1872, May 13, 1872, both in Adams Papers.

13. Kaledin, *Mrs. Henry Adams*, 32; Dykstra, *Clover Adams*, 5, 48–49.

14. HA, *Education*, 906; HA to Jacob Cox, November 8, 1869, in *Letters*, ed. Levenson, 2: 60.

15. HA to Charles Gaskell, March 26, 1872, May 20, 1872, in *Letters*, ed. Levenson, 2: 133, 137.

16. Kaledin, *Mrs. Henry Adams*, 70; Dykstra, *Clover Adams*, 56.

17. Donald, *Sumner*, 2: 539–540; CS to Wendell Phillips, March 10, 1872, in *Letters of Sumner*, ed. Palmer, 2: 580; Charles Town (VA) *Spirit of Jefferson*, January 10, 1871; Hoogenboom, *Outlawing the Spoils*, 111.

18. "The Political Campaign of 1872," *North American Review* (1872): 407; *New York Herald*, July 19, 1869; New York *Sun*, July 31, 1869; Bellevue (LA) *Bossier Banner*, August 21, 1869; Carson City *Daily State Register*, May 11, 1871; *Memphis Daily Appeal*, July 18, 1871; McConnelsville (OH) *South-Eastern Independent*, July 21, 1871; *New Orleans Republican*, July 18, 1871; *Knoxville Daily Chronicle*, August 8, 1871.

19. *New York Herald*, March 28, 1872, April 25, 1872; *New-York Tribune*, April 10, 1872; *New Orleans Republican*, March 29, 1872; *Chicago Tribune*, April 28, 1872; Albany (OR) *State Rights Democrat*, May 3, 1872; Richmond *Daily Dispatch*, April 27, 1872; *Washington Evening Star*, March 25, 1872; *Yorkville (SC) Enquirer*, April 4, 1872; Columbia *Daily Phoenix*, April 27, 1872; *Charleston Daily News*, March 16, 1872; *Jonesboro (TN) Herald and Tribune*, April 11, 1872.

20. CFA Diary, April 16, 1872, April 18, 1872, both in Adams Papers.

21. *Albany Register*, April 19, 1872; *Charleston Daily News*, April 19, 1872; CFA Diary, April 24, 1872, Adams Papers.

22. CFA2, *Adams*, 392; Washington *Evening Star*, April 25, 1872; *Wilmington Journal*, May 3, 1872; Ravenna (OH) *Democratic Press*, May 2, 1872.

23. Lexington (MO) *Weekly Caucasian*, April 27, 1872; Richmond *Daily Dispatch*, April 26, 1872; Alexandria *Daily State Journal*, April 25, 1872; *New York Herald*, April 28, 1872; *Alexandria Gazette*, April 26, 1872.

24. *Proceedings of the Liberal Republican Convention* (New York, 1872), 3; *Charleston Daily News*, April 26, 1872, April 29, 1872; San Francisco *Elevator*, April 27, 1872; Washington *Evening Star*, May 8, 1872; Washington *Daily National Republican*, April 27, 1872; *Alexandria Gazette*, April 26, 1872; Alexandria *Daily State Journal*, April 25, 1872; *Wheeling Daily Intelligencer*, April 25, 1872; *Knoxville Daily Chronicle*, April 28, 1872; *Wilmington (NC) Journal*, May 3, 1872.

25. CFA Diary, May 1, 1872, Adams Papers; Washington *Evening Star*, April 30, 1872; *Charleston Daily News*, May 3, 1872; *Bellows Falls (VT) Times*, May 10, 1872; *Centre (PA) Reporter*, May 3, 1872; Brattleboro *Vermont Phoenix*,

May 10, 1872; Richmond *Daily Dispatch*, April 30, 1872; *New York Herald*, May 1, 1872; Washington *New National Era*, May 2, 1872; *Chicago Tribune*, May 3, 1872; J. Laurence Laughlin, "The New Party," *Atlantic Monthly* (1884): 838; *Proceedings of the Liberal Republican Convention*, 22.

26. *Charleston Daily News*, May 11, 1872; *New York Herald*, April 8, 1872, May 4, 1872; Washington *Evening Star*, May 3, 1872, May 9, 1872; *Abbeville (SC) Press and Banner*, May 8, 1872; Washington *Daily National Republican*, April 13, 1872; *Nashville Union and American*, May 4, 1872; *Proceedings of the Liberal Republican Convention*, 29. On Adams's efforts to get Irish-born but naturalized US citizens out of Kilmainham, see his letters to W. Jackson, April 9, 1867, and W. B. West, April 23, 1867, both in Adams Papers.

27. CFA Diary, May 18, 1872, May 25, 1872, CFA to WHS, June 5, 1872, all in Adams Papers.

28. *Chicago Tribune*, May 9, 1872; *New-York Tribune*, May 4, 1872; Washington *New National Era*, May 16, 1872; *New York Herald*, May 10, 1872, May 11, 1872; *Nashville Union and American*, May 9, 1872; *Bradford (VT) National Opinion*, May 17, 1872; Columbia *Daily Phoenix*, May 16, 1872; *Knoxville Weekly Chronicle*, May 15, 1872; CFA to Miron Winslow, May 26, 1872, Adams Papers.

29. Simpson, *Political Education*, 81; Kirkland, *Adams*, 162; *Springfield Daily Republican*, May 8, 1872; CFA Diary, March 20, 1874, January 1, 1875, both in Adams Papers.

30. Kaledin, *Mrs. Henry Adams*, 71; O'Toole, *Five of Hearts*, 17; HA to Charles Gaskell, June 23, 1872, in *Letters*, ed. Levenson, 139–141 and n. 2; CFA Diary, June 27, 1872, Adams Papers.

31. Dusinberre, *Adams*, 69; Marian Adams to Ellen Gurney, September 5, 1872, in *The Letters of Mrs. Henry Adams*, ed. Ward Thoron (New York, 1937), 30; Dykstra, *Clover Adams*, 64.

32. Dusinberre, *Adams*, 69; Dykstra, *Clover Adams*, 64; CFA Diary, February 1, 1873, Adams Papers.

33. O'Toole, *Five of Hearts*, 22–23; Otto Friedrich, *Clover: The Tragic Love Story of Clover and Henry Adams and Their Brilliant Life in America's Gilded Age* (New York, 1979), 167.

34. Alexandria *Daily State Journal*, February 14, 1872; Washington *New National Era*, February 29, 1872; Duberman, *Adams*, 378–383; HA to Charles Gaskell, August 29, 1872, in *Letters*, ed. Levenson, 2: 147; CFA Diary, November 13, 1872, Adams Papers.

35. Stern, *When the Guns Roared*, 344; CFA2, *Adams*, 396, 400–401; CFA Diary, August 27, 1872, August 28, 1872, November 4, 1872, November 13, 1872, all in Adams Papers.

36. CFA2, *Adams*, 390–391; Ravenna (OH) *Democratic Press*, August 3, 1871; *Nashville Union and American*, July 9, 1872; Richmond *Daily Dispatch*, July 11, 1872.

37. HA to CFA, October 13, 1872, in *Letters*, ed. Levenson, 2: 150; New Orleans *Weekly Louisianan*, November 2, 1872.

38. Mitchell Snay, *Horace Greeley and the Politics of Nineteenth-Century America* (Lanham, 2011), 180–181; CFA Diary, December 1, 1872, Adams Papers.

39. Frederick Douglass, *Grant or Greeley—Which? Facts and Arguments for the Consideration of Colored Citizens of the United States* (Harrisburg, 1872); Brookhiser, *America's First Dynasty*, 140; unidentified newspaper clipping, circa 1880, CFA Diary, November 14, 1872, November 27, 1872, all in Adams Papers.

40. CFA, *Memorial Address of Charles Francis Adams on the Life, Character, and Services of William H. Seward* (New York, 1873); *Albany Evening Journal*, April 17, 1873; CFA Diary, March 11, 1874, March 13, 1874, March 16, 1874, November 6, 1874, all in Adams Papers.

41. Simpson, *Political Education*, 86; CFA Diary, February 13, 1873, March 25, 1874, December 16, 1874, all in Adams Papers.

42. CFA Diary, November 4, 1874, January 20, 1875, both in Adams Papers; *Chicago Daily Tribune*, August 2, 1875; Washington *National Republican*, August 3, 1875.

43. Duberman, *Adams*, 390–391; Kirkland, *Adams*, 162–163; *Memphis Daily Appeal*, February 17, 1875; Washington *Evening Star*, February 13, 1875; HA to Charles Gaskell, February 15, 1875, HA to Henry Cabot Lodge, June 4, 1876, in *Letters*, ed. Levenson, 2: 217, 272.

44. Nagel, *Descent from Glory*, 243–244.

45. Roy Morris, *Fraud of the Century: Rutherford B. Hayes, Samuel Tilden, and the Stolen Election of 1876* (New York, 2003), 83, 145; Ari Hoogenboom, *Rutherford B. Hayes: Warrior and President* (Lawrence, 1995), 266; HA to Henry Cabot Lodge, August 5, 1876, August 31, 1876, in *Letters*, ed. Levenson, 2: 285, 289.

46. Michael Holt, *By One Vote: The Disputed Presidential Election of 1876* (Lawrence, 2008), 45; Ravenna (OH) *Democratic Press*, October 5, 1876; *Alexandria Gazette*, September 18, 1876; Austin *Weekly Democratic Statesman*, September 28, 1876; Canton *Stark County Democrat*, September 28, 1876.

47. *Leavenworth Colored Radical*, November 16, 1876; CFA Diary, November 8, 1876, January 2, 1877, both in Adams Papers.

48. CFA Diary, November 9, 1876, November 10, 1876, November 11, 1876, November 16, 1876, November 17, 1876, all in Adams Papers. On election-year violence, see Egerton, *Wars of Reconstruction*, 312–316.

49. CFA Diary, December 18, 1876, December 31, 1876, CFA to William Armory, December 16, 1881, all in Adams Papers.

50. E. W. Stoughton, "The 'Electoral Conspiracy' Bubble Exploded," *North American Review* (1877): 196; CFA Diary, February 17, 1877, April 17, 1877, CFA to Samuel Tilden, March 5, 1877, all in Adams Papers.

51. Samuels, *Adams: Middle Years*, 7; Beringause, *Brooks Adams*, 63; CFA Diary, July 15, 1877, Adams Papers.

52. Kaledin, *Mrs. Henry Adams*, 66–67.

53. CFA Diary, January 2, 1877, June 20, 1877, CFA2 Diary, June 20, 1877, all in Adams Papers.

54. Samuels, *Young Henry Adams*, 296–297; Samuels, *Adams: Middle Years*, 11, 141; Dykstra, *Clover Adams*, 74–75, 81–82.

55. Dykstra, *Clover Adams*, 91–92.

56. HA, *The Life of Albert Gallatin* (Philadelphia, 1879); Wills, *Adams*, 98–99; *Nation*, August 21, 1879, 128, 145.

57. HA to Charles Gaskell, July 9, 1881, HA to Justin Winsor, June 6, 1881, in *Letters*, ed. Levenson, 2: 428, 430; CFA Diary, February 23, 1873, December 31, 1874, March 11, 1877, November 2, 1880, all in Adams Papers.

58. HA, *Democracy: An American Novel* (New York, 1880); Samuels, *Adams: Middle Years*, 89; O'Toole, *Five of Hearts*, 73; Gilley, "Democracy and Henry Adams," *Biography* 14 (1991): 354.

59. Arline Tehan, *Henry Adams in Love: The Pursuit of Elizabeth Sherman Cameron* (New York, 1983), 60; Kaledin, *Mrs. Henry Adams*, 169–170; Samuels, *Adams: Middle Years*, 68; *Washington Critic*, December 14, 1885.

60. Nagel, *Descent from Glory*, 326–327; Dykstra, *Clover Adams*, 127–129; HA to John Hay, April 8, 1883, in *Letters*, ed. Levenson, 2: 497.

61. HA, *Esther: A Novel* (New York, 1884); Samuels, *Adams: Middle Years*, 224.

62. Friedrich, *Clover*, 299–305; Kaledin, *Mrs. Henry Adams*, 220; Dykstra, *Clover*, 155; Samuels, *Adams: Middle Years*, 224–239.

63. Samuels, *Adams: Middle Years*, 269–270; Kaledin, *Mrs. Henry Adams*, 170.

64. Chalfant, *Better in Darkness*, 435; Beringause, *Brooks Adams*, 69–70.

65. BA, *The Emancipation of Massachusetts: The Dream and the Reality* (Boston, 1886); *Springfield (OH) Globe-Republic*, April 16, 1885; Kirkland, *Adams*, 210; Lehighton (PA) *Carbon Advocate*, May 31, 1879; *Chicago Daily Tribune*, December 7, 1878; *New-York Tribune*, September 17, 1878; *Cincinnati Star Eagle*, October 22, 1878; Anderson, *Brooks Adams*, 43.

66. Nagel, *Descent from Glory*, 252–253; Chalfant, *Better in Darkness*, 568; HA to Rebecca Dodge, September 7, 1889, in *Letters*, ed. Levenson, 3: 197.

67. Samuel Flagg Bemis, "Henry Adams, 2nd," *Proceedings of the Massachusetts Historical Society* 70 (1950): 279–280; CFA2 Diary, December 3, 1873, July 17, 1875, July 30, 1875, all in Adams Papers.

68. Maggor, *Brahmin Capitalism*, 45; Adams Cooke, "'An Unpardonable Bit of Folly and Impertinence': Charles Francis Adams Jr., American Anti-Imperialists, and the Philippines," *New England Quarterly* 83 (2010): 321; CFA2, *Autobiography*, 191.

69. Washington *Grit*, June 21, 1884; *Los Angeles Daily Herald*, December 24, 1889; Lawrence *Western Recorder*, June 20, 1884; CFA2 Diary, April 30, 1884, May 3, 1884, May 4, 1884, all in Adams Papers; CFA2, *Autobiography*, 191–192; Nagel, *Descent from Glory*, 310.

70. DeCanino, *Democracy and the Origins*, 191; Indianapolis *Freeman*, February 2, 1889; Kirkland, *Adams*, 159–160.

71. Dykstra, *Clover Adams*, 162–163.

72. Dykstra, *Clover Adams*, 189; Samuels, *Adams: Middle Years*, 264; HA to Robert Cunliffe, March 25, 1885, in *Letters*, ed. Levenson, 2: 590.

73. Dykstra, *Clover Adams*, 204–205; Chalfant, *Better in Darkness*, 500.

74. Chalfant, *Better in Darkness*, 504–506; Nagel, *Descent from Glory*, 281; CFA2 Diary, December 6, 1885, Adams Papers.

75. HA to Elizabeth Cameron, December 25, 1885, HA to John Hay, December 17, 1885, in *Letters*, ed. Levenson, 2: 643, 645; Washington *Evening Star*, December 7, 1885; New York *Sun*, December 9, 1885, December 13, 1885, March 21, 1886; Washington *Sunday Herald*, December 20, 1885; *Alexandria Gazette*, December 7, 1885; *Washington Critic*, December 9, 1885; Washington *National Republican*, December 10, 1885; Samuels, *Adams: Middle Years*, 327.

76. New York *Sun*, November 22, 1886; Washington *Evening Star*, November 22, 1886; *New York Times*, November 22, 1886; Washington *National Republican*, November 22, 1886; La Crosse *Wisconsin Labor Advocate*, November 26, 1866; HA to Theodore Dwight, November 24, 1886, HA to Charles Gaskell, December 12, 1886, HA to Robert Cunliffe, January 17, 1887, in *Letters*, ed. Levenson, 3: 46–48, 53; CFA2 Diary, November 21, 1886, Adams Papers.

77. New Haven *Morning Journal and Courier*, November 22, 1886; HA to JQA2, in *Letters*, ed. Levenson, 3: 50.

78. *Wichita Eagle*, June 8, 1889; *Iola (KS) Register*, June 14, 1889; CFA2 Diary, June 6, 1889, Adams Papers; Nagel, *Descent from Glory*, 300; HA to Wayne MacVeagh, July 22, 1888, HA to Elizabeth Cameron, June 2, 1889, in *Letters*, ed. Levenson, 3: 129, 179.

79. HA to Eliza Lippitt, June 16, 1889, HA to CFA2, February 21, 1896, in *Letters*, ed. Levenson, 3: 182, 4: 376.

EPILOGUE

1. *New York Times*, October 28, 1871; BA and HA, *The Degradation of the Democratic Dogma* (New York, 1920), 3–4.

2. Levenson, "Etiology of Israel Adams," 579; Nagel, *Descent from Glory*, 306.

3. New York *Evening World*, August 14, 1894; Nagel, *Descent from Glory*, 306–307; Washington *Evening Star*, August 14, 1894; *Asheville Daily Citizen*, August 14, 1894.

4. *Jersey City News*, August 14, 1894; *New-York Tribune*, August 15, 1874, July 14, 1900; New York *Sun*, July 14, 1900; *Washington Times*, May 17, 1911; *New York Times*, June 12, 1954.

5. Samuels, *Adams: Middle Years*, 124, 465, n. 52; Anderson, *Brooks Adams*, 215, n. 23; HA to John Hay, October 4, 1895, HA to Charles Gaskell, July 31, 1896, in *Letters*, ed. Levenson, 4: 337, 409.

6. Lawrence *Historic Times*, August 1, 1891; *Leavenworth Advocate*, November 15, 1890, December 6, 1890; *Washington Bee*, December 26, 1891; CFA2, *Richard Henry Dana: A Biography* (Boston, 1891); CFA2, *Autobiography*, 194–198.

7. Rebecca Scott, "A Cuban Connection: Edwin F. Atkins, Charles Francis Adams, Jr., and the Former Slaves of Soledad Plantation," *Massachusetts Historical Review* 9 (2007): 23–24; Cooke, "'Unpardonable Bit of Folly and Impertinence,'" 313; CFA2, "An Undeveloped Function," *American Historical Review* 7 (1902): 203–232.

8. L. Moody Simms, "Charles Francis Adams Jr. and the Negro Question," *New England Quarterly* 41 (1968): 437; Paul Nagel, "Reconstruction, Adams Style," *Journal of Southern History* 52 (1986): 9–10; CFA2, "Reflex Light on Africa," *Century* 52 (1906): 107.

9. CFA2, *Lee at Appomattox and Other Papers* (Boston, 1902); *Savannah Tribune*, June 21, 1902.

10. Nagel, "Reconstruction, Adams Style," 11; DeGruccio, "Manhood, Race, and Failure," 672; CFA2, *Autobiography*, 206–207; CFA2, *Lee's Centennial* (Cambridge, 1907), 33.

11. Nagel, "Reconstruction, Adams Style," 13; *Cleveland Gazette*, August 1, 1906; *St. Louis Palladium*, June 20, 1903; Chicago *Broad Axe*, May 5, 1906; St. Paul *Appeal*, June 2, 1906; Indianapolis *Freeman*, June 2, 1906, August 25, 1906.

12. Nagel, *Descent from Glory*, 301; CFA2, *Charles Francis Adams* (Boston, 1900); Kirkland, *Adams*, 206–207; HA to Elizabeth Cameron, March 5, 1900, in *Letters*, ed. Levenson, 5: 102.

13. HA, *History of the United States during the First Administration of Thomas Jefferson* (New York, 1889); HA to BA, February 3, 1909, February 18, 1909, in *Letters*, ed. Levenson, 6: 217, 226–229; Beringause, *Brooks Adams*, 308.

14. BA, *The Law of Civilization and Decay: An Essay on History* (New York, 1895), 178; BA, *America's Economic Supremacy* (New York, 1900); BA, *The New Empire* (New York, 1902); Beringause, *Brooks Adams*, 242; Timothy Donovan, *Henry Adams and Brooks Adams: The Education of Two American Historians* (Norman, 1961), 74, 96; HA to Elizabeth Cameron, September 25, 1894, in *Letters*, ed. Levenson, 4: 212.

15. HA to Lucy Baxter, October 27, 1896, in *Letters*, ed. Levenson, 4: 435; Coffeyville (KS) *American*, October 1, 1898; Tehan, *Adams in Love*, 124–125; O'Toole, *Five of Hearts*, 325–326.

16. HA, *Mont-Saint Michel and Chartres* (Boston, 1913 ed.), 180, 235; O'Toole, *Five of Hearts*, 379–380; HA to Louisa Hooper, April 30, 1901, HA to BA, February 17, 1909, in *Letters*, ed. Levenson, 5: 246, 6: 224.

17. Nagel, *Descent from Glory*, 339; BA and HA, *The Degradation of the Democratic Dogma* (New York, 1920), 103.

18. Nagel, *Descent from Glory*, 315; CFA2, *Autobiography*, 9, 16, 124, 137, 190; New York *Sun*, October 12, 1919.

19. Kirkland, *Adams*, 220–221; HA to Elizabeth Cameron, March 26, 1915, in *Letters*, ed. Levenson, 6: 690; *Honolulu Star Bulletin*, March 20, 1915; Philadelphia *Evening Public Ledger*, March 20, 1915; *Bridgeport Evening Farmer*, March 20, 1915.

20. L. G. Walker, "Henry Adams's 1912 Stroke: A Misunderstood Illness," *New England Quarterly* 71 (1998): 284–285; O'Toole, *Five of Hearts*, 392.

21. Walker, "Adams's 1912 Stroke," 289; O'Toole, *Five of Hearts*, 392; Tehan, *Adams in Love*, 264; Washington *Evening Star*, March 27, 1918; New York *Sun*, March 28, 1918; *New-York Tribune*, March 29, 1918.

22. HA to Elizabeth Cameron, October 16, 1896, in *Letters*, ed. Levenson, 4: 431; Nagel, *Descent from Glory*, 376–377; Beringause, *Brooks Adams*, 387–388; Washington *Evening Star*, February 14, 1927.

23. BA and HA, *Degradation*, 34.

24. Samuels, *Adams: Middle Years*, 314.

25. HA to CFA2, November 10, 1911, in *Letters*, ed. Levenson, 4: 480; Nagel, *Descent from Glory*, 357.

INDEX

DOUGLAS R. EGERTON is a professor of history at Le Moyne College. The award-winning author of eight previous books, including *Thunder at the Gates* and *The Wars of Reconstruction*, he lives in Fayetteville, New York.